OXFORD MONOGRAPHS IN
INTERNATIONAL LAW

General Editor: PROFESSOR VAUGHAN LOWE,
*Chichele Professor of Public International Law in
the University of Oxford and Fellow of All Souls College, Oxford*

Investment Treaty Arbitration and Public Law

OXFORD MONOGRAPHS IN INTERNATIONAL LAW

The aim of this series is to publish important and original pieces of research on all aspects of international law. Topics that are given particular prominence are those which, while of interest to the academic lawyer, also have important bearing on issues which touch upon the actual conduct of international relations. Nonetheless, the series is wide in scope and includes monographs on the history and philosophical foundations of international law.

RECENT TITLES IN THE SERIES

International Organisations and their Exercise of Sovereign Powers
Dan Sarooshi

Differential Treatment in International Environmental Law
Lavanya Rajamani

Peremptory Norms in International Law
Alexander Orakhelashvili

Defining Terrorism in International Law
Ben Saul

Human Rights in International Criminal Proceedings
Salvatore Zappalà

Universal Jurisdiction
International and Municipal Legal Perspectives
Luc Reydams

International Human Rights and Islamic Law
Mashood A. Baderin

Investment Treaty Arbitration and Public Law

GUS VAN HARTEN

OXFORD
UNIVERSITY PRESS

Great Clarendon Street, Oxford OX2 6DP

Oxford University Press is a department of the University of Oxford.
It furthers the University's objective of excellence in research, scholarship,
and education by publishing worldwide in

Oxford New York

Auckland Cape Town Dar es Salaam Hong Kong Karachi
Kuala Lumpur Madrid Melbourne Mexico City Nairobi
New Delhi Shanghai Taipei Toronto

With offices in

Argentina Austria Brazil Chile Czech Republic France Greece
Guatemala Hungary Italy Japan Poland Portugal Singapore
South Korea Switzerland Thailand Turkey Ukraine Vietnam

Oxford is a registered trade mark of Oxford University Press
in the UK and in certain other countries

Published in the United States
by Oxford University Press Inc., New York

© Gus Van Harten, 2007

The moral rights of the author have been asserted

Crown copyright material is reproduced under Class Licence
Number C01P0000148 with the permission of OPSI
and the Queen's Printer for Scotland

Database right Oxford University Press (maker)

First published 2007

All rights reserved. No part of this publication may be reproduced,
stored in a retrieval system, or transmitted, in any form or by any means,
without the prior permission in writing of Oxford University Press,
or as expressly permitted by law, or under terms agreed with the appropriate
reprographics rights organization. Enquiries concerning reproduction
outside the scope of the above should be sent to the Rights Department,
Oxford University Press, at the address above

You must not circulate this book in any other binding or cover
and you must impose the same condition on any acquirer

British Library Cataloguing in Publication Data

Data available

Library of Congress Cataloging in Publication Data

Van Harten, Gus.
 Investment treaty arbitration and public law / Gus Van Harten.
  p. cm.— (Oxford monographs in international law)
 Includes bibliographical references and index.
 ISBN 978–0–19–921789–2 (hardback : alk. paper) 1. Investments,
Foreign—Law and legislation. 2. Arbitration and award, International.
3. Commercial treaties. I. Title
 K3830.V36 2007
 346.07—dc22
                                                      2006100844

Typeset by Newgen Imaging Systems (P) Ltd., Chennai, India
Printed in Great Britain
on acid-free paper by
Antony Rowe Ltd., Chippenham, Wiltshire

ISBN 978–0–19–921789–2

1 3 5 7 9 10 8 6 4 2

General Editor's Preface

Some of the most important substantive developments in international law are taking place in the arbitral tribunals that are adjudicating upon claims arising from bilateral investment treaties. Questions such as the limits of the right of a state to regulate its economy, the balancing of private rights against public interests, and the adequacy of governmental proceedings to meet the emerging requirement of 'transparency' in international law are being raised in, and settled by, these tribunals. Indeed, this is perhaps the most active and rapidly developing of all areas of international law at this moment. The paradox is that these questions of enormous significance to the public order of states are being decided by tribunals whose members are appointed by the investor and the government in dispute and whose proceedings, and even whose very existence, may be private, often with little or no opportunity for public comment upon or scrutiny of the proceedings.

This fine study by Dr Van Harten addresses the issues arising from this private adjudication of questions of public order. He analyses the issues of principle arising from this phenomenon, and the measures that are being taken to increase the opportunities for public participation in these arbitrations. Readers may not agree with all of his views and conclusions, but as tribunals struggle with these crucial issues they can only be helped by the clarity and insights of this robust and timely study.

AVL
Oxford
October 2006

Preface

This book is an analytical and institutional study of the recently emerged system of investment treaty arbitration. Its central claim is that the system is unlike other regimes of public law in that it uses the model of private arbitration rather than that of a tenured judiciary to decide finally what legislatures, public administrations, and courts may lawfully do in the exercise of regulatory powers. Moreover, for this reason the system is flawed, above all because it submits the sovereign authority and budgets of states to formal control by adjudicators who may be suspected—because they are untenured and because only one class of parties can bring claims—of interpreting investment treaties broadly in order to expand the system's appeal to potential claimants and, in turn, their own prospects for future appointment. And while this perceived bias may be effectively dispelled by the reputations of individual arbitrators for fairness and balance, this is none the less an unreliable basis on which to found a system that could otherwise make an important contribution to the legal system of a global economy.

This is no doubt a controversial claim and it is not one that I expected to make when I embarked on this project. My original aim was to show comprehensively that the system is a 'public law' phenomenon as contrasted against other perspectives on the system, and that it is more akin to domestic administrative or constitutional law than to the other potential comparators of commercial arbitration, human rights, and classical public international law. In constructing the argument, however, and especially in light of comments received from the anonymous reviewers of the book, it became clear that there was a more important case to be made about the system's integrity as a form of adjudicative government. Many criticisms, not all valid, have been levelled against investment treaty arbitration, particularly in the debates since the late 1990s in the United States and Canada about NAFTA arbitration, in many other developed countries about the OECD's proposal for a Multilateral Agreement on Investment, and more recently in those developing and former communist countries that have been most targeted by investor claims. In this book, the objective is to provide a more focused and detailed explanation for why certain criticisms, above all those regarding judicial independence, are particularly germane to the present system, and not to other international regimes, because of its unique use of private arbitration and state liability in the regulatory sphere.

It is not enough to criticize without offering alternatives and so, in the end, the book makes a case for political reform. In particular, the analytical discussion supports and culminates in a proposal for institutional reform that would, it is argued, satisfy the principles of judicial decision-making that are lacking in the present system. The proposal that is elaborated is not the only avenue available to remedy the system's problems, of course, but in my estimation it would at least introduce an adequate degree of judicial accountability and independence, without which the system's promise of the rule of law in a global economy is vacuous.

The book is aimed at a mixed audience although its tone and orientation is generally critical and academic. An effort has been made to express ideas in an accessible way and not to assume detailed prior knowledge, although the writing may prove dense at times and for this I ask the reader's tolerance and forgiveness. For practitioners, the book offers a framework by which to analyse investment disputes and characterize the adjudicative process, with implications for the interpretation of key concepts and standards and for the use of domestic public law as an analogous source of legal principles and doctrines. Detailed case references are included in Chapters 4, 5, and 6 of the book, in particular regarding the issues of parallel claims and forum-shopping, the core standards of review, and the interpretive stances adopted by different tribunals in cases to date.

It may be helpful to disclose at this stage a few points about referencing. In the notes the broad approach has been to list relevant sources in chronological order although there are exceptions to this, such as where sources that exemplify the point that is made in the body of the text are listed ahead of more general references. With respect to investment treaty cases, I have separated cases pursuant to the North American Free Trade Agreement from those pursuant to other investment treaties where there appeared to be value in doing so, mainly on the ground that NAFTA Chapter 11 is developing its own self-contained and generally more rigorous jurisprudence. Finally, in the references, I have typically erred in favour of inclusion—where the subject-matter has received significant attention elsewhere.

Many (probably the great majority) of investment treaty awards, and all those reviewed in this study, are publicly available although in some cases only via the internet. My practice has been to include award publication details for as many of these five reporters as possible: ICSID Review—Foreign Investment Law Journal (ICSID Rev), International Legal Materials (ILM), International Law Reports (ILR), ICSID Reports (ICSID Rep), and World Trade and Arbitration Materials. In rare cases, details for other reporters are also listed. Where awards or case materials are available only via the internet, I have attempted to refer the reader to as many of the widely used websites as possible, noting the case number or (where no case number is available) the arbitration rules under which the claim was filed. For readability, with respect to investment treaty awards, I refer in the text and bibliography to abbreviated names of websites rather than the pinpoint website address, with the full address details laid out in the List of Key Websites that follows the List of Abbreviations (below). For other documents that are available only by internet, I have included the pinpoint address as of 9 September 2006. Note that investment treaty awards are also broadly classified in the references as relating to the 'Merits', 'Jurisdiction', 'Damages', or other matters, with priority given in this order where an award deals with more than one of these subjects.

Those working in this field would be much the poorer without the freely accessible Investment Treaty News (ITN) newsletter, which is produced by Luke Eric Peterson and funded, as I understand, by public interest organizations and foundations. I have found this service to be a valuable resource. Also, in accessing the text of awards and other materials, my personal preference is to use Andrew Newcombe's 'Investment Treaty Arbitration' website for investment treaty awards and Todd Weiler's 'NAFTA Claims' website for awards and materials in NAFTA arbitration.

The original research for the book was conducted from 2002 to 2006 during my PhD studies in Law at the London School of Economics. Although this book is based on my PhD thesis, it has undergone substantial revision largely in response to the astute comments and criticisms of the anonymous reviewers at Oxford University Press. I also thank Sally McCann, Jodi Towler, and the other members of the editorial team at OUP for their care and attention to the manuscript, and especially John Louth for commissioning and shepherding the book to publication. I am deeply indebted to my PhD supervisors: Martin Loughlin and Deborah Cass, both of whom showed a dedicated interest in my work and provided many fresh ideas and insights. My PhD examiners, Peter Muchlinski and Sol Picciotto, carefully reviewed the thesis, and their thoughtful advice led to numerous improvements. I also benefited from discussions with other faculty members and colleagues; in particular, I thank Joanna Benjamin, Chris Greenwood, Virginia Mantouvalou, Loukas Mistelis, Antoine Romanetti, Rick Rawlings, Ken Shadlen, Gerry Simpson, Francis Snyder, and N'Gunu Tiny. Further, I wish to thank the many practitioners who took the time to speak to me about their work and the system, especially Sir Jeremy Carver, Norah Gallagher, Meg Kinnear, and J Christopher Thomas. All opinions expressed and any errors made in the book are, of course, entirely my own.

During my PhD studies, I received generous financial support from the Social Sciences and Humanities Research Council of Canada, the UK Overseas Research Students Awards Scheme, the LSE Research Studentship Fund, and the Sir Richard Stapley Educational Trust. I also received funding from the William Robson Memorial Fund at LSE towards the publication of my thesis as a book. I am very grateful for this support. Further, I acknowledge that during my PhD studies earlier work of mine on the topic was published in the European Journal of International Law (vol 17, 121, with Martin Loughlin), the Review of International Political Economy (vol 12, 600), Arbitration International (vol 21, 493), and International Trade Law and Regulation (vol 9, 139).

I reserve special thanks firstly to the Honourable Dennis R O'Connor, Associate Justice of the Ontario Court of Appeal, with whom I had the pleasure to work for several years, and to the other judges of the Court of Appeal under whom I clerked, all of whom instilled in me a high level of respect for judicial institutions and for the integrity of individual judges. I also wish to thank the lawyers and other staff with whom I worked on the Walkerton Inquiry and the Arar Inquiry in

Canada, especially Paul Cavalluzzo, Marc David, Ron Foerster, Brian Gover, and Freya Kristjanson for their insights into the practice and the politics of law. My greatest debt is to my family and above all my parents, who have supported and encouraged me in every possible way, and to the inspiring memory of my grandfather, Vic Hugh, to whom this book is dedicated. Lastly, I wish to thank Susanne, whose generosity of spirit and enthusiasm for my work I do not deserve, but very truly appreciate.

Contents

List of Abbreviations	xiii
List of Key Websites	xvii
Table of Cases (Investment Arbitration; International; Domestic)	xix
Table of Domestic Statutes	xxvii
Table of Treaties	xxix

1. Introduction — 1
 The system of investment treaty arbitration   3
 The scope and complexity of the system   6
 The exceptionality of the system   8

2. A Return to the Gay Nineties? — 12
 Historical Background   13
  The context of post-colonial conflict   13
  The proposals for a multilateral investment code   18
 The Emergence of the System   24
  The explosion of claims   24
  The role of arbitration treaties   34
  Explanations for the emergence of the system   38
 Conclusion   44

3. From Contract to Public Law — 45
 The Analytical Framework   46
  The public–private distinction   46
  Sovereignty and regulatory adjudication   48
 The Origins of the Treaty Structure   50
  The establishment of international commercial arbitration   50
  The expansion into the regulatory sphere   54
 Investment Treaty Arbitration as Regulatory Adjudication   58
  The character of international commercial arbitration   59
  The specific consent: arbitration as contract   62
  The general consent: arbitration as governing arrangement   63
  The investor's consent   68
 Conclusion   70

4. Scope and Standards of Review — 72
 The Scope of Investment Treaty Arbitration   73
 The Standards of Review   80
  National treatment   83

The minimum standard of treatment 86	
Expropriation 90	
Conclusion	93

5. The Transformation of International Law — 95

The Individualization of Claims	96
The Prospective Consent	99
The Dynamic of State Liability	101
The Far-reaching Nature of Claims	109
The removal of the duty to exhaust local remedies 110	
The facilitation of forum-shopping 113	
International Enforceability	117
Conclusion	119

6. Approaches and Interpretations — 121

The Discretion of Arbitrators	122
The Interpretive Approaches of Arbitrators	124
The analogy to commercial arbitration 124	
The analogy to public international law 131	
The investor rights approach 136	
The public law framework 143	
Conclusion	149

7. The Businessman's Court — 152

Four Criteria of Public Law Adjudication	153
Accountability 153	
Openness 159	
Coherence 164	
Independence 167	
The Options for Reform	175
The limits of domestic responses 175	
An international investment court 180	

Bibliography   185
Index   209

List of Abbreviations

AC	Appeal Cases Law Reports (United Kingdom)
ACHR	American Convention on Human Rights
AJIL	American Journal of International Law
All ER	All England Law Reports
ASEAN	Association of Southeast Asian Nations
B & C	Barnewall & Cresswell's King's Bench Reports (United Kingdom)
B & S	Best & Smith's Queen's Bench Reports (United Kingdom)
BCAC	British Columbia Appeal Cases (Canada)
BC CA	British Columbia Court of Appeal (Canada)
BCLR	British Columbia Law Reports (Canada)
Beav	Beavan's Rolls Court Reports (United Kingdom)
BIT	bilateral investment treaty
CA	Court of Appeal (United Kingdom)
CCC	Canadian Criminal Cases
CELR	Canadian Environmental Law Reports
CIEL	Center for International Environmental Law
CML Rev	Common Market Law Review (Europe)
Cons TS	Consolidated Treaty Series
CPR	Canadian Patent Reporter
CTS	Canadian Treaty Series
CUP	Cambridge University Press
DC The Hague	District Court of the Hague (Netherlands)
DDC	United States District Court for the District of Columbia
DFAIT	Department of Foreign Affairs and International Trade (Canada)
DLR	Dominion Law Reports (Canada)
ECHR	European Convention on Human Rights
ECJ	European Court of Justice
ECLAC	Economic Commission for Latin American and the Caribbean
ECR	European Court Reports
ECtHR	European Court of Human Rights
EJIL	European Journal of International Law
ER	English Reports
ESC	Economic and Social Council (United Nations)
EU	European Union
Eur TS	European Treaty Series
FCR	Federal Court Reports (Canada)
FDI	foreign direct investment
GA	General Assembly (United Nations)
GAOR	Official Records of the General Assembly (United Nations)
GATS	General Agreement on Trade in Services
GATT	General Agreement on Tariffs and Trade
HL	House of Lords (United Kingdom)

HLC	Clark & Finnelly's House of Lords Reports (United Kingdom)
ICC	International Chamber of Commerce
ICJ	International Court of Justice
ICLQ	International and Comparative Law Quarterly
ICSID	International Centre for Settlement of Investment Disputes
ICTY	International Criminal Tribunal for the Former Yugoslavia
IHRR	International Human Rights Reports
IJC	International Joint Commission (Canada–United States)
ILC	International Law Commission
ILM	International Legal Materials
ILR	International Law Reports
IMF	International Monetary Fund
ITA	Investment Treaty Arbitration
Iran–US CTR	Iran–US Claims Tribunal Reports
KB	King's Bench Law Reports (United Kingdom)
LN	League of Nations
LNTS	League of Nations Treaty Series
LSE	London School of Economics
MAI	Multilateral Agreement on Investment
MFN	most favoured nation
NAFTA	North American Free Trade Agreement
NC	North Carolina
Nfld	Newfoundland and Labrador
NGO	non-governmental organization
NYU	New York University
OAC	Ontario Appeal Cases (Canada)
OECD	Organization for Economic Co-operation and Development
OLRC	Ontario Law Reform Commission (Canada)
Ont CA	Court of Appeal for Ontario (Canada)
Ont SCJ	Ontario Superior Court of Justice (Canada)
OR	Ontario Reports (Canada)
OUP	Oxford University Press
PCIJ	Permanent Court of International Justice
QB	Queen's Bench Law Reports (United Kingdom)
RIAA	Reports of International Arbitral Awards
RPR	Real Property Reports (Canada)
RSC	Revised Statutes of Canada
S Ct	Supreme Court Reporter (United States)
SCC	Stockholm Chamber of Commerce
SCR	Supreme Court Reports (Canada)
SICE	Sistema de Información sobre Commercio Exterior (Foreign Trade Information System)
Swan	Swanston's Chancery Reports (United Kingdom)
Swed Svea CA	Swedish Svea Court of Appeal
TRIMs	Trade-Related Investment Measures
UAE	United Arab Emirates
UK	United Kingdom

UKTS	United Kingdom Treaty Series
UN	United Nations
UNCITRAL	United Nations Commission on International Trade Law
UNCTAD	United Nations Conference on Trade and Development
UNDP	United Nations Development Programme
UNTS	United Nations Treaty Series
US	United States of America
US (case citations)	United States Supreme Court Reports
USC	United States Code
USTR	United States Trade Representative
Wheat	Wheaton's Supreme Court Reports (United States)
WLR	Weekly Law Reports (United Kingdom)
WTO	World Trade Organization

List of Key Websites

Department of Foreign Affairs and International Trade (Canada) (DFAIT) www.international.gc.ca/tna-nac/gov-en.asp (awards and documents in NAFTA claims against Canada).

International Centre for the Settlement of Investment Disputes (ICSID) www.worldbank.org/icsid/cases/cases.htm (awards in ICSID arbitrations).

Investment Claims www.investmentclaims.com (awards in investment treaty arbitrations).

Investment Treaty Arbitration (ITA) ita.law.uvic.ca/news.htm (awards in investment treaty arbitrations).

NAFTA Claims www.naftaclaims.com (awards and documents in NAFTA arbitrations).

US State Department www.state.gov/s/l/c3741.htm (awards and documents in NAFTA claims against the United States).

Table of Cases

INVESTMENT ARBITRATION

ADF Group Inc v United States of America (Procedural Order No 2) (11 July 2001),
  online: State Department, NAFTA Claims. 129
ADF Group Inc v United States of America (Merits) (9 January 2003), 18 ICSID Rev 195,
  6 ICSID Rep 470, 15(3) World Trade and Arb Mat 55. .... 21, 65, 78–9, 86, 88, 99,
     132–3, 136, 145–6, 149
AES Corporation v Argentine Republic (Jurisdiction) (26 April 2005), ICSID Case No ARB/02/17,
  online: ITA, Investment Claims. 125
AGIP SpA v People's Republic of Congo (Merits) (30 November 1979), 21 ILM 726,
  67 ILR 318, 1 ICSID Rep 306. 24
Aguas Argentinas, SA v Argentine Republic (Participation by Amicus Curiae) (19 May 2005),
  ICSID Case No ARB/03/19, online: ICSID, ITA, Investment Claims. 163
Aguas del Tunari SA v Republic of Bolivia (Jurisdiction) (21 October 2005), 18(2)
  World Trade and Arb Mat 271. .... 116, 138, 148, 163
Aguas Provinciales de Santa Fe SA v Argentine Republic (Participation by Amicus Curiae)
  (17 March 2006), ICSID Case No ARB/03/17, online: ICSID, ITA, Investment Claims..... 163
Amco Asia Corp v Republic of Indonesia (Decision) (24 June 1982), ICSID Case No ARB/81/1
  [unpublished]. 172
Amco Asia Corp v Indonesia (Jurisdiction) (25 September 1983), 23 ILM 351, 89 ILR 379,
  1 ICSID Rep 389. 125
American Manufacturing & Trading Inc v Republic of Zaire (Merits) (21 February 1997),
  36 ILM 1534, 5 ICSID Rep 14. 89
Asian Agricultural Products Ltd (AAPL) v Sri Lanka (Merits) (27 June 1990), 30 ILM 577,
  4 ICSID Rep 246. .... 24, 30, 106, 137
Autopista Concesionada de Venezuela v Bolivarian Republic of Venezuela (Jurisdiction)
  (27 September 2001), 16 ICSID Rev 469. 79
Azinian (Robert) et al v United Mexican States (Merits) (1 November 1999), 14 ICSID
  Rev 538, 39 ILM 537, 5 ICSID Rep 272. .... 93, 118, 133, 136, 141, 143, 145–6, 149
Azurix Corp v Argentine Republic (Jurisdiction) (8 December 2003), 43 ILM 262, 16(2)
  World Trade and Arb Mat 111. .... 71, 77, 111, 115, 136–7
Azurix Corp v Argentine Republic (Merits) (14 July 2006), ICSID Case No ARB/01/12,
  online: ITA, Investment Claims. 89, 93, 138
Bogdanov (Iurii) et al v Moldova (Merits) (22 September 2005), SCC Rules, online: ITA,
  Investment Claims. 24, 113, 139
*Banro American Resources, Inc and Société Aurifère du Kivu et du Maniema SARL v Democratic
  Republic of the Congo* (Jurisdiction) (1 September 2000), 17 ICSID Rev 382. 130
Bayindir Insaat Turizm Ticaret Ve Sanayi AŞ v Islamic Republic of Pakistan (Jurisdiction)
  (14 November 2005), 18(1) World Trade and Arb Mat 163. 79
BP America Production Co v Argentine Republic (Jurisdiction) (27 July 2006), ICSID Case
  No ARB/04/8, online: ITA. 47, 165
Canfor Corporation v United States of America (Jurisdiction) (6 June 2006), UNCITRAL Rules,
  online: State Department, ITA, NAFTA Claims. 69, 79, 112
Ceskoslovenska Obchodni Banka v Slovak Republic (Jurisdiction) (24 May 1999),
  14 ICSID Rev 251, 17(3) World Trade and Arb Mat 189. .... 116, 124–5, 138
Champion Trading Company v Arab Republic of Egypt (Jurisdiction) (21 October 2003),
  19 ICSID Rev 275. .... 111, 113

CME Czech Republic BV v Czech Republic (Merits) (13 September 2001), 14(3)
World Trade and Arb Mat 109. . . . . 7–8, 89, 92, 109, 114–15, 125, 137
CME Czech Republic BV v Czech Republic (Damages) (14 March 2003), 15(4)
World Trade and Arb Mat 83 and 245. . . . . 7, 110, 115, 130, 134, 142–3, 145
CMS Gas Transmission Company v Argentine Republic (Jurisdiction) (17 July 2003),
42 ILM 788, 7 ICSID Rep 492. . . . . 26, 41, 66, 70, 73, 77, 110–11, 115, 136–7
CMS Gas Transmission Company v Argentine Republic (Merits) (12 May 2005),
44 ILM 1205, 17(5) World Trade and Arb Mat 63. . . . . 3, 8, 83, 138
Compañía de Aguas del Aconquija SA & Vivendi Universal v Argentine Republic (Decision on
Challenge to the President) (3 October 2001), 17 ICSID Rev 168, 125 ILR 46,
6 ICSID Rep 330. 172
Compañía de Aguas del Aconquija SA & Vivendi Universal v Argentine Republic (Annulment)
(3 July 2002), 41 ILM 1135, 125 ILR, 58, 6 ICSID Rep 340. 115–16
Compañía del Desarrollo de Santa Elena, SA v Republic of Costa Rica (Merits)
(17 February 2000), 15 ICSID Rev 169, 39 ILM 317, 5 ICSID Rep 157, 13(1)
World Trade and Arb Mat 81. . . . . 18, 68, 71, 92, 137
Continental Casualty Company v Argentine Republic (Jurisdiction) (22 February 2006),
ICSID Case No ARB/03/9, online: ITA 66, 77, 113, 138
Crompton Corp v Government of Canada (Notice of Claim) (6 November 2001),
online: DFAIT, NAFTA Claims. 85
Empresas Lucchetti, SA v Lucchetti Peru, SA (Merits) (7 February 2005),
19 ICSID Rev 359, 17(3) World Trade and Arb Mat 161. . . . . 4, 146
Encana Corporation v Republic of Ecuador (Merits) (3 February 2006), London Court of
International Arbitration Administered Case No UN 3481. . . . . 84, 112, 115, 134, 145–6
Enron Corporation v Argentina Republic (Jurisdiction) (2 August 2004),
ICSID Case No ARB/01/3, online: ICSID, ITA, Investment Claims. 97, 111, 132
Ethyl Corporation v Government of Canada (Investor's Submissions) (2 October 1997),
UNCITRAL Rules, online: DFAIT, NAFTA Claims. 86, 99
Ethyl Corporation v Government of Canada (Procedural Orders) (13 October 1997 and
undated), UNCITRAL Rules, online: DFAIT, NAFTA Claims. 162
Ethyl Corporation v Government of Canada (Jurisdiction) (24 June 1998), 38
ILM 708. . . . . 65–6, 78–9, 125
Eureko v Republic of Poland (Merits) (19 August 2005), UNCITRAL Rules, online: ITA,
Investment Claims. 89, 92, 138
Fedax NV v Republic of Venezuela (Jurisdiction) (11 July 1997), 5 ICSID Rep 186,
37 ILM 1378. . . . . 73, 79, 116–17
Feldman Karpa (Marvin Roy) v United Mexican States (Jurisdiction) (6 December 2000),
18 ICSID Rev 469, 7 ICSID Rep 327. . . . . 102, 114, 118, 138
Feldman Karpa (Marvin Roy) v United Mexican States (Procedural Order No 5)
(6 December 2000), ICSID Case No ARB(AF)/99/1, online: NAFTA Claims. 161
Feldman Karpa (Marvin Roy) v United Mexican States (Merits) (16 December 2002),
18 ICSID Rev 488, 42 ILM 625, 7 ICSID Rep 341, 15(3) World Trade and
Arb Mat 157. . . . . 66, 68, 71, 73, 84–5, 93, 122, 165
Fireman's Fund Insurance Company v United Mexican States (Jurisdiction) (17 July 2003), 15(6)
World Trade and Arb Mat 3. . . . . 98, 115, 133
GAMI Investments, Inc v Government of the United Mexican States (Merits) (15 November 2004),
44 ILM 545, 17(2) World Trade and Arb Mat 127. . . . . 70, 77, 86, 92, 99, 113, 115,
118, 132, 134, 136, 138, 145, 165
Gardella (Adriano) v Côte d'Ivoire (Merits) (29 August 1979), 1 ICSID Rep 283. 24
Generation Ukraine Inc v Ukraine (Merits) (16 September 2003), 44 ILM 404. . . . . 93, 134
Genin (Alex) and Others v Republic of Estonia (Merits) (25 June 2001), 17 ICSID Rev 395,
6 ICSID Rep 304. . . . . 111, 144, 146

Investment Arbitration xxi

Glamis Gold, Ltd v United States of America (Participation by Amicus Curiae)
  (16 September 2005), UNCITRAL Rules, online: State Department,
  NAFTA Claims. 162
Gruslin (Philippe) v Malaysia (Merits) (27 November 2000), 5 ICSID Rep 484. 78
Holiday Inns SA v Morocco (Jurisdiction) (12 May 1974), 1 ICSID Rep 645. 24
International Thunderbird Gaming Corporation v United Mexican States (Merits)
  (26 January 2006), 18(2) World Trade and Arb Mat 59. . . . . 70, 88, 110, 123, 144
Joy Mining Machinery Ltd v Arab Republic of Egypt (Jurisdiction) (6 August 2004),
  19 ICSID Rev 486, 44 ILM 73. . . . . 79, 112, 146
Kaiser Bauxite Company v Jamaica (Jurisdiction) (6 July 1975), 114 ILR 144,
  1 ICSID Rep 296. 24
Lanco International Inc v Argentine Republic (Jurisdiction) (8 December 1998),
  40 ILM 457. . . . . 63, 77, 111
Lauder (Ronald S) v Czech Republic (Final Award) (3 September 2001), (2002) 4 World
  Trade and Arb Materials 35. . . . . 8, 112
Lemire (Joseph Charles) v Ukraine (Settlement), ICSID Case No ARB(AF)/98/1, online: ITA 4
Loewen Group, Inc and Raymond L Loewen v United States of America (Jurisdiction)
  (5 January 2001), 7 ICSID Rep 421. 161
Loewen Group, Inc and Raymond L Loewen v United States of America (Merits) (26 June 2003),
  42 ILM 811, 7 ICSID Rep 442, 15(5) World Trade and Arb Mat 97. . . . . 4, 65, 88, 118, 130,
  133–6, 140, 143–7, 149, 174
Maffezini (Emilio Agustín) v Kingdom of Spain (Jurisdiction) (25 January 2000),
  16 ICSID Rev 212, 124 ILR 9. . . . . 77, 81, 109, 138
Metalclad Corporation v United Mexican States (Merits) (30 August 2000), 16 ICSID Rev 168,
  40 ILM 36, 5 ICSID Rep 212, 13(1) World Trade and Arb Mat 45. . . . . 4, 65, 83, 88, 92,
  109, 137, 139, 146
Methanex Corporation v United States of America (Jurisdiction) (7 August 2002), 14(6)
  World Trade and Arb Mat 109. . . . . 65, 67, 132–3, 144
Methanex Corporation v United States of America (Participation by Amicus Curiae) (15 January
  2001), UNCITRAL Rules, online: State Department, ITA, NAFTA Claims. 162
Methanex Corporation v United States of America (Merits) (3 August 2005), 44 ILM 1345, 17(6)
  World Trade and Arb Mat 61. . . . . 93, 123, 146
Middle East Cement Shipping and Handling Co SA v Arab Republic of Egypt (Merits)
  (12 April 2002), 18 ICSID Rev 602, 7 ICSID Rep 173. . . . . 70, 89, 111
Mondev International Ltd v United States of America (Merits) (11 October 2002), 42 ILM 85, 6
  ICSID Rep 192, 15(3) World Trade and Arb Mat 273. . . . . 66, 87–8, 102, 115, 118, 123,
  125, 136, 141, 145–6
MTD Equity Sdn Bhd v Republic of Chile (Merits) (25 May 2004), 44 ILM 91. . . . . 83, 89, 138
Noble Ventures v Romania (Merits) (12 October 2005), ICSID Case No ARB/01/11,
  online: ITA, Investment Claims. 86, 106, 133, 138, 144
Occidental Exploration and Production Company v Republic of Ecuador (Merits) (1 July 2004),
  17(1) World Trade and Arb Mat 165. . . . . 4, 83, 86, 89, 111, 137
Olguín (Eudoro Armando) v Republic of Paraguay (Merits) (26 July 2001), 18 ICSID Rev 143,
  6 ICSID Rep 164. . . . . 81, 89, 93, 114
Petrobart Ltd v Kyrgyz Republic (Merits) (29 March 2005), SCC Rules, SCC Arbitration
  Institute Case No 126/2003. . . . . 77, 111, 138
Plama Consortium Limited v Republic of Bulgaria (Jurisdiction) (8 February 2005),
  20 ICSID Rev 262, 44 ILM 721, 17(4) World Trade and Arb Mat 215. . . . . 81, 133
Pope & Talbot Inc v Government of Canada (Jurisdiction) (26 January 2000),
  UNCITRAL Rules, online: DFAIT, NAFTA Claims. 78–9
Pope & Talbot Inc v Government of Canada (Investor's Submissions) (28 January 2000),
  UNCITRAL Rules, online: DFAIT, NAFTA Claims. 86, 99

Pope & Talbot Inc v Government of Canada (Merits, Phase 1) (26 June 2000), 13(4)
    World Trade and Arb Mat 19. . . . . 80, 92–3, 146
Pope & Talbot Inc v Government of Canada (Canada's Submissions) (10 October 2000),
    UNCITRAL Rules, online: DFAIT, NAFTA Claims. 88
Pope & Talbot Inc v Government of Canada (Merits, Phase 2) (10 April 2001),
    13(4) World Trade and Arb Mat 61. . . . . 85–6, 88, 99, 124, 126,
                                                                                         132, 139, 146, 161–2
Pope & Talbot Inc v Government of Canada (Letter from Presiding Arbitrator)
    (17 September 2001), UNCITRAL Rules, online: DFAIT, NAFTA Claims. 127
Pope & Talbot Inc v Government of Canada (Investor's Submissions) (14 December 2001),
    UNCITRAL Rules, online: DFAIT, NAFTA Claims. 86, 99, 127
Pope & Talbot Inc v Government of Canada (Damages) (31 May 2002), 41 ILM 1347, 14(6)
    World Trade and Arb Mat 44. . . . . 83, 127
PSEG Global Inc v Republic of Turkey (Jurisdiction) (4 June 2004), 44 ILM 465. 111
Salini Costruttori SpA and Italstrade SpA v Kingdom of Morocco (Jurisdiction) (23 July 2001),
    42 ILM 609, 6 ICSID Rep 400. . . . . 79, 140, 144
Salini Costruttori SpA and Italstrade SpA v Hashemite Kingdom of Jordan (Jurisdiction)
    (29 November 2004), 20 ICSID Rev 148, 44 ILM 573. 81
Saluka Investments BV v Czech Republic (Merits) (17 March 2006), 18(3) World Trade and
    Arb Mat 166 . . . . 7, 79, 93, 117, 134, 143, 145
SD Myers, Inc v Government of Canada (Procedural Order No 3 and 11) (10 June 1999 and
    11 November 1999), UNCITRAL Rules, online: DFAIT, NAFTA Claims. 161–2
SD Myers, Inc v Government of Canada (Investor's Submissions) (20 July 1999),
    UNCITRAL Rules, online: DFAIT, NAFTA Claims. 86, 99
SD Myers, Inc v Government of Canada (Merits) (13 November 2000), 40 ILM 1408, 15(1)
    World Trade and Arb Mat 184. . . . . 4, 78–9, 88–9, 93, 102, 136,
                                                                                         141, 145–6, 149
SD Myers, Inc v Government of Canada (US Submissions) (18 September 2001),
    UNCITRAL Rules, online: State Department, NAFTA Claims. 80
SD Myers, Inc v Government of Canada (Damages) (21 October 2002), 15(1)
    World Trade and Arb Mat 103. . . . . 78–9, 83
SGS Société Générale de Surveillance v Pakistan (Jurisdiction) (6 August 2003),
    18 ICSID Rev 301, 42 ILM 1290, 8 ICSID Rep 406, 16(2)
    World Trade and Arb Mat 167. . . . . 79, 110–11, 122, 132–5, 143–4,
                                                                                         146, 165, 174
SGS Société Générale de Surveillance v Philippines (Jurisdiction) (29 January 2004),
    8 ICSID Rep 518, 16(3) World Trade and Arb Mat 91. . . . . 57, 79–80, 125, 130, 134,
                                                                                         138, 142, 165
Sedelmayer (Franz) v Russian Federation (Merits) (7 July 1998), SCC Rules, online: ITA,
    Investment Claims. 112, 115, 138
Sempra Energy International v Argentine Republic (Jurisdiction) (11 May 2005), ICSID Case No
    ARB/02/16, online: ICSID, ITA, Investment Claims. 77, 111, 113, 115, 132, 138
Siemens AG v Argentine Republic (Jurisdiction) (3 August 2004),
    44 ILM 138. . . . . 77, 81, 98, 111, 115, 136–9
Soufraki (Hussein Nuaman) v United Arab Emirates (Jurisdiction) (7 July 2004), 17(1)
    World Trade and Arb Mat 129. 114
Southern Pacific Properties (Middle East) Ltd v Arab Republic of Egypt (Jurisdiction)
    (14 April 1988), 3 ICSID Rep 131. . . . . 24, 30
Tecnicas Medioambientales Tecmed, SA v United Mexican States (Merits) (29 May 2003),
    19 ICSID Rev 158, 43 ILM 133. . . . . 71, 81, 83, 89, 92, 126,
                                                                                         136–7, 144

Tokios Tokelès v Ukraine (Jurisdiction) (29 April 2004), 20 ICSID Rev 205, 16(4)
World Trade and Arb Mat 75.................................. 110, 115–16, 130, 132–4, 138
Tradex Hellas SA v Republic of Albania (Merits) (29 April 1999), 14 ICSID Rev 161,
5 ICSID Rep 47. 116
United Parcel Service of America, Inc v Government of Canada (Jurisdiction) (22 November
2002), UNCITRAL Rules, online: DFAIT, ITA, NAFTA Claims. 73, 88, 102, 132–3,
141–2, 157
United Parcel Service of America Inc v Government of Canada (Participation by Amicus Curiae)
(1 August 2003), UNCITRAL Rules, online: DFAIT, NAFTA Claims. 130, 162
United Parcel Service of America, Inc v Government of Canada (Investor's Submissions)
(23 March 2005), UNCITRAL Rules, online: DFAIT, NAFTA Claims................. 86, 99
Vacuum Salt Products, Ltd v Republic of Ghana (Jurisdiction) (16 February 1994),
9 ICSID Rev 72, 20 Ybk Comm'l Arb 11. 115
Waste Management, Inc v United Mexican States (Jurisdiction) (2 June 2000),
15 ICSID Rev 214, 40 ILM 56, 121 ILR 30............................ 65, 69, 70, 133, 138
Waste Management, Inc v United Mexican States (Jurisdiction) (26 June 2002), 41 ILM 1315,
6 ICSID Rep 549, 14(6) World Trade and Arb Mat 203............................ 88, 118
Waste Management Inc v United Mexican States (Merits) (30 April 2004), 43 ILM
967, 16(4) World Trade and Arb Mat 3........................ 65, 92–3, 110, 114–16, 118,
134, 136–9, 144–6, 149
Wena Hotels Ltd v Arab Republic of Egypt (Jurisdiction) (25 May 1999), 41 ILM 881,
6 ICSID Rep 74. 115
Wena Hotels Ltd v Arab Republic of Egypt (Merits) (8 December 2000), 41 ILM 896,
6 ICSID Rep 89... 139, 141

INTERNATIONAL

Administrative Decision No V (1924), 7 RIAA 119, 19 AJIL 612 (US–Germany Mixed Claims
Commission)... 49, 96, 98, 112
Ambatielos Claim (Greece v United Kingdom) (1956), 12 RIAA 83. 96
Amoco International Finance Corp v Iran (1987), 15 Iran-US CTR 189..................... 109
Anglo-Iranian Oil Company (United Kingdom v Iran), [1952] ICJ Rep 93. 97
Barcelona Traction, Light and Power Co (Belgium v Spain), [1970] ICJ
Rep 3, 9 ILM 227.. 49, 77, 96–7, 112–13
*Brasserie du Pêcheur SA v Germany; Secretary of State for Transport, ex parte Factortame
Ltd and Others* (No 46 & 48/93), (1996) 1 CML Rev 889...................... 104, 147–8
Caire Claim (France v Mexico) (1929), 5 RIAA 516.. 106
Case Concerning the Payment of Various Serbian Loans Issued In France (France v Serbia) (1921),
PCIJ Ser A, No 20.. 96
The Chorzow Factory (Germany v Poland) (1928), PCIJ Ser A, No 17....................... 109
Corfu Channel (Merits) *(United Kingdom v Albania)*, [1949] ICJ Rep 4..................... 106
Elettronica Sicula SpA (United States v Italy), [1989] ICJ Rep 14. .... 97, 112, 133–4
Fabiani Case (France v Venezuela) (1896), 10 RIAA 33.................................... 102
Francovich and Bonifaci v Republic of Italy (No 6 and 9/90), [1991] ECR I-5357, (1993)
2 CML Rev 66.. 104, 147–9
Hauer v Rheinland-Pfatz (No 44/79), [1979] ECR 3727, (1980) 3 CML Rev 42............... 90
In the Matter of Cross-border Trucking Services (Merits) (6 February 2001), 13(3)
World Trade and Arb Mat 121... 85, 106
Interhandel Case (Switzerland v United States), [1959] ICJ Rep 6............................ 96
Iran–United States No A/18 (1984), 5 Iran–US CTR 251, 23 ILM 489...................... 97
Janes Claim (United States v Mexico) (1926), 4 RIAA 82................................... 105

Jurisdiction of the Courts of Danzig (Advisory Opinion) (1928), PCIJ Ser B, No 15. . . . . 120, 140
Köbler v Austria (No C-224/01), [2003] ECR I-10239, 3 CML Rev 28. 104
Laboratoires Pharmaceutiques Bergaderm and Goupil v Commission (No 352/98),
 [2000] ECR I-5291. 148
LaGrand (Merits) (*Germany v United States*), [2001] ICJ Rep 466, 40 ILM 1069. . . . . 120, 140, 142
Legal Consequences of the Construction of a Wall in the Occupied Palestinian Territory (Advisory
 Opinion) (9 July 2004), ICJ General List No 131. . . . . 105, 120, 140
Mavrommattis Palestine Concessions (*Greece v Great Britain*) (1924), PCIJ Ser A, No 2. . . . . . 49, 96–7
Neer Claim (*United States v Mexico*) (1926), 4 RIAA 60. 87–8
Norweigen Loans (*France v Norway*), [1957] ICJ Rep 9. 110
Nottebohm (*Liechtenstein v Guatemala*), [1955] ICJ Rep 4. . . . . 49, 96–7, 114
R v Ministry of Agriculture and Fisheries, ex parte Hedley Lomas (Ireland) Ltd (No 5/94),
 [1996] ECR I-2553. 104
R v Treasury, ex parte British Telecommunications (No 392/93), [1996]
 ECR I-1631, 3 WLR 203. 107
Rewe-Zentral Finanz eG v Lanschwirtschaftskammer für das Saarland (No 33/76),
 [1976] ECR 1989. 149
Salomone Haim v Kassenzahnärztliche Vereinigung Nordrhein (No 424/97),
 [2000] ECR I-5123. 104
Sporrong and Lönnroth v Sweden, Eur Ct HR Ser A, No 52, [1983] EHRR 35. 90
Status of Eastern Carelia (Advisory Opinion) (1923), PCIJ Ser B, No 5. 96
Tabacalera Boquerón SA v Paraguay (1997), Inter-Am Comm HR, Rep No 47/97,
 Annual Report of the Inter-American Commission on Human Rights: 1987,
 OEA/Ser.L/V/II.98/Doc7/rev (1998) 225. 104
Texaco Overseas Petroleum Co and California Asiatic Oil Co v Libya (Merits) (1977),
 53 ILR 389, 17 ILM 1. 130
Tippetts v TAMS-AFFA (1985), 6 Iran–US CTR 219. 106
Union Bridge Company Claim (*United States v Great Britain*) (1924), 6 RIAA 138. 106
WTO Appellate Body Report, *EC Measures Concerning Meat and Meat Products (Hormones)*,
 WTO Doc WT/DS26/AB/R and WT/DS48/AB/R (16 January 1998). 133

DOMESTIC

A&L Investments Ltd v Ontario (Minister of Housing) (1993) 13 OR (3rd) 799,
 32 RPR (2nd) 1 (Ont CA). 90
Anns v Merton (1977) [1978] AC 728, 2 All ER 492. 108
Attorney-General v De Keyser's Royal Hotel, Ltd [1920] AC 508. 90
Attorney-General v Leveller Magazine Limited [1979] AC 440. 161
Attorney-General of Canada v SD Myers, Inc [2004] 3 FCR 368, 5 CELR (3rd)
 166 (Fed Ct TD). 156
Authorson (Litigation Guardian of) v Canada (Attorney-General) [2003] 2 SCR 40,
 227 DLR (4th) 385. 66
Baccus v SRL Servicio Nacional del Trigo [1957] 1 QB 438 (CA). 62
Banco Nacional de Cuba v Sabbatino (1964) 376 US 398, 3 ILM 381. 118
Bank of United States v Planter's Bank of Georgia (1824) 9 Wheat 904 (US Sup Ct). 62
Blad v Bamfield (1674) 3 Swan 604, 36 ER 992. 117
Blanco (8 February 1873) Rec 1er Supp 61. 107
Bremen v Zapata Offshore Co (1972) 407 US 1, 92 S Ct 1907. 155
British Columbia v Tener [1985] 1 SCR 533, 17 DLR (4th) 1. 90
Brown v British Columbia (Minister of Transportation and Highways [1994] 1 SCR 420,
 112 DLR (4th) 1. 108

Domestic

Chromalloy Aeroservices v Arab Republic of Egypt (1996) 939 F Supp 907, 12(4)
  Int'l Arb R B-1 (DDC)... 157
Claim against the Empire of Iran (1963) 45 ILR 57 (Ger Fed Const Ct)....................... 47
CME Czech Republic BV v Czech Republic (2003) 15(5) World Trade and Arb Mat 171
  (Swed Svea CA).. 7
I Congreso del Partido [1983] 1 AC 244 (HL).. 47
Corporacion Transnacional de Inversiones v STET International (1999) 45 OR (3rd) 183
  (Ont SCJ), aff'd 49 OR (3rd) 414 (Ont CA)................................. 155
Council of Canadians v Canada (8 July 2005, Pepall J, Docket No 01-CV-208141)
  (Ont SCJ).. 69, 176
Czarnikow v Roth, Schmidt & Co [1922] 2 KB 478................................. 61
Dalehite v United States (1953) 364 US 15... 108
Duke of Brunswick v King of Hannover (1844) [1848] 6 Beav 1, 2 HLC 1.................... 117
Ecuador v Occidental Exploration and Production Co [2005] 2 Lloyd's Rep 240 (QB).......... 158
Ecuador v Occidental Exploration and Production Co [2006] 1 Lloyd's Rep 773 (QB).......... 156
France Fenwick and Co v R [1927] 1 KB 458... 90
Fray v Blackburn (1863) 3 B & S 576, 122 ER 217 (QB)................................... 108
Gallagher v Lynn [1937] AC 863.. 90
Garnett v Ferrand (1827) 6 B & C 611, 108 ER 576 (KB)................................. 108
Gulf Canada Resources Ltd v Arochem International Inc (1992) 66 BCLR (2nd) 113,
  43 CPR (3rd) 390... 60
Gulf Canada Resources Ltd v Arochem International Inc (1992) 11 BCAC 145,
  43 CPR (3rd) 390 (BC CA).. 155
Hilmarton I (1995) 20 Ybk Comm'l Arb 663.. 157
Home Office v Harman [1983] 1 AC 280.. 161
Indian Towing Co v United States (1955) 350 US 61.................................. 108
Lucas v South Carolina Coastal Council (1992) 505 US 1003............................ 90
Manitoba Fisheries Ltd v R [1979] 1 SCR 101, 88 DLR (3rd) 462......................... 90
Mitsubishi Motors Corp v Soler Chrysler Plymouth Inc (1985) 473 US 614............ 62, 155
Nielsen v Kamloops [1984] 2 SCR 2, 10 DLR (4th) 641................................. 108
Oetjen v Central Leather Co (1918) 246 US 297.. 117
Pennsylvania Central Transportation Company v City of New York (1978) 438 US 104............ 90
Quintette Coal Ltd v Nippon Steel Corp (1990) 50 BCLR (2nd) 207 (BC CA)................ 155
R v Valente (No 2) [1985] 2 SCR 673, 23 CCC (3rd) 193, 24 DLR (4th) 161............... 173
Republic of Argentina v Weltover (1992) 504 US 607...................................... 47
Republic of Ghana v Telekom Malaysia Berhad (18 October 2004 and 5 November 2004,
  No HA/RK 2004.667 and HA/RK 2004.788) (DC The Hague) 172
Scherk v Alberto-Culver Co (1974) 417 US 506... 155
Scott v Scott [1913] AC 417... 161
Shearson/American Express, Inc v McMahon (1987) 482 US 220........................... 155
Sonatrach v Ford Bacon & Davis Inc (1990) 11 Ybk Comm'l Arb 370........................ 157
Swinamer v Nova Scotia (Attorney General) [1994] 1 SCR 445, 112 DLR (4th) 18............. 108
Trendtex Trading Corp v Central Bank of Nigeria [1977] QB 529(CA).................. 46, 62
United Mexican States v Metalclad Corporation (2001) 89 BCLR (3rd) 359,
  38 CELR 284, 13(5) World Trade and Arb Mat 219 (BC Sup Ct)................ 103, 156
United Mexican States v Marvin Roy Feldman Karpa (2003) 16(2) World Trade and
  Arb Mat 237 (Ont SCJ).. 125, 156
United Mexican States v Marvin Roy Feldman Karpa (2005) 193 OAC 216,
  248 DLR (4th) 443 (Ont CA).. 125, 156

Table of Domestic Statutes

Arbitration Act 1996 (UK). 155
Bipartisan Trade Promotion Authority Act 2002 (USA). 40
Código de Comercio, Title IV, c 1–9 (Commercial Arbitration) (Mexico). 155
Commercial Arbitration Act, RSC 1985, c 17 (2nd Supp) (Canada). 155
Crown Proceedings Act 1947 (UK). 107
Emergency Law No 25.561 (6 January 2002) (Argentina). 1
Federal Arbitration Act 1925 (USA). 129, 155
Federal Tort Claims Act 1946 (USA). 107
Foreign Sovereign Immunities Act 1976 (USA). 46
International Commercial Arbitration Act, RSBC 1996, c 233 (British Columbia). 156
National Decree No 256/2002 (9 February 2002) (Argentina). 1
State Immunity Act 1978 (UK). 46
United Nations Foreign Arbitral Awards Convention Act, RSC 1985, c 16 (Canada). 129

Table of Treaties

Accord entre la Confédération suisse et la République des Philippines concernant la promotion et la protection réciproque des investissements (the Switzerland—Philippines BIT) (Manille, 31 March 1997; entered into force 23 April 1999). 29, 76
Accord entre la Confédération suisse et la République du Pakistan concernant la promotion et la protection réciproque des investissements (the Switzerland–Pakistan BIT) (Berne, 11 July 1995; entered into force 6 May 1996). 29, 76
Accord entre le Gouvernement de la République Française et le Gouvernement de la République Argentine sur l'encouragement et la protection réciproques des investissements (the France–Argentina BIT) (Paris, 3 July 1991; entered into force 3 March 1993). 29, 76, 170
Acuerdo para la promoción y la protección reciproca de inversiones entre el Reino de España y la República Argentina (the Spain–Argentina BIT) (Buenos Aires, 3 October 1991; entered into force 28 September 1992). 29, 76
Acuerdo para la promoción y protección reciproca de inversiones entre los Estados Unidos Mexicanos y el Reino de España (the Spain–Mexico BIT) (Mexico City, 22 June 1995; entered into force 18 December 1996). 29, 76, 128, 170
Agreement among the Government of Brunei Darussalam, the Republic of Indonesia, Malaysia, the Republic of the Philippines, the Republic of Singapore and the Kingdom of Thailand for the Promotion and Protection of Investments (ASEAN Agreement for the Promotion and Protection of Investments) (Manila, 15 December 1987; 27 ILM 612). 26, 171
Agreement between the Government of the United Kingdom of Great Britain and Northern Ireland and the Government of the Arab Republic of Egypt for the promotion and protection of investments (the UK–Egypt BIT) (London, 11 June 1975, UKTS No 97 (1976); Cmd 6638; entered into force 24 February 1976). 29, 76
Agreement between the Government of the United Kingdom of Great Britain and Northern Ireland and the Government of the Democratic Socialist Republic of Sri Lanka for the promotion and protection of investments (the UK–Sri Lanka BIT) (Colombo, 13 February 1980; UKTS No 14 (1981); Cmd 8186; entered into force 18 December 1980). 29, 76, 170
Agreement between the Government of the United Kingdom of Great Britain and Northern Ireland and the Government of the Republic of India (the UK–India BIT) (London, 14 March 1994; UKTS No 27 (1995); Cmd 2797; entered into force 6 January 1995). 37, 102, 171
Agreement between the Hellenic Republic and the Arab Republic of Egypt for the promotion and reciprocal protection of investments (the Greece–Egypt BIT) (Athens, 16 July 1993; entered into force 6 April 1995). 29, 58, 76
Agreement on encouragement and reciprocal protection of investments between the Kingdom of the Netherlands and the Republic of Bolivia (the Netherlands–Bolivia BIT) (10 March 1992; entered into force 1 November 1994). 29, 58, 76, 171
Agreement on encouragement and reciprocal protection of investments between the Kingdom of the Netherlands and the Czech and Slovak Republic (the Netherlands–Czech Republic BIT) (22 October 1991; entered into force 19 December 1992). 7, 29, 58, 76, 171
Agreement on encouragement and reciprocal protection of investments between the Kingdom of the Netherlands and the Republic of Venezuela (the Netherlands–Venezuela BIT) (22 October 1991; entered into force 1 November 1993). 29, 76, 170
Agreement on Trade-Related Investment Measures (the TRIMs Agreement) (annex IA of the Agreement Establishing the World Trade Organization) (15 April 1994; *Final Act Embodying the Results of the Uruguay Round of Multilateral Trade Negotiations* (1994) 139). 21, 75

Table of Treaties

American Convention on Human Rights (ACHR) (1144 UNTS 123; entered into force 18 July 1978). 103
Charter of Economic Rights and Duties of States, GA Res 3281, UN GAOR, 29th Sess, Supp No 31, UN Doc A/9631 (1974) 50, 14 ILM 251. 17
Charter of the United Nations (26 June 1945; UKTS No 67 (1946) (not published in the UNTS); entered into force 24 October 1945). 119, 140
Chile-United States Free Trade Agreement (6 June 2003; online: USTR http://www.ustr.gov/Trade_Agreements/Bilateral/Chile_FTA/Final_Texts/Section_Index.html). 164
Convenio entre la República Argentina y la Union Economica Belgo-Luxemburguesa para la promoción y la protección de inversiones (the Belgium–Argentina BIT) (Brussels, 28 June 1990; entered into force 20 May 1994). 29, 76
Convenio entre la República del Perú y la República del Paraguay sobre promoción y protección de inversiones (the Peru–Paraguay BIT) (Lima, 31 January 1994; entered into force 18 December 1994). 29, 76
Convention for the Protection of Human Rights and Fundamental Freedoms (the European Convention on Human Rights [ECHR]) (4 November 1950; Eur TS 5, 213 UNTS 222; entered into force 3 September 1953). 103, 136, 159
Convention on the Settlement of Investment Disputes Between States and Nationals of Other States (the ICSID Convention) (Washington, 18 March 1965; 4 ILM 524; entered into force 14 Oct 1966). 5, 27, 34–6, 38, 55–8, 79, 96, 118–19, 129, 132, 139,
154–5, 157, 160, 163, 170–1, 176, 181
Convention on the Execution of Foreign Arbitral Awards (the Geneva Convention of 1927) (Geneva, 26 September 1927; 92 LNTS 302, 27 AJIL 1 (1929); entered into force 25 July 1929). 51, 56
Declaration of the Government of the Democratic and Popular Republic of Algeria concerning the Settlement of Claims by the Government of the United States of America and the Government of the Islamic Republic of Iran (the Algiers Declaration) (Algiers, 19 January 1981; 20 ILM 230 (1981)). 100
Declaration on the Establishment of a New International Economic Order, GA Res 3201, UN GAOR, 6th Spec Sess, Supp No 1, UN Doc A/9559 (1974) 3, 13 ILM 715. 17
Declaration on the Human Rights of Individuals Who are not Nationals of the Country in which They Live, GA Res 40/144, UN GAOR, 40th Sess, Supp No 53, UN Doc A/40/53 (1985) 252. 140–1
The Dominican Republic–Central America–United States Free Trade Agreement (CAFTA) (Washington, 5 August 2004; entered into force 1 March 2006 [US, El Salvador], 1 April [Honduras, Nicaragua], and 1 July 2006 [Guatemala]; 16(6) World Trade and Arb Mat 87). 26, 40, 164
Energy Charter Treaty (annex I of the Final Act of the European Energy Charter Conference) (Lisbon, 17 December 1994; 34 ILM 373). 26, 29–30, 37, 40, 76, 81–2, 114
European Convention on International Commercial Arbitration (21 April 1961; 484 UNTS 364). 54
European Convention on State Immunity (16 May 1972; 74 Euro TS, 11 ILM 470; entered into force 11 June 1976). 46
Final Act of the United Nations Conference on Trade and Employment: Havana Charter for an International Trade Organization (the Havana Charter), UN Conference on Trade and Employment, UN Doc 1948 II.D.4.1 (1948). 20, 23
General Agreement on Trade in Services (the GATS) (15 April 1994; 33 ILM 44). 21, 75
Inter-American Convention on International Commercial Arbitration (the Panama Convention) (Panama, 30 January 1975; 14 ILM 336). 54, 58, 118–19, 129, 155
International Covenant on Civil and Political Rights (16 December 1966; 999 UNTS 171, 61 AJIL 870; entered into force 23 March 1976). 103
Morocco-United States Free Trade Agreement (Washington, 15 June 2004; online: USTR: http://www.ustr.gov/Trade_Agreements/Bilateral/Morocco_FTA/Section_Index.html). 164

Table of Treaties

North American Free Trade Agreement (NAFTA) (17 December 1992; 32 ILM 296 and 605; entered into force 1 January 1994). 3–4, 25–32, 34, 37, 40, 57–8, 61, 64–70, 76, 79–82, 84, 86, 88, 92, 99, 101–3, 113–14, 116, 118–19, 123, 126–32, 134, 136, 140–1, 145–7, 154, 156–7, 160–5, 169, 173–9

Peru-United States Trade Promotion Agreement (Washington, 12 April 2006; online: USTR http://www.ustr.gov/Trade_Agreements/Bilateral/Peru_TPA/Section_Index.html). 164

Protocol on Arbitration Clauses in Commercial Matters (the Geneva Protocol of 1923) (Geneva, 24 September 1923; 20 AJIL 194 (1926); entered into force 28 July 1924). 50–1

Protocolo de Colonia para la Promoción y Protección Recíproca de Inversiones en el MERCOSUR (the Colonia Protocol) (17 January 1994, adopted by Mercosur/CMC/Dec No 11/93; not in force; online: SICE http://www.sice.oas.org/Trade/MRCSR/colonia/pcolonia_s.asp). 26

Resolution on Permanent Sovereignty Over Natural Resources, GA Res 1803, UN GAOR, 17th Sess, Supp No 17, UN Doc A/5217 (1962) 15, 57 AJIL 710. 17

Rome Statute of the International Criminal Court (Statute of the ICC) (Rome, 17 July 1998; 2187 UNTS 3). 69, 182

Singapore–United States Free Trade Agreement (Washington, 6 May 2003; online: USTR http://www.ustr.gov/Trade_Agreements/Bilateral/Singapore_FTA/Section_Index.html). 40, 164

Softwood Lumber Agreement between the Government of Canada and the Government of the United States of America (Washington, 29 May 1996; CTS 1996/16, 35 ILM 1195; entered into force 29 May 1996). 126

Statute of the International Court of Justice (Statute of the ICJ) 59 Stat 1055. 182

Statute of the International Criminal Tribunal for the Former Yugoslavia (Statute of the ICTY) (annex to UN Security Council Res No 827) (25 May 1993, 32 ILM 1203 (1993)). 182

Tratado entre la República Federal de Alemania y la República Argentina sobre promoción y protección recíproca de inversiones (the Germany–Argentina BIT) (Bonn, 9 April 1991; entered into force 8 November 1993). 29, 76, 170

Treaty between the United States of America and the Argentine Republic concerning the reciprocal encouragement and protection of investment (the US–Argentina BIT) (Washington, 14 November 1991; entered into force 20 October 1994). 30, 76, 170

Treaty between the United States of America and the Republic of Ecuador concerning the reciprocal encouragement and protection of investment (the US–Ecuador BIT) (Washington, 27 August 1993; entered into force 11 May 1997). 29–30, 76

Treaty between the Government of the United States of America and the Government of Romania concerning the reciprocal encouragement and protection of investment (the US-Romania BIT) (Bucharest, 28 May 1992; entered into force 15 January 1994). 29–30, 76

Treaty of Amity, Commerce and Navigation between Great Britain and the United States (the Jay Treaty) (19 November 1794; 52 Cons TS 243; entered into force 28 October 1795). 100–1

Treaty on Free Trade Between the Republic of Colombia, the Republic of Venezuela and the United Mexican States (13 June 1994; entered into force 1 January 1995; online: SICE http://www.sice.oas.org/trade/go3/G3INDICE.asp). 26

Treaty with the Czech and Slovak Federal Republic concerning the reciprocal encouragement and protection of investment (the US–Czech Republic BIT) (Washington, 22 October 1991; entered into force 19 December 1992). 29–30, 76, 169

Understanding on Rules and Procedures Governing the Settlement of Disputes (the WTO Dispute Settlement Understanding) (15 April 1994; 33 ILM 112). 103

United Nations Convention on the Law of the Sea (Montego Bay, 10 December 1982; 21 ILM 1261; entered into force 16 November 1994). 103

United Nations Convention on the Recognition and Enforcement of Foreign Arbitral Awards (the New York Convention) (New York, 10 June 1958; 330 UNTS 3; entered into force 7 June 1959). 5, 34–6, 38, 51–8, 61, 118–19, 128–9, 155–8, 165, 176, 181

UN Basic Principles on the Independence of the Judiciary (adopted by the Seventh United Nations Congress on the Prevention of Crime and the Treatment of Offenders, Milan, 26 August–6 September 1985; endorsed by GA Res 40/32 and 40/146, UN GAOR, 40th Sess, UN Doc A/RES/40/32 and A/RES/40/146 (1985)). 167–8, 180

Universal Declaration of Human Rights, GA Res 217A, UN GAOR, 3rd Sess, Part I, UN Doc A/810 (1948) 71. .... 141, 150

Vienna Convention on the Law of Treaties (Vienna, 22 May 1969; 1155 UNTS 331; entered into force 27 January 1980). 66

1

Introduction

Argentina's economy collapsed in December 2001. It had been in a major slump since the Asian financial crisis of 1998, largely because its currency regime—which pegged the peso to the US dollar—had crippled Argentine exporters against their foreign competitors. From mid-2001, (US)$20 billion was moved out of Argentina in speculation of a devaluation of the peso and, in late November, the country's central bank reserves fell by $2 billion in a single day amidst massive capital flight. In response, the government froze bank accounts and imposed wage and capital controls. In turn, on 7 December, the International Monetary Fund blocked the release of $2 billion to Argentina, blaming the government's failure to impose austerity measures and other reforms. This sent the economy into free-fall. Jobs disappeared en masse as hundreds of businesses went bankrupt. Wages of government workers were cut by 40 per cent and $3 billion in private pensions was redirected by the government to service the national debt. Argentinians blockaded streets and beat at the doors of the banks in desperation. Popular insurrection was espoused at 'neighbourhood assemblies' where anger was directed at the 'tens of billions taken away by the power suppliers [and] the profits that the telephone companies gained every year'. In just two weeks at the end of December five presidents were forced from office. That month, 30 people died in street protests and looting, and by January the government was distributing emergency food aid.[1]

In the face of financial catastrophe, the newly appointed government of President Duhalde announced on 6 January 2002 that it would allow the peso to decline in value against the dollar, thus cutting national savings by 70 per cent overnight, and attempt to renegotiate the country's debt 'in order to guarantee the operation of the National State in accordance with available resources'.[2] For many

---

[1] M Barrow, 'Argentina puts bankers to the test' *The Times* (7 August 2001) 21; P Wheatcroft, 'Argentina loan' *The Times* (23 August 2001) 23; G Gamini, 'Argentina faces debt default as IMF stops loan' *The Times* (7 December 2001) 21; L Paterson, 'Argentina holds make-or-break talks with IMF' *The Times* (8 December 2001) 56; G Gamini, 'Rioters killed as Argentina slides into chaos' *The Times* (20 December 2001) 17; S Calloni, 'Frágil, el equilibrio politico, económico y social en Argentina' *La Jornada* [Mexico] (21 January 2002). See also JF Hornbeck, 'The Argentine Financial Crisis: A Chronology of Events' (US Congressional Research Service Report No RS21130, 31 January 2002).

[2] Emergency Law No 25.561 (6 January 2002) (Argentina); National Decree No 256/2002 (9 February 2002) (Argentina).

months afterwards, Argentina was mired in severe crisis, described by the *Economist* as 'a decline without parallel' and 'an economic collapse to match the Great Depression of the 1930s'.³ By November 2002 more than half the population was living in poverty. However, by 2004 the value of the peso stabilized and the economy began to recover. And, early in 2005, the government reached an agreement with bondholders to restructure over $100 billion in debt, paying about 34 cents on the dollar.⁴ The reforms of early 2002 thus proved successful in at least averting a total collapse and allowing the country to emerge, in the words of the government, 'with its republican form of government intact'.⁵

Yet an important chapter in this story is still unfolding. Since 2001 foreign investors in Argentina—such as Enron and Azurix of the United States; Vivendi and Suez of France; Siemens of Germany; Gas Natural of Spain; and National Grid of the United Kingdom—have brought dozens of legal claims against the country under an obscure system of international arbitration, established by an array of investment treaties concluded in the 1990s between Argentina and the major capital-exporting states of Western Europe and North America. By 2006 more than 30 claims were pending against Argentina for an estimated $17 billion in claimed compensation, amounting to nearly the entire annual budget of the national government.⁶ Many of the firms had purchased assets in the utilities sectors—water, gas, electricity—in the heydey of the privatizations of the early 1990s, when President Carlos Menem and his finance minister, Domingo Cavallo, carried out a shock programme of liberalization, deregulation, and sale of state assets. At the time, the privatization contracts signed by many foreign investors stipulated that utility rates would be denominated in dollar-pegged pesos and that they would rise or fall alongside the US producer price index. Ten years later, at the nadir of the economic crisis, the government ordered utility rates to be translated into devalued pesos and then frozen so that wage earners and businesses could afford basic services. This left the finances of many investors in tatters.

---

³ 'A decline without parallel-Argentina's collapse' *The Economist* (2 March 2002); 'Liberty's great advance' *The Economist* (28 June 2003).

⁴ U Goni, 'Debt-ridden middle classes ready to desert Argentina' *The Sunday Times* (6 January 2002) 24; T Walker, 'Argentina panics as banks close' *The Sunday Times* (21 April 2002) 25; G Gamini, 'Argentina slides deeper into mire of debt' *The Times* (15 November 2002) 22; T Hennigan, 'Argentina defaults on $2.9 billion debt' *The Times* (10 September 2003) 13; A Thomson, 'Argentina revels in power of peso' *The Financial Times* (30 June 2005) 43.

⁵ *CMS Gas Transmission Company v Argentine Republic* (Application for Annulment) (8 September 2005), ICSID Case No ARB/01/8, para 23, online: ITA.

⁶ LE Peterson, 'Argentine bondholders girding for multi-billion dollar investment treaty claim' *Investment Law and Policy News Bulletin* (10 June 2005); V Lowe, 'Some Comments on Procedural Weaknesses in International Law' (2004) 98 Am Soc'ty Int'l L Proc 37, 39. One group of foreign bondholders announced that it would bring a claim on behalf of its members for an estimated $25 billion, although the claim apparently never materialized: A Thomson, 'Argentine creditors toughen stance' *The Financial Times* (17 February 2005) 39; OC Pell, White & Case LLP, 'Recent Argentine Legislation and Argentine Bondholders' (Memorandum to the Global Committee of Argentine Bondholders, 15 February 2005).

The question underlying these claims by foreign firms is in a sense very straightforward: who should bear the cost of losses suffered by investors during the crisis and subsequent reforms? Did the Argentine government act rashly or unfairly burden foreign companies in its 'pesofication' of the monetary system? Or were the companies foolish to purchase the assets and assume debt in foreign currency on the risk that an economic collapse might provoke emergency restructuring by the state? An initial answer was provided in May 2005 by the investment treaty tribunal in *CMS v Argentina*, when three arbitrators ordered Argentina to pay $133 million to CMS Energy, a US-based investor in the gas sector.[7] The arbitrators concluded among other things that, regardless of whether the government acted in good faith in adopting policies that harmed CMS Energy's business, Argentina bore an 'objective' responsibility under international law to ensure a stable and predictable business environment for foreign investors, even in the midst of financial meltdown.[8] Further, the arbitrators decided that the investor's right to compensation was not extinguished or moderated by circumstances of public emergency.[9]

In contrasting these controversial findings of the *CMS v Argentina* tribunal against the tumultuous social and economic breakdown in Argentina, my aim is not to argue that the award was incorrect in law and imprudent in policy (although in my view it probably was), but rather to show that private arbitrators have a new-found power to review and discipline states, and to convey an impression of how this power interacts with the lives of ordinary people and the way they are governed. It is true that the raft of claims against Argentina was an exceptionally dramatic episode in the recent expansion of investment treaty arbitration[10] but it remains indicative of a much wider phenomenon.

The system of investment treaty arbitration

Little more than a decade ago, investment treaty arbitration was virtually unknown beyond the circles of those who were involved, one way or another, in the negotiation of investment treaties. The system entered the public mindset in the mid-1990s after several claims were brought by investors under Chapter 11 of the North American Free Trade Agreement (NAFTA) and, eventually, under numerous bilateral investment treaties. Since then, the system has expanded rapidly. In the last ten years investors have launched more than 150 claims under investment treaties, mainly against developing and former communist countries,

---

[7] *CMS Gas Transmission Company v Argentine Republic* (Merits) (12 May 2005), 44 ILM 1205, 17(5) World Trade and Arb Mat 63 [cited as *CMS v Argentina*], para 53–6.
[8] *CMS v Argentina* (n 7 above) para 274–84.   [9] *CMS v Argentina* (n 7 above) para 387–92.
[10] The term 'investment treaty arbitration' (or 'investor–state arbitration') refers to compulsory arbitration, pursuant to an investment treaty, between a state and an investor at the option of the latter. The term also distinguishes 'treaty' arbitration from the contract- or legislation-based variants of investment arbitration.

and most are still pending. This has generated a fourteen-fold spike in the rate of claims at the World Bank's Centre for Settlement of Investment Disputes (ICSID), for example.[11] Moreover, the subject-matter of claims under investment treaties has engaged a very diverse range of business and regulatory concerns. Under NAFTA, claims were brought against Canada, Mexico, or the US in disputes arising from a Canadian parliamentary ban on hazardous waste exports, a Mexican state governor's designation of an ecological park, and a Mississippi judge's conduct of a jury trial.[12] Under bilateral investment treaties, tribunals have been established to resolve disputes involving the issuance of radio broadcasting licences in the Ukraine, the annulment of permits for an industrial plant in Peru, and the denial of VAT refunds in the oil sector in Ecuador.[13]

The question at the heart of this book is what is the essential character and significance of this new system? In response, three claims are advanced. The first is that the advent of investment treaty arbitration is a revolutionary development in international adjudication. The second is that the system's crucial importance is that—unlike any other form of international arbitration—it is a method of public law adjudication, meaning that it is used to resolve *regulatory* disputes between individuals and the state as opposed to reciprocal disputes between private parties or between states. Third, and most troubling, is that the system's unique use of private arbitration in the regulatory sphere conflicts with cherished principles of judicial accountability and independence in democratic societies; in effect, it taints the integrity of the legal system by contracting out the judicial function in public law.

The more detailed argument in support of these claims may be summarized as follows. States, by concluding investment treaties that allow foreign investors (for the most part multinational firms[14]) to advance international claims against

---

[11] During the 10 years from 1996 to 2005, 166 claims by investors were registered at ICSID, compared to 35 in the previous 30 years. So recent is the explosion of claims under investment treaties that the UN Conference on Trade and Development could not long ago report: 'There is very little known on the use that countries and investors have made of [bilateral investment treaties]: they have been invoked in a few international arbitrations, and presumably in diplomatic correspondence and investor demands. Their most significant function appears to be that of providing signals of an attitude favouring FDI.' UNCTAD, *Trends in International Investment Agreements: An Overview* (UNCTAD Series on Issues in International Investment Agreements, 1999) 47.

[12] *SD Myers, Inc v Government of Canada* (Merits) (13 November 2000), 40 ILM 1408, 15(1) World Trade and Arb Mat 184; *Metalclad Corporation v United Mexican States* (Merits) (30 August 2000), 16 ICSID Rev 168, 40 ILM 36, 5 ICSID Rep 212, 13(1) World Trade and Arb Mat 45; *Loewen Group, Inc and Raymond L Loewen v United States of America* (Merits) (26 June 2003), 42 ILM 811, 7 ICSID Rep 442, 15(5) World Trade and Arb Mat 97.

[13] *Lemire (Joseph Charles) v Ukraine* (Settlement), ICSID Case No ARB(AF)/98/1, online: ITA; *Empresas Lucchetti, SA and Lucchetti Peru, SA v Republic of Peru* (Jurisdiction) (7 February 2005), 19 ICSID Rev 359, 17(3) World Trade and Arb Mat 161, para 18–21; *Occidental Exploration and Production Company v Republic of Ecuador* (Merits) (1 July 2004), 17(1) World Trade and Arb Mat 165, para 32.

[14] However extensive their actual business operations, foreign investors are typically complex legal entities organized as networks of companies (or other legal entities) which I shall refer to as multinational firms or multinational enterprises. As defined by the Organization for Economic Co-operation

Introduction 5

states have given arbitrators the authority to resolve regulatory disputes between investors and the state. This authority is in certain respects more powerful than that of any court, domestic or international, because the system piggybacks on the rules and structure of international commercial arbitration instead of adopting a more conventional court-based model. First, as with the public law competence of the courts, arbitrators have comprehensive jurisdiction to review sovereign acts of the state by applying broadly worded standards of review that are open to a range of interpretations and, as such, they are empowered to resolve core matters of public law. Second, because investment treaties utilize the enforcement structure of the New York Convention and the ICSID Convention, the awards of arbitrators are more widely enforceable than any other adjudicative decision in public law. Third, the laws of the major enforcing countries in North America and Europe were revised in the 1980s and 1990s (for the distinct objective of promoting international commercial arbitration) to direct domestic courts to defer to foreign arbitration awards; as a result, arbitrators interpret and apply public law with limited court supervision. Finally, arbitrators are able to award damages as a public law remedy without having to apply the various limitations on state liability that evolved in domestic legal systems to balance the objectives of deterrence and compensation against the competing principles of democratic choice and governmental discretion.

In doing this, states have enabled privately contracted adjudicators to determine the legality of sovereign acts and to award public funds to businesses that sustain loss as a result of government regulation. This undermines basic hallmarks of judicial accountability, openness, and independence. Above all, the lack of security of tenure of arbitrators in a one-sided system of state liability, in which only investors bring the claims and only states pay damages for breach of the treaties, makes the adjudicator dependent on prospective claimants and thus biased, in an objective sense, against respondent governments. That is, because they receive appointments only if investors bring claims, arbitrators may reasonably be perceived as having a financial stake in interpreting investment treaties so as to

and Development (OECD) in its *Guidelines for Multinational Enterprises* (2000) 17–18, multinational enterprises: 'usually comprise companies or other entities established in more than one country and so linked that they may co-ordinate their operations in various ways. While one or more of these entities may be able to exercise a significant influence over the activities of others, their degree of autonomy within the enterprise may vary widely from one multinational enterprise to another. Ownership may be private, state or mixed.' An inherent aspect of multinational firms is their ability to make decisions about the allocation of capital and about production and distribution that transcend the boundaries of national regulation. The integral part played by such firms in organizing capital flows reflects their role as agents of globalization and makes them central actors in investment arbitration. S Timberg, 'International Combines and National Sovereigns' (1947) 95 U Penn L Rev 575, 577–8; AA Fatouros, 'On Domesticating Giants: Further Reflections on the Legal Approach to Transnational Enterprise' (1976) 15 U Western Ontario L Rev 151, 152–4; M Wilkins, 'Defining a Firm: History and Theory' in P Hertner and G Jones (eds) *Multinationals: Theory and History* (1986) 80–1; S Picciotto, 'Introduction: What Rules for the World Economy?' in S Picciotto and R Mayne (eds) *Regulating International Business* (1999) 6–7.

expand the system's compensatory promise for investors. And while the domestic courts of either the host or the home state may be seen to be biased in the resolution of an international investment dispute, it is a step backward to replace them with adjudicators who are perceptibly dependent on private interests in ways that tenured judges are not.

The scope and complexity of the system

Three additional points may be highlighted at this introductory stage. The first is that, while investment treaty arbitration is not a *global* regime in the absence of bilateral investment treaties (BITs) between major capital-exporting states or a multilateral investment code, it should none the less be understood as an international system that is elaborate and well entrenched, that has wide geographic scope, and that governs the bulk of the capital flows into developing and former communist countries. In particular, the system is constituted by the hundreds of bilateral and regional investment treaties currently in force (and mostly concluded in the 1990s[15]) that share three key characteristics. First, each treaty that is part of the system authorizes foreign investors to make and seek enforcement of claims for money damages against the state parties without the claims being vetted by the investor's home state or by an international organization. Second, sovereign acts of the states parties are subjected to broad standards of review that apply to a wide range of governmental activity, giving arbitrators a comprehensive jurisdiction to award compensation to international business in the regulatory sphere. Third, disputes are resolved using a private model of adjudication that originates in the rules and enforcement structure of international commercial arbitration, presenting major challenges to public law principles of judicial accountability, openness, and independence. By consenting to an array of treaties that share these characteristics, most states have by now plugged themselves into the system and, in so doing, they have integrated into their governing apparatus a uniquely international and privately modelled system of public law adjudication.

This leads to the second point that I wish to highlight at this stage. It is that the significance of the system in relation to public law must not be underestimated, although the sheer complexity of the system—incorporating, as it does, a multitude of investment treaties, several major conventions on international arbitration, various sets of arbitration rules, and the domestic arbitration laws of as many as 165 countries—may tend to mask its character in this respect. A review of a recent and quite infamous case may offer a glimpse of this complexity as well as the power that the system bestows on arbitrators. In March 2003 a tribunal

---

[15] UNCTAD, *Bilateral Investment Treaties—1959–1999* (New York: United Nations, 2000) 1 (the number of bilateral investment treaties rose from 385 in 1989 to 1,857 by 1999); UNCTAD, *World Investment Report 2004* (New York: United Nations, 2004) 221 (2,265 bilateral investment treaties were concluded by the end of 2003, involving 175 countries).

constituted in Sweden ordered the Czech Republic to pay (US)$353 million to an investor that owned a Czech TV broadcasting business.[16] The investor was a Dutch company, CME Czech Republic, that was in turn owned by the cosmetics billionaire Ralph Lauder, an American citizen.[17] The tribunal ordered the Czech Republic to pay damages to Mr Lauder's company after finding that the Czech government, by issuing regulatory advice that prompted CME to divest itself of a popular TV station, had violated the country's bilateral investment treaty with the Netherlands.[18] After failing to have the award set aside in the Swedish courts, the Czechs committed to pay it in full, lest they suffer yet more harm to their reputation in the capital markets.[19] Further, following the claim, other foreign firms brought or threatened claims against the Czech Republic in cases ranging from the collapse of a domestic bank, to an unsuccessful bid for a mobile telephone network, to the seizure of a jet by Czech customs authorities in lieu of back taxes owed by the foreign owner.[20]

For present purposes, the *CME* case is significant for two reasons. First, the case is revealing because the award of $353 million placed an enormous strain on the public finances of the Czech Republic. The amount was roughly equal to the country's entire health-care budget[21] and, adjusted for population size and gross national income, it was equivalent to an award of $19 billion against the United Kingdom, $26 billion against Germany, or $131 billion against the United States.[22] Second, just ten days before the award was issued, a parallel claim by

---

[16] *CME Czech Republic BV v Czech Republic* (Merits) (13 September 2001), 14(3) World Trade and Arb Mat 109 [cited as *CME* (Merits)].

[17] B Von Hase, 'Do the Right Thing' *The Times Magazine* [London] (13 September 2003) 50.

[18] Agreement on encouragement and reciprocal protection of investments between the Kingdom of the Netherlands and the Czech and Slovak Republic (the Netherlands–Czech Republic BIT) (22 October 1991; entered into force 19 December 1992). The treaty violation arose from the Czech government's regulatory treatment of a Czech TV network that was owned by CME. According to the tribunal, the government in effect destroyed the investment by issuing an interpretation of the law that forced CME to give up its ownership share.

[19] *CME Czech Republic BV v Czech Republic* (2003) 15(5) World Trade and Arb Mat 171 [cited as *CME* (Judgment)] (Swed Svea CA). The Czech Republic applied to set aside the award before the Swedish court of appeal, rather than the Czech courts, because Sweden had been chosen by the arbitration tribunal as the legal seat of the arbitration (the actual hearings were held in Düsseldorf, Germany). LE Peterson, 'Swedish court affirms award against Czech Republic; damages could be taxable' *Investment Law and Policy Weekly News Bulletin* (16 May 2003).

[20] *Saluka Investments BV v Czech Republic* (Merits) (17 March 2006), 18(3) World Trade and Arb Mat 166. S François-Poncet and C Mouawad, 'Final Arbitral Award Rendered in 2003 in SCC Case 49/2002' (2004) 2004:1 Stockholm Arbitration Report 141; LE Peterson, 'Investors emboldened by arbitral verdict against Czech Republic' *Investment Law and Policy Weekly News Bulletin* (11 April 2003); Z Kawaciukova, 'State ordered to pay 10 billion Kc' *The Prague Post* (19 March 2003); R Anderson, 'Tribunal to rule on Czech bank failure' *Financial Times* (8 April 2005) 27.

[21] T Kellner, 'The Informer: Call It the Ronald Lauder Tax', 171(9) *Forbes Magazine* (28 April 2003).

[22] *CME Czech Republic BV v Czech Republic* (Damages) (14 March 2003), 15(4) World Trade and Arb. Mat. 83 and 245, para 80 (separate opinion of I Brownlie). As an aside, in 2006 Ralph Lauder reportedly paid $135 million for Gustav Klimt's *Portrait of Adele Bloch-Bauer I*, the highest price ever paid for a painting: C Vogel, 'Lauder Pays $135 Million, a Record, for a Klimt Portrait' *The New York Times* (19 June 2006).

Mr Lauder himself based on the same case against the Czech Republic, but initiated six months earlier under a Czech-United States investment treaty, was *dismissed* by a separate tribunal.[23] In reviewing the conduct of the Czech broadcasting authorities—very soon after to be condemned by the *CME* tribunal as 'interference', 'coercion', and an 'intentional undermining' of Mr Lauder's investment[24]—this earlier tribunal concluded that it 'did not see any inconsistent conduct on the part of the Media Council which would amount to an unfair and inequitable treatment', that Mr Lauder's allegation was 'rather vague', and that Mr Lauder had acquiesced in his regulatory treatment by failing to 'commence any administrative or other proceedings before the appropriate courts of the Czech Republic in the course of which the issue of the overall attitude of the Media Council in this affair . . . could be addressed and decided'.[25] Thus, two starkly conflicting decisions were issued in the same dispute under similarly worded investment treaties. Mr Lauder, the American investor, lost his personal claim on the basis that the Czech Republic's breach of the treaty was 'too remote to qualify as a relevant cause for the harm'.[26] But Mr Lauder, the Dutch investor, was able to collect damages through a holding company in the Netherlands.[27]

As such, the case demonstrated two peculiarities of the system as a public law phenomenon: its invitation to forum-shopping by investors and, by implication, its vulnerability to the troubling outcome of conflicting awards; as well as the potentially severe fiscal consequences of the power of arbitrators to decide that a state has broken the law and to punish it by ordering payment of compensation to a foreign investor.

The exceptionality of the system

The third point to stress at this stage is that the system is a highly exceptional development in the context of international law. Of course, it is not surprising that disputes may arise between foreign investors and states in a global economy. International investment disputes have existed for as long as people in one country acquired business interests in another, and much of the great social and economic change of the nineteenth and twentieth centuries—European industrialization, the growth of international business, socialist revolution and Third World decolonization, the establishment of new states, the rise and fall of the Soviet Union—expanded the conditions in which investment disputes could

---

[23] *Lauder (Ronald S) v Czech Republic* (Final Award) (3 September 2001), (2002) 4 World Trade and Arb Materials 35 [cited as *Lauder*].   [24] *CME* (Merits) (n 16 above) para 582, 593, and 611.
[25] *Lauder* (n 23 above) para 261, 273, 287, and 295.   [26] *Lauder* (n 23 above) para 235.
[27] The Czech Republic's application to set aside the award on this point was rejected by the Swedish court of appeal on the basis that Ralph Lauder and CME—the Dutch company controlled by Mr Lauder—were different parties and that their claims could therefore proceed concurrently, even though the substance of the claims was the same: *CME* (Merits) (n 16 above) para 426-33. The Swedish court of appeal was also influenced by the fact that the Czech Republic had refused, at an

arise.²⁸ To what minimum standard of treatment are foreign investors entitled under international law? To what degree can states support their own industries at the expense of outside competition? Under what conditions can a government expropriate, or regulate, the property of a multinational firm? These questions have driven and plagued debates about international law for well over a century.

On the other hand, it is most surprising that individual investors can now, rather suddenly in the historical context, trigger the compulsory arbitration of international investment disputes. For most of the twentieth century, international courts and tribunals rarely had jurisdiction over disputes concerning state regulation of foreign nationals. Students of international law will be well aware that such disputes were customarily resolved by dispute resolution between states.²⁹ This might result in a claim of diplomatic protection by the home state of a foreign national against the state whose conduct was in doubt, but such claims were typically settled by negotiation and, exceptionally, by adjudication between states. Moreover, once the states involved arrived at a resolution, individuals were left without further remedy under international law.³⁰ Thus, foreign investors like other foreign nationals relied on their home state to represent their interests in the international sphere and, faced with 'the arbitrary whim or caprice of state officials' or 'the most flagrant spoliations of private property', they sometimes suffered greatly for this dependence.³¹

These customary arrangements may appear unfair but it should be remembered that they follow from an elemental principle of international society; that is, that a state is the legal representative of the population of its territory.³² As the legal framework of state-based representation is altered by states, and individuals are allowed to bring claims on their own behalf, some very important questions arise. One set of questions, not the primary focus of this book, springs from the selectivity of such a system. If foreign investors are permitted to claim compensation under international law, why not a migrant worker who is denied access to

early stage, the investor's offer to consolidate the two claims: *CME* (Judgment) (n 19 above) 210 and 242.

²⁸ AA Fatouros, 'International Law and the Third World' (1964) 50 Virg L Rev 783, 783–94; PT Muchlinski, *Multinational Enterprises and the Law* (Oxford: Blackwell, 1999) 10–11.

²⁹ JG Merrills, *International Dispute Settlement* (3rd edn, Cambridge: CUP, 1998) 114–15; J Collier and V Lowe, *The Settlement of Disputes in International Law* (Cambridge: CUP, 1999) 6–7.

³⁰ JL Brierly, *The Law of Nations* (6th edn, Oxford: Clarendon Press, 1963) 277 ('He has no remedy of his own, and the state to which he belongs may be unwilling to take up his case for reasons which have nothing to do with its merits; and even if it is willing to do so, there may be interminable delays before, if ever, the defendant state can be induced to let the matter go to arbitration ... ').

³¹ Quoting, respectively, MS McDougal, HD Lasswell, and L Chen, 'Nationality and Human Rights: The Protection of the Individual in External Arenas' (1973) 83 Yale LJ 900, 906; WL Penfield, 'Address: Is the Forcible Collection of Contract Debts in the Interest of International Justice and Peace?' (1907) 1 Am Soc'ty Int'l L Proc 129, 131.

³² WW Willoughby, *The Fundamental Concepts of Public Law* (New York: Macmillan, 1924) 307; B Kingsbury, 'Sovereignty and Inequality' (1998) 9 EJIL 599, 601 (noting that state sovereignty is the 'means by which people can express, and be deemed to have expressed, consent to the application of international legal norms and to international institutional competences').

the rights and entitlements of domestic employees, or a refugee who is denied asylum and deported to torture, or an indigenous people whose land is polluted and livelihood destroyed by a multinational firm? None of these alternative scenarios is on the political agenda and, beyond the European Union, nearly all states have strongly resisted the idea of allowing non-investors any such legal status.[33] At present, therefore, the advent of investment treaty arbitration stands out, not as the vanguard of a broad movement to protect individuals in international law, but as an anomalous and exceptionally potent system that protects one class of individuals by constraining the governments that continue to represent everyone else. Designed in this way, the system disadvantages those individuals who stand to benefit from business regulation that is now foreclosed by investment treaties or from other public initiatives, the cost of which is made too high or uncertain by the threat of investor claims.

For these reasons, it is right to subject investment treaty arbitration to careful scrutiny in light of its character not simply as an international system but as a unique form of public law adjudication; that is, as a treaty-based regime that uses rules and structures of international law and private arbitration to make governmental choices regarding the regulatory relationship between individuals and the state. Towards this end, much of this book inquires into the system as it stands: after reviewing the system's historical background in Chapter 2, Chapters 3–5 deal with the fundamental distinction between investment treaty arbitration and commercial arbitration, with the wide-ranging governmental discretion that is wielded by arbitrators, and with the novelty of the system in international law. On the other hand, as is by now fairly clear, the book also incorporates an edge of criticism of the system; from this perspective, Chapter 6 evaluates, and for the most part rejects, the interpretive approaches adopted by arbitrators to date, and Chapter 7 presents the argument that the system fails to satisfy basic standards of judging in public law and elaborates a proposal for reform.

In this last regard, it should be emphasized that the target of criticism in this book is neither the global economy nor foreign investors nor the employment of international law and adjudication to strengthen the confidence of international business or resolve regulatory disputes involving the state. Rather, the target of criticism is the particular way in which states have used a private method of international adjudication to resolve claims that should be finally determined by

---

[33] Important reforms have taken place to elevate the international status of individuals, especially in human rights law, but they differ greatly in their scope and effectiveness from the right of investors to bring claims under investment treaties; moreover even in EU law, individuals must exhaust local remedies before bringing a claim against a state, whereas many investment treaties remove this duty. D Shelton, *Remedies in International Human Rights Law* (Oxford: OUP, 1999) 137–8; EB Weiss, 'Invoking State Responsibility in the Twenty-first Century' (2002) 96 AJIL 798, 809–11 and 815; J Thornton, 'Environmental Liability—A Shrinking Mirage or the Most Realistic Attempt So Far' (2003) J Planning & Enviro L 272. On the duty to exhaust local remedies, see J Paulsson, *Denial of Justice in International Law* (Cambridge: CUP, 2005) 8–9; as well as the discussion in Ch 5 below, p 110–13.

courts, whether domestic or international. Consensual arbitration is broadly suitable as a means to settle disputes between companies or between states, but it is fundamentally inadequate as a substitute for the public courts in the regulatory domain. As I shall argue, the courts *and only the courts* should have the final authority to interpret the law that binds sovereign power and to stipulate the appropriate remedies for sovereign wrongs that lead to business loss.

2
A Return to the Gay Nineties?

Over the course of the twentieth century, the major capital-exporting states advanced numerous proposals for a multilateral[1] treaty that would codify liberal standards of investor protection[2] under international law. Many of these envisaged the use of international adjudication for purposes of review and enforcement, although most did not go so far as to contemplate the compulsory arbitration of claims brought directly by investors. In any event, all of them were ultimately dropped in the face of opposition by capital-importing states, setting the stage for the evolution of today's more eclectic collection of bilateral and regional investment treaties.

One example of a proposed multilateral treaty, the International Convention for the Mutual Protection of Private Property Rights in Foreign Countries, aptly illustrates the historical position of the developing world. The draft convention provided for extensive legal protection of private foreign investors, for an international court to resolve disputes (as well an arbitration tribunal to determine the amount of compensation due in cases of expropriation), and for economic sanctions against states that did not abide by decisions of the international court.[3] The proposal was aired by capital-exporting states in 1957 at an economic conference in San Francisco. It was not warmly received. One conference delegate, Miguel Cuaderno, then Governor of the Central Bank of the Philippines, cautioned that it would allow private investors to dominate the economic, if not political, affairs of underdeveloped nations.[4] Guillermo Belt, representing pre-revolutionary Cuba, rejected the treaty as 'a return to the Gay Nineties'.[5] He was referring to the period of rampant imperialism that characterized the late nineteenth century. But he might as well have been presaging the future, for the 1990s witnessed the emergence of a system

---

[1] In this book, the term 'multilateral' is reserved for investment treaties that are open to or intended for signature by any state. Investment treaties concluded between two states are referred to as 'bilateral' investment treaties (BITs) and those between more than two states (whether or not as part of a broader trade agreement) as 'regional' investment treaties.

[2] Substantive provisions in investment treaties are sometimes divided into standards of 'protection' and 'liberalization': eg UNCTAD, *World Investment Report 1996* (Geneva: United Nations, 1997) 189–94. In this book, for simplicity, all such provisions are referred to simply as standards of review or of 'investor protection'.

[3] AS Miller, 'Protection of Private Foreign Investment by Multilateral Convention' (1959) 53 AJIL 371, 374.   [4] Miller (n 3 above), citing *The New York Times* (16 October 1957).
[5] Miller (n 3 above), citing *Time Magazine* (28 October 1957).

with greater scope and potential to protect investors, by controlling governments, than any adjudicative regime since direct colonial arrangements were dismantled.

The failure of proposals for a multilateral investment code in the twentieth century pushed the major capital-exporting countries (ie Western European states, the US, and Japan) and international business organizations to push for alternatives. Their efforts yielded fruit as the post-colonial era evolved into a global market in which most developing countries compete vigorously to attract outside investment. In the 1990s, in particular, capital-importing states[6] saw fit to conclude hundreds of investment treaties, most of which provide for compulsory investment arbitration. As a whole, these treaties constitute today's system of investment treaty arbitration because they allow foreign investors to bring claims for damages against states based on liberal standards of investor protection, and to seek enforcement of damages awards across the globe. Also, and exceptionally, they allow such claims to be resolved by private arbitrators rather than an international court.

Historical Background

The context of post-colonial conflict

Let us begin by reviewing the historical background of the conflict between capital-exporting and capital-importing states. Although the modern setting for investment treaty arbitration differs from that of a century ago, the 'international'

---

[6] As a broad category, 'capital-importing' refers here to 111 states whose inward stock of foreign direct investment (FDI) exceeded their outward stock in 2004 by a ratio of at least 2 to 1 [UNCTAD, *World Investment Report 2005* (New York: United Nations, 2005) annex table B.2]. These included: Algeria, Angola, Argentina, Armenia, Azerbaijan, Bahrain, Bangladesh, Barbados, Belarus, Belize, Benin, Bermuda, Bolivia (1990 data), Brazil, Brunei Darussalam, Bulgaria (2000 data), Burkina Faso, Burundi, Cambodia, Cameroon, Cape Verde, Central African Republic, Chad, Chile, China, Colombia, Comoros, Costa Rica, Côte d'Ivoire, Croatia, Czech Republic, Cyprus, Dominican Republic, Ecuador, Equatorial Guinea, Egypt, El Salvador, Estonia, Ethiopia, Fiji, Gambia, Ghana, Greece, Guatemala, Guinea, Guinea-Bissau, Guyana, Haiti, Hungary, India, Indonesia (2000 data), Iran (2000 data), Ireland, Israel, Jamaica, Jordan (1990 data), Kazakhstan (2000 data), Kenya, Kyrgyzstan (2000 data), Latvia, Lao, Lebanon, Lesotho, Lithuania, Macao, Madagascar, Malawi, Malaysia, Mali, Malta, Mauritania, Mauritius, Mexico, Moldova, Morocco, Mozambique, Namibia, Netherlands Antilles, New Zealand, Nicaragua, Niger, Nigeria, Oman, Pakistan, Papua New Guinea, Paraguay, Peru, Philippines, Poland, Qatar, Romania, Rwanda, Saudi Arabia, Senegal, Seychelles, Slovakia, Slovenia, Sri Lanka, Swaziland, Thailand, Togo, Trinidad and Tobago, Tunisia, Turkey, Uganda, United Arab Emirates, Uruguay, Vanuatu, Venezuela, Yemen, and Zimbabwe. In addition, 10 other states are included as borderline cases where their inward stock of FDI exceeded their outward stock in 2004 by less than 2 to 1, but their outward stock was less than (US)$100 billion: Aruba, Bahamas, Cayman Islands, Gabon, Liberia, Panama, Portugal, Russian Federation, South Africa, and South Korea. Of these 121 countries, 25 major capital-importers emerge with an inward FDI stock of over $25 billion: China ($245 billion), Ireland ($229 billion), Mexico ($183 billion), Brazil ($151 billion), Russian Federation ($98 billion), Bermuda ($78 billion), Portugal ($65 billion), Poland ($61 billion), Hungary ($60 billion), Czech Republic ($56 billion), South Korea

character of investment disputes remains rooted in colonial and post-colonial conflict over foreign ownership and control of local resources and assets.[7] Then, as now, most cross-border investment emanated from Europe and the US, and foreign-owned assets were predominantly owned by Western companies.[8] Thus, the modern origins of investment law and arbitration lie in the late nineteenth and early twentieth centuries, during which most of the world was organized into European empires and large amounts of Western capital flowed abroad.[9] During this period, the legal and institutional framework for the resolution of investment disputes was obviously very different from today's. Regulatory authority in colonial territories emanated from an imperial capital.[10] Disputes between investors and local authorities were resolved within the imperial legal system and, when subject to adjudication, they fell under the jurisdiction of its courts and administrators.[11] Imperial law authorized and regulated the conduct of business across the empire, and the law generally ensured a high degree of business freedom in order

($55 billion), Argentina ($54 billion), Chile ($54 billion), New Zealand ($50 billion), Thailand ($49 billion), Malaysia ($46 billion), South Africa ($46 billion), Venezuela ($44 billion), India ($39 billion), Cayman Islands ($36 billion), Turkey ($35 billion), Israel ($33 billion), Nigeria ($31 billion), Vietnam ($29 billion), Greece ($27 billion).

On the other hand, 'capital-exporting' refers to 20 states whose outward FDI stock exceeded their inward stock in 2004: Austria, Botswana, British Virgin Islands, Canada, Denmark, Finland, France, Germany, Iceland, Italy, Japan, Kuwait (2000 data), Libya, Netherlands, Norway, Sweden, Switzerland, Taiwan, United Kingdom, United States. It also refers to 6 borderline cases whose inward stock exceeded their outward stock in 2004 by less than 2 to 1, but whose outward stock was more than $100 billion: Australia, Belgium, Hong Kong, Luxembourg, Singapore, and Spain. Of these 26 states, 16 major capital-exporters emerge with an outward stock of over $100 billion: United States ($2.02 trillion), United Kingdom ($1.38 trillion), Germany ($830 billion), France ($770 billion), Netherlands ($550 billion), Hong Kong ($410 billion), Switzerland ($390 billion), Japan ($370 billion), Canada ($370 billion), Spain ($330 billion), Italy ($280 billion), Belgium ($250 billion), Sweden ($200 billion), Luxembourg ($180 billion), Australia ($170 billion), and Singapore ($100 billion).

Finally, 49 countries were not classified due to insufficient data: Afghanistan, Anguilla, Antigua and Barbuda, Bhutan, Congo, Congo (Democratic Republic of), Cuba, Djibouti, Dominica, Eritrea, Falkland Islands (Malvinas), Georgia, Gibraltar, Grenada, Honduras, Iraq, Maldives, Mongolia, Montserrat, Myanmar (Burma), Nepal, North Korea, Palestinian Territory, Saint Kitts and Nevis, Saint Lucia, Saint Vincent and the Grenadines, Sào Tomé and Principe, Serbia and Montenegro, Sierra Leone, Sudan, Suriname, Syria, Tanzania, Timor-Leste, Turks and Caicos Islands, Vietnam, Zambia, and 12 island states in Oceania.

[7] AA Fatouros, 'International Law and the Third World' (1964) 50 Virg L Rev 783, 783–94.

[8] The significant historical exception is Japan: PT Muchlinski, *Multinational Enterprises and the Law* (Oxford: Blackwell, 1999) 28–9. DR Young, 'Governmental Regulation of Foreign Investment' (1969) 47 Texas L Rev 421, 425–6; UNCTAD, *World Investment Report 2004* (Geneva: United Nations, 2004) xviii (developed countries continue to account for over 90% of total outward FDI) and annex table A.I.3, A.III.5, A.III.12, B.2, and B.4.

[9] E Hobsbawm, *Industry and Empire* (London: Penguin, 1968) 129–31; I Brownlie, *Principles of Public International Law* (6th edn, Oxford: OUP 2003) 500.

[10] AV Dicey, *An Introduction to the Study of the Law of the Constitution* [1885] (London: Macmillan (8th edn, London: Macmillan, 1915) 51–61; R Jackson, 'Sovereignty in World Politics: A Glance at the Conceptual and Historical Landscape' (1999) 47 Pol Studies 431, 441–4.

[11] SM Hill, 'Growth of International Law in Africa' (1990) 16 LQ Rev 249, 256–9; Dicey (n 10 above) 47 and 55–8.

to facilitate the economic penetration of colonized areas.[12] Where native authorities or peoples interfered with the activities of investors in the colonial era, they risked confrontation with the empire.

Not all non-Western territories were directly colonized at this time. Even so, in an environment of rapid industrialization, European and American business acquired extensive interests in those territories that were not directly colonized, which at times led to disputes with local authorities.[13] In some cases, the Western powers used military force to impose capitulation treaties on other states, including China, Persia, Egypt, and the Ottoman Empire, so as to force open these economies to foreign commerce and industry.[14] Thus, the Anglo-Turkish Convention of 1838 granted European investors the right to establish themselves in the Ottoman Empire, lowered tariffs, and removed internal barriers to trade.[15] In response, Ottoman control of outside investment disintegrated and, by the 1850s, European business dominated the Ottoman economy, having secured extensive concessions in mining, railroad and port construction, coastal navigation, banking, and public utilities.[16] Where disputes arose between the Ottoman authorities and a foreign investor, Ottoman court proceedings were supervised by foreign consular officials who had either ultimate authority or veto power over the local judge.[17] Foreign investors maintained the nationality of their home country and their property was protected by its laws.[18] Thus, beyond the colonies themselves, investor protection was provided by the extraterritorial application of European or American law,[19] and the threat or employment of force was available to ensure business security.

---

[12] SKB Asante, *Transnational Investment Law and National Development* (1981) 24; Y Ghai, R Luckham, and F Snyder, 'Introduction' in Y Ghai, R Luckham, and F Snyder (eds) *The Political Economy of Law* (Oxford: OUP, 1987) 8; PT Muchlinski, 'The Rise and Fall of the Multilateral Agreement on Investment: Where Now?' (2000) 34 Int'l Lawyer 1033, 1034–5. Governing powers were in many cases granted directly to a chartered colonial company: Hill (n 11 above) 258–9 and 264; JH Latané, 'Address' (1907) Am Soc'ty Int'l L Proc 100, 136.

[13] GS Jones, 'The History of US Imperialism' in R Blackburn (ed) *Ideology in Social Science* (Glasgow: Fontana/Collins, 1972) 228–30; Muchlinski (n 12 above) 1034–5.

[14] WE Grigsby, 'The Mixed Court of Egypt' (1896) 12 LQ Rev 252; AM Latter, 'The Government of Foreigners in China' (1903) 19 LQ Rev 316; JK Fairbank, *The United States and China* (Cambridge, Mass: Harvard University Press, 1959) 120–3; WR Johnston, *Sovereignty and Protection: A Study of British Jurisdictional Imperialism in the Late Nineteenth Century* (Durham, NC: Duke University Press, 1973) 29; C Lipson, *Standing Guard-Protecting Foreign Capital in the Nineteenth and Twentieth Centuries* (Berkeley: University of California Press, 1985) 13–14; JAG Roberts, *A History of China* (London: Macmillan, 1999) 162–8; A Anghie, 'Finding the Peripheries: Sovereignty and Colonialism in Nineteenth-Century International Law' (1999) 40 Harv Int'l LJ 1, 41.

[15] C Issawi, *The Economic History of Turkey 1800–1914* (Chicago: University of Chicago Press, 1980) 5; Lipson (n 14 above) 13.   [16] Quoting Lipson (n 14 above) 14.

[17] Alternatively, disputes involving foreigners were subject to the jurisdiction of a mixed court on which foreign judges sat in the majority: Grigsby (n 14 above) 253–4. See also MO Hudson, 'The Rendition of the International Mixed Court at Shanghai' (1927) 21 AJIL 451, 454–5.

[18] Johnston (n 14 above) 29; Issawi (n 15 above) 5; Lipson (n 14 above) 13–14.

[19] N Krisch, 'International Law in Times of Hegemony' (2005) EJIL 369, 401–2; Muchlinski (n 12 above) 1034–5; AA Fatouros, 'On Domesticating Giants: Further Reflections on the Legal Approach to Transnational Enterprise' (1976) 15 U Western Ontario L Rev 151, 166.

Of course, even in the nineteenth century, some countries managed to avoid or escape extraterritorial law as well as formal colonization, primarily in Latin America and later Japan.[20] In such cases, where the law was not directly imposed by a foreign power, investment disputes were transformed into inter-state disputes.[21] Likewise, during the twentieth century, more investment disputes were transformed into international disputes as colonial empires receded and extraterritorial arrangements were replaced by more reciprocal treaty arrangements.[22] These circumstances encouraged, for example, the establishment of mixed claims commissions to resolve conflicts over the treatment of foreign investment, especially between Western business and states in Latin America.[23] Thus, when the government of Cipriano Castro in Venezuela announced that it would not repay its debts to European creditors, a naval armada was dispatched by Germany, Great Britain, and Italy to blockade Caracas and bombard coastal facilities. Under this pressure, the Venezuelans agreed to repay the debt, subject to international arbitration, with preference given to the creditors of countries that had committed military force to enforce the claims.[24] Episodes such as these encouraged the negotiation of the Porter Convention of 1907, which barred states from using force to collect debts, although again only if the debtor state consented to international arbitration to resolve disputes with foreign creditors.[25]

International arbitration thus emerged as a less costly and less odious alternative to the use of force in international economic affairs. As the century progressed, and legal prohibitions on the use of force were strengthened and expanded, international arbitration became yet more attractive as a means for the major capital-exporting states to achieve protection for foreign assets owned by their nationals. On the other hand, many developing countries remained hostile towards arbitration, given its historical association with domination by the great powers and the fact that it was commonly imposed simply as another vehicle of discipline and control. For newly independent states, one aspect of their efforts to

---

[20] MJ Farrelly, 'Recent Questions of International Law: Japan and European Consular Jurisdiction' (1894) 10 LQ Rev 254, 266–7; A Alvarez, 'Latin America and International Law' (1909) 3 AJIL 269.   [21] Muchlinski (n 12 above) 1034–5.

[22] W Peter, *Arbitration and Renegotiation of International Investment Agreements* (The Hague: Kluwer Law International, 1995) 6–7. The new arrangements were based on the European model of bilateral commercial treaties dating from at least the eighteenth century, which were founded on commitments to mutual recognition of non-discrimination in trade in goods and to the unhindered carrying on of business in each state's territory: RR Wilson, 'Post-War Commercial Treaties of the United States' (1949) 43 AJIL 262, 263 and 277; H Walker, 'Treaties for the Encouragement and Protection of Foreign Investment: Present United States Practice' (1956) 5 Am J Comp L 229, 230–1; R Dolzer and M Stevens, *Bilateral Investment Treaties* (The Hague: Kluwer Law International, 1995) 10–11.   [23] Brownlie (n 9 above) 500.

[24] M Hood, *Gunboat Diplomacy 1895–1905* (London: George Allen & Unwin, 1975) 187–8; G Morón, *A History of Venezuela* (London: George Allen & Unwin, 1964) 185–7.

[25] L Drago, 'State Loans in Their Relations to International Policy' (1907) 1 AJIL 692; J Paulsson, *Denial of Justice in International Law* (Cambridge: CUP, 2005) 22–3.

gain more control over their resources was to demand that investment disputes within their territory be resolved in their own courts, based on their own laws.[26] These aspirations reached a high water-mark in the 1960s and 1970s with the assertion of the ideal of permanent sovereignty over natural resources and the proposal for a New International Economic Order.[27] That said, the campaign of the developing world for greater sovereign control over the domestic economy can be traced back much further to the Calvo doctrine[28] and Drago doctrine[29] of the late nineteenth century. The Latin American post-colonial experience, in particular, foreshadowed more recent divisions between capital-exporting and capital-importing states.

Contemporary investment treaties differ from extraterritorial and colonial legal regimes in many respects. They are not imposed by direct force and they apply international law rather than a foreign domestic law to regulate states. They also subject disputes to adjudication by international tribunals instead of imperial courts or foreign consuls. On the other hand, investment treaties apply standards of review—to protect foreign investment from state regulation—that are based on a Western conception of international law that was long resisted by the Third World, and the typical contemporary arbitrator is a Western professional.[30] So, while investment treaty arbitration is unique, one should not lose sight of its ancestry or the fact that early international arbitrations of investment disputes sometimes followed in the wake of foreign invasion and occupation.[31] In this light, it is not that surprising that investment treaty arbitration is viewed with hesitation, not to say suspicion, in many quarters, including among

---

[26] International Law Commission, *Summary Records of the 9th Session*, 1957, UN Doc A/CN.4/106, [1957] 1 Ybk Int'l Law Comm 155, para 45–51 (comment by P Nervo); W Friedmann, *Law in a Changing Society* (London: Stevens & Sons, 1959) 454–5; Fatouros (n 7 above) 802–4; AF Abbott, 'Latin America and International Arbitration Conventions: The Quandary of Non-Ratification' (1976) 17 Harv Int'l LJ 131, 136–7.

[27] Resolution on Permanent Sovereignty Over Natural Resources, GA Res 1803, UN GAOR, 17th Sess, Supp No 17, UN Doc A/5217 (1962) 15, 57 AJIL 710; Declaration on the Establishment of a New International Economic Order, GA Res 3201, UN GAOR, 6th Spec Sess, Supp No 1, UN Doc A/9559 (1974) 3, 13 ILM 715; Charter of Economic Rights and Duties of States, GA Res 3281, UN GAOR, 29th Sess, Supp No 31, UN Doc A/9631 (1974) 50, 14 ILM 251. J Castaneda, 'The Underdeveloped Nations and the Development of International Law' (1961) 15 Int'l Org 38, 39; K Hossain, 'Introduction' in K Hossain and SR Chowdhury (eds) *Permanent Sovereignty over Natural Resources in International Law* (London: Pinter, 1984) ix–xix.

[28] Asserting that the use of force to protect foreign investors was prohibited and that, upon entering a state's territory, foreign investors had to respect local laws and subject themselves to domestic courts. The only protection to which investors were entitled under international law was the same treatment as that enjoyed by nationals. C Calvo, *Le Droit international* (5th edn, Paris: A Rousseau, 1896) 118–64; AS Hershey, 'The Calvo and Drago Doctrines' (1907) 1 AJIL 26; DR Shea, *The Calvo Clause* (Minneapolis: University of Minnesota Press, 1955) 9–21.

[29] Drago (n 25 above); Hershey (n 28 above).

[30] GM Wilner, 'Acceptance of Arbitration by Developing Countries' in TE Carbonneau (ed) *Resolving Transnational Disputes Through International Arbitration* (Charlottesville: University of Virginia Press, 1984) 286.   [31] Fatouros (n 7 above) 817–18.

constituencies in developed countries that support more extensive regulation of multinational firms.³²

The proposals for a multilateral investment code

Customary international law, based on principles of sovereign equality and independence, is less favourable to foreign investors than was its colonial and quasi-colonial antecedents. As the age of European empire receded, investors were not only deprived of direct imperial protection but were also left without a right to bring claims under international law against states in whose territory their assets were located.³³ An investment dispute was an international dispute, to be settled through diplomacy or, exceptionally, by inter-state adjudication.³⁴ Only the home state of an investor could bring an international claim and the investor had to accept the outcome agreed to by its state.³⁵ More fundamentally, host states could simply decline to consent to international adjudication in the event of a dispute with a foreign investor and, where they did consent, the investor could take part in the adjudication only if the home state and the host state agreed to a process that gave individuals this capacity.³⁶ Thus, political bargains could be struck at the expense of foreign investors and powerful states could choose to ignore claims on behalf of nationals of weaker states. Needless to say, the security of their investors' assets always remained a priority for the former colonial powers, but investors themselves were nevertheless at the mercy of their governments; their interests subsumed in a formal sense within the home state's calculus of its own interest.

This situation was less desirable for international business and, in some respects, for the major capital-exporting states. However, their efforts to establish

---

³² MO Hudson, *International Tribunals* (Washington: Carnegie Endowment for International Peace and the Brookings Institution, 1944) 457; Peter (n 22 above) 205; M Sornarajah, 'The Climate of International Arbitration' (1991) 8(2) J Int'l Arb 47, 63; VL Been and JC Beauvais, 'The Global Fifth Amendment: NAFTA's Investment Protections and the Misguided Quest for an International "Regulatory Takings" Doctrine' (2003) 78 NYU L Rev 30, 128–39.

³³ Fatouros (n 7 above) 795–6.

³⁴ Brownlie (n 9 above) 500; JG Merrills, 'The Means of Dispute Settlement' in MD Evans (ed) *International Law* (2nd edn, Oxford: OUP, 2006) 543.

³⁵ Hudson (n 32 above) 67–9 and 198; UNCTAD, *Bilateral Investment Treaties in the Mid-1990s* (Geneva: United Nations, 1998) 89–90; Muchlinski (n 8 above) 534–6.

³⁶ In a number of cases, states have consented under diplomatic pressure to adjudicate disputes with foreign nationals after the dispute has arisen, with varying degrees of participation in the proceedings by individuals. Hudson (n 32 above) 3–6 and 196–7; Brownlie (n 9 above) 500 (noting that in the century after 1840 some 60 mixed claims commissions were established to resolve disputes arising from injury to the interests of aliens, including between Mexico and the US in 1839, 1848, 1868, and 1923; between Venezuela and 10 other states in 1903, and between Great Britain and the US in 1853, 1871, and 1908). See also eg *Compañía del Desarrollo de Santa Elena, SA v Republic of Costa Rica* (Merits) (17 February 2000), 15 ICSID Rev 169, 39 ILM 317, 5 ICSID Rep 157, 13(1) World Trade and Arb Mat 81, para 25 (based on a consent to investment arbitration by Costa Rica after the dispute had arisen, prompted by the United States' blocking of a $175 million loan to Costa Rica by the Inter-American Development Bank).

and enforce international standards of investor protection were regarded by capital-importing states, including many in Europe, as discriminatory toward domestic investors and as an unacceptable challenge to their regulatory autonomy.[37] In this context, major Western states pushed alongside their business lobbies[38] for a treaty that would guard foreign investors from expropriation and other interference by host states.[39] The first proposal, in 1929, was the Draft Convention on the Treatment of Foreigners, which was prepared by officials from the League of Nations and the International Chamber of Commerce.[40] It was ambitious in scope given that, in the words of one observer, it applied 'not only to the exercise of all economic activity' but also 'to civil and legal rights, to the acquisition, preservation and transmission of property by foreigners and to fiscal charges both exceptional and normal'.[41] On the other hand, it was also more modest in its vision of investor protection than contemporary investment treaties, particularly in its provisions for investment disputes to be resolved by inter-state adjudication rather than direct investor claims. Thus, following custom at the time, it conceptualized investment disputes in terms of the relationship between states. Despite this, the proposal was rejected after some countries objected, in particular, to the breadth of the guarantee of national treatment for investors.[42]

After the Second World War the inclusion of a multilateral investment code within the remit of the International Trade Organization was mooted and later

[37] Castaneda (n 27 above) 39–41; Abbott (n 26 above) 137; SKB Asante, 'International Law and Foreign Investment: A Reappraisal' (1988) 37 ICLQ 588, 591–5; SKB Asante, 'International Law and Investments' in M Bedjaouni (ed) *International Law: Achievements and Prospects* (Paris and Dordrecht: UNESCO and Martinus Nijhoff, 1991) 669–73. Similar arguments have been made in the case of developed capital-importing countries: eg VL Been and JC Beauvais (n 32 above) 128–39.

[38] The leading lobby organization of private investors is the International Chamber of Commerce, supported by national organizations such as the US Council on International Business, the National Association of Manufacturers, and the National Foreign Trade Council: eg ICC, 'Fair Treatment for Foreign Investments: International Code' (ICC Brochure No 129, 1949); National Association of Manufacturers, 'The Havana Charter for an International Trade Organization' (1949); National Foreign Trade Council, 'Position of the NTC with Respect to the Havana Charter for an ITO' (1950); ICC, 'Multilateral rules for investment' (Doc No 103/179, Rev, 30 April 1996); ICC, 'ICC's expectation regarding a WTO investment agreement' (Policy statement of the ICC Commission on Trade and Investment Policy, 7 March 2003); DM Price, Testimony Before the Subcommittee on Trade of the House Committee on Ways and Means, Hearing on the Summit of the Americas and Prospects for Free Trade in the Hemisphere (Statement on behalf of the US Council for International Business, 8 May 2001).

[39] M Hart, 'A Multilateral Agreement on Foreign Direct Investment—Why Now?' in P Sauvé and D Schwanen (eds) *Investment Rules for the Global Economy* (Toronto: CD Howe Institute, 1996) 50–6; Muchlinski (n 8 above) 573–4; Muchlinski (n 12 above) 1035–7.

[40] League of Nations, 'Responsibility of States for Damage Caused in Their Territory to the Person or Property of Foreigners', Conference for the Codification of International Law, Bases of Discussion, vol 3, LN Doc C.75.M.69.1929.V (1929) [cited as Draft Convention of 1929]. AK Kuhn, 'The International Conference on the Treatment of Foreigners' (1930) 24 AJIL 570.

[41] Kuhn (n 40 above) 571. On the other hand, the Draft Convention of 1929 was more limited than contemporary investment treaties in that it did not apply to corporate investors or to the pre-establishment phase of an investment.

[42] EM Borchard, ' "Responsibility of States," At the Hague Codification Conference' (1930) 24 AJIL 517, 530.

abandoned during the post-war negotiations on the international economy.[43] The proposal was slated for negotiation 'at the insistence of influential American business groups', according to one commentator; however, the final draft of the investment provisions of the Havana Charter of 1948 diverged widely from the business lobby's original proposal.[44] Article 12 of the Havana Charter declared the rights of states to take steps 'to ensure that foreign investment is not used as a basis for interference in its internal affairs or national policies' and 'to determine whether and to what extent and upon what terms it will allow future foreign investments'.[45] There was no mention of compensation for expropriation or of compulsory arbitration, among other business priorities. In part because of the regulatory flexibility that it afforded to states, the Havana Charter was rejected by business groups and eventually abandoned after the US Administration declined to submit it to Congress for ratification.[46]

A further proposal for a multilateral treaty was floated by major capital-exporting states in 1959, boosted by the post-war recovery in Western Europe and the global re-emergence of German firms, in particular. The Abs–Shawcross Draft Convention on Investments Abroad was an amalgam of proposals by investor organizations in Germany and the UK, and it reflected investor interests to a greater extent than did the Draft Convention of 1929 or the Havana Charter.[47] Described as the 'Magna Carta' of private investors, it was intended 'to help remove the disregard of vested foreign rights and interests in international business'[48] and included liberal standards to protect investment, including guarantees of economic freedom for investors and a broadly worded protection from expropriation. Perhaps most importantly, it introduced the notion of an investor being able to bring a treaty claim against a state before an arbitration tribunal, the members of which would be appointed by the investor, the host state, and either the President of the International Court of Justice or the UN Secretary-General.[49] Thus, the proposal utilized the model of international

---

[43] C Wilcox, *A Charter for World Trade* (New York: Macmillan, 1949); W Diebold, 'The End of the ITO' in *Essays in International Finance*, no 16 (Princeton: Princeton University Press, 1952); Hart (n 39 above) 52–6.

[44] Quoting AA Fatouros, 'An International Code to Protect Private Investment—Proposals and Perspectives' (1961) 14 U Toronto LJ 77, 80. BA Wortley, *Expropriation in Public International Law* (Cambridge: CUP, 1959) 149.

[45] Final Act of the United Nations Conference on Trade and Employment: Havana Charter for an International Trade Organization (the Havana Charter), UN Conference on Trade and Employment, UN Doc 1948 II.D.4.1 (1948), art 12.

[46] Diebold (n 43 above) 18–19; JH Jackson, WJ Davey, and AO Sykes, Jr, *Legal Problems of International Economic Relations* (4th edn, St Paul, Minn: West Group, 2002) 213; Hart (n 39 above) 54.

[47] The text of the Draft Convention is reproduced in H Abs and H Shawcross, 'The Proposed Convention to Protect Private Foreign Investment' (1960) 9 J Public L 115. G Schwarzenberger, 'The Abs–Shawcross Draft Convention on Investments Abroad: A Critical Commentary' (1960) 9 J Public L 147; Fatouros (n 44 above) 87–90. [48] Miller (n 3 above) 371 (fn 1) and 378.

[49] Text of the Draft Convention, reproduced in Abs and Shawcross (n 47 above), art VII(2) and annex.

arbitration to settle regulatory disputes between investors and the state and, in this regard, it was a progenitor of the contemporary system.

Once again, the Abs–Shawcross proposal did not result in a multilateral treaty, mainly because of spirited opposition by capital-importing states. It re-emerged in the 1967 Draft Convention on the Protection of Foreign Property of the Organization for Economic Co-operation and Development (OECD) but this also did not achieve any formal status, although it did serve as a model for early European bilateral treaties that provided for compulsory arbitration of investor claims.[50] Also, both instruments mark an early shift in strategy by European capital-exporting countries towards bilateral negotiations, as their governments surmised that a favourable multilateral treaty was unlikely in the face of Third World assertion of greater autonomy. Thus, in the 1970s, the promotion of multilateral investment rules centred on the OECD and was mainly limited to less ambitious, non-enforceable instruments.[51] In the 1980s a proposal for a multilateral investment treaty at the Uruguay Round of GATT negotiations was also opposed by developing states and rejected in its broad form.[52] So, while the WTO Agreements do apply to investment in important ways, mainly under the General Agreement on Trade in Services[53] and the Agreement on Trade-Related Investment Measures,[54] these agreements are far more modest in terms of the protection of assets of foreign investors than bilateral and regional investment treaties.[55] Above all, the WTO system does not allow direct claims by investors, relying exclusively on state-to-state dispute settlement.

After the Uruguay Round, the investor lobby—and especially the US Council for International Business, a national affiliate of the International Chamber of Commerce—pushed for renewed negotiations toward a 'high standard, liberal investment regime', this time at the OECD.[56] This led to the controversial

[50] Dolzer and Stevens (n 22 above) 2.
[51] S Dillon, *International Trade and Economic Law in the European Union* (Oxford: Hart, 2002) 100.   [52] Muchlinski (n 12 above) 1039.
[53] General Agreement on Trade in Services (the GATS) (15 April 1994; 33 ILM 44).
[54] Agreement on Trade-Related Investment Measures (the TRIMs Agreement) (annex IA of the Agreement Establishing the World Trade Organization) (15 April 1994), *Final Act Embodying the Results of the Uruguay Round of Multilateral Trade Negotiations* (1994) 139.
[55] The GATS, by regulating cross-border services supplied 'by commercial presence', deals with market access by investors but is limited to economic sectors positively listed by the host state. Further, the GATS does not have other investment standards such as a minimum standard of treatment or expropriation. Likewise, the TRIMs Agreement is limited to investment measures related to trade in goods only: art 1. The TRIMs Agreement imposes significant restrictions on performance requirements but does not constrain the authority of states in a general way, as under investment treaties. *ADF Group Inc v United States of America* (Merits) (9 January 2003), 18 ICSID Rev 195, 6 ICSID Rep 470, 15(3) World Trade and Arb Mat 55, para 125 (noting Mexico's submission that, other than the GATS and the TRIMs Agreement, WTO law does not address foreign investment disciplines, and that work on the relationship between trade and investment is at an early stage). Dillon (n 51 above) 96–7, 101, and 114; P Civello, 'The TRIMs Agreement: A Failed Attempt at Investment Liberalization' (1999) 8 Minn J Global Trade 97; E Kentin, 'Prospects for Rules on Investment in the New WTO Round' (2002) 29 Leg Issues Econ Integration 61.
[56] E Smythe, 'Domestic and International Sources of Regime Change: Canada and the Negotiation of the OECD Multilateral Agreement on Investment' (Paper presented to the Annual

Multilateral Agreement on Investment (MAI), drafted by the OECD Secretariat for consideration by the OECD member states.[57] In the first place, the members of the OECD are almost exclusively capital-exporting states and the OECD was seen as a favourable forum in which differences among those states could be resolved in favour of investors before opening the treaty to ratification by developing states on an individual basis, at which time the bargaining power of the latter would be much weaker than at the Uruguay Round.[58] In terms of its actual content, the MAI was in many respects the culmination of decades of efforts by capital-exporting countries and international business to consolidate high level investor protection at the global level. Yet the ambitiousness of the MAI stoked public opposition in the OECD countries as well as capital-importing states, and various NGO coalitions—based especially in the environmental sector—pushed Western governments to reject it on the grounds that it would hamper proactive regulation and democratic decision-making.[59] At the same time tensions arose in the negotiations about whether the MAI should reflect a US or more modest European model, the former implying a broader definition of investment and the extension of national treatment to the pre-establishment stage.[60] Eventually, the investor lobby also cooled to the idea, fearing that a watered-down multilateral treaty could be worse than none at all.[61] The MAI was finally abandoned after France, with the support of some other OECD countries, withdrew from the negotiations.[62]

The final instalment of this brief history of proposed multilateral treaties brings us to the WTO's Cancun ministerial conference in 2003, where investment was included as one of the four 'Singapore issues'. The inclusion of investment in the negotiations led to a major conflict between developed and developing member states, with the latter arguing that liberal investment rules would restrict their ability to pursue industrial and development policies.[63] The conference ended when

---

Meeting of the Canadian Political Science Association, St John's, Nfld, 8 June 1997) 9–10; S Picciotto, 'A Critical Assessment of the MAI' in S Picciotto and R Mayne (eds) *Regulating International Business* (Houndmills: Macmillan, 1999); Muchlinski (n 12 above) 1037–9; A Walter, 'NGOs, Business, and International Investment: The Multilateral Agreement on Investment, Seattle, and Beyond' (2001) 7 Glob Governance 51, 58–60.

[57] *The MAI Negotiating Text*, OECD, Paris (1998) [cited as *MAI*].
[58] P Juillard, 'MAI: A European View' (1998) 31 Cornell Int'l LJ 477, 479.
[59] C Lalumière and J-P Landau, 'Report on the Multilateral Agreement on Investment (MAI)' (Interim report to the Government of France, September 1998); Smythe (n 56 above) 19–20; Walter (n 56 above) 61–3.
[60] Juillard (n 58 above) 480–3; Muchlinski (n 12 above) 1047–8; Dillon (n 51 above) 97–9.
[61] P Malanczuk, 'State–State and Investor–State Dispute Settlement in the OECD Draft Multilateral Investment Agreement' (2000) 3 J Int'l Econ L 417, 418; Walter (n 56 above) 63–4.
[62] H Scoffield, 'France pulls out of MAI talks' *The Globe and Mail* [Toronto] (15 October 1998) B1; Muchlinski (n 12 above) 1048–9.
[63] International Centre for Trade and Sustainable Development and International Institute for Sustainable Development, 'The Singapore Issues: Investment, Competition Policy, Transparency in Government Procurement and Trade Facilitation' (Doha Round Briefing Series, vol 2(6), August 2003) 1–4.

developing states flatly rejected a draft ministerial text calling for modalities 'that will allow negotiations on a multilateral investment framework to start'.[64] In this case, as in the others, it proved impossible to reach agreement on the issue of multilateral investment rules, even when the negotiating mandate at Cancun was moderated by a WTO statement that any rules on investment 'should reflect in a balanced manner the interests of home and host countries, and take due account of the development policies and objectives of host governments as well as their right to regulate in the public interest'.[65] Negotiations, to put it mildly, were at an impasse.

The litany of failed proposals for a multilateral code reflects the enduring conflict that pits the major capital-exporting countries and international business against capital-importing states represented most prominently in recent years by countries such as Brazil, Egypt, India, Malaysia, and Uganda.[66] Investor-friendly proposals have been rejected time and again by capital-importing countries and, of late, by various lobbies in developed countries themselves.[67] On the other hand, alternative proposals that affirmed the right of states to regulate foreign investors—primarily the Havana Charter—were abandoned by the US and international capital.[68] It is puzzling, therefore, that most developing countries have been willing, especially in the 1990s, to concede to the present system of investment treaty arbitration which is in many respects as rigorous and intrusive as the proposed MAI. Put differently, even without a multilateral code, capital-exporting states have managed to achieve, through networks of bilateral and regional treaties, the high level of protection for foreign investors that they long sought on behalf of international business.[69]

---

[64] WTO, *Draft Cancún Ministerial Text*, 2nd rev, 13 September 2003, WTO Doc JOB(03)/150/Rev.2 (2003) 3. J Hillary, 'Divide and Rule: The EU and US Response to Developing Country Alliances at the WTO' (Report for Action Aid International, 2004) 7–12.

[65] WTO, *Doha Ministerial Declaration*, 20 November 2001, WTO Doc WT/MIN(01)/DEC/1 (2001) para 22.

[66] Wortley (n 44 above) 119–26; Peter (n 22 above) 217–18 and 329–31; Muchlinski (n 8 above) 173, 501–14, and 573–4; Hillary (n 64 above) 7.

[67] Fatouros (n 44 above) 101 (arguing in 1961 that capital-importing states will not accept obligations without corresponding undertakings by capital-exporting states as to the amount of foreign investment to be forthcoming, and that most proposals are one-sided: 'They provide for the protection of the investors' interests without attempting to safeguard the host state's interests. There is no convincing justification for this bias . . . . [A code] should attempt to regulate comprehensively the whole relationship between host state and foreign investors. Otherwise, such a code might be construed as limiting the former's powers without restricting the latter's freedom of action.'); Muchlinski (n 12 above) 1035–8 and 1050–1; Picciotto (n 56 above) 99–100; Walter (n 56 above) 58–60.

[68] LH Woolsey, 'The Problem of Foreign Investment' (1948) 42 AJIL 121, 126–8; Diebold (n 43 above) 18–19; Fatouros (n 44 above) 80 and 101; Hart (n 39 above) 54.

[69] MS Bergman, 'Bilateral Investment Protection Treaties: An Examination of the Evolution and Significance of the US Prototype Treaty' (1983) 16 NYU J Int'l L & Pol 1, 3–4 and 8–9; M Sornarajah, *The Pursuit of Nationalized Property* (Dordrecht: Martinus Nijhoff, 1986) 38–9; KJ Vandevelde, 'The Bilateral Treaty Program of the United States' (1988) 21 Cornell Int'l LJ 201; JW Salacuse, 'BIT by BIT: The Growth of Bilateral Investment Treaties and their Impact on Foreign Investment in Developing Countries' (1990) 14 Int'l Lawyer 655, 657; UNCTAD (n 35 above) 8–10.

The Emergence of the System

The explosion of claims

We turn now to the emergence of the present system. It is necessary at the outset to distinguish investment *treaty* arbitration from other forms of prospective investment arbitration. This is best done by examining the state's consent. States can consent to the arbitration of future disputes with foreign investors in three ways: by contract, by domestic legislation, and by treaty.[70] The form of a state's consent is significant because it correlates strongly with the positioning of investment arbitration in the private or public sphere, and in the domestic or international sphere. Thus it points to the character of the adjudicative authority that is exercised by arbitrators.

First, a state can accept an arbitration clause in a contract with a foreign investor, in which case the state is typically regarded as acting in a private capacity and its consent as limited to a commercial relationship with another private party.[71] Second, a state can consent to investment arbitration by enacting a law that authorizes foreign investors to submit any investment dispute with the state to international arbitration.[72] Third, a state can conclude a treaty that likewise provides for the compulsory arbitration of disputes with foreign investors.[73] In the latter two cases, the state consents *generally* to investment arbitration, pursuant to either domestic law or international law.[74] The state's consent is general because it authorizes the arbitration of any future dispute concerning the state's exercise of public authority in relation to foreign investors, at the option of the

---

[70] AR Parra, 'The Role of ICSID in the Settlement of Investment Disputes' (1999) 16(1) ICSID News 5; UNCTAD, *Dispute Settlement: Investor–State*, UNCTAD Series on Issues in International Investment Agreements (New York: United Nations, 2003) 53.

[71] Early ICSID arbitrations were typically founded on consents recorded, in the traditional manner, by a clause in an investment contract: eg *Holiday Inns SA v Morocco* (Jurisdiction) (12 May 1974), 1 ICSID Rep 645; *Kaiser Bauxite Company v Jamaica* (Jurisdiction) (6 July 1975), 114 ILR 144, 1 ICSID Rep 296; *Gardella (Adriano) v Côte d'Ivoire* (Merits) (29 August 1979), 1 ICSID Rep 283; *AGIP SpA v People's Republic of Congo* (Merits) (30 November 1979), 21 ILM 726, 67 ILR 318, 1 ICSID Rep 306.

[72] eg *Southern Pacific Properties (Middle East) Ltd v Arab Republic of Egypt* (Jurisdiction) (14 April 1988), 3 ICSID Rep 131 [cited as *SPP*], 161. Parra (n 70 above) (noting that, during 1965 to 1999, 30 countries included references to ICSID in domestic investment legislation).

[73] eg *Asian Agricultural Products Ltd (AAPL) v Sri Lanka* (Merits) (27 June 1990), 30 ILM 577, 4 ICSID Rep 246 [cited as *AAPL*], para 2–6.

[74] J Paulsson, 'Arbitration without Privity' (1995) 10 ICSID Rev 232, 233 and 240. When the consent is given in domestic legislation, it is subject to domestic law and can be withdrawn or amended according to domestic law: I Delupis, *Finance and Protection of Investments in Developing Countries* (Epping: Gower Press, 1973) 27. On the other hand, when the consent is given in a treaty, it is subject to the terms of the treaty and can only be withdrawn or amended with the consent of the states parties or by abrogation of the treaty: *Bogdanov (Iurii) et al v Moldova* (Merits) (22 September 2005), SCC Rules, 8–9, online: ITA, Investment Claims.

investor.[75] Unlike contract-based arbitration, which relies on the specific consents of private parties, both legislation- and treaty-based arbitration engage disputes within the regulatory sphere. They expose the state to claims by a broad class of potential claimants in relation to any governmental activity affecting foreign investors, in the absence of a contract between an individual investor and the state.[76]

The character of the state's consent is discussed in detail in Chapter 3 of this book. Suffice it to say here that the general consent transforms investment arbitration from a sub-category of commercial arbitration, based on a reciprocal legal relationship between the disputing parties, into a type of governing arrangement. The present study focuses on treaty-based investment arbitration because it most clearly involves the use of private arbitration as a governing arrangement at the international level. As such, it raises special concerns about the delegation of adjudicative authority to arbitrators who are insulated from domestic judicial review. These concerns are not present, or at least not prevalent, in contract-based arbitration because such arbitration does not usually determine core questions of public law. Further, the concerns are not as significant in the case of legislation-based arbitration because the delegation of authority to arbitrators is subject to direct control by the legislature or courts of the delegating state. Treaty-based arbitration goes much further in its removal of investment arbitration from the legal domain of a state's own governing institutions and in the delegation of core elements of the judicial function in public law to private arbitrators, in both the public and the international sphere.

The first treaties to incorporate general consents by states to investment arbitration were a handful of bilateral investment treaties (BITs) signed in the late 1960s.[77] In the 1970s and 1980s general consents in BITs became more common

---

[75] eg under NAFTA Chapter 11 each NAFTA state 'consents to the submission of a claim' by investors of another NAFTA state 'in accordance with the procedures set out in this Agreement': North American Free Trade Agreement (NAFTA) (17 December 1992; 32 ILM 296 and 605; entered into force 1 January 1994), art 1116 and 1117 (providing for the general consents of the NAFTA states), and art 1120(2) (incorporating the applicable arbitration rules, as selected by the investor when filing a claim, as arbitration 'procedures'). Paulsson (n 74 above) 256; TW Wälde, 'Investment Arbitration Under the Energy Charter Treaty—From Dispute Settlement to Treaty Implementation' (1996) 12 Arb Int'l 429, 434–6; A Afilalo, 'Constitutionalization Through the Back Door: A European Perspective on NAFTA's Investment Chapter' (2001) 34 NYU J Int'l L & Pol 1, 4; JC Thomas, 'Notes on Investor-State Arbitration in the North American Context' (Address to the International Bar Association conference, San Francisco, 9–14 September 2003) 2–4.
[76] Paulsson (n 74 above) 233.
[77] Dolzer and Stevens (n 22 above) 126 (noting that earlier BITs, such as the Germany–Pakistan BIT of 1959, did not provide for compulsory arbitration of investor claims, and that the first BIT to include an ICSID clause was a Netherlands–Indonesia BIT, signed in 1968, followed by Italy's BITs with Chad and Côte d'Ivoire, both signed in 1969). At the same time, in 1969, ICSID published a set of model BIT clauses in order to encourage states to consent to treaty-based investment arbitration: *Model Clauses Relating to the Convention on the Settlement of Investment Disputes Designed for Use in Bilateral Investment Agreements* (1969), 8 ILM 1341.

though not universal.[78] Only in the 1990s did the inclusion of general consents to investment treaty arbitration become the rule.[79] Thus it is not possible to identify investment treaty arbitration as a system until the 1990s, during and after which roughly 2,000 bilateral investment treaties were concluded of about 2,400 now signed.[80] Also, a number of important regional treaties were concluded in the 1990s, including the North American Free Trade Agreement (NAFTA)[81] and the Energy Charter Treaty,[82] both of which authorized investor claims in relation to specific provisions on investment.[83] NAFTA, in particular, was a watershed in the 1990s' wave of treaties because it applies to extensive capital flows between Canada, Mexico, and the US.[84] It has led to more investor claims and a more comprehensive body of awards than has any other investment treaty[85] and the

---

[78] UNCTAD (n 35 above) 8–10; AR Parra, 'ICSID and Bilateral Investment' (2000) 17(1) ICSID News 7 (noting that the first BITs that incorporated general consents were concluded in the late 1960s. Then 86 BITs were concluded by European countries during the 1970s, usually including the consent of each state to the submission to ICSID of 'any dispute', between the state and a national of the other state party, regarding investment. In the 1980s another 211 BITs were concluded, including some with developing countries that had previously refrained (such as China), and the US launched its BIT programme).

[79] UNCTAD (n 35 above) 10 and 89–90; UNCTAD, *Trends in International Investment Agreements: An Overview*, UNCTAD Series on Issues in International Investment Agreements (New York: United Nations, 1999) 10 and 45–6.

[80] *CMS Gas Transmission Company v Argentine Republic* (Jurisdiction) (17 July 2003), 42 ILM 788, 7 ICSID Rep 492 [cited as *CMS*], para 45. UNCTAD (n 79 above) 44; UNCTAD, *Bilateral Investment Treaties—1959–1999* (New York: United Nations, 2000) 1 and 4 (reporting that the number of BITs quintupled during the 1990s, from 385 in 1989 to 1,857 by 1999, involving 102 countries in 1989 and 173 countries in 1999); UNCTAD (n 8 above) xix (reporting that by 2004 most countries had concluded investment treaties with their principal investment partners). See also UNCTAD, 'Occasional Note: Many BITs Have Yet to Enter Into Force' (New York, United Nations, 2005) 1–2 (noting that several hundred of the BITs signed in the 1990s have not been ratified).

[81] NAFTA (n 75 above) art 1116 and 1117.

[82] Energy Charter Treaty (annex I of the Final Act of the European Energy Charter Conference) (Lisbon, 17 December 1994; 34 ILM 373), art 26 (adopted by approximately 50 countries, mostly OECD members, Central and Eastern European countries, and members of the Commonwealth of Independent States; and broadly applying to the energy sector).

[83] Paulsson (n 74 above) 233; Wälde (n 75 above) 434–6. Other regional treaties that authorize compulsory investment arbitration include: Agreement among the Government of Brunei Darussalam, the Republic of Indonesia, Malaysia, the Republic of the Philippines, the Republic of Singapore and the Kingdom of Thailand for the Promotion and Protection of Investments (ASEAN Agreement for the Promotion and Protection of Investments) (Manila, 15 December 1987; 27 ILM 612), art X; Protocolo de Colonia para la Promoción y Protección Recíproca de Inversiones en el MERCOSUR (the Colonia Protocol) (17 January 1994, adopted by Mercosur/CMC/Dec No 11/93; not in force), art 9(2) and (4); Treaty on Free Trade Between the Republic of Colombia, the Republic of Venezuela and the United Mexican States (13 June 1994; entered into force 1 January 1995), art 17–17 and 17–18; The Dominican Republic–Central America–United States Free Trade Agreement (CAFTA) (Washington, 5 August 2004; entered into force 1 March 2006 [US, El Salvador], 1 April [Honduras, Nicaragua], and 1 July 2006 [Guatemala]; 16(6) World Trade and Arb Mat 87), art 10.17 and 10.18.

[84] M Trebilcock and R Howse, *The Regulation of International Trade* (London: Routledge, 1995) 295–7; AM Rugman and M Gestrin, 'A Conceptual Framework for a Multilateral Agreement on Investment: Learning from the NAFTA' in P Sauvé and D Schwanen (eds) *Investment Rules for the Global Economy* (Toronto: CD Howe Institute, 1996) 156–62.

[85] To August 2006 there have been 41 notices of intent by investors to submit a claim under NAFTA Chapter 11, of which at least 22 have led to arbitration proceedings. Of these, 13 have

early NAFTA experience drew attention to the availability of investment treaty arbitration and helped to trigger the rapid growth in claims under other treaties.[86] Exceptionally, under NAFTA, there have been multiple claims against each state party, including claims against major capital-exporting states.

Also in the 1990s ratifications of the ICSID Convention,[87] which rose gradually in the 1980s, accelerated following the accession of former communist and major developing countries, and ICSID emerged as the leading forum for investment treaty arbitration.[88] Moreover, although not central to the emergence of the system in general, investment treaties expanded in the 1990s beyond conventional relationships between capital-exporting and capital-importing states to include many new treaties among developing and former communist states.[89] Before the 1990s nearly all investment treaties were concluded between major capital-exporting and capital-importing countries, usually based on the model BITs of the former.[90]

Of course, in any system that incorporates hundreds of different treaties, variations in the text of individual treaties will create diversity, complexity, and a degree of uncertainty about the actual obligations assumed by states.[91] In particular, there are important differences among treaties in terms of their scope, the standards of review, and the choice of arbitration rules and institutions.[92] The BITs of Western European countries, unlike US-modelled BITs, do not normally extend

---

resulted in final awards on the merits, including 2 in claims against Canada, 7 in claims against Mexico, and 4 in claims against the United States. Of the 13 awards on the merits to date, damages were awarded in 2 claims against Canada and 2 claims against Mexico. Each of the four claims against the United States was unsuccessful.

[86] Been and Beauvais (n 32 above) 44–5.

[87] Convention on the Settlement of Investment Disputes Between States and Nationals of Other States (the ICSID Convention) (Washington, 18 March 1965; 4 ILM 524; entered into force 14 Oct 1966). A Broches, 'Development of International Law by the International Bank for Reconstruction and Development' (1965) 59 Am Soc'ty Int'l L Proc 33, 34–8; M Hirsh, *The Arbitration Mechanism of the International Centre for Settlement of Investment Disputes* (Dordrecht: Martinus Nijhoff, 1993) 11–15; JG Merrills, *International Dispute Settlement* (3rd edn, Cambridge: CUP, 1998) 113; C Schreuer, *The ICSID Convention: A Commentary* (2001).

[88] ICSID www.worldbank.org/icsid/constate/constate.htm (reporting that, by 25 January 2006, 143 states had ratified the ICSID Convention, including Turkey (ratification in 1989), China (1993), Argentina (1994), Venezuela (1995), and, most recently, Syria (2006)). However, some significant capital-importers, such as Brazil, Canada, India, Mexico, and South Africa, have not signed the ICSID Convention, and others have excluded important economic sectors such as oil and natural gas from their consents to ICSID jurisdiction.   [89] UNCTAD (n 79 above) 33–4.

[90] Peter (n 22 above) 332–3; Juillard (n 58 above) 477. After the ICSID Convention was concluded more and more capital-exporting countries adopted policies in favour of BITs with capital-importing states, culminating in the US adoption of a BIT programme in the early 1980s: Bergman (n 69 above) 3–4. For texts of model BITs, see UNCTAD, *International Investment Instruments: A Compendium*, vol 3 (New York: United Nations, 1996).

[91] UNCTAD (n 35 above) 139–40 (noting that differences in the language of investment treaties reflect the fact that the treaties were negotiated in different time periods, with innovations by one country tending to be adopted in later treaties by other countries); UNCTAD (n 2 above) 166; D Schneiderman, 'Investment Rules and the New Constitutionalism' (2000) 25 Law & Social Inq 757, 781.

[92] Paulsson (n 74 above) 240; Dolzer and Stevens (n 22 above) 26, 33–4, 57–8, 64; UNCTAD (n 35 above) 139–40; UNCTAD (n 79 above) 53–86; UNCTAD (n 8 above) 223–4.

national treatment to the pre-establishment stage of investment (ie to the period before an investor has entered the host economy) or apply specific prohibitions on performance requirements, for example.[93] Importantly, some treaties remove or alter the duty of investors to exhaust local remedies, while others remain silent on the matter, while still others contain a fork-in-the-road clause that may oblige investors to choose between domestic remedies and a claim under the treaty.[94] Lastly, the general consents of states to compulsory arbitration are in some cases contained in, and limited to, the investment provisions of a regional trade agreement rather than a BIT per se.[95] Given these variations, it is not possible to reach firm legal conclusions about how a particular dispute will be resolved without examining in detail the language, structure, and negotiating history of the relevant treaty.

But in spite of the variations, there remains an entrenched system of investment treaty arbitration designed to protect investors from the exercise of public authority. It is not a global system in the absence of BITs between capital-exporting states or a multilateral code.[96] Even so, the wide geographic coverage and flexible accessibility of existing treaties has taken investment treaty arbitration beyond a collection of disparate dispute settlement mechanisms and established it as a general adjudicative system in the regulatory sphere.[97] The key unifying feature of the treaties, as such, is their use of the compulsory arbitration of investor claims as a type of governing arrangement and, by implication, the delegation of comprehensive adjudicative authority to arbitrators.[98] And where regional trade agreements are also subject to compulsory investment arbitration, they too should be viewed as part of the treaty network that makes up the system.[99]

In practical terms, not all investment treaties are equal in the degree to which they may lead to claims by investors against the states parties. Some treaties govern

---

[93] Dolzer and Stevens (n 22 above) 79–80; UNCTAD, *Admission and Establishment*, UNCTAD Series on Issues in International Investment Agreements (New York: United Nations, 1999) 17–18 and 26–8.   [94] UNCTAD (n 70 above) 29–34.

[95] For instance, the positioning of NAFTA's investment chapter alongside 19 other chapters on topics such as trade in goods, intellectual property rights, and government procurement, which do not provide for compulsory arbitration of investor claims, may have implications for how the investment provisions are interpreted. JC Thomas, 'Investor–State Arbitration Under NAFTA Chapter Eleven' (Paper presented to the NAFTA Chapter 11 Investor–State Disputes: Litigating Against Sovereigns conference, Canadian Bar Association, March 2000) 5–7.

[96] Malanczuk (n 61 above) 436–7; CN Brower, CH Brower II, and JK Sharpe, 'The Coming Crisis in the Global Adjudicative System' (2003) 19 Arb Int'l 415, 415–18.

[97] JW Salacuse, 'Toward a Global Treaty on Foreign Investment: The Search for a Grand Bargain' in N Horn (ed) *Arbitrating Foreign Investment Disputes* (The Hague: Kluwer Law International, 2004) 68–70; UNCTAD (n 8 above) 221.

[98] UNCTAD (n 79 above) 45–6; Schneiderman (n 91 above) 769–70 and 781; Z Douglas, 'The Hybrid Foundations of Investment Treaty Arbitration' (2003) 74 Brit Ybk Int'l L 151, 159.

[99] Salacuse (n 97 above) 35–6; M-F Houde and K Yannaca-Small, 'Relationships between International Investment Agreements' (OECD Working Paper on International Investment No 2004/1, May 2004) 5–6. The text of the NAFTA investment chapter, for example, was based on the US model bilateral investment treaty. Since NAFTA was concluded both the US and Canada have used Chapter 11 as the starting-point for their other investment treaties. JW Boscariol, 'Canada and the New International Investment Regime—Canada's Foreign Investment Protection Agreements'

far more flows of capital than do others. Judging from the early trend in investor claims, however, the key treaties are those concluded between the major capital-exporting states and either developing or former communist countries that host substantial foreign-owned assets. For this reason, in examining the specific provisions of investment treaties, the present study gives special attention to NAFTA; the Energy Charter Treaty; and the following BITs: Belgium–Argentina, France–Argentina, Germany–Argentina, Greece–Egypt, Netherlands–Bolivia, Netherlands–Czech Republic, Netherlands–Venezuela, Peru–Paraguay, Spain–Argentina, Spain–Mexico, Switzerland–Pakistan, Switzerland–Philippines, United Kingdom–Egypt, United Kingdom–Sri Lanka, United States–Argentina, United States–Czech Republic, United States–Ecuador, and United States–Romania.[100] These were selected in order to give a manageable sampling of significant treaties—'significant' in that each has founded at least one jurisdictional award

(Presentation to the Canadian Bar Association—Ontario International Law Section, March 1999); JA Soloway, 'Environmental Regulation as Expropriation: The Case of NAFTA's Chapter 11' (2000) 33 Can Bus LJ 92, 99–100; M Kantor, 'The New Draft Model US BIT: Noteworthy Developments' (2004) 21 J Int'l Arb 382, 382.

[100] NAFTA (n 75 above); Energy Charter Treaty (n 82 above); Convenio entre la República Argentina y la Union Economica Belgo-Luxemburguesa para la promoción y la protección de inversiones (the Belgium–Argentina BIT) (Brussels, 28 June 1990; entered into force 20 May 1994); Accord entre le Gouvernement de la République Française et le Gouvernement de la République Argentine sur l'encouragement et la protection réciproques des investissements (the France–Argentina BIT) (Paris, 3 July 1991; entered into force 3 March 1993); Tratado entre la República Federal de Alemania y la República Argentina sobre promoción y protección recíproca de inversiones (the Germany–Argentina BIT) (Bonn, 9 April 1991; entered into force 8 November 1993); Agreement between the Hellenic Republic and the Arab Republic of Egypt for the promotion and reciprocal protection of investments (the Greece–Egypt BIT) (Athens, 16 July 1993; entered into force 6 April 1995); Agreement on encouragement and reciprocal protection of investments between the Kingdom of the Netherlands and the Republic of Bolivia (the Netherlands–Bolivia BIT) (10 March 1992; entered into force 1 November 1994); Agreement on encouragement and reciprocal protection of investments between the Kingdom of the Netherlands and the Czech and Slovak Republic (the Netherlands–Czech Republic BIT) (22 October 1991; entered into force 19 December 1992); Agreement on encouragement and reciprocal protection of investments between the Kingdom of the Netherlands and the Republic of Venezuela (the Netherlands–Venezuela BIT) (22 October 1991; entered into force 1 November 1993); Convenio entre la República del Perú y la República del Paraguay sobre promoción y protección de inversiones (the Peru–Paraguay BIT) (Lima, 31 January 1994; entered into force 18 December 1994); Acuerdo para la promoción y la protección reciproca de inversiones entre el Reino de España y la República Argentina (the Spain–Argentina BIT) (Buenos Aires, 3 October 1991; entered into force 28 September 1992); Acuerdo para la promoción y protección reciproca de inversiones entre los Estados Unidos Mexicanos y el Reino de España (the Spain–Mexico BIT) (Mexico City, 22 June 1995; entered into force 18 December 1996); Accord entre la Confédération suisse et la République du Pakistan concernant la promotion et la protection réciproque des investissements (the Switzerland–Pakistan BIT) (Berne, 11 July 1995; entered into force 6 May 1996); Accord entre la Confédération suisse et la République des Philippines concernant la promotion et la protection réciproque des investissements (the Switzerland–Philippines BIT) (Manille, 31 March 1997; entered into force 23 April 1999); Agreement between the Government of the United Kingdom of Great Britain and Northern Ireland and the Government of the Arab Republic of Egypt for the promotion and protection of investments (the UK–Egypt BIT) (London, 11 June 1975, UKTS No 97 (1976); Cmd 6638; entered into force 24 February 1976); Agreement between the Government of the United Kingdom of Great Britain and Northern Ireland and the Government of the Democratic Socialist Republic of Sri Lanka for the promotion and protection of investments (the UK–Sri Lanka BIT) (Colombo, 13 February 1980; UKTS No 14 (1981); Cmd 8186; entered

pursuant to an investor claim—as opposed to a comprehensive database of the whole system.

As discussed, the genesis of investment treaty arbitration as a mechanism to regulate states based on the delegation of adjudicative authority to arbitrators lies in the general consent of the state, which originates in the late 1960s. Yet the system came of age only in the 1990s, as evidenced by the explosive growth of investor claims in the last decade. Thus whereas sporadic arbitrations have taken place at ICSID since the 1970s, the first ICSID awards that were based on a general consent of the respondent state (pursuant to a statute and a treaty, respectively) were issued in 1988 and 1990.[101] Previously, ICSID awards were typically based on the mutual consents of an investor and a host state in a contract or in an agreement to arbitrate made after the dispute had arisen.[102] This changed only in the 1990s when the rapid proliferation investment treaties fuelled a burst of claims under NAFTA, the Energy Charter Treaty, and BITs. After 1996 in particular 'the floodgates ... seemed to open', according to one ICSID staff member.[103] From 1996 to 2005 ICSID registered 166 claims, compared to 35 claims in the previous three decades, and the trend appears to be sustaining. By July 2006 there were 111 claims pending, more than all the claims registered at ICSID during its entire history until 2002. Many of these claims were made against the beleaguered Argentinians in the aftermath of the country's economic crisis, explaining the spike in claims in 2003. Nevertheless, the rate of claims remains relatively high, now averaging between 25 and 30 per year, and they are distributed among several different capital-importing regions.

Moreover, the growth at ICSID is only part of the story of rapid expansion.[104] For one, it does not include cases in which an investor and a state settle a dispute after the claim is threatened but before the claim is registered by ICSID. More importantly, ICSID is the only international forum that is required to publicize claims. Others, such as the Court of Arbitration of the International Chamber of Commerce and *ad hoc* tribunals established under the UNCITRAL Rules, allow for claims to be kept confidential, in the traditional of commercial arbitration,

---

into force 18 December 1980); Treaty between the United States of America and the Argentine Republic concerning the reciprocal encouragement and protection of investment (the US–Argentina BIT) (Washington, 14 November 1991; entered into force 20 October 1994); Treaty with the Czech and Slovak Federal Republic concerning the reciprocal encouragement and protection of investment (the US–Czech Republic BIT) (Washington, 22 October 1991; entered into force 19 December 1992); Treaty between the United States of America and the Republic of Ecuador concerning the reciprocal encouragement and protection of investment (the US–Ecuador BIT) (Washington, 27 August 1993; entered into force 11 May 1997); Treaty between the Government of the United States of America and the Government of Romania concerning the reciprocal encouragement and protection of investment (the US–Romania BIT) (Bucharest, 28 May 1992; entered into force 15 January 1994).

[101] *SPP* (n 72 above); *AAPL* (n 73 above).

[102] Until 1984 ICSID arbitrations were based on consents recorded in the traditional manner by a clause in an investment contract or a post-dispute *compromis*. Since then, dozens of claims have been submitted to ICSID by investors lacking a prior contractual relationship with the host state and relying on domestic legislation or a treaty to establish the state's consent to international arbitration. Parra (n 70 above). [103] Parra (n 78 above).

[104] Brower *et al* (n 96 above) 416.

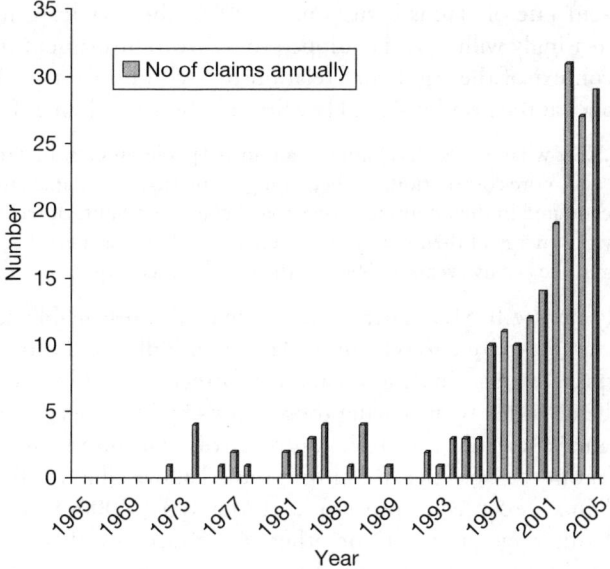

Fig. 1. ICSID claims registered annually: 1965–2005

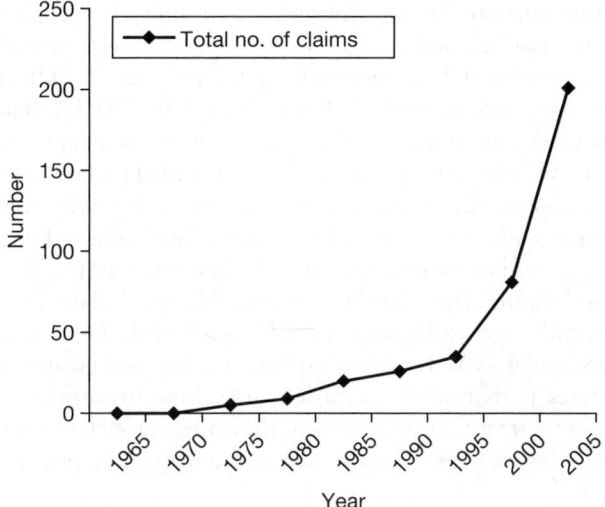

Fig. 2. ICSID claims registered in total: 1965–2005

unless both of the disputing parties agree to the public release of information. For this reason, it is not possible to assess fully the extent to which investment treaty arbitration has expanded[105] although at minimum the ICSID experience suggests

[105] An important exception is NAFTA, under which the states parties have adopted a general practice of publishing materials that relate to Chapter 11 arbitration regardless of the applicable arbitration rules: Free Trade Commission, *Notes of Interpretation of Certain Chapter 11 Provisions* (31 July

that the present rate of claims is sustainable.[106] At the very least, it reveals that firms are increasingly willing and equipped to resort to investment treaty arbitration in the context of the regulatory relationship with host states. According to one practitioner at the London-based law firm Herbert Smith in 2002:[107]

> I do think . . . that what we see developing is an unstoppable process. In particular, this is because more and more corporations are becoming aware that, quite apart from what they might have negotiated in their contracts, they may have direct rights of recourse bestowed upon them by the energy of their own governments . . . . And I suspect that what we have seen emerging in the last five years will be just the tip of the iceberg.

Based mainly on the ICSID experience, one may also reasonably conclude that the primary targets of investor claims to date are middle-sized capital-importing countries, especially in Latin America and the former Soviet Bloc. A fairly reliable picture can be obtained by reviewing those claims by investors that have led to a widely available[108] award on jurisdiction by a tribunal (on the assumption that uncertainty about the existence of claims is rooted above all in the likelihood that numerous claims are settled in private) as of March 31, 2006. In sum, 75 claims had reached this stage at ICSID or other institutions by this time, of which 30 claims were brought against Latin American countries, 16 against the former Soviet Bloc, 10 against countries in the Middle East and North Africa, 8 against Asian countries, and 8 against Canada or the United States. Just 2 claims were filed against sub-Saharan African countries and only 1 against a Western European country. Further, of these 75 claims, 76 per cent were brought against a lower-middle or upper-middle income country and the average GDP per capita of the respondent state was (US)$11,148 (or $8,363 if NAFTA claims against Canada and the US are omitted). Small-sized and low-income countries have generally avoided claims, with no jurisdictional awards issued to date against Central American or Caribbean countries, and only two involving sub-Saharan Africa. Likewise, countries with very large markets—including Western Europe and the large developing or former communist states (China, India, Brazil, Russia)—have managed to avoid claims. There has been an award in just 1 claim against Russia, 1 against Spain, and 8 against Canada or the US, each of the latter targeted by the other's investors under NAFTA. One explanation for this greater exposure of middle-sized states is that small countries rarely host investments substantial enough to warrant a treaty claim (although they often face claims under investment contracts) whereas large countries have more bargaining power to refuse to

---

2001), 13(6) World Trade and Arb Mat 139, art A, online: DFAIT www.dfait-maeci.gc.ca/tna-nac/NAFTA-Interpr-en.asp.

[106] A Cosbey *et al*, 'Investment and Sustainable Development' (Report by the International Institute for Sustainable Development, 2004) 15–16.

[107] C McLachlan, 'Commentary: The Broader Context' (2002) 18 Arb Int'l 339, 343.

[108] Widely available meaning available online: ICSID; ITA (Investment Treaty Arbitration); or NAFTA Claims.

Table 1. Claims leading to an award on jurisdiction, per country

Country	No of claims	GNP/ capita (US$)[a]	World Bank classification[b]
Algeria	1	6,107	Lower middle income
Argentina	13	12,106	Upper middle
Bolivia	1	2,587	Lower middle
Bulgaria	1	7,731	Lower middle
Burundi	1	648	Low
Canada	4	30,677	High
Chile	2	10,274	Upper middle
Congo	1	697	Low
Czech Rep	3	16,357	Upper middle
Ecuador	2	3,641	Lower middle
Egypt	4	3,950	Lower middle
Estonia	1	13,539	Upper middle
Jordan	1	4,320	Lower middle
Kyrgyzstan	1	1,751	Low
Latvia	2	10,270	Upper middle
Malaysia	1	9,512	Upper middle
Mexico	9	9,168	Upper middle
Moldova	1	1,510	Low
Morocco	2	4,004	Lower middle
Myanmar	1	na	Low
Pakistan	3	2,097	Low
Paraguay	1	4,684	Lower middle
Peru	1	5,260	Lower middle
Philippines	1	4,321	Lower middle
Poland	1	11,379	Upper middle
Romania	1	7,277	Lower middle
Russian Fed	1	9,230	Upper middle
Slovakia	1	13,494	Upper middle
Spain	1	22,391	High
Sri Lanka	2	3,778	Lower middle
Turkey	1	6,772	Upper middle
UAE	1	22,420	High
Ukraine	3	5,491	Lower middle
US	4	37,562	High
Venezuela	1	4,919	Upper middle
	Total 75	Avg $11,148 (adjusted by no of claims per country) Avg $8,363 (excluding Canada and US)	Low 8 (10.7%) Lower middle: 21 (28.0%) Upper middle: 36 (48.0%) High 10 (13.3%)

[a] United Nations Development Programme, *Human Development Report 2005* (New York: United Nations, 2005) 219.
[b] World Bank Country Classification Data 2004.

conclude investment treaties in the first place, or to deter claims by investors seeking to maintain favourable relations with the government of a major market.

The role of arbitration treaties

Investment treaty arbitration is established by bilateral and regional investment treaties, but all such treaties also incorporate the wider framework of international arbitration for certain purposes. In particular, investment treaties rely on existing instruments of international arbitration—primarily the ICSID Convention of 1965[109] and the New York Convention of 1958[110]—to supply an institutional structure and procedural paradigm for investor–state arbitration and to authorize the recognition and enforcement of awards by domestic courts.[111] These instruments pre-date the present system largely because the use of international arbitration to resolve disputes involving private parties was conventionally reserved for commercial disputes. I discuss this aspect of the system in more detail in Chapter 3 of this book; what follows is merely a brief introduction to the role of the ICSID Convention and New York Convention and to the conduct of an investor–state arbitration.

The ICSID Convention played an integral role in the system's establishment because it created a forum—the World Bank's International Centre for Settlement of Investment Disputes (ICSID)—and a body of rules dedicated to investor–state arbitration.[112] Importantly, many investment treaties delegate to the ICSID Administrative Council or Secretary-General the authority to appoint presiding arbitrators of investment treaty tribunals where the disputing parties do not otherwise agree on who should be appointed.[113] There is also an ICSID Secretariat to register and administer arbitrations, and an ICSID annulment process for the review of ICSID awards that is designed to replace domestic judicial review in this regard.[114] More broadly, ICSID is able to call upon the World Bank to add weight to investment treaty awards, given the World Bank's influence over access to international credit by most capital-importing countries.[115] In each case,

---

[109] ICSID Convention (n 87 above).
[110] United Nations Convention on the Recognition and Enforcement of Foreign Arbitral Awards (the New York Convention) (New York, 10 June 1958; 330 UNTS 3; entered into force 7 June 1959).
[111] UNCTAD (n 35 above) 62–4 and 97–8; KJ Vandevelde, 'The Political Economy of a Bilateral Investment Treaty' (1998) 92 AJIL 621, 621; Parra (n 78 above). Note that 'recognition' of an arbitration award by a court serves to bar fresh proceedings by the other disputing party; 'enforcement' refers to the court's application of legal sanctions, including seizure of property and other assets, forfeit of bank accounts, or imprisonment: A Redfern and M Hunter, *Law and Practice of International Commercial Arbitration* (4th edn, London: Sweet & Maxwell, 2004) 434–5.
[112] ICSID, *Rules of Procedure for Arbitration Proceedings*, revised 26 September 1984 and 1 January 2003 (original rules 1968), reprinted in *Convention, Regulations and Rules* (Washington: ICSID, 2003) 93 [cited as ICSID Rules].
[113] eg NAFTA (n 75 above) art 1124(1); US–Czech Republic BIT (n 100 above), art VI(3)(b)(ii); Spain–Mexico BIT (n 100 above), title 4(3) (app).   [114] Muchlinski (n 8 above) 551–3.
[115] Delupis (n 74 above) 3; Peter (n 22 above) 321; Redfern and Hunter (n 111 above) 431–2.

ICSID plays a critical role in housing and promoting investment treaty arbitration, although states do not register their consent to arbitrate investor claims by ratifying the ICSID Convention itself.

Another aspect of ICSID should be mentioned. Under the ICSID Convention, access to ICSID arbitration was originally limited to states and to investors of those states that were signatories of the ICSID Convention. Thus, where an investor and a state consented to ICSID arbitration, the arbitration could take place only if the investor's home state and the respondent state were parties to the ICSID Convention. This naturally restricted ICSID's availability and appeal to non-party states and their investors. To remedy this, the ICSID system was opened to disputes involving non-signatory states in 1978 by the creation of the ICSID Additional Facility.[116] The Additional Facility authorized ICSID to administer disputes involving non-signatory states and their investors.[117] It also extended the scope of ICSID arbitration to include disputes that did not arise directly out of an investment as long as the dispute related to a transaction that had 'features that distinguish it from an ordinary commercial transaction'.[118] That said, the Additional Facility is not governed by the ICSID Convention and, as a result, an award under the Additional Facility does not come within the ICSID enforcement system.[119] Instead, it would normally be enforceable under the New York Convention and other instruments of commercial arbitration.[120] Thus the Additional Facility allows access to ICSID facilities by states (or their investors) that are unwilling to relinquish ultimate control over investment arbitration to the ICSID system of annulment and enforcement.

In sum, the ICSID Convention is the starting-point of contemporary investment arbitration because it opened the way for treaties that establish the general consents of states to compulsory arbitration of regulatory disputes, and more

---

[116] *Rules Governing the Additional Facility for the Administration of Proceedings by the Secretariat of the International Centre for Settlement of Investment Disputes*, revised 1 January 2003 (original rules 1978), 1 ICSID Rep 213 [cited as ICSID Additional Facility Rules]. The Additional Facility was established by a majority decision of the ICSID Administrative Council of 27 September 1978: 1 ICSID Rep 218.

[117] ICSID Additional Facility Rules (n 116 above) art 2.

[118] ICSID Additional Facility Rules (n 116 above) art 2 and 4(3). When it approved the Additional Facility, the ICSID Administrative Council commented that the following transactions are distinguishable from 'an ordinary commercial transaction': 'Economic transactions which (a) may or may not, depending on their terms, be regarded by the parties as investments for the purposes of the [ICSID] Convention, which (b) involve long-term relationships or the commitment of substantial resources on the part of either party, and which (c) are of special importance to the economy of the State party, can be clearly distinguished from ordinary commercial transactions. Examples of such transactions can be found in various forms of industrial cooperation agreements and major civil works contracts.'
ICSID Additional Facility Rules, reprinted in (1993) 1 ICSID Rep 217, 220 (art 4(3), commentary).

[119] ICSID Additional Facility Rules (n 116 above) art 3 and 53. Instead, an Additional Facility arbitration award is subject to the rules of recognition and enforcement of the seat of the arbitration (art 3, commentary and art 20).

[120] ER Leahy, 'Enforcement of Arbitral Awards Issued by the Additional Facility of the International Centre of Settlement of Investment Disputes (ICSID)' (1985) 2(3) J Int'l Arb 15, 15–16.

broadly to the use of international arbitration to regulate states in their sovereign capacity.[121] This role must not be overstated, however.[122] First, ICSID arbitration does not encompass the system of investment treaty arbitration as a whole because some arbitrations take place in forums other than ICSID,[123] under different arbitration rules,[124] and subject to other appointing authorities.[125] Above all, the ICSID Convention did not establish the all-important general consents of states.[126] Thus, while the seed of the present system was planted with the ICSID Convention, the system did not fully emerge until investment treaties were concluded in large numbers in the 1990s.

The New York Convention is the founding treaty of international arbitration although its role was originally focused on the commercial sphere. I discuss this treaty in more detail in later chapters of the book; suffice it to say here that the New York Convention provided the impetus for the arbitration industries that have developed in many countries alongside the expansion of international commerce. In recent decades, in particular, the business of commercial arbitration has nourished a growing number of national arbitration centres that rely on standardized rules of arbitration. Importantly, the institutional and conceptual infrastructure of the New York Convention provided a ready-made model of arbitration that was adopted in the ICSID Convention for the purpose of resolving investor claims against states. Also, once incorporated into investment treaties themselves, the New York Convention also offered a framework, alongside the ICSID Convention, for the international enforcement of awards with limited supervision by domestic courts. In these respects, the New York Convention and the ICSID Convention are the two key multilateral arbitration treaties that undergird the system of investment treaty arbitration.

Tribunals usually conduct investor–state arbitrations in a similar way regardless of whether they are authorized to act under the auspices of the ICSID Convention or the New York Convention. Typically, an arbitration begins with the investor's notice of a claim which is provided to the respondent state, to a relevant arbitration

---

[121] B Stern, 'Comments—International Economic Relations and the MAI Dispute Settlement System' (1999) 16(2) J Int'l Arb 118, 127–8.

[122] eg Malanczuk (n 61 above) 436–7 (arguing that there is a modern standard as to the non-applicability of the local remedies rule under the ICSID Convention, without referring to BITs).

[123] eg the International Court of Arbitration of the International Chamber of Commerce or the Arbitration Institute of the Stockholm Chamber of Commerce.

[124] eg UN, *Arbitration Rules of the United Nations Commission on International Trade Law*, UN GA Res 31/98, UN GAOR, 31st Session, Supp No 17, UN Doc A/31/17, c V, s C (1976) [cited as UNCITRAL Rules]; *Rules of Arbitration of the International Chamber of Commerce*, revised 1 January 1998 (original rules 1922) [cited as ICC Rules], online: ICC www.iccwbo.org/court/english/arbitration/rules.asp; *Rules of the Arbitration Institute of the Stockholm Chamber of Commerce*, revised 1 April 1999 [cited as SCC Rules], online: SCC www.sccinstitute.com/uk/Rules.

[125] eg the President of the International Court of Justice.

[126] ICSID Convention (n 87 above) preamble ('Declaring that no Contracting State shall by the mere fact of its ratification, acceptance or approval of this Convention and without its consent be deemed to be under any obligation to submit any particular dispute to conciliation or arbitration').

institution (such as ICSID), and in some cases to the home state or to other states parties to the treaty. In the normal course, once a claim is filed, a tribunal of three arbitrators is established, with one arbitrator each appointed by the investor and the respondent state, respectively, and a president appointed by agreement or, where agreement is not possible, by an outside appointing authority (or, in arbitrations governed by the UNCITRAL Rules, the president is normally appointed by agreement of the two party-appointed arbitrators). Designated appointing authorities include ICSID, the International Court of Justice, the International Chamber of Commerce, and the Stockholm Chamber of Commerce.[127] In terms of the conduct of the actual arbitration, BITs initially authorized the filing of investor claims only under the ICSID Arbitration Rules; however, later treaties incorporated other rules such as the UNCITRAL Rules, the ICSID Additional Facility Rules, and the ICC Rules.[128] Where a treaty incorporates more than one set of rules, investors may choose the rules under which to file a claim, although the different sets of rules are very similar in how they govern an arbitration.

Once a tribunal is constituted, the arbitration generally proceeds as follows.[129] First, the tribunal resolves procedural matters; most importantly, the tribunal selects the jurisdictional seat of the arbitration, which, in turn, determines the domestic law that will govern applications to set aside the agreement to arbitrate or an arbitration award. The tribunal also resolves other matters such as the disclosure of documents, the degree of openness of the proceedings, and any challenge to the impartiality of an arbitrator. Once these preliminary matters are settled, the tribunal hears the respondent state's objections to the tribunal's jurisdiction or to the admissibility of the claim. These objections usually raise various issues, such as whether the claimant is an 'investor' who has made an 'investment' under the treaty. Where the tribunal finds that it has jurisdiction, the arbitration proceeds to the merits of whether the respondent state violated one or more of the standards of review that protect foreign investors under the treaty. If a violation is found to have caused loss to the investor, the tribunal may award compensation to the

---

[127] eg NAFTA (n 75 above) art 1124(1) (designating the Secretary-General of ICSID as appointing authority); Agreement between the Government of the United Kingdom of Great Britain and Northern Ireland and the Government of the Republic of India (UK–India BIT) (London, 14 March 1994, UKTS No 27 (1995), Cmd 2797, entered into force 6 January 1995), art 9(3)(c)(ii) (designating the President of the International Court of Justice); Greece–Egypt BIT (n 100 above) art 10(2) (designating the President of the Court of International Arbitration of the International Chamber of Commerce in Paris); Netherlands–Czech Republic BIT (n 100 above) art 8(4) (designating the President of the Arbitration Institute of the Stockholm Chamber of Commerce).

[128] eg NAFTA (n 75 above) art 1120(1) (allowing an investor to choose to file a claim under any of the UNCITRAL Rules, the ICSID Rules, or the ICSID Additional Facility Rules which, in turn, will govern the arbitration); Energy Charter Treaty (n 82 above) art 26(4) (allowing an investor to choose from the UNCITRAL Rules, the ICSID Rules, the ICSID Additional Facility Rules, or the SCC Rules).

[129] GN Horlick and AL Marti, 'NAFTA Chapter 11B: A Private Right of Action to Enforce Market Access through Investments' (1997) 14(1) J Int'l Arb 43; TW Wälde (n 75 above) 449–56; MJ Staff and CW Lewis, 'Arbitration Under NAFTA Chapter 11: Past, Present, and Future' (2003) 25 Houston J Int'l L 301, 308–16; UNCTAD (n 70 above) 40–64.

investor, as well as costs to either party. Finally, should the state refuse to comply with the award, the investor may pursue enforcement against the state's assets in the state itself or in other countries, most commonly under the ICSID Convention or the New York Convention.

Explanations for the emergence of the system

The emergence of investment treaty arbitration has taken place alongside wider trends commonly associated with the global economy,[130] the most important of which are the rise of multinational firms[131] and the liberalization of international financial markets.[132] First, it is perhaps trite to observe that multinational firms have in the post-war era assumed a central role in planning and financing economic activity, extracting natural resources, producing goods, delivering services, employing labour, researching and developing new technology, and marketing products.[133] They organize most cross-border private capital flows, often within their own corporate structure,[134] and they exercise a great deal of influence over governmental decisions in a range of pertinent areas, including the deregulation of capital flows.[135] As the key 'investors' in the global economy, multinational firms and their lobbyists have been the major players, other than states, in the promotion and negotiation of investment treaties.

[130] Including the internationalization of economic activity, the development of new communications and transportation technology, the withdrawal of the state from various activities, and the rise in power of non-state actors. AA Fatouros, 'Transnational Enterprise in the Law of State Responsibility' in RB Lillich (ed) *International Law of State Responsibility for Injuries to Aliens* (Charlottesville: University Press of Virginia, 1983) 361–3; S Picciotto, 'Introduction: What Rules for the World Economy?' in S Picciotto and R Mayne (eds) *Regulating International Business* (Houndmills: Macmillan, 1999) 9–10; Muchlinski (n 8 above) 35–8; AC Aman, 'The Limits of Globalization and the Future of Administrative Law: From Government to Governance' (2001) 8 Ind J Global Legal Studies 379, 379–84; S Sassen, 'Globalization or Denationalization?' (2003) 10 Rev Int'l Pol Econ 1, 5–6. On 'globalization' see generally D Held and A McGrew, 'Globalization' (1999) 5 Glob Governance 483, 490–4; PT Muchlinski, 'Globalisation and Legal Research' (2003) 37 Int'l Lawyer 221, 221–5.

[131] NS Rodley, 'Corporate Nationality and the Diplomatic Protection of Multinational Enterprises: The *Barcelona Traction* Case' (1971) 47 Indiana LJ 70, 71–2 and 84–5; Fatouros (n 19 above) 154–6; M Sornarajah, *The International Law on Foreign Investment* (Cambridge: CUP, 1994) 51; Hart (n 39 above) 39–44; Muchlinski (n 8 above) 25–33.

[132] R Kozul-Wright and R Rowthorn, 'Spoilt for Choice? Multinational Corporations and the Geography of International Production' (1998) 14 Ox Rev Econ Policy 74, 84–5; C Deblock and D Brunelle, 'Globalization and New Normative Frameworks—The Multilateral Agreement on Investment', Cahier de recherche 98–2 (Groupe de recherche sur l'intégration continentale, Université de Québec à Montréal, 1998) 5–8; J Kelsey, 'The Denationalization of Money: Embedded Neoliberalism and the Risks of Implosion' (2003) 12 Social & Leg Studies 155, 158.

[133] J Dunning, *International Production and the Multinational Enterprise* (London: Allen & Unwin, 1981); UNCTAD (n 8 above) xvii.

[134] RJ Mataloni, Jr, 'A Guide to BEA Statistics on US Multinational Companies' (March 1995) Survey Current Bus 38, 48; Picciotto (n 130 above) 6–7.

[135] J Braithwaite and P Drahos, *Global Business Regulation* (Cambridge: CUP, 2000) 488–91; Walter (n 56 above) 52–3; A Prakash, 'Beyond Seattle: Globalization, the Nonmarket Environment and Corporate Strategy' (2002) 9 Rev Int'l Pol Econ 513, 520–1.

The present system is also a legal outcome of the removal of domestic controls on capital flows and the corresponding expansion of an international market for private investment.[136] Obviously, without the massive growth in cross-border capital flows since the 1980s, there would be much less pressure on capital-exporting states to secure legal protection for foreign assets acquired by their nationals.[137] Similarly, without an international market in which capital is highly mobile, there would be less pressure on capital-importing states to attract foreign investors by making concessions in investment treaties and elsewhere. Finally, since most deregulated capital flows are controlled by multinational enterprises, including global financial firms, there is a higher level of interest by major private actors in the direct control of regulatory disputes with host states.[138] Investment treaties are in this respect an offshoot of the expansion of international capital.

However, the negotiation of hundreds of investment treaties involves more than a simple division of interests between capital-exporting and capital-importing states. In multilateral negotiations, it is at times possible to identify negotiating blocs based on this dichotomy, but the position of many capital-importers has shifted dramatically from the 1970s' high water-mark of Third Worldism. Many developing countries have adopted a conscious and in some cases very successful economic strategy based in part on opening themselves to foreign investment. One may presume that this is done because governments view integration into the global economy as a better development strategy than the alternatives[139] and, in this regard, it is an error to overlook or dismiss the role and various benefits of foreign investment in domestic growth and national competitiveness.[140] Further, besides well-known investment platforms or tax havens such as Hong Kong and the British Virgin Islands, some Asian and oil-rich states have become important sources of capital for the West. Finally, a small number of former colonies have reconfigured their economies to such an extent as to become international centres of capital in their own right, supporting multinational firms and playing an important cross-border investment role in regional settings, if not the world.[141]

---

[136] Picciotto (n 130 above) 7–9; World Bank, *World Development Report 1999/2000* (Oxford: OUP, 2000) 71–2; A Baines, 'Capital Mobility and European Financial and Monetary Integration: A Structural Analysis' (2002) 28 Rev Int'l Studies 337, 347.

[137] B Eichengreen *et al*, 'Liberalizing Capital Movements: Some Analytical Issues', Economic Issues No 17 (IMF, 1999).

[138] Peter (n 22 above) 381–2 and 388; J Bhagwati, 'The Capital Myth: The Difference between Trade in Widgets and Dollars' (1998) 77(3) For Affairs 7, 11–12.

[139] Peter (n 22 above) 13–14; Rugman and Gestrin (n 84 above) 159–62; UNCTAD, *World Investment Report 2003* (New York: United Nations, 2003) 87 and 106.

[140] ME Porter, *The Competitive Advantage of Nations* (New York: The Free Press, 1990) 548–9, 670–1, and 678–80; UNCTAD (n 141 above) 139, fn 138; MP Todaro and SC Smith, *Economic Development* (8th edn, Harlow: Pearson, 2003) 638–44.

[141] UNCTAD (n 8 above) xviii (reporting that TNCs from developing countries' share of global FDI flows rose from less than 6% in the mid-1980s to 11% in the late 1990s, before falling to 7% during 2001–3). Some developing countries invest more abroad than some developed ones: Singapore (36% of gross fixed capital formation during 2001–3), Chile (7%), and Malaysia (5%), compared to the US (7%), Germany (4%), and Japan (3%)).

Reflecting this dynamic, many investment treaties were concluded in the 1990s among developing and former communist countries.

In the same vein, most capital-exporting states are also important destinations of foreign investment. The US, in particular, is a huge capital-importer as well as exporter.[142] In turn, developed countries have, in some cases, belatedly come to the realization that the implications of a general consent in an investment treaty are more far-reaching and perhaps less one-sided than once thought.[143] To a significant degree, therefore, political pressures have developed in some capital-exporting states to moderate investor protection in order to preserve space for domestic decision-making on labour rights, public health, and environmental protection. Notably, the targeting of the United States by Canadian investors in claims under NAFTA provoked heated debate in the US Congress and Administration about whether the US investment treaty programme threatens domestic democracy and regulation.[144]

In these circumstances, the distinction between capital-exporters and capital-importers has become a bit blurred. Even so, this homogenizing trend can also be overstated, at the risk of downplaying the distinctive positions occupied by states in relation to investment treaty arbitration.[145] Is it so surprising that a major developed country can be the subject of investor claims in a world of large, diversified multinational firms and deregulated capital flows? The breadth and potency of the constraints imposed by investment treaties virtually ensures this result. Further, few treaties—namely, NAFTA and the Energy Charter Treaty—expose major capital-exporting states to claims in actual practice. Barring some innovative forum-shopping by investors, it is likely that the great majority of claims will continue to be brought by Western firms against governments in Latin America, the former Soviet Bloc, the Middle East, Africa, and Asia. The most common scenario is for claims to be brought under an investment treaty between a capital-importing country and a major capital-exporting state for which the former is not itself a significant source of investment.[146] In this scenario, the capital-importing

---

[142] Muchlinski (n 8 above) 30; UNCTAD (n 8 above) xix (reporting that the US was the world's largest FDI recipient until 2003, when it was surpassed by China).

[143] D Brown, 'Commentary' in LR Dawson (ed) *Whose Rights? The NAFTA Chapter 11 Debate* (Ottawa: Centre for Trade Law and Policy, 2002) 40–1.

[144] This led to the modification of the US Administration's trade negotiating authority under the Bipartisan Trade Promotion Authority Act 2002, Div B, Title XXI, Trade Act of 2002, Pub L No 107–210, 116 USC 933, s 2102(3), and to some limitations on the scope and substance of investor protection in the Singapore–United States Free Trade Agreement (Washington, 6 May 2003); and CAFTA (n 83 above). L Sek, 'Fast-Track Authority for Trade Agreements (Trade Promotion Authority): Background and Developments in the 107th Congress' (US Congressional Research Service Report No IB10084, 17 January 2002) 1–2; R Singh, 'The Impact of the Central American Free Trade Agreement on Investment Treaty Arbitrations: A Mouse that Roars?' (2004) 21 J Int'l Arb 329, 329–34.

[145] PG Cerny, 'Paradox of the Competition State: The Dynamics of Political Globalization' (1997) 32 Gov't and Opposition 251, 259–67; Kozul-Wright and Rowthorn (n 132 above) 76–8.

[146] Kozul-Wright and Rowthorn (n 132 above) 88; Soloway (n 99 above) 99; UNCTAD (n 141 above) 95.

state assumes major liabilities to multinational firms without securing any legal advantage under the treaty for its own nationals. Extended to hundreds of treaties, the effect is to regulate capital-importing states intensively without imposing binding obligations on home states or investors. This reflects the evolution of a treaty-based system in which the negotiating agenda was always driven by the usual suspects in Western Europe and North America.[147]

So, why did developing countries consent to so many investment treaties in the last two decades? No doubt, each individual country has its own reasons for concluding an investment treaty, calling for a detailed study of specific countries and treaties that is beyond the scope of this book. The modest aim here is simply to highlight some overarching conditions and trends that appear connected to the emergence of investment treaty arbitration. First is the evolution of the discussion of the role of multinational enterprises in domestic economies from a somewhat speculative and jingoistic debate in the 1960s and 1970s to a more careful analysis of the costs and benefits of foreign investment.[148] Alongside this, the 1980s and 1990s brought much greater commitment to integration and liberalization in many countries,[149] led by the Thatcher and Reagan Administrations, and in international financial institutions like the World Bank and the International Monetary Fund.[150] These political conditions favoured the negotiation of investment treaties while prompting other reforms that enable foreign investment, such as the removal of capital controls and privatization of state-owned assets.[151] In many countries, a torrent of BITs was concluded in a short period after the government adopted a liberal economic policy, based partly on encouraging foreign investment and committing to a high level of investor protection.[152]

Importantly, while the conclusion of BITs can have important signalling effects for investors, there is no clear evidence that they actually draw in foreign investment.[153] Even if such evidence existed, however, the emergence of the system is

[147] Dolzer and Stevens (n 22 above) 12–14; Muchlinski (n 12 above) 1049; CG Garcia, 'All the Other Dirty Little Secrets: Investment Treaties, Latin America, and the Necessary Evil of Investor–State Arbitration' (2004) 16 Florida J Int'l L 301, 316.
[148] TJ Farer, 'Economic Development Agreements: A Functional Analysis' (1971) 10 Colum J Transnat'l L 200, 200; Hart (n 39 above) 78–84; UNCTAD (n 2 above) 131–2; Muchlinski (n 8 above) 11; A Mody and AP Murshid, 'Growing Up with Capital Flows' (IMF Working Paper, Doc No WP/02/75, 2002) 3–5.
[149] Muchlinski (n 12 above) 10–11 and 93; Kelsey (n 132 above) 158.
[150] UNCTAD (n 2 above) 131–2; D Kalderimis, 'IMF Conditionality as Investment Regulation: A Theoretical Analysis' (2004) 13 Social & Leg Studies 103, 107.
[151] K Williams, 'British Re-Nationalization and Regulation: The Government's Liability to Shareholders' (1993) 14 U Penn J Int'l Bus L 243, 243–4; Muchlinski (n 12 above) 10–11 and 203–4.
[152] eg *CMS* (n 80 above) para 60 (noting that, in the early 1990s, invitations from Argentina to foreign investors to purchase state assets expressly mentioned the protection available to foreign investors under BITs). Dolzer and Stevens (n 22 above) 12; World Bank, *World Development Report 2005* (Washington, DC: IBRD, 2004) 176–8.
[153] M Hallward-Driemeier, 'Do Bilateral Investment Treaties Attract Foreign Direct Investment? Only a Bit ... and They Could Bite' (World Bank Policy Research Working Paper No 3121, Washington, June 2003) 4–5 and 22–3; P Egger and M Pfaffermayr, 'The Impact of

still extraordinary when one considers that the investor lobby has heralded the supposedly universal benefits of investor protection since the 1920s, and yet only in the 1980s and 1990s did its lobbying efforts bear real fruit. What this indicates is that structural factors coalesced during this period to intensify the pressures on capital-importing countries to make legal concessions to attract foreign private capital.[154] The key factors in this regard are: tight international credit and the Third World debt crisis, the legacy of capital flight that often followed financial deregulation, the thinning out of bargaining options after the fall of the Soviet Union, and reductions in Western official aid.[155] Each of these factors contributed to a bargaining environment in which increased mobility put international capital in a stronger position to demand concessions from host states. Added to this was pressure from financial institutions, both public and private, and from the governments of capital-exporting states.[156] Thus, from the 1980s, the World Bank and IMF reportedly began to link evaluations of a country's creditworthiness and policy compliance to its level of openness to investment,[157] whereas capital-exporting states have tied the availability of national insurance for foreign investment to the existence of an investment treaty with the recipient state.[158] These varied developments have enhanced the clout and prestige of private investors in a global capital market in which most states compete, whether eagerly or desperately, to attract investment or support the business strategies of 'their own' multinational firms.[159]

Bilateral Investment Treaties on Foreign Direct Investment' (2004) 32 J Comp Economics 788; J Tobin and S Rose-Ackerman, 'Foreign Direct Investment and the Business Environment in Developing Countries: the Impact of Bilateral Investment Treaties' (Working paper, Yale University, 3 January 2005); J Hewko, 'Foreign Direct Investment—Does the Rule of Law Matter?' (Report to the Carnegie Endowment for International Peace, Rule of Law Series, Report No 26, April 2002) 6–9.

[154] Smythe (n 56 above) 5–8; KJ Vandevelde, 'Sustainable Liberalism and the International Investment Regime' (1998) 19 Mich J Int'l L 373, 386–90; A Walter, 'Globalisation and Policy Convergence: the Case of Direct Investment Rules' in RA Higgott et al (eds) *Non-State Actors and Authority in the Global System* (London: Routledge, 2000).

[155] Fatouros (n 7 above) 795; Hart (n 39 above) 79; UNCTAD (n 79 above) 29–30; S Haggard, *Developing Nations and the Politics of Global Integration* (Washington, DC: Brookings Institution, 1995) 6–7; C Thomas, 'Balance-of-Payments Crises in the Developing World: Balanced Trade, Finance and Development in the New Economic Order' (2000) 15 Am U Int'l L Rev 1249, 1263; M Sornarajah, *The Settlement of Foreign Investment Disputes* (Boston: Kluwer, 2001) 12.

[156] Peter (n 22 above) 388; Bhagwati (n 138 above) 11–12.

[157] LC Situmbeko and J Jones Zulu, 'Zambia: Condemned to debt' (Report by the World Development Movement, April 2004) 52 (reporting that Zambia's Investment Act of 1993, which increased legal protection for foreign investors, was introduced as a condition of a World Bank privatization and structural reform credit that year).

[158] Delupis (n 74 above) 37 and 136–50; Dolzer and Stevens (n 22 above) 12–13 and 156–7; CK Dalrymple, 'Politics and Foreign Direct Investment: The Multilateral Investment Guarantee Agency and the Calvo Clause' (1996) 29 Cornell Int'l LJ 161, 186; Muchlinski (n 8 above) 514–19.

[159] Vandevelde (n 111 above) 633–5; O Morrissey, 'Investment and Competition Policy in the WTO: Issues for Developing Countries' (2001) 20 Development Policy Rev 63, 64–5.

A compelling explanation for the expansion of investment treaty arbitration, therefore, lies in the dynamic of inter-state competition.[160] States conclude investment treaties to attract investment, but the degree to which any one treaty makes a state more attractive to investors depends on the extent to which the treaty provides more favourable treatment than that offered by other destinations. States with less to offer in terms of their domestic market, resources, or workforce must compensate by conceding more legal rights to investors.[161] The trade-off is that these states are left with a narrower range of policy options directly to support domestic growth or resist wider competitive pressures in relation to levels of taxation, subsidization, and regulation of capital in general.[162] Cumulatively, the proliferation of treaties intensifies the pressures on all states to attract capital by liberalizing investment standards. Likewise, the conclusion of a series of 'high-standard' treaties by one major capital-exporter pressures other capital-exporting states to obtain comparable protection for their own firms. As more states accept more intrusive constraints, the bar rises as to what qualifies as a hospitable investment climate.[163] The outcome, as Guzman argues, is a 'bidding up' of state concessions to international capital.[164]

An outstanding question is the role played by the major capital-exporting states in establishing this system. It is not surprising, given the history, that such states would favour a system that ensures high-level investor protection, especially if one concludes that the system operates in a rather lop-sided way that favours multinational firms over respondent states. But why would Western countries, having such rich traditions of judicial openness and independence, push for the use of private arbitration to resolve what are clearly regulatory disputes? Why not establish an international judicial body, more like the International Court of Justice or the WTO Appellate Body, as proposed in the Abs–Shawcross proposal of 1959, for example? This question is reserved for Chapter 7, given its close

---

[160] WW Bratton *et al*, 'Introduction: Regulatory Competition and Institutional Evolution' in WW Bratton *et al* (eds) *International Regulatory Competition and Coordination* (Oxford: Clarendon, 1996) 4, 13–14, 49, and 54–5; Y Dezaley, 'Between the State, Law, and the Market: The Social and Professional Stakes in the Construction and Definition of a Regulatory Arena' in WW Bratton *et al* (eds) *International Regulatory Competition and Coordination* (Oxford: Clarendon, 1996) 61–2; S Picciotto (n 56 above) 92–3.

[161] Walter (n 154 above); Been and Beauvais (n 32 above) 121.

[162] Kozul-Wright and Rowthorn (n 132 above) 86–7; S Sassen, 'Losing Control? The State and the New Geography of Power?' (1999) 1 Global Dialogue 78, 83–7; Muchlinski (n 8 above) 222–3; RS Avi-Yonah, 'Globalization, Tax Competition, and the Fiscal Crisis of the Welfare State' (2000) 113 Harv L Rev 1573, 1575–9; Prakash (n 135 above) 514–15.

[163] Been and Beauvais (n 32 above) 124. A dynamic of inter-state competition is written into investment treaties themselves through the standard of most favoured nation treatment, which requires states to make their commitments under one investment treaty available under others. This establishes a systemic assumption in favour of expanding protection to investors as a wider group.

[164] AT Guzman, 'Why LDCs Sign Treaties That Hurt Them: Explaining the Popularity of Bilateral Investment Treaties' (1998) 38 Virg J Int'l L 639, 671–2.

connection to a key argument of the book: that investment treaties delegate the core judicial function in public law to arbitrators.

Conclusion

The discussion in this chapter introduced investment law and arbitration by examining the historical conflict between capital-exporting and capital-importing countries over proposals for a multilateral investment treaty, and by arguing that this legal conflict is interwoven with the social and economic history of European expansion and colonialism, and the corresponding efforts of newly independent countries to achieve greater regulatory autonomy over foreign-owned assets within their territory. In addition, an overview was provided of the present system of investment treaty arbitration and the manner in which its use has expanded as multinational firms have capitalized on the opportunity to bring claims against middle-sized developing and former communist states. Finally, some explanations were offered why capital-importing countries have agreed in bilateral and regional treaties to accept an intensity of adjudicative supervision and investor protection that they long opposed at the multilateral level.

The conclusion of so many investment treaties during the 1990s supports the conclusion that many states joined at that time in a broad convergence of opinion and strategy about how international law should be used to encourage investment and protect business in the global economy. Indeed, it could be said that an important diplomatic failure of the twentieth century was the failure to afford international adjudication a more integral role in earlier stages of economic globalization. Some might suggest that, with investment treaty arbitration, states have at last rectified this. The underlying question in this book is whether the adjudicative model that was chosen by states—involving the private arbitration of regulatory disputes—is the appropriate one.

3
From Contract to Public Law

Investment treaty arbitration is often approached as a form of reciprocally consensual adjudication between an investor and a state. The argument of this chapter is that it should instead be viewed as a mechanism of adjudicative review in public law. This is the case for two reasons: first, the system is established by a sovereign act of the state; second, it is predominantly used to resolve disputes arising from the exercise of sovereign authority.[1] Put differently, the subject-matter of investment treaty arbitration is a class of disputes arising from the state's relationships with individuals who are subject to the exercise of public authority by the state. This is very different from the consensual arbitration of conventional international disputes (between states) or commercial disputes (between private parties) in which both disputing parties are equally capable of possessing legal rights and obligations. As a public law system, investment treaty arbitration engages the regulatory relationship between state and individual, rather than a reciprocal relationship between juridical equals. Indeed, unlike any other form of international arbitration, it gives private arbitrators a comprehensive jurisdiction over disputes within the regulatory sphere.

This argument is presented in three stages. The chapter begins with an outline of the methodology that is used to distinguishing 'public' from 'private' in international arbitration and an elaboration of underlying assumptions regarding juridical sovereignty and regulatory adjudication. The discussion then turns to the historical evolution of the treaty structure for international commercial arbitration and to its transplantation by investment treaties into the regulatory sphere. Finally, the conceptual foundations of commercial arbitration are explored as a basis for comparison to investment treaty arbitration, with particular focus on the nature of the state's consent in both contexts. The unifying theme is that the compulsory[2] arbitration of individual claims under investment treaties should be

---

[1] A Chayes, 'The Role of the Judge in Public Law Litigation' (1976) 89 Harv L Rev 1281, 1294–5 and 1302; D Cohen and JC Smith, 'Entitlement and the Body Politic: Rethinking Negligence in Public Law' (1986) 64 Can Bar Rev 1, 7–8; D Shelton, *Remedies in International Human Rights Law* (Oxford: OUP, 1999) 39 and 47–50.

[2] MO Hudson, *International Tribunals* (Washington: Carnegie Endowment for International Peace and the Brookings Institution, 1944) 75 ('compulsory jurisdiction ... may be said to exist only where a particular tribunal, either pre-existing or susceptible of being brought into existence without the concurrence of the parties to the dispute, is endowed with power to decide a dispute upon the application of a single party').

understood not in terms of the conceptual framework of private law but as a uniquely internationalized form of governing arrangement.

The Analytical Framework

The public–private distinction

The argument begins with the premiss that it is both possible and useful to distinguish between the public (or sovereign) and private (or commercial) nature of disputes that are resolved by adjudication. Of course, there is always grey when differentiating black from white, and so it is with the public–private distinction. But the presence of grey does not mean that black and white do not exist. When a legislature expropriates property, leading to a dispute with its private owner, the passage of the legislation is quintessentially a sovereign act and the resulting dispute is quite clearly a dispute within the public sphere.[3] Alternatively, when the government contracts with a company to tend the lawn in front of Parliament, the government's conclusion of the contract is a commercial act of the state, one that any private party could carry out, and its resolution by arbitration can credibly be positioned within the private domain.

As with any system of classification, it may be difficult to pinpoint the difference between public and private in specific cases. But the distinction is nevertheless drawn in all modern legal systems, including public international law, because the recognition of any unique subject—here, 'the state'—necessitates a description of that subject.[4] The distinction is present, for example, in the principle of sovereign immunity, which posits, in absolute terms, that one state's authority is not subject to adjudication in another state's courts.[5] In this regard, many states recognize an exception to the general principle of sovereign immunity with respect to commercial acts of the state that removes the shield of sovereign immunity from the private business conduct of the state.[6] To apply this restrictive doctrine, various tests are adopted to distinguish sovereign acts (*jure imperii*) from commercial acts (*jure gestionis*), but in all cases a distinction is made in order to determine the scope of a state's immunity.[7]

---

[3] JA Rabkin, *Law Without Nations?* (Princeton: Princeton University Press, 2005) 330
[4] eg International Law Commission, 'Draft Articles on Responsibility of States for Internationally Wrongful Acts', *Report of the International Law Commission on the Work of Its Fifty-third Session*, UN GAOR, 56th Sess, Supp No 10, annex, UN Doc A/56/10 (2001) 43 [cited as ILC Draft Articles], art 4 and 5.
[5] R Von Hennigs 'European Convention on State Immunity and Other International Aspects of Sovereignty Immunity' (2001) 9 Willamette J Int'l L & Disp Resolution 185, 186–7.
[6] *Trendtex Trading Corp v Central Bank of Nigeria* [1977] QB 529, 557–8 (CA) [cited as *Trendtex*]. GR Delaume 'Sovereign Immunity and Transnational Arbitration' (1987) 3 Arbitration Int'l 28, 28–9.
[7] eg European Convention on State Immunity (16 May 1972; 74 Euro TS, 11 ILM 470; entered into force 11 June 1976), art 7(1); Foreign Sovereign Immunities Act 1976, 28 USC, 847 F Supp 61 (USA), s 1605(a); State Immunity Act 1978 (UK), s 3.

One technique for drawing the public–private distinction is to examine the character of relevant acts of the state and ask whether they are acts that the state alone, as the juridical sovereign, can carry out. Thus, in *I Congreso del Partido*, Lord Wilberforce relied on an assessment of the nature of state acts rather than their purpose as a basis for defining the scope of sovereign immunity, supported by this statement from German Federal Constitutional Court in the *Claim against the Empire of Iran Case*:[8]

As a means for determining the distinction between acts jure imperii and jure gestionis one should rather refer to the nature of the state transaction or the resulting legal relationships, and not to the motive or purpose of the state activity. It thus depends upon whether the foreign state has acted in exercise of its sovereign authority, that is in public law, or like a private person, that is in private law.

This method of distinguishing is formalistic in that it makes it imperative to define the uniqueness of the state as an entity. By adopting it, one need not downplay various critiques of the distinction between public and private power or deny that sovereign acts benefit some individuals and groups more than others, or suggest that the private acts of state and non-state actors cannot hold great significance for the public at large.[9] Nor is it suggested here that all investment disputes can be credibly classified as public or private;[10] indeed, in the case of investment arbitration, significant grey areas between public and private exist in arbitrations pursuant to stabilization clauses in investment contracts or umbrella clauses in investment treaties.[11] The aim here is rather to show as clearly as possible that the establishment of international arbitration as an adjudicative mechanism to resolve regulatory disputes between states and individuals is a major departure from the conventional use of international arbitration in the private sphere. Indeed, the proclivity of some commentators to overlook the uniqueness of the sovereign as a juridical entity tends to mask the importance of investment treaty arbitration as a rare expression of public law on the international plane.[12]

---

[8] *I Congreso del Partido* [1983] 1 AC 244, 267 (HL), citing *Claim against the Empire of Iran* (1963), 45 ILR 57, 80 (Ger Fed Const Ct). See also *Republic of Argentina v Weltover* (1992) 504 US 607, 613–14.

[9] J Freeman, 'The Private Role in Public Governance' (2000) 75 NYU L Rev 543, 547–9; A Claire Cutler, 'Critical Reflections on the Westphalian Assumptions of International Law and Organization: A Crisis of Legitimacy' (2001) 27 Rev of Int'l Studies 133, 138; D Mullan and A Ceddia, 'The Impact on Public Law of Privatization, Deregulation, Outsourcing, and Downsizing: A Canadian Perspective' (2003) 10 Ind J Global Legal Studies 199, 245.

[10] C Harlow, '"Public" and "Private" Law: Definition Without Distinction' (1980) 43 Mod L Rev 241.

[11] eg *BP America Production Co v Argentine Republic* (Jurisdiction) (27 July 2006), ICSID Case No ARB/04/8, para 108–9, online: ITA. AC Sinclair, 'The Origins of the Umbrella Clause in the International Law of Investment Protection' (2004) 20 Arb Int'l 411; F Orrego Vicuña, 'Of Contracts and Treaties in the Global Market' (2004) 8 Max Planck Ybk UN Law 341.

[12] eg CN Brower, CH Brower II, and JK Sharpe, 'The Coming Crisis in the Global Adjudicative System' (2003) 19 Arb Int'l 415, 415 (characterizing all investment disputes as commercial disputes).

Sovereignty and regulatory adjudication

As framed, the public–private distinction boils down to a series of assumptions about juridical sovereignty and its relationship to adjudication. Briefly, they are as follows. Sovereignty is a conceptual framework for understanding the representative relationship between the state and the people in its territory and, as such, for organizing the public sphere.[13] Sovereignty means that the state is treated as the entity that represents a group of people in relation to the members of the group and to other states.[14] Sovereignty is a matter of authority not control; it is a concept not an attribute.[15] In ideal terms, sovereignty implies external autonomy and internal control on the part of the state but neither fully exists in reality.[16] Rather, sovereignty is a tool for thinking about how people are organized as political entities. As such, it is a foundational concept of both public international law and domestic public law.[17] As a sovereign in the international sphere, a state is the representative of a population and territory; in the domestic sphere, the state is the repository of the collective authority to make governmental decisions.

A particular class of disputes may arise between the state and individuals who are subject to the exercise of the uniquely sovereign authority by the state. For present purposes, I shall refer to these disputes as 'regulatory' disputes and distinguish them from other 'public' disputes (ie between states or between different entities of a state) on the ground that they involve a claim made directly against the state by a private party. More importantly, regulatory disputes can be distinguished from 'private' disputes that arise between individuals acting in a private capacity (although the relationship between those individuals may itself be subject to state regulation).[18] Thus, in commercial arbitration, a party's consent to arbitrate takes place within the private sphere not because the consent is irrelevant to the public in general but because the disputing parties, acting in a private capacity, have agreed to use a particular method of dispute resolution in disputes arising between themselves.[19] They have agreed, in a manner endorsed by the state, to insulate the

---

[13] FW Maitland, 'The Crown as Corporation' (1901) 17 LQ Rev 131, 131–3 and 138; Q Skinner, 'Hobbes and the Purely Artificial Person of the State' (1999) 7 J Pol Phil 1, 1–3; I Brownlie, *Principles of Public International Law* (6th edn, Oxford: OUP, 2003) 119 and 289.

[14] R Jackson, 'Sovereignty in World Politics: A Glance at the Conceptual and Historical Landscape' (1999) 47 Pol Studies 431, 453.

[15] AV Dicey, *An Introduction to the Study of the Law of the Constitution* [1885] (8th edn, London: Macmillan, 1915) 27–34; Jackson (n 14 above) 432–3; A Sweet Stone, 'Islands of Transnational Governance' in M Shapiro and A Sweet Stone (eds) *Law, Politics, and Judicialization* (Oxford: OUP, 2002) 323.   [16] M Loughlin, *The Idea of Public Law* (Oxford: OUP, 2003) 76 and 84.

[17] C Eagleton, *The Responsibility of States in International Law* (New York: NYU Press, 1928) 4, 28, and 35–6; A James, *Sovereign Statehood: The Basis of International Society* (London: Allen & Unwin, 1986) 267–9; Loughlin (n 16 above) 58–60 and 83; C Warbrick, 'States and Recognition in International Law' in MD Evans (ed) *International Law* (2nd edn, Oxford: OUP, 2006) 222–4.

[18] Chayes (n 1 above) 1282–4.

[19] AS Rau, 'Integrity in Private Judging' (1997) 38 South Texas L Rev 455, 486–7; A Redfern and M Hunter, *Law and Practice of International Commercial Arbitration* (4th edn, London: Sweet & Maxwell, 2004) 7–8 and 131.

adjudication of their dispute from the courts and subject it instead to arbitration. In contrast, the submission of sovereign decisions to review by an adjudicative process amounts to a policy choice by the state to use that particular method of adjudication as part of its governing apparatus.[20] Public law adjudication is distinct from reciprocally consensual adjudication in the private sphere because the state acts in a sovereign capacity when it consents to the adjudication and because the relevant dispute arises from the exercise of sovereign authority by the state.

Conventionally, in international law, regulatory disputes were adjudicated by domestic courts acting on the basis of domestic law.[21] Domestic public law conventionally dealt with the internal authority of the state: how sovereign authority was constituted, delegated, and exercised within the state's territory;[22] in contrast, international law dealt with the external authority of the state: how relations and disputes among states were governed and resolved.[23] It is true that, in international law, adjudication was occasionally used to resolve disputes arising from one state's treatment of a national of another state and in such cases international adjudication engaged the regulatory relationship between the state and foreign nationals. But the degree to which this could take place was limited by doctrines of sovereign consent and immunity and by the duty to exhaust local remedies.[24] Regulatory disputes in a state's territory were presumed to fall within the exclusive domain of the state's legal system subject to minimum standards of international law and disputes could not be adjudicated at the international level without the host state's consent. Also, an international claim on behalf of a foreign national had to be brought by the home state and was treated, in principle, as the home state's claim.[25] These rules followed from customary assumptions about the nature of the state's authority in its territory and the manner in which it could be controlled by the arrangements of other states for adjudicating regulatory disputes.

Where the regulatory relationship was directly subject to adjudication in customary international law, a dispute was converted in conceptual terms from a regulatory dispute between the host state and an individual into a dispute between

---

[20] M Damaška, 'Activism in Perspective' (1983) 92 Yale LJ 1189, 1191–2; Loughlin (n 16) 5 and 12.

[21] I Delupis, *Finance and Protection of Investments in Developing Countries* (Epping: Gower Press, 1973) 123; W Peter, *Arbitration and Renegotiation of International Investment Agreements* (The Hague: Kluwer Law International, 1995) 167–9; D Lemieux and A Stuhec, *Review of Administrative Action Under NAFTA* (Scarborough: Carswell, 1999) 146.

[22] S de Smith and R Brazier, *Constitutional and Administrative Law* (8th edn, London: Penguin, 1998) 6–7 and 503; Loughlin (n 16 above) 84.

[23] TJ Lawrence, *The Principles of International Law* (London: Macmillan & Co, 1923) 2–3; MN Shaw, *International Law* (5th edn, Cambridge: CUP, 2003) 121.

[24] See the discussion in Ch 5 below, p 110–13.

[25] *Mavrommattis Palestine Concessions* (*Greece v Great Britain*) (1924), PCIJ Ser A, No 2, 12; *Administrative Decision No V* (1924), 7 RIAA 119, 19 AJIL 612, 626–7 (US–Germany Mixed Claims Commission); *Nottebohm* (*Liechtenstein v Guatemala*), [1955] ICJ Rep 4, 24; *Barcelona Traction, Light and Power Co* (*Belgium v Spain*), [1970] ICJ Rep 3, 9 ILM 227, para 78–9.

juridical equals (ie states). The regulatory relationship was thus made reciprocal in the manner of private law adjudication. With the advent of individual claims under investment treaties, often without the duty to exhaust local remedies, regulatory disputes are directly subjected to international arbitration such that the state and the aggrieved individual face each other directly as disputing parties. Thus, the regulatory relationship becomes subject to an individualized form of international adjudication that is no longer reciprocally constituted. This transformation marks the genesis of investment treaty arbitration as a governing arrangement. It has implications for well-established principles of public law, including the principle of legislative supremacy, as discussed below and in Chapter 5 of this book. Suffice it to say at this point that by compelling the state to arbitrate future disputes arising from sovereign acts, investment treaties bestow upon arbitrators a comprehensive jurisdiction to resolve investor–state disputes in the regulatory sphere.

The Origins of the Treaty Structure

The establishment of international commercial arbitration

States have only lately extended the treaty framework for international arbitration to encapsulate regulatory claims by individuals. Originally, international arbitration was established to resolve disputes between states. It was championed in particular as an alternative to the use of force in diplomatic relations. In this context, arbitration was subject to the rules that applied to inter-state disputes under international law: individuals were not allowed to bring claims since their interests were formally represented by their home state. However, as international business expanded in phases over the course of the twentieth century, states progressively gave individuals a more direct role in international arbitration by adopting it as a vehicle for the resolution of commercial disputes. In doing so, their primary aim was not to control the regulation of business by states but to facilitate commerce between firms from different countries.

The roots of international commercial arbitration can be traced to the Geneva Protocol of 1923,[26] which was drawn up at the League of Nations in response to an initiative by the International Chamber of Commerce and signed by 17 states, mostly in Europe.[27] In this treaty, states agreed to recognize agreements by private parties, located in different jurisdictions, to submit disputes that might arise between them to binding arbitration.[28] At the same time, states qualified this

---

[26] Protocol on Arbitration Clauses in Commercial Matters (the Geneva Protocol of 1923) (Geneva, 24 September 1923; 20 AJIL 194 (1926); entered into force 28 July 1924).

[27] A Nussbaum, 'Treaties on Commercial Arbitration' (1942) 56 Harv L Rev 219, 221–2 and 234–6; Redfern and Hunter (n 19 above) 67.

[28] Geneva Protocol of 1923 (n 26 above) art 1 and 4.

From Contract to Public Law

arrangement by agreeing to enforce an award only if it was made within the enforcing state's own territory and by limiting the treaty to commercial disputes.[29] Thus, among other things, states preserved domestic judicial control over the scope of international commercial arbitration, including the degree to which it could displace domestic courts' authority over regulatory disputes.

The ambit of international commercial arbitration was expanded in the Geneva Convention of 1927,[30] in which states agreed to enforce arbitration awards made in each other's territory.[31] This internationalized the enforcement of awards by allowing a successful party to enforce an arbitration award against assets of the losing party in the territory of any state party to the treaty.[32] Awards became portable: they could be used to chase assets of a losing party across many parts of the globe. None the less, international commercial arbitration remained subject to important restrictions.[33] To enforce an award, the successful party still had to show that it was consistent with the laws of the state in which enforcement was sought as well as the state in which the arbitration was held.[34] Further, the subject-matter of the award had to be 'capable of settlement' under the law of the state in which enforcement was sought,[35] and states retained the right to limit their enforcement obligations to commercial disputes.[36]

In the early 1950s, the International Chamber of Commerce—among other organizations—lobbied for a more ambitious treaty to replace the Geneva Convention of 1927, and in 1958 states responded by concluding the United Nations Convention on the Recognition and Enforcement of Foreign Arbitral Awards (the New York Convention).[37] The negotiating history of the New York Convention reflects an underlying tension between the aims of states to expand recognition of commercial arbitration, on the one hand, and the need to preserve domestic judicial autonomy, on the other. In the words of the UN drafting committee: 'it would be desirable to establish a new convention which, while going further than the Geneva Convention in facilitating the enforcement of foreign arbitral awards, would at the same time maintain generally recognized principles

---

[29] Redfern and Hunter (n 19 above) 67–8.
[30] Convention on the Execution of Foreign Arbitral Awards (the Geneva Convention of 1927) (Geneva, 26 September 1927; 92 LNTS 302, 27 AJIL 1 (1929); entered into force 25 July 1929).
[31] Nussbaum (n 27 above).   [32] Redfern and Hunter (n 19 above) 68 and 454.
[33] Redfern and Hunter (n 19 above) 454–5 (noting that the award was enforceable only if (1) the award was made pursuant to an agreement to which the Geneva Protocol of 1923 applied and (2) the award was made in the territory of a state party, and (3) the parties to the award were subject to the jurisdiction of one of the states parties to the Geneva Convention of 1927).
[34] Geneva Convention of 1927 (n 30 above) art 1(c).
[35] Geneva Convention of 1927 (n 30 above) art 1(b). Also, the award had to be consistent with the agreement to arbitrate and with the applicable procedural rules (art 1(c) and 2(c)), and recognition and enforcement had to be consistent with the public policy and the principles of law of the country where enforcement was sought (art 1(e)).
[36] See the list of reservations by the states parties in (1929) 27 AJIL 1, 11.
[37] United Nations Convention on the Recognition and Enforcement of Foreign Arbitral Awards (the New York Convention) (New York, 10 June 1958; 330 UNTS 3; entered into force 7 June 1959). AJ Van den Berg, *The New York Convention of 1958* (Antwerp: Kluwer, 1981).

of justice and respect the sovereign rights of States'.[38] To advance the first of these objectives, the New York Convention expanded the scope for the enforcement of arbitration awards. States undertook to recognize arbitration agreements that dealt with future disputes arising out of a defined legal relationship, whether or not the relationship was contractual.[39] Also, the New York Convention removed the requirement that an award had to comply with the laws of the state in which enforcement was sought. Instead, awards had only to comply with the laws of the state in which the arbitration was held, subject to basic standards of consent and due process. By agreeing to enforce awards on this basis, states relinquished a significant degree of judicial control over awards issued by arbitration tribunals established in foreign jurisdictions. Largely for this reason, the New York Convention has been described as 'the single most important pillar on which the edifice of international arbitration rests' and as 'perhaps ... the most effective instance of international legislation in the entire history of commercial law'.[40]

Today, the New York Convention has wide geographic coverage. More than 120 states have ratified the treaty, such that it now offers a wide range of jurisdictions in which the successful party in an arbitration can seek enforcement of an award against the loser's assets. Even so, the New York Convention fell short of the International Chamber of Commerce's original proposal for a 'fully international' award that would be globally enforceable without any review by domestic courts in the jurisdiction where the arbitration was held.[41] Moreover, award enforcement under the New York Convention remained limited to those disputes that were deemed capable of settlement by arbitration, and to awards that were consistent with the public policy of the country in which enforcement was sought.[42] Thus, domestic courts retained broad authority to limit the enforcement of awards; moreover, the treaty continued to allow states to limit their obligations to commercial disputes.[43]

Domestic courts in different countries interpreted these restrictions on the scope of international commercial arbitration in different ways.[44] This prompted renewed efforts to harmonize domestic laws dealing with international commercial arbitration.[45] To this end, in 1985, the UN Commission on International

---

[38] *Report of the Committee on the Enforcement of International Arbitral Awards*, UN ESC, UN Doc E/AC.42/4/Rev.1 (28 March 1955) 5.
[39] New York Convention (n 37 above) art II.1 and II.3. Redfern and Hunter (n 19 above) 68–9.
[40] Quoting, respectively, G Wetter, 'The Present Status of the International Court of Arbitration of the ICC: An Appraisal' (1990) 1 Am Rev Int'l Arb 91, 93; MJ Mustill, 'Arbitration: History and Background' (1989) 6(2) J Int'l Arb 43, 43.   [41] Redfern and Hunter (n 19 above) 68, fn 83.
[42] New York Convention (n 37 above) art II(1) and V(2)(a) and (b).
[43] New York Convention (n 37 above) art I(3). This was one of two permitted reservations. The other was a reciprocity reservation by which states could limit recognition to awards made in states that also recognized the treaty. By 2001, 39 of 125 states parties had entered a commercial reservation and 68 had entered a reciprocity reservation.
[44] *Note by the Secretariat: Further Work in respect of International Commercial Arbitration*, UN, UN Doc A/CN.9/169 (11 May 1979) 109.
[45] *Report of the Secretary-General: Analytical Compilation of Comments by Governments and International Organizations on the Draft Text of a Model Law on International Commercial Arbitration*, UN, UN Doc A/CN.9/263 and Add.1–3 (1985) [cited as *Comments by Governments*], 84.

From Contract to Public Law 53

Trade Law (UNCITRAL) produced the Model Law on International Commercial Arbitration[46] in order (once again) to facilitate the recognition and enforcement of foreign arbitration awards. The Model Law was designed to be used by states as a basis for domestic legislation that would establish a special regime in domestic law for international commercial arbitration.[47] It directs domestic courts to recognize and enforce an award 'irrespective of the country in which it was made' and without any requirement for reciprocity, subject to minimum requirements of consent and due process.[48] It also adopts broad definitions of the concepts of 'international' and 'commercial', and explicitly gives arbitration tribunals the authority to rule on their own jurisdiction.[49] Importantly, the Model Law extends the provisions of the New York Convention that limit judicial discretion to refuse to recognize and enforce awards in the place of enforcement so as to encompass the setting aside of awards by the courts in the place of the arbitration.[50]

In each respect, the drafting of the Model Law by UNCITRAL addressed a number of business complaints about domestic court supervision of commercial arbitration pursuant to the New York Convention.[51] Since the Model Law was published, approximately 40 states in both the industrialized and the developing world have used it to reform their legislation on commercial arbitration in order to provide for greater judicial deference to foreign arbitration awards.[52] To the extent that it encouraged a more uniform approach to enforcement, the Model Law enhanced the portability of New York Convention awards. Even so, states may still elect to limit the Model Law to commercial disputes and thus to the private realm.[53]

Before it produced the Model Law, the UN Commission on International Trade Law sought to promote international commercial arbitration by producing

---

[46] *Model Law on International Commercial Arbitration*, 21 June 1985, UNCITRAL, UN Doc A/40/17, annex I, 24 ILM 1302 [cited as UNCITRAL Model Law]. *Comments by Governments* (n 45 above) 84.

[47] *Report of the Secretary-General: Analytical Commentary on Draft Text of a Model Law on International Commercial Arbitration*, UN, UN Doc A/CN.9/264 (25 March 1985), 16 Ybk UNCITRAL 104 [cited as *Model Law Report*], 7.

[48] UNCITRAL Model Law (n 46 above) art 34–6.

[49] UNCITRAL Model Law (n 46 above) art 1(3) and 16.   [50] Mustill (n 40 above) 52.

[51] *Report of the Secretary-General: Possible Features of a Model Law on International Commercial Arbitration*, UN, UN Doc A/CN.9/207 (14 May 1981), (1981) 12 Ybk UNCITRAL 77.

[52] Mustill (n 40 above) 51–3; M Tenenbaum, 'International Arbitration of Trade Disputes in Mexico—The Arrival of the NAFTA and New Reforms to the Commercial Code' (1995) 12(1) J Int'l Arb 53, 59–60 and 73–4; S Kierstead, 'Referral to Arbitration Under Article 8 of the UNCITRAL Model Law: The Canadian Approach' (1998) 31 Can Bus LJ 98, 99–102; L Biucovic, 'Impact of the Adoption of the Model Law in Canada: Creating a New Environment for International Arbitration' (1998) 30 Can Bus LJ 376, 381; K-H Böckstiegel, 'An Introduction to the New German Arbitration Act Based on the UNCITRAL Model Law' (1998) 14 Arb Int'l 19, 28–31; Redfern and Hunter (n 19 above) 70–1; H Smit and V Pechota, *World Arbitration Reporter*, vol 2 (Huntington, NY: Juris, 2002); R Nishikawa, 'Arbitration Law Reform in Japan' (2004) 21 J Int'l Arb 303, 305–6. The list of grounds upon which an award may be set aside by a domestic court under art 36 of the UNCITRAL Model Law (n 46 above) was imported from the list of grounds upon which an award may be denied recognition and enforcement under art V of the New York Convention (n 37 above).

[53] UNCITRAL Model Law (n 46 above) art 1(1).

the UNCITRAL Arbitration Rules of 1976.[54] The UNCITRAL Rules are worth mentioning because they are often incorporated into investment treaties as one of the sets of procedures under which an investor may choose to file a claim.[55] Thus, the UNCITRAL Rules—like other sets of arbitration rules that are incorporated into the system in this way[56]—are used to govern the conduct of investment treaty arbitration, including important issues such as the appointment of arbitrators, the selection of the jurisdictional seat of the arbitration, the level of openness of the proceedings, and the binding nature of an award.[57] Notably, the UNCITRAL Rules like other rules were written with reference to contract-based arbitration relating to international trade. As such, they provide a further example of how investment treaties incorporate rules that originate in reciprocally consensual adjudication rather than the public law process of a court.[58]

The expansion into the regulatory sphere

By concluding the New York Convention, as complemented by the UNCITRAL Model Law and other instruments,[59] states established arbitration as an alternative

---

[54] *Arbitration Rules of the United Nations Commission on International Trade Law*, UN GA Res 31/98, UN GAOR, 31st Sess, Supp No 17, UN Doc A/31/17, c V, s C (1976) [cited as UNCITRAL Rules], preamble (stating that the UNCITRAL Rules were adopted as a set of 'rules for *ad hoc* arbitration that are acceptable in countries with different legal, social and economic systems' and that 'would significantly contribute to the development of harmonious economic relations').

[55] UNCTAD, *Dispute Settlement: Investor–State*, UNCTAD Series on Issues in International Investment Agreements (New York: United Nations, 2003) 35.

[56] ICSID, *Rules of Procedure for Arbitration Proceedings*, revised 26 September 1984 and 1 January 2003 (original rules 1968), reprinted in *Convention, Regulations and Rules* (Washington: ICSID, 2003) [cited as ICSID Rules] 93; *Rules Governing the Additional Facility for the Administration of Proceedings by the Secretariat of the International Centre for Settlement of Investment Disputes*, revised 1 January 2003 (original rules 1978), 1 ICSID Rep 213 [cited as ICSID Additional Facility Rules]; *Rules of Arbitration of the International Chamber of Commerce*, revised 1 January 1998 (original rules 1922) [cited as ICC Rules], online: ICC www.iccwbo.org/court/english/arbitration/rules.asp; and *Rules of the Arbitration Institute of the Stockholm Chamber of Commerce*, revised 1 April 1999 [cited as SCC Rules], online: SCC www.sccinstitute.com/uk/Rules.

[57] The most important difference between the UNCITRAL Rules and other sets of rules is that the UNCITRAL Rules are not connected to an established institutional structure and they provide for the presiding arbitrator of tripartite tribunals to be appointed by the two party-appointing arbitrators, rather than the disputing parties. PT Muchlinski, *Multinational Enterprises and the Law* (Oxford: Blackwell, 1999) 540.

[58] eg *Report of the Secretary-General: Preliminary Draft Set of Arbitration Rules for Optional Use in Ad Hoc Arbitration Relating to International Trade (UNCITRAL Arbitration Rules)*, UN, UN Doc A/CN.9/97 (4 November 1974), 6 Ybk UNCITRAL 163, 164.

[59] eg European Convention on International Commercial Arbitration (21 April 1961; 484 UNTS 364) (applying to international arbitrations whether or not the states from which the parties come are European); Inter-American Convention on International Commercial Arbitration (the Panama Convention) (Panama, 30 January 1975; 14 ILM 336) (modelled on the New York Convention and applying to various Latin American countries that have not ratified the New York Convention).

method for the resolution of commercial disputes between private parties.⁶⁰ Most importantly, the New York Convention established a space in which international arbitration could operate beyond the direct control of domestic courts.⁶¹ Even so, to the extent that international arbitration was used to resolve individual claims, it was limited to relations within what may loosely be called the private sphere. As a private or 'alternative' method of adjudication, arbitration was subject to the preferences of the disputing parties, allowing for the use of rules of confidentiality and arbitrator appointment that are anathema to a judicial process in public law. But the jurisdiction of tribunals did not extend in general to disputes arising from the state's exercise of public authority over individuals. Rather, it was limited by the terms of the agreement to arbitration between the disputing parties and by the scope of their private legal relationship. A critical aspect of investment treaties is that they extend the private model of adjudication that is endorsed by the New York Convention and the UNCITRAL Model Law into the regulatory sphere by giving arbitrators a comprehensive jurisdiction to resolve investor claims against the state.

The first multilateral treaty in which states clearly contemplated the expansion of international arbitration to encompass regulatory disputes between states and investors was the Convention on the Settlement of Investment Disputes of 1965 (the ICSID Convention),⁶² which established the World Bank's International Centre for Settlement of Investment Disputes (ICSID). For ICSID to have jurisdiction, both the state and the investor must consent to ICSID arbitration by contract, statute, or treaty.⁶³ In the latter two cases, the authority for ICSID arbitration originates in a general consent of the state, which allows ICSID arbitrators to exercise adjudicative authority in the regulatory sphere in ways that arbitrators acting under the New York Convention never could. This is the most important feature of the ICSID Convention: it laid a conceptual foundation for states to extend investment arbitration beyond contract and to use it in a generalized way as a governing arrangement.

In the negotiation of the New York Convention during the 1950s there were proposals to expand international commercial arbitration by broadening the treaty's definition of the term 'commercial'. These proposals were motivated by

---

⁶⁰ AF Abbott, 'Latin America and International Arbitration Conventions: The Quandary of Non-Ratification' (1976) 17 Harv Int'l LJ 131, 139; M Sornarajah, 'The UNCITRAL Model Law: A Third World Viewpoint' (1989) 6(4) J Int'l Arb 7, 14.
⁶¹ Redfern and Hunter (n 19 above) 440–1.
⁶² Convention on the Settlement of Investment Disputes Between States and Nationals of Other States (the ICSID Convention) (Washington, 18 March 1965; 4 ILM 524; entered into force 14 October 1966). A Broches, 'Development of International Law by the International Bank for Reconstruction and Development' (1965) 59 Am Soc'ty Int'l L Proc 33, 34–8; M Hirsh, *The Arbitration Mechanism of the International Centre for Settlement of Investment Disputes* (Dordrecht: Martinus Nijhoff, 1993) 11–15; JG Merrills, *International Dispute Settlement* (3rd edn, Cambridge: CUP, 1998) 113. See generally C Schreuer, *The ICSID Convention: A Commentary* (Cambridge: CUP, 2001).   ⁶³ Schreuer (n 62 above) 191–224.

the growing importance of state entities in international trade.[64] Negotiators from Western states in particular pressed for a treaty that would clearly apply not only to private firms but also to state agencies where they entered into international contracts.[65] In the end, the treaty applied to state agencies, but states retained the right to limit their obligations to commercial disputes.[66] Also, it was reported by the negotiators of the treaty that the treaty's application to state entities did not need to be expressly limited to cases in which the state was acting in a private capacity on the basis that such language 'would be superfluous and that a reference in the present report [of the drafting committee] would suffice'.[67] Therefore, to the extent that the New York Convention encompassed disputes involving the state, it was broadly limited to those which involved the state's activities in a private capacity.[68] The treaty extended to contract-based investment arbitration but not to investment arbitration in the public sphere based on the general consent.

Unlike the New York Convention, the ICSID Convention does not expressly limit ICSID arbitration to commercial disputes between investors and states; thus it allows the use of investment arbitration as public law adjudication. In particular, the ICSID Convention extends the jurisdiction of ICSID tribunals to

---

[64] Besides this factor, some states and the International Chamber of Commerce took the view that the use of the term commercial in the Geneva Convention of 1927 was uncertain and that this made it difficult for the parties to an arbitration agreement to predict whether their agreement would be upheld: eg *Comments by Governments on the draft Convention on the Recognition and Enforcement of Foreign Arbitral Awards*, UN ESC, UN Doc E/2822/Add.4 (3 April 1956) 4 (comment by the United Kingdom); *Report by the Secretary-General on the Recognition and Enforcement of Foreign Arbitral Awards*, annex I and II, UN ESC, UN Doc E/2822 (31 January 1956) [cited as *Award Enforcement Report*], 13 (annex I, comment by Switzerland) and 7 (annex II, comment by the ICC).

[65] eg *Award Enforcement Report* (n 64 above) 11 (Annex I, comment by Austria).

[66] Although this should not be taken to mean that the treaty was intended to encompass the public sphere for those states that did not make such a reservation. The negotiating history of the New York Convention indicates that this was not the intention: eg *Report of the Committee on the Enforcement of International Arbitral Awards*, UN ESC, UN Doc E/AC.42/SR.3 (Third Meeting, 23 March 1955) [cited as *Draft Convention Report*], 6 (comment by Belgium); *Award Enforcement Report* (n 64 above) 23 (annex II, comment by the Society of Comparative Legislation) and 5–6 (comment by the ICC).

[67] Quoting *Draft Convention Report* (n 66 above) 7. The negotiating history of Article I of the New York Convention reveals an intention both to extend the treaty to the commercial activities of state agencies and to limit the treaty to the private sphere: eg *Award Enforcement Report* (n 64 above) 11 (annex I, comment by Austria) and 9 (annex II, comment by the Society of Comparative Legislation); *Draft Convention Report* (n 66 above) 7 (comment by Belgium).

[68] Tension about the appropriate scope of international commercial arbitration also arose during the negotiation of the UNCITRAL Model Law with respect to the definition of the term commercial: *Comments by Governments* (n 45 above) 57 (comment by the United States) and 57–8 (comment by UNCTAD). The compromise that was reached was to avoid either defining the term commercial in the text of the Model Law or leaving the definition to domestic law, as in the case of the New York Convention. Instead, a footnote was included with art 1(1) to provide guidance on the possible meaning of the term, which stated, *inter alia*, that commercial relationships included 'investment' (*Model Law Report* (n 47 above) 11). The inclusion of this language in a footnote rather than the text highlighted the discretion of states to decide for themselves whether to include an expanded definition in their domestic legislation. See also *Model Law Report* (n 47 above) 10; *Comments by Governments* (n 45 above) 84 (comment by the ICC).

'any legal dispute arising directly out of an investment',[69] without restricting the definition of the term 'investment'.[70] As a result, the scope of ICSID arbitration is left to the legal instrument that authorizes the arbitration and, under most investment treaties, the concept of investment is defined broadly, as discussed in Chapter 4 of this book. This has extended the scope of ICSID arbitration beyond contractual disputes to a very wide range of regulatory disputes between investors and states.[71] A key innovation of the ICSID Convention, therefore, was its flexibility in relation to the types of claims by individuals against the state that were considered suitable for arbitration.

In the decades since the ICSID Convention was concluded states have ratified hundreds of investment treaties, all of which transplant the original model of consensual arbitration into the regulatory sphere. In investment treaty arbitration, as in commercial arbitration, a tribunal is constituted to adjudicate a claim initiated by a private party.[72] The tribunal has the authority to rule on its own jurisdiction and to admit the claim.[73] Often the tribunal selects the jurisdictional seat of the arbitration and, consequently, the domestic law under which the arbitration takes place.[74] Upon finding that it has jurisdiction, a tribunal determines the facts of the dispute and applies the applicable law in order to resolve issues arising from the facts.[75] If the tribunal finds that the respondent state breached an applicable legal standard, the tribunal may award damages to the claimant investor; alternatively, the tribunal may dismiss the claim.[76] An award is binding on both the claimant and the respondent and, although it does not establish binding precedent, it may have persuasive value in future cases.[77] Further, an award is insulated from judicial review by domestic courts. Generally, courts may set aside an award only in the event of a jurisdictional error or gross procedural impropriety, and not, crucially, where the tribunal has erroneously interpreted the law.[78]

---

[69] ICSID Convention (n 62 above) art 25.

[70] eg *First Preliminary Draft of a Convention on the Settlement of Investment Disputes, Annotated Text*, World Bank, UN Doc SID/63–15 (9 August 1963) 16 (art II, comment), reprinted in ICSID, *Convention on the Settlement of Investment Disputes between States and Nationals of Other States— Documents Concerning the Origins and the Formulation of the Convention*, vol 2 (World Bank, 1968) 149; World Bank, *Report of the Executive Directors on the Convention on the Settlement of Investment Disputes Between States and Nationals of Other States* (18 March 1965), reprinted in *Convention, Regulations and Rules* (Washington: ICSID, 2003) para 27.

[71] Put differently, the notion of an investment dispute under the ICSID Convention overlaps with the concept of a commercial dispute under the New York Convention: *SGS Société Générale de Surveillance v Philippines* (Jurisdiction) (29 January 2004), 8 ICSID Rep 518, 16(3) World Trade and Arb Mat 91, para 10.

[72] North American Free Trade Agreement (NAFTA) (17 December 1992; 32 ILM 296 and 605; entered into force 1 January 1994), art 1123 and 1124.

[73] ICSID Convention (n 62 above) art 41; UNCITRAL Model Law (n 46 above) art 16; UNCITRAL Rules (n 54 above) art 21(1) and (2); ICSID Additional Facility Rules (n 56 above) art 46. See also *Model Law Report* (n 47 above) 37.

[74] UNCITRAL Rules (n 54 above) art 16(1); ICSID Additional Facility Rules (n 56 above) art 21 of sch C; UNCITRAL Model Law (n 46 above) art 20.

[75] NAFTA (n 72 above) art 1131.   [76] NAFTA (n 72 above) art 1135.

[77] NAFTA (n 72 above) art 1136(2) and 1136(4).

[78] See the discussion in Ch 7 below, p 154–8.

Thus, like commercial arbitration, investment treaties allow claims to be brought by a private party before a tribunal, the members of which may be appointed by the disputing parties. The proceedings are based on rules originating in private arbitration[79] and the main remedy is a damages award that can be enforced under the New York Convention and other instruments of commercial arbitration.[80] In addition, many arbitrations are heard by private arbitration centres, other than ICSID, which are governed not by states but by business organizations. In some cases investment treaties grant these centres the authority to appoint presiding arbitrators.[81] Above all, the authority to resolve a regulatory dispute is given to private arbitrators whose status and background differ significantly from judges in that they are appointed on a case-by-case basis and thus may be seen to have a financial stake in the promotion of investment treaty arbitration as a institution. I return to these issues in Chapter 7 of this book. Suffice it to say that in each respect, and to a somewhat varying degree, states have used investment treaties to inject into the regulatory domain a private model of adjudication that was originally designed for the resolution of commercial disputes, and thus to establish a uniquely private method of government at the international level.

Investment Treaty Arbitration as Regulatory Adjudication

Given the extent to which investment treaties incorporate a private model of adjudication, investment treaty arbitration may appear little different from commercial arbitration.[82] But it is a mistake to confuse the two. As elaborated below, commercial arbitration is constituted by an agreement between private parties to

---

[79] eg ICSID Rules (n 56 above); UNCITRAL Rules (n 54 above); and ICC Rules (n 56 above). See eg NAFTA (n 72 above) art 1120(1) (giving investors the choice of filing a claim under the ICSID Rules, the ICSID Additional Facility Rules, or the UNCITRAL Rules).

[80] New York Convention (n 37 above); Panama Convention (n 59 above); UNCITRAL Model Law (n 46 above). Arbitrations pursuant to the ICSID Rules are subject to recognition and enforcement under the ICSID Convention (n 62 above), which provides an enforcement structure for investment arbitration generally, as opposed to an enforcement structure that was clearly originally intended for international commercial arbitration alone. However, all other investment treaty arbitrations—including those pursuant to the ICSID Additional Facility Rules, the UNCITRAL Rules, and the ICC Rules—are subject to recognition and enforcement under the New York Convention and other instruments of international commercial arbitration.

[81] eg treaties establishing the Court of Arbitration of the International Chamber of Commerce as appointing authority: Agreement on encouragement and reciprocal protection of investments between the Kingdom of the Netherlands and the Republic of Bolivia (the Netherlands–Bolivia BIT) (10 March 1992; entered into force 1 November 1994), art 9(4); Agreement between the Hellenic Republic and the Arab Republic of Egypt for the promotion and reciprocal protection of investments (the Greece–Egypt BIT) (Athens, 16 July 1993; entered into force 6 April 1995), art 10(2). See also eg Agreement on encouragement and reciprocal protection of investments between the Kingdom of the Netherlands and the Czech and Slovak Republic (the Netherlands–Czech Republic BIT) (22 October 1991; entered into force 19 December 1992), art 8(4) (establishing the Arbitration Institute of the Stockholm Chamber of Commerce as appointing authority).

[82] Chayes (n 1 above) 1282–4; Redfern and Hunter (n 19 above) 1–12.

arbitrate disputes between themselves and its authority derives from the autonomy of individuals to order their private affairs as they wish.[83] Investment treaty arbitration, in contrast, originates in the authority of the state to use adjudication to resolve regulatory disputes between individuals and the state.[84] It is both constituted by a sovereign act of the state and used to resolve disputes that arise from sovereign acts or omissions of the state. Thus, at its root, the misapprehension of investment treaty arbitration as commercial arbitration confuses public for private authority.

The character of international commercial arbitration

Let us examine more closely the conceptual foundations of international commercial arbitration. Commercial arbitration is a private form of adjudication authorized by the will of the disputing parties[85] and it is governed by principles that follow from the presumed supremacy of party autonomy.[86] This principle posits that the voluntary decisions of individuals about their own affairs should be respected by the state. Honouring party autonomy means respecting the decisions of those who, in doing business with one another, agree to arbitrate disputes, thus creating an 'agreement to arbitrate' which is the 'foundation stone' of international commercial arbitration.[87] The arbitration exists as a result of the agreement of the parties and the authority for the arbitration is a matter of contract.[88]

Commercial arbitration arose as an alternative to the public courts.[89] Individuals could agree to have disputes between them resolved by arbitrators rather than judges. The use of arbitration may be preferable because it is faster than the courts, it is governed by rules chosen by the parties, or it can be kept confidential.[90] At the international level, arbitration could be used to fill gaps between legal systems and

[83] Redfern and Hunter (n 19 above) 131.
[84] EV Abbot, 'The Police Power and the Right to Compensation' (1889) 3 Harv L Rev 189; LL Fuller, 'Consideration and Form' (1941) 41 Colum L Rev 799, 806–8; Chayes (n 1 above) 1294–5 and 1302.
[85] *Report of the Secretary-General: Possible Features of a Model Law on International Commercial Arbitration*, UN, UN Doc A/CN.9/207 (14 May 1981), (1981) 12 Ybk UNCITRAL 77 [cited as *Preliminary Model Law Report*] 78 ('Probably the most important principle on which the model law should be based is the freedom of the parties in order to facilitate the proper functioning of international commercial arbitration according to their expectations. This would allow them to freely submit their disputes to arbitration and to tailor the 'rules of the game' to their specific needs.'). See also UNCITRAL Model Law (n 46 above) art 19(1).
[86] Fuller (n 84 above) 806–8; Redfern and Hunter (n 19 above) 265–7; LY Fortier, 'Delimiting the Spheres of Judicial and Arbitral Power' (2000) 80 Can Bar Rev 143, 147–8.
[87] Redfern and Hunter (n 19 above) 131.
[88] L Fuller, 'The Forms and Limits of Adjudication' (1978) 92 Harv L Rev 353, 392–3; Rau (n 19 above) 486–7. But see H-L Yu and L Shore, 'Independence, Impartiality, and Immunity of Arbitrators—US and English Perspectives' (2003) 52 ICLQ 935, 965–7.
[89] Y Dezeley and B Garth, *Dealing in Virtue: International Commercial Arbitration and the Construction of a Transnational Legal Order* (Chicago: University of Chicago Press, 1996) 27–30.
[90] United States Department of Commerce, Office of the Chief Counsel for International Commerce, *International Arbitration* (1998); Redfern and Hunter (n 19 above) 22–8.

avoid problems in enforcing decisions of foreign courts.[91] For states, one reason to endorse international commercial arbitration was to facilitate the speedy and efficient resolution of cross-border business disputes.[92] International commercial arbitration could be structured so as to take place in a neutral jurisdiction that did not favour one party over the other.[93] This facilitated commerce by building confidence in the prospects for fair, prompt, and effective adjudication among actors from different countries.

The principle of party autonomy calls for the parties' agreement to arbitrate to be respected by states and, in particular, by domestic courts.[94] It follows that the agreement to arbitrate should be honoured by the home state of each disputing party as well as by other states. Likewise, the process should be insulated from oversight by domestic courts within the bounds of consent and basic procedural fairness.[95] Where an arbitration falls within the scope of the agreement to arbitrate, an application by the unsuccessful party to stay the arbitration or set aside an award should generally be dismissed.[96] Likewise, an award should be enforced by the courts so long as the process was not seriously unfair and so long as the arbitration did not exceed the scope of the parties' agreement.[97] That is, no one state's conception of justice or policy should be imposed on the parties where it conflicts with their mutual agreement to arbitrate.[98]

This does not mean that the state does not exercise public authority in relation to arbitration.[99] All arbitration tribunals depend on the authority of states to compel a party to submit to binding adjudication and on their coercive power to enforce awards.[100] Tribunals may rely on the authority of domestic courts to order a party to respect an arbitration agreement,[101] to compel attendance of witnesses

---

[91] Redfern and Hunter (n 19 above) 22–3.

[92] *Report of the Committee on the Enforcement of International Arbitral Awards*, UN ESC, UN Doc. E/AC.42/SR.1–3 (First Meeting, 1 March 1955) 5–6.

[93] Here, 'neutrality' refers to neutrality between the disputing parties, not between the state and an investor in a regulatory dispute.

[94] *Preliminary Model Law Report* (n 85 above) 78. Lord Saville, 'Denning Lecture 1995: Arbitration and the Courts' (1995) 61 Arbitration: J Institute of Chartered Arbitrators 157, 157.

[95] A Bucher, 'Court Intervention in Arbitration' in R Lillich and CN Brower (eds) *International Arbitration in the 21st Century: Towards Judicialization and Uniformity?* (Ardsley, NY: Transnational Publishers, 1994) 29; Redfern and Hunter (n 19 above) 271–2 and 328–9.

[96] eg *Gulf Canada Resources Ltd v Arochem International Inc* (1992) 66 BCLR (2nd) 113, 43 CPR (3rd) 390, para 43. Kierstead (n 52 above) 101–2.

[97] Redfern and Hunter (n 19 above) 444–7.

[98] Rau (n 19 above) 539; Redfern and Hunter (n 19 above) 419–21 and 456–9.

[99] Fuller (n 84 above) 808–9; WM Reisman, *Systems of Control in International Adjudication and Arbitration* (Durham: Duke University Press, 1992) 1; DM Gruner, 'Accounting for the Public Interest in International Arbitration: The Need for Procedural and Structural Reform' (2003) 41 Colum J Transnat'l L 923, 924; EH Bouzari, 'The Public Policy Exception to Enforcement of International Arbitral Awards: Implications for Post-NAFTA Jurisprudence' (1995) 30 Texas Int'l LJ 205, 214 and 221.

[100] Dezaley and Garth (n 89 above) 120–3; Redfern and Hunter (n 19 above) 11–12, 65–6, and 328–9; Yu and Shore (n 88 above) 964 and 967.

[101] UNCITRAL Model Law (n 46 above) art 8 and 11(4).

or production of documents,[102] to enforce interim measures,[103] or as an ultimate resort in case of a deadlock.[104] Thus, commercial arbitration could itself be viewed as a form of governing arrangement in that it depends on the state to make it compulsory.[105] And, as such, one might surmise that it is legitimate for the state to override agreements to arbitrate in order to limit the use of arbitration for various reasons, such as to protect the interests of the weaker parties, third parties, or the public.[106] Even so, most states—both to facilitate their own firms' participation in commerce and, in some cases, to support their national arbitration industry— have limited their interference with private agreements to arbitrate.[107] And, where the domestic character of courts forecloses the making of reliable commitments between companies that are based in different jurisdictions, state support for international commercial arbitration is critical for the legal framework of a global market economy. Nevertheless, the decision of a private party to consent to compulsory arbitration remains portentous: 'By agreeing to arbitrate, parties give up one of the basic rights of the citizens of any civilised community—that is to say, the right to go to their own courts of law'.[108]

This conceptual framework characterizes commercial arbitration as an autonomous system that is separate from the public sphere. Arbitration is defined or endorsed by the state as 'private' based on the sovereign decision to respect the autonomous decisions of commercial actors to displace the courts' competence and replace it with a mutually constructed alternative.[109] The state itself, acting through the legislature or the courts, identifies the parameters of private adjudication as distinct from the regulatory activity of the state and from the use of adjudication to define the legal boundaries of sovereign authority. So long as a dispute exists within this construction of the private sphere, individuals may agree to withdraw a particular dispute or legal relationship from the primary jurisdiction of the state's courts and subject it instead to arbitration. In turn, the courts are directed to give deference to arbitration, from the stage of recognizing an

---

[102] UNCITRAL Model Law (n 46 above) art 6, 8, and 27.

[103] NAFTA (n 72 above) art 1134; UNCITRAL Model Law (n 46 above) art 17.

[104] UNCITRAL Model Law (n 46 above) art 11(4) (appointment of arbitrators). *Preliminary Model Law Report* (n 85 above) 78.

[105] Redfern and Hunter (n 19 above) 328–9. Adjudicative authority is the authority to order a final remedy or sanction backed by the coercive power of the state and, as such, all adjudication involves the exercise of public authority, even where it deals with legal relationships in the private sphere that do not raise matters of public concern.

[106] *Czarnikow v Roth, Schmidt & Co* [1922] 2 KB 478, 488. MS Rosenthal, 'Arbitration in the Settlement of International Trade Disputes' (1946) 11 Law & Contemporary Problems 808, 832; OM Fiss, 'Against Settlement' (1984) 93 Yale LJ 1073, 1085–6; Rau (n 19 above) 512; MA Scodro, 'Arbitrating Novel Legal Questions: A Recommendation for Reform' (1996) 105 Yale LJ 1927, 1947–9.

[107] As demonstrated by the number of states that have ratified the New York Convention (more than 120) and passed domestic legislation based on the UNCITRAL Model Law (more than 40).

[108] A Redfern and M Hunter, *Law and Practice of International Commercial Arbitration* (3rd edn, London: Sweet & Maxwell, 1999) 5 (this statement does not appear in the 4th edn).

[109] Redfern and Hunter (n 19 above) 138–9 and 256.

agreement to arbitrate to that of executing an award. What is important here is not whether this is a comprehensive and precise description of commercial arbitration. What is important is that this framework cannot be maintained when arbitration is used to resolve regulatory disputes, as demonstrated by an examination of the different ways in which the state consents, respectively, to contract- and treaty-based investment arbitration.

The specific consent: arbitration as contract

Commercial arbitration originates in the consent of private parties, acting in a private capacity. This consent can be given either after the dispute has arisen or in advance. Where the consent is given after the dispute has arisen, it is specific to the dispute; where the consent is given in advance, it is specific to the relationship between the parties. In either case, the consent is limited to a particular dispute or relationship between private parties. The degree of specificity of the consent to arbitration affects the breadth of the jurisdiction of an arbitration tribunal and the degree to which the disputing parties have conceded their right to adjudicate a particular dispute in the courts.[110] In principle, arbitration that is authorized by an agreement to arbitrate based on a specific consent cannot go beyond the private relationship between the disputing parties. That is, the subject-matter of the dispute cannot affect the interests of either third parties or the state in the regulatory sphere because neither third parties nor the state (acting in a sovereign capacity) have consented to the arbitration.[111]

This does not mean that a state cannot specifically consent to private arbitration. On the contrary, a state can consent to private arbitration like any other private party when the state acts in a private capacity. Public officials may contract with a company for the supply of goods or services and agree to arbitrate disputes arising from the contract.[112] Where the state consents to arbitration in a contract, the arbitration is typically a form of commercial arbitration (albeit unique in that it involves the state as a private party).[113] The state's consent flows from its entry into private domain.[114] It is specific to the dispute or to the relevant commercial

---

[110] Redfern and Hunter (n 19 above) 8–9.

[111] In some cases a private arbitration may affect third parties or the state, although the degree to which this is the case is usually regulated by the state. Since the 1980s, for example, the US Supreme Court has adopted a pro-arbitration stance by allowing the arbitration of disputes that engage the interests of third parties and the general public: *Mitsubishi Motors Corp v Soler Chrysler Plymouth Inc*, 473 US 614, 627–37 (1985).

[112] eg *Baccus v SRL Servicio Nacional del Trigo* [1957] 1 QB 438 (CA) (regarding the arbitration of a dispute arising from a sales contract between a private company and an agency of the Spanish government).

[113] JP Carver, 'The Strengths and Weaknesses of International Arbitration Involving a State as a Party: Practical Implications' (1985) 1 Arb Int'l 179, 180; SJ Toope, *Mixed International Arbitration— Studies in Arbitration Between States and Private Persons* (Cambridge: Grotius Publications, 1990) 391–400; C Larsen, 'International Commercial Arbitration' *ASIL Insights* (April 1997) 1.

[114] *Bank of United States v Planter's Bank of Georgia* (1824) 9 Wheat 904, 907 (US Sup Ct); *Trendtex* (n 6 above) 557–8.

relationship and, in principle, it does not engage the interests of third parties or investors in general or the public at large.

International commercial arbitration may be used to resolve disputes between states and foreign investors, in which case it is a form of contract-based investment arbitration pursuant to a commercial relationship.[115] Contracts between states and foreign investors—variably called investment agreements, economic development agreements, or state contracts—often include arbitration clauses[116] and most of these contracts (although not all[117]) involve the state acting in a private capacity. In contract-based investment arbitration involving the state, the principle of party autonomy plays a central role because the dispute is between private parties. The dispute is an investment dispute within the private sphere or, alternatively, a commercial dispute that happens to involve the state as a disputing party.

A state's specific consent to the arbitration of investment disputes could have important implications for governmental decision-making by that state, but these implications are dwarfed by the consequences of investment arbitration based on a general consent. Investment arbitration pursuant to a contract is much more predictable and manageable than its treaty and legislation-based variants because its subject-matter is confined to a specific dispute, investor, or project, and because the contracting parties and the disputing parties are the same.[118] Thus, the state has a relatively clear sense of what it has agreed to arbitrate. Also, because the state acts in a private capacity when it consents to contract-based investment arbitration, such arbitration is less likely to engage matters of public concern.

The general consent: arbitration as governing arrangement

Under investment treaties, states consent generally to the compulsory arbitration of disputes with foreign investors *as a group*.[119] The option to arbitrate is thus open to any natural or legal person who satisfies the conditions for initiating a claim. This incorporates within the system a broad class of potential claimants whose identity is unknown to the state at the time of the state's consent[120] and a wide range of potential disputes arising from any exercise of sovereign authority that affects the assets of a foreign investor. In making a general consent, the state does not act in a private capacity; rather, the state exercises an authority that it alone

---

[115] Redfern and Hunter (n 19 above) 55.   [116] Peter (n 21 above) 1–2.

[117] SKB Asante, *Transnational Investment Law and National Development* (Lagos: University of Lagos, 1981) 65 and 69; M Sornarajah, *The Settlement of Foreign Investment Disputes* (Boston: Kluwer, 2001) 5.

[118] JG Merrills, 'The Means of Dispute Settlement' in MD Evans (ed) *International Law* (2nd edn, Oxford: OUP, 2006) 542.

[119] *Lanco International Inc v Argentine Republic* (Jurisdiction) (8 December 1998), 40 ILM 457, para 43. J Paulsson, 'Arbitration without Privity' (1995) 10 ICSID Rev 232, 256; TW Wälde, 'Investment Arbitration Under the Energy Charter Treaty—From Dispute Settlement to Treaty Implementation' (1996) 12 Arb Int'l 429, 434–6.   [120] Paulsson (n 119 above) 233.

possesses as a representative entity in the international sphere.[121] Only the state can consent generally to arbitration because only the state has the authority to regulate individuals in its territory and to authorize the compulsory adjudication of disputes between the state and individuals who are subject to its regulatory authority. In this respect, the general consent transforms international arbitration from a form of reciprocally consensual adjudication into a governing arrangement.[122]

In an insightful article published over a decade ago, Paulsson described investment treaty arbitration as 'arbitration without privity'.[123] The label has been widely adopted.[124] However, it is somewhat misleading because it likens the general consent of a state (arbitration without privity) to the specific consent of a private party in a commercial arbitration (arbitration with privity). The analytical framework remains one of private law; although investment arbitration via the general consent lacks privity it is still understood in terms of an agreement to arbitrate between the parties to the dispute. Alternatively, the general consent is sometimes described as a 'standing offer' by the state to arbitrate disputes with foreign investors.[125] The offer is standing because an investor can capitalize on the opportunity to bring a claim at any time. This label is also somewhat misleading because it too borrows from the language of private law. However, it does at least hint at the degree to which the general consent opens international adjudication to a wide class of potential claimants and disputes.

One way to illustrate the significance of the general consent is to consider how a state, by the vehicle of the specific consent, could commit to the level of investor protection and state liability that flows from a general consent. To do so, the state would have to conclude a separate agreement to arbitrate with each foreign investor in its territory, and with every foreign investor considering entering its territory.[126] Thus, for Mexico to achieve something comparable to its general consent to the compulsory arbitration of investor claims under the North American Free Trade Agreement (NAFTA), it would have to enter into a separate contract

---

[121] WW Willoughby, *The Fundamental Concepts of Public Law* (New York: Macmillan, 1924) 307; WI Jennings, *The Law and the Constitution* (London: University of London Press, 1959) 312; W Friedmann, *Law in a Changing Society* (London: Stevens & Sons, 1959) 351.

[122] C Harlow and R Rawlings, *Law and Administration* (London: Butterworths, 1997) 5 and 41–5; Lemieux and Stuhec (n 21 above) 151–2; Loughlin (n 16 above) 6, 78, and 82.

[123] Paulsson (n 119 above).

[124] eg J Werner, 'The Trade Explosion and Some Likely Effects on International Arbitration' (1997) 14 J Int'l Arb 5, 6; AK Bjorklund, 'Contract Without Privity: Sovereign Offer and Investor Acceptance' (2001) 2 Chi J Int'l L 183; AR Parra, 'ICSID and Bilateral Investment' (2000) 17(1) ICSID News 7. But see M Sornarajah, 'Power and Justice in Foreign Investment Arbitration' (1997) 14 J Int'l Arb 103, 127.

[125] JC Thomas, 'Investor–State Arbitration Under NAFTA Chapter Eleven' (Paper presented to the NAFTA Chapter 11 Investor–State Disputes: Litigating Against Sovereigns conference, Canadian Bar Association, Toronto, March 2000) 17–18; Schreuer (n 62 above) 210; O Spiermann, 'Individual Rights, State Interests and the Power to Waive ICSID Jurisdiction under Bilateral Investment Treaties' (2004) 20 Arb Int'l 179, 180.

[126] Many investment treaties include, in the definition of investor, those entities that are seeking to make an investment in the host state: eg NAFTA (n 72 above) art 1139 ('investor of a Party').

with every natural or legal person with US or Canadian nationality who directly or indirectly owns or controls (or who was seeking directly or indirectly to own or control) assets in Mexico. The suggestion that Mexico might do so is absurd, revealing the sheer scope of the obligations and liabilities that flow from the general consent. This also highlights how the moniker of 'arbitration without privity' downplays the role of investment treaty arbitration as a governing arrangement by characterizing the general consent as a type of blanket contractual obligation on the part of the state to all existing and future investors. In effect, the latter approach negates the state's regulatory role by reducing the entire universe of interactions between states and investors to a series of commercial relationships.

The general consent is a uniquely sovereign act, in particular, because of the nature of the disputes to which the consent relates. By consenting generally to investment treaty arbitration, the state submits itself to a particular mechanism for controlling its own regulatory conduct. Typically, investment treaty tribunals apply standards that constrain the acts of the state's legislature, administration, and judiciary.[127] The passage or amendment of legislation is a sovereign act, as is the imposition of mandatory rules by executive government or the final resolution of a dispute by a domestic court.[128] These acts are possible only if one accepts the uniqueness of the state as the representative of a political group; no private entity can carry them out without having been delegated the authority to do so by the state. Thus, in investment treaty arbitration, it is not only the act of consent that is sovereign but also the acts or omissions that generate disputes with foreign investors and that are subject to review.

---

[127] Under most investment treaties this is inherent in the international obligations assumed by the state. In the case of NAFTA, however, Chapter 11 arbitration expressly applies to 'state measures' including 'any law, regulation, procedure, requirement or practice' of the states parties: NAFTA (n 72 above) art 201(1). *Ethyl Corporation v Government of Canada* (Jurisdiction) (24 June 1998), 38 ILM 708 [cited as *Ethyl*], para 65; *Waste Management, Inc v United Mexican States* (Jurisdiction) (2 June 2000), 15 ICSID Rev 214, 40 ILM 56, 121 ILR 30 [cited as *Waste Management No 1*], para 11–14 (dissenting opinion); *Methanex Corporation v United States of America* (Jurisdiction) (7 August 2002), 14(6) World Trade and Arb Mat 109 [cited as *Methanex*], para 25–32; *ADF Group Inc v United States of America* (Merits) (9 January 2003), 18 ICSID Rev 195, 6 ICSID Rep 470, 15(3) World Trade and Arb Mat 55 [cited as *ADF*], para 56–9; *Loewen Group, Inc and Raymond L Loewen v United States of America* (Merits) (26 June 2003), 42 ILM 811, 7 ICSID Rep 442, 15(5) World Trade and Arb Mat 97 [cited as *Loewen*], para 39–40 and 218; *Waste Management Inc v United Mexican States* (Merits) (30 April 2004), 43 ILM 967, 16(4) World Trade and Arb Mat 3 [cited as *Waste Management No 2*], para 174.

As such, investment treaties generally constrain all branches of government and all levels of government by imputing responsibility for the conduct of sub-national governments to the state as a whole. NAFTA (n 72 above) art 105 (providing explicitly that the states parties shall 'ensure that all necessary measures are taken' to give effect to the treaty, including its observance by sub-national governments, subject to exceptions for certain sub-national measures). *Metalclad Corporation v United Mexican States* (Merits) (30 August 2000), 16 ICSID Rev 168, 40 ILM 36, 5 ICSID Rep 212, 13(1) World Trade and Arb Mat 45, para 73; *ADF* (above) para 164–5; *Loewen* (above) para 40, 53, and 123. MA Luz, 'NAFTA, Investment and the Constitution of Canada: Will the Watertight Compartments Spring a Leak' (2001) 32 Ottawa L Rev 35, 84; RG Dearden, 'Arbitration of Expropriation Disputes between an Investor and the State under the North American Free Trade Agreement' (1995) 29 J World Trade 113, 121.

[128] Harlow and Rawlings (n 122 above) 605; Loughlin (n 16 above) 80.

The broad application of investment treaties to sovereign acts has profound implications for domestic public law, especially because arbitrators are empowered to award damages as a remedy, even if the actual impact on governmental decision-making is difficult to assess, given the confidentiality that surrounds the system and the near-impossibility of assessing whether and in what sectors policy initiatives have been abandoned or modified by states in order to avert or settle claims. Most important are the implications for domestic systems of democratic choice as represented in domestic law, for example, by the principle of legislative supremacy.[129] In most democracies, legislative decisions are supreme but for constraints imposed by the constitution as interpreted by the courts.[130] Typically, the courts will limit the availability of damages as a remedy for unconstitutional acts of the legislature out of respect for the functionality of government and for electoral decision-making.[131] Under investment treaties, however, legislative decisions are reviewable just like any other state measure and, as such, arbitrators may decide that legislation is unlawful and award damages as a remedy in public law.[132] The state cannot plead that its acts were justified or that state liability is precluded under domestic law because the state agreed to subject itself to treaty arbitration based on the terms of the treaty.[133]

There is nothing startling about this from the international perspective, given that a basic principle of international law is that a state cannot rely on its own law and governing structure to evade an international obligation.[134] Also, the principle of the unity of the state, consistent with the state's representative status, makes the state responsible for the acts of all its constituent elements regardless of how sovereign authority is subdivided in domestic law. Applied as a system of legal relationships among states, these principles permit states to make agreements

---

[129] F Pollock, 'Sovereignty in English Law' (1894) 8 Harv L Rev 243, 243–4; Dicey (n 15 above) 3–4 and 36–9; J Goldsworthy, *The Sovereignty of Parliament* (Oxford: Clarendon, 1999) 1–2.

[130] eg *Authorson (Litigation Guardian of) v Canada (Attorney General)* [2003] 2 SCR 40, 227 DLR (4th) 385, para 48–57. Dicey (n 15 above) 4, 18–19, 68–72, and 103; MT Ahmedouamar, 'The Liability of the Government in France as a Consequence of its Legal Activities' (1983) 11 Int'l J Legal Info 1, 5.

[131] D Mullan, 'Damages for Violation of Constitutional Rights—A False Spring?' (1995) 6 Nat'l J Constitutional Law 105, 126; C Harlow, 'Francovich and the Problem of the Disobedient State' (1996) 2 Eur LJ 199, 213.

[132] eg *Ethyl* (n 127 above) para 65; *CMS Gas Transmission Company v Argentine Republic* (Jurisdiction) (17 July 2003), 42 ILM 788, 7 ICSID Rep 492 [cited as *CMS*], para 108; *Continental Casualty Company v Argentine Republic* (Jurisdiction) (22 February 2006), ICSID Case No ARB/03/9, para 25 and 64, online: ITA.

[133] eg *Mondev International Ltd v United States of America* (Merits) (11 October 2002), 42 ILM 85, 6 ICSID Rep 192, 15(3) World Trade and Arb Mat 273, para 154 (a local authority's immunity from suit for interference with contractual relations, under domestic law, does not protect a state from NAFTA Chapter 11 claims because NAFTA has its own remedy of compulsory investment arbitration to which no local statutory immunity would apply); *Feldman Karpa (Marvin Roy) v United Mexican States* (Merits) (16 December 2002), 18 ICSID Rev 488, 42 ILM 625, 7 ICSID Rep 341, 15(3) World Trade and Arb Mat 157 [cited as *Feldman*], para 78.

[134] Vienna Convention on the Law of Treaties (Vienna, 22 May 1969; 1155 UNTS 331; entered into force 27 January 1980), art 27. *CMS* (n 132 above) para 108. ILC Draft Articles (n 4 above) art 3 and 4.

with each other as distinct units in the international sphere.[135] What is important about investment treaty arbitration is that it applies these principles in the context of *regulatory* disputes between states and investors as opposed to reciprocal disputes between states, or between private parties. The effect is to trump the principle of legislative supremacy and, in the result, to alter a central tenet of representative democracy.[136] Thus, international principles like the unity of the state are transformed from rules that facilitate and enforce inter-state bargains into a vehicle for arbitrators to sanction the decisions of elected officials, with limited judicial oversight.

The primary argument of this chapter focuses on the uniqueness of the state as a representative entity so as to distinguish investment treaty arbitration from commercial arbitration, highlighting in particular the sovereign nature of both the state's consent and the acts that trigger disputes with investors. However, many commentators draw the same distinction by examining the wide-ranging implications of investment treaty arbitration for the public (including the impact on legislative decision-making, as just discussed).[137] It is true that investment arbitration, where it originates in sovereign authority, tends to affect matters of public concern that go well beyond those arising from the state's involvement in a particular commercial relationship.[138] Above all, because it determines the legality of the exercise of public authority in individual cases, regulatory adjudication is more likely to engage the public interest.[139] Moreover, by assessing these wider implications, one highlights the significance of a state's decision to register a general consent to compulsory arbitration, and thus shift governmental discretion to international tribunals and foreign courts, as a major policy decision in its own right.[140]

---

[135] Lawrence (n 23 above) 51.

[136] C Harlow, *State Liability: Tort Law and Beyond* (Oxford: OUP, 2004) 62; Rabkin (n 3 above) 40–1.

[137] C Tollefson, 'Metalclad v. United Mexican States Revisited: Judicial Oversight of NAFTA's Chapter Eleven Investor-State Claim Process' (2002) 11 Minn J Global Trade 183, 204–5.

[138] CH Brower II, 'Investor-State Disputes Under NAFTA: The Empire Strikes Back' (2001) 40 Colum J Transnat'l L 43, 45; Brower *et al* (n 12 above) 418.

[139] By way of illustration, the jurisdictional hearings in the *Methanex* arbitration under NAFTA, in which the US was the respondent, were attended by 9 US government departments and agencies, including the Department of State, US Trade Representative, Department of Commerce, Department of Justice, Department of Treasury, Department of Labor, Environmental Protection Agency, California Environmental Protection Agency, and California State Water Resources Control Board: *Methanex* (n 127 above) para 16 and 49. See also Werner (n 124 above) 9–10; E Obadia, 'ICSID, Investment Treaties and Arbitration: Current and Emerging Issues' (2001) 18(2) ICSID News 4, 4; BM Cremades and DJA Cairns, 'The Brave New World of Global Arbitration' (2002) 3 J World Investment 173, 208; J Werner, 'Making Investment Arbitration More Certain—A Modest Proposal' (2003) 4 J World Investment 767.

[140] For a taste of the debate on the degree to which investment treaty arbitration constrains the state and on the costs and benefits: M Barlow and T Clark, *MAI: The Multilateral Agreement on Investment and the Threat to Canadian Sovereignty* (Toronto: Stoddart: 1997); D Schneidermann, 'Investment Rules and the New Constitutionalism' (2000) 25 Law and Social Inquiry 757; CN Brower and LA Steven, 'Who Then Should Judge? Developing the International Rule of Law under

Nevertheless, the focus on the consequences of investment treaties is less compelling as a basis for distinguishing investment treaty arbitration as a unique form of adjudication because it raises the question of why the resolution of some regulatory disputes may, in some cases, be less important to the public interest than the resolution of a commercial dispute.[141] For example, it is debatable whether the *Feldman* tribunal's award under NAFTA Chapter 11 of (US)$1.7 million in damages against Mexico, for Mexico's decision not to rebate taxes to cigarette exporters,[142] is more significant for Mexicans than the resolution of a contractual dispute worth hundreds of millions of dollars between Mexico's state oil company and a major foreign buyer. Some commercial disputes in the private sphere simply affect public concerns to a greater degree than some investment disputes in the regulatory sphere. Thus, the special character of investment treaty arbitration is more precisely identified by examining the role of sovereign authority in the system's establishment and in the origins of the relevant disputes. Because these disputes are triggered by sovereign acts, they are of interest to the general public, but the reverse is not always true.

The investor's consent

The focus thus far has been on the significance of the state's consent in investment treaty arbitration. However, some commentators and arbitrators look to the investor's consent in order to locate the system within the private sphere.[143] They do so by merging the investor's consent with the state's consent to create a classical agreement to arbitrate, as in a commercial arbitration. This conceptual approach is critically analysed in this section.

The investor's consent is best viewed as the acceptance of an opportunity provided by the state to foreign investors as a group. In particular, the investor's consent accepts an opportunity to seek damages via international arbitration for a state's alleged breach of an international standard. The investor's consent has no meaning in the absence of the original consent of the state. This differentiates the investor's consent in investment treaty arbitration from the consent of a disputing party in commercial arbitration. Under investment treaties, the investor's consent is made possible by an inter-state bargain rather than by a private agreement and it relates to a regulatory dispute rather than a commercial dispute.

To illustrate further, in investment treaty arbitration an investor decides whether to resort to arbitration only after a dispute with the state has arisen. The consent is thus retrospective: it is specific to a dispute arising from the regulatory relationship.[144] Unlike the state, the investor does not agree to the compulsory

---

NAFTA Chapter 11' (2001) 2 Chi J Int'l L 193; IA Laird, 'NAFTA Chapter 11 Meets Chicken Little' (2001) 2 Chi J Int'l L 223.

[141] Fuller (n 88 above) 357.   [142] *Feldman* (n 133 above).

[143] eg Schreuer (n 62 above) 233. See generally Rau (n 19 above) 386–7; Toope (n 113 above) 389.

[144] The investor's consent is akin to a party's conclusion of an agreement to arbitrate—or *compromis*—after a dispute has arisen. See also *Compañia del Desarrollo de Santa Elena, SA v Republic of*

arbitration of future disputes with the host state or with individuals affected by the investor's business activities. Tribunals do not have general jurisdiction to award damages against multinational firms for violations of treaty standards that regulate international investors. Generally speaking, only states are sanctioned and only investors are compensated.[145] Indeed, investors cannot consent generally to investment arbitration in the regulatory sphere as does the state.[146] As private parties, investors are subject to the exercise of public authority by the state; the reverse is never true. For a foreign investor to be sanctioned via compulsory international arbitration in the regulatory sphere would require the consent of the investor's home state, not the investor.[147] Under investment treaties, the investor's consent is always specific, just as the state's consent is always general.

This does not mean that the investor's consent is insignificant. Depending on the terms of the relevant treaty, the submission of a dispute to arbitration has important ramifications for the investor as well as the state. For example, it may affect the availability of alternative remedies under domestic law: some treaties contain 'fork in the road' provisions that require claimants to choose between a treaty claim and domestic remedies. In the case of NAFTA, to initiate a claim an investor must waive legal remedies in both the host state and the other NAFTA states.[148] Both types of provisions establish the exclusivity of investment treaty arbitration as a method to challenge acts of a host state or to seek damages as a remedy.[149] In both cases, they require investors as a condition of their access to

---

Costa Rica (Merits) (17 February 2000), 15 ICSID Rev 169, 39 ILM 317, 5 ICSID Rep 157, 13(1) World Trade and Arb Mat 81 [cited as *Santa Elena*] (providing an example of an ICSID arbitration based on a host state's specific consent to the arbitration given after the dispute had arisen). M Habicht, *Post-War Treaties for the Pacific Settlement of International Disputes* (Cambridge: Harvard University Press, 1931) 1041–3.

[145] This is 'generally speaking' only because some investment treaties allow counter-claims by the respondent state after an investor has made a claim under the treaty.

[146] For an investor to consent generally to compulsory international arbitration in the regulatory sphere, the investor would have to exercise public authority over foreign nationals. However, investors can only exercise public authority where such authority has been delegated to the investor by a state. To illustrate, colonial companies were once given wide-ranging powers to govern foreign territories on behalf of the home state. In such circumstances, the investor acted as a public entity and any general consent made by the investor would be on behalf of the home state. MJ Farrelly, 'Recent Questions of International Law: The British Government and the Chartered Companies in Africa' (1894) 10 LQ Rev 254, 263.

[147] Such as in the case of the International Criminal Court, whose jurisdiction is limited (but for cases referred to the court by the UN Security Council) to those acts of individuals that were committed either within the territory of a state party or by a national of a state party: Rome Statute of the International Criminal Court (Statute of the ICC) (Rome, 17 July 1998; 2187 UNTS 3), art 12(2).

[148] NAFTA (n 72 above) art 1121. The waiver has two elements. First, the investor must waive the right to pursue domestic proceedings in any NAFTA state (including the investor's home state); second, the investor retains the right to pursue domestic legal proceedings in the host state alone that do not involve the payment of damages. In particular, the investor may pursue 'proceedings for injunctive, declaratory or other extraordinary relief, not involving the payment of damages'. *Waste Management No 1* (n 127 above) para 18–30.

[149] *Council of Canadians v Canada* (8 July 2005, Pepall J, Docket No 01-CV-208141), para 53 (Ont SCJ). *Waste Management No 1* (n 127 above) para 27; *Canfor Corporation v United States of America* (Jurisdiction) (6 June 2006), UNCITRAL Rules, para 237, online: State Department, ITA,

investment treaty arbitration to relinquish rights that are otherwise available under domestic law.[150]

These conditions of access to the system are stipulated by the states parties to the relevant investment treaty as part of their agreement to establish investment treaty arbitration as a governing arrangement. In this context, the investor's consent is more akin to the decision of an individual to seek damages against the state in domestic public law than to the decision of an individual to seek damages against another individual in private law or to the consent of a disputing party in commercial arbitration. The conditions that attach to the investor's consent flow not from an agreement to which the investor is a party but from an inter-state bargain. It is a consent of privilege rather than reciprocal obligation.

Conclusion

In this chapter, I have reviewed how investment treaties transplant the existing arrangements for international commercial arbitration into the regulatory sphere. I have also presented an argument for why investment treaty arbitration should be viewed as a form of public law adjudication based on the system's original and ongoing connection to sovereign authority. In this regard, the system is best understood as a uniquely internationalized arm of the governing apparatus of states, one that employs arbitration to review and control the exercise of public authority in relation to international business. As a governing arrangement, investment treaty arbitration forms part of the institutions and processes that apply to the relationship between those who govern and those who are governed; between state officials and bodies, on the one hand, and private individuals, on the other.[151]

NAFTA Claims. For the host state, this exclusivity precludes investors from going to foreign courts to resolve regulatory disputes in the territory of the host state and limits the prospect of state liability to that of a damages award by a NAFTA tribunal. Foreign investors sometimes seek judicial relief before the courts of their own state in the event of a regulatory dispute abroad. To illustrate, the Iran–US Claims Tribunal was established as part of an agreement to release American hostages held in Iran in January 1981, in return for the release of Iranian assets that were frozen in the US and the suspension by presidential order of hundreds of commercial lawsuits that were pending in the US in relation to Iran. A fund of one billion dollars was released by the US to a depository bank, to be held in escrow, and amounts awarded to US claimants by the tribunal were discharged from that account, which Iran undertook to keep topped up: Redfern and Hunter (n 19 above) 60–1.

[150] Although the degree of exclusivity that the treaty provides is, of course, subject to interpretation and limitation by tribunals: eg *Waste Management No 1* (n 127 above) para 13–14 and 59 (dissenting opinion); *GAMI Investments, Inc v Government of the United Mexican States* (Merits) (15 November 2004), 44 ILM 545, 17(2) World Trade and Arb Mat 127, para 38; *International Thunderbird Gaming Corporation v United Mexican States* (Merits) (26 January 2006), 18(2) World Trade and Arb Mat 59, para 118. *Middle East Cement Shipping and Handling Co SA v Arab Republic of Egypt* (Merits) (12 April 2002), 18 ICSID Rev 602, 7 ICSID Rep 173, para 71; *CMS* (n 132 above) para 80.

[151] An adjudicator's authority to resolve a dispute, like the authority of other individuals who exercise public authority, is a part of the apparatus for governing within a state. Damaška (n 20 above) 1191–2.

In many states, adjudication plays an important and expanding role in regulating relations between individuals and the state.[152] One of the core functions of the judiciary is to constrain the exercise of sovereign authority by executive government and, under many constitutions, by the legislature.[153] When a judge invokes his or her public law competence to resolve a dispute between the state and a person or organization that is subject to regulation by the state, he or she determines matters such as the legality of governmental activity, the degree to which individuals should be protected from regulation, and the appropriate role of the state.[154] The role of arbitrators under investment treaties is essentially the same.

Whether it is determined by domestic or international standards, the resolution of a regulatory dispute is intrinsically a matter of public law.[155] For this reason, investment treaty arbitration most resembles the domestic adjudication of individual claims against the state under administrative or constitutional law.[156] However, investors are able to invoke international principles and standards—originally developed in the context of a legal relationship between juridical equals—that are not typically employed in the adjudication of a regulatory dispute under domestic law.[157] Moreover, their claims for damages are resolved by privately contracted adjudicators according to rules that are in many respects alien to public law. But to what extent does this mixture of private form and regulatory substance amount to an actual authority to review and discipline states? This is the subject of the next chapter.

---

[152] M Shapiro, 'The Globalization of Law' (1993) 1 Ind J Global Legal Studies 37, 47–50; JHH Weiler, 'Epilogue: Towards a Common Law of International Trade' in JHH Weiler (ed) *The EU, the WTO, and the NAFTA* (Oxford: OUP, 2000) 201–2.   [153] Loughlin (n 16 above) 30 and 85.

[154] JHH Weiler (n 152 above) 202; M Koskenniemi, 'What Is International Law For?' in MD Evans (ed) *International Law* (2nd edn, Oxford: OUP, 2006) 66–7.

[155] Loughlin (n 16 above) 5 and 88.

[156] Brownlie (n 13 above) 503–4; B Kingsbury, N Krisch, and RB Stewart, 'The Emergence of Global Administrative Law' (2005) 68 Law & Contemporary Problems 15, 25–6, and 55–7.

[157] eg *Feldman* (n 133 above) para 62 (invoking the international principle of estoppel in claims arising from boundary disputes); *Santa Elena* (n 144 above) para 35 (international standard of compensation, calculated without accounting for existing environmental legislation that would restrict the commercial development of expropriated property); *Tecnicas Medioambientales Tecmed, SA v United Mexican States* (Merits) (29 May 2003), 19 ICSID Rev 158, 43 ILM 133, para 70–1 and 173 (international principle of good faith); *Azurix Corp v Argentine Republic* (Jurisdiction) (8 December 2003), 43 ILM 262, 16(2) World Trade and Arb Mat 111, para 34 (international principle of unity of the state).

4
Scope and Standards of Review

Arbitrators resolved cases of great public importance long before the advent of investment treaty arbitration, in the context of both commercial arbitration and dispute settlement among states. However, in these other contexts, a state is able to assess and control the extent to which a clause in a particular contract, or its consent to the arbitration of a specific dispute, will subject matters of governmental concern to compulsory arbitration. The significance of investment treaties is that they give arbitrators a comprehensive jurisdiction over a very broad class of potential disputes with foreign investors, which are thus removed from the domain of domestic courts. The next set of questions that arises is, just how broad is this class of disputes, and do they really engage core elements of public law? That is, how far does the writ of arbitrators actually run?

The content of the judicial function of arbitrators under investment treaties lies partly in the scope of the review mechanism and the content of the standards[1] of review. The 'scope' of investment treaty arbitration here refers to the range of state activity that is subject to control by the system.[2] In this chapter, I review the notion of 'investment' in contemporary treaties to demonstrate that the system affords to arbitrators a broad jurisdiction over a wide range of sovereign acts. In addition, I argue that the treaties typically apply broadly framed standards of review by looking at three key standards—national treatment, the minimum standard of treatment, and compensation for expropriation—which reveal the interpretive and governmental discretion that is delegated to arbitrators. It should be said that the aim here is not to demarcate precisely the boundaries of arbitrator authority or the meaning of particular standards, a Herculean task in itself, but merely to show that within those boundaries a wide expanse of regulatory activity is subject to intensive review.

---

[1] The term 'standards' is used rather than 'rules' to refer to the substantive obligations that states assume in investment treaties in order to reflect the level of generality at which those obligations are expressed. D Kennedy, 'Form and Substance in Private Law Adjudication' (1976) 89 Harv L Rev 1685, 1687–1701; JP Trachtman, 'The Domain of WTO Dispute Resolution' (1999) 40 Harv Int'l LJ 333, 334.

[2] UNCTAD, *Scope and Definition*, UNCTAD Series on Issues in International Investment Agreements (New York: United Nations, 1999).

The Scope of Investment Treaty Arbitration

The scope of investment treaty arbitration can be demonstrated by a review of the key concept of 'investment'.[3] Investment treaties limit the jurisdiction of tribunals to disputes that relate to investment,[4] although the term is usually defined broadly enough to encompass a wide range of economic activity that is subject to state regulation, including economic activity not covered by other trade agreements or by conventional notions of foreign direct investment.[5] By implication, a broad range of governmental activity is brought within the supervisory discretion of arbitrators.

In conventional trade law, the primary subject of regulation was trade in 'goods'.[6] In this context, international standards applied to state measures that affected tangible products with distinct physical characteristics.[7] As a result, trade rules could be defined in relation to state measures that affect the movement of identifiable tangible products, normally when they cross a border.[8] This led to a system of trade regulation that was based on elaborate systems of product classification as well as detailed lists of permissible tariffs and quotas for different categories of products. Over time, states expanded the rules to encompass measures that had the equivalent effect of a tariff or quota and this complicated the matter.[9]

---

[3] These are not the only aspects of jurisdiction under investment treaties. For example, the concept of 'investor'—a jurisdictional concept—may be defined broadly so as to open investment treaty arbitration to multinational firms that organize their ownership of assets through an international structure of holding companies: see the discussion in Ch 5 below, p 113–15. A tribunal's characterization of the treaty's substantive standards of review may also be treated as a matter of jurisdiction: *United Parcel Service of America, Inc v Government of Canada* (Jurisdiction) (22 November 2002), UNCITRAL Rules [cited as *UPS*], para 37, online: DFAIT, ITA, Investment Claims.

[4] UNCTAD, *World Investment Report 1996* (Geneva: United Nations, 1997) 173–4; UNCTAD (n 2 above) 15–23.

[5] *Feldman Karpa (Marvin Roy) v United Mexican States* (Merits) (16 December 2002), 18 ICSID Rev 488, 42 ILM 625, 7 ICSID Rep 341, 15(3) World Trade and Arb Mat 157 [cited as *Feldman*], para 96; *Fedax NV v Republic of Venezuela* (Jurisdiction) (11 July 1997), 37 ILM 1378, 5 ICSID Rep 186, para 24; *CMS Gas Transmission Company v Argentine Republic* (Jurisdiction) (17 July 2003), 42 ILM 788, 7 ICSID Rep 492 [cited as *CMS* (Jurisdiction)], para 52. R Dolzer and M Stevens, *Bilateral Investment Treaties* (The Hague: Martinus Nijhoff, 1995) 26; J Paulsson, 'Arbitration without Privity' (1995) 10 ICSID Rev 232, 238–9; P Juillard, 'MAI: A European View' (1998) 31 Cornell Int'l LJ 477, 483; CM Correa, 'Bilateral Investment Agreements: Agents of New Global Standards for the Protection of Intellectual Property Rights?' (Report for GRAIN, August 2004) 6–7.

[6] M Trebilcock and R Howse, *The Regulation of International Trade* (3rd edn, London: Routledge, 2005) 23–4 and 27–8.

[7] JH Dalhuisen, *Dalhuisen on International Commercial, Financial and Trade Law* (Oxford: Hart, 2000) 351.

[8] L Ehring, 'De Facto Discrimination in WTO Law: National and Most-Favored-Nation Treatment—or Equal Treatment?' (Jean Monnet Working Paper No 12/01, New York University School of Law, 2001) 1.

[9] JH Jackson, *The World Trading System* (2nd edn, Cambridge, Mass: MIT Press, 1997) 49–50; JHH Weiler, 'Epilogue: Towards a Common Law of International Trade' in JHH Weiler (ed) *The EU, the WTO, and the NAFTA* (Oxford: OUP, 2000) 201 and 205–6.

Even so, the standards remained connected to cross-border movements of tangible products and thus relatively definable.

Identifying an investment is more difficult. Goods are products; investment is a concept.[10] Investment involves decisions, acts, and motives: the contribution of capital to a business venture for profit or return (for example).[11] Also, cross-border investment takes place within a broader environment than the mere movement of tangible things. Walker comments that investment is 'a process inextricably woven into the fabric of human affairs generally' and that it is 'inadequately dealt with unless set in the total "climate" in which it is to exist'.[12] A system that controls the exercise of public authority over investment has the potential to impact on a much wider range of economic activity than does a system that regulates trade in goods.[13]

Indeed, if the term investment is not narrowly defined from the start, using detailed and precise language, it has the potential to encompass an extremely wide range of economic activity.[14] Take the example of water.[15] Water could be classified as a good or product that moves across borders; ie as bottled water or bulk water. In this case, the state measures that related to international trade in water as a good would be those that affected the movement of bottled or bulk water across an international border. Likewise, investments that related to international trade in water *as a good* would be those in which capital is committed to an endeavour to move water across borders for a return. The characterization of water as a good—and of investment as the commitment of capital to the trade of water as a good—narrows the range of economic activity that is affected by international standards.

By widening the concept of water-related investment, it is possible dramatically to expand the scope of the economic (and regulatory) activity that is affected. Hydroelectricity, commercial shipping, the manufacture of goods, mining, agriculture: all involve the use of water as an economic activity and all are regulated by the state.[16] All involve the expenditure of capital and all are subject to regulation

---

[10] W Peter, *Arbitration and Renegotiation of International Investment Agreements* (The Hague: Kluwer Law International, 1995) 18–19.

[11] M Daly, 'Some Taxing Questions for the Multilateral Agreement on Investment (MAI)' (1997) 20 World Economy 787, 788.

[12] H Walker, 'Treaties for the Encouragement and Protection of Foreign Investment: Present United States Practice' (1956) 5 Am J Comp L 229, 244.

[13] BB Ramaiah, 'Towards a Multilateral Framework on Investment' (1997) 6 Transnat'l Corp 117, 118–19; A Afilalo, 'Constitutionalization Through the Back Door: A European Perspective on NAFTA's Investment Chapter' (2001) 34 NYU J Int'l L & Pol 1, 7; UNCTAD, *World Investment Report 2003* (New York: United Nations, 2003) 99–101.

[14] A Landsmeer, 'Movement of Capital and Other Freedoms' (2001) 28 Legal Issues of Economic Integration 57, 67–9.

[15] International Joint Commission, *Protection of the Waters of the Great Lakes—Final Report to the Governments of Canada and the United States* (IJC, February 2002); PH Gleick et al, 'The New Economy of Water' (Report for the Pacific Institute for Studies in Development, Environment, and Security, 2002) 11–14; A Ostrovsky, R Speed, and E Tuerk, 'GATS, Water and the Environment' (Report for the Center for International Environmental Law and the World Wide Fund for Nature, 2003) 23–4.

[16] Ostrovsky *et al* (n 15 above) 22.

for reasons of resource management, pollution control, public health, and so on. This reflects the nature of water as an essential resource. It also indicates the differences between applying international standards to water either as a good, as an investment relating to a good, or as an investment in general.

The World Trade Organization agreements that govern investment, as opposed to trade in goods, tend to limit the scope of the idea of investment in important ways. For instance, the Agreement on Trade-Related Investment Measures applies only to investments that are themselves connected to trade in goods; that is, to cross-border movement of tangible products.[17] More broadly, the General Agreement on Trade in Services (GATS) applies to trade in services, including services that are supplied by a foreign company through a commercial presence in the jurisdiction of the consumer.[18] As such, the GATS applies to investments that are connected to intangible products.[19] Even so, unlike investment treaties, the GATS is a bottom-up (or positive list) agreement under which states must expressly consent to the application of GATS standards in specific sectors and modes of supply.[20]

If investment treaties were bottom-up treaties like the GATS, then states could limit their commitments to particular sectors of investment or investors and, where a state did not make express commitments in a particular field, the treaty would be presumed not to apply. But investment treaties are top-down (negative list) agreements, so states may not limit their obligations to particular areas of economic activity relating to investment. Instead, the treaties apply generally to any type of investment that is not expressly excluded. This makes the treaty definition of investment vital to determining the scope of investment treaty arbitration.

Over time, investment treaties have expanded their definition of investment so that it now covers a very wide range of economic and regulatory activity connected to foreign-owned or foreign-controlled assets.[21] The precise wording of the definition varies among treaties, although contemporary treaties typically refer to 'every kind of asset' or 'every kind of investment' that is 'directly or indirectly

---

[17] Agreement on Trade-Related Investment Measures (the TRIMs Agreement) (annex IA of the Agreement Establishing the World Trade Organization) (15 April 1994), art 1, *Final Act Embodying the Results of the Uruguay Round of Multilateral Trade Negotiations* (1994) 139. S Dillon, *International Trade and Economic Law in the European Union* (Oxford: Hart, 2002) 101.

[18] General Agreement on Trade in Services (the GATS) (15 April 1994; 33 ILM 44), art I(2) ('For the purposes of this Agreement, trade in services is defined as the supply of a service: . . . (c) by a service supplier of one Member, through commercial presence in the territory of any other Member; . . . '). UNCTAD, *World Investment Report 2004* (Geneva: United Nations, 2004) 222–3.

[19] Dalhuisen (n 7 above) 351; UNCTAD (n 18 above) 145.

[20] The GATS is a bottom-up agreement because its most significant obligations apply only to those service sectors positively identified by the respective state party. UNCTAD (n 13 above) 148–9.

[21] Over time, the definition of investment in investment treaties has expanded to include eg 'associated activities' of investment and short-term capital flows. JE Pattison 'The United States–Egypt Bilateral Investment Treaty: A Prototype for Future Negotiations' (1983) 16 Cornell Int'l LJ 305, 316–17; Dolzer and Stevens (n 5 above) 27–31; UNCTAD (n 13 above) 99–101.

owned' by an investor, and specifically list the following items:[22]
(1) tangible and intangible property;[23]
(2) shares, bonds, and other interests in companies;[24]

---

[22] Compiled from the following treaties: Convenio entre la República Argentina y la Union Economica Belgo-Luxemburguesa para la promoción y la protección de inversiones (the Belgium–Argentina BIT) (Brussels, 28 June 1990; entered into force 20 May 1994), art 1(2); Tratado entre la República Federal de Alemania y la República Argentina sobre promoción y protección recíproca de inversiones (the Germany–Argentina BIT) (Bonn, 9 April 1991; entered into force 8 November 1993), art 1(1); Agreement between the Hellenic Republic and the Arab Republic of Egypt for the promotion and reciprocal protection of investments (the Greece–Egypt BIT) (Athens, 16 July 1993; entered into force 6 April 1995), art 1(1); Accord entre le Gouvernement de la République Française et le Gouvernement de la République Argentine sur l'encouragement et la protection réciproques des investissements (the France–Argentina BIT) (Paris, 3 July 1991; entered into force 3 March 1993), art 1(1); Acuerdo para la promoción y la protección reciproca de inversiones entre el Reino de España y la República Argentina (the Spain–Argentina BIT) (Buenos Aires, 3 October 1991; entered into force 28 September 1992), art I(2); Acuerdo para la promoción y protección reciproca de inversiones entre los Estados Unidos Mexicanos y el Reino de España (the Spain–Mexico BIT) (Mexico City, 22 June 1995; entered into force 18 December 1996), art I(2); Agreement on encouragement and reciprocal protection of investments between the Kingdom of the Netherlands and the Republic of Bolivia (the Netherlands–Bolivia BIT) (10 March 1992; entered into force 1 November 1994), art 1(a); Agreement on encouragement and reciprocal protection of investments between the Kingdom of the Netherlands and the Czech and Slovak Republic (the Netherlands–Czech Republic BIT) (22 October 1991; entered into force 19 December 1992), art 1(a); Agreement on encouragement and reciprocal protection of investments between the Kingdom of the Netherlands and the Republic of Venezuela (the Netherlands–Venezuela BIT) (22 October 1991; entered into force 1 November 1993), art 1(a); Convenio entre la República del Perú y la República del Paraguay sobre promoción y protección de inversiones (the Peru–Paraguay BIT) (Lima, 31 January 1994; entered into force 18 December 1994), art 1(1); Accord entre la Confédération suisse et la République du Pakistan concernant la promotion et la protection réciproque des investissements (the Switzerland–Pakistan BIT) (Berne, 11 July 1995; entered into force 6 May 1996), art 1(2); Accord entre la Confédération suisse et la République des Philippines concernant la promotion et la protection réciproque des investissements (the Switzerland–Philippines BIT) (Manille, 31 March 1997; entered into force 23 April 1999), art I(2); Agreement between the Government of the United Kingdom of Great Britain and Northern Ireland and the Government of the Arab Republic of Egypt for the promotion and protection of investments (the UK–Egypt BIT) (London, 11 June 1975, UKTS No 97 (1976); Cmd 6638; entered into force 24 February 1976), art 1(a); Agreement between the Government of the United Kingdom of Great Britain and Northern Ireland and the Government of the Democratic Socialist Republic of Sri Lanka for the promotion and protection of investments (the UK–Sri Lanka BIT) (Colombo, 13 February 1980; UKTS No 14 (1981); Cmd 8186; entered into force 18 December 1980), art 1(a); Treaty between the United States of America and the Argentine Republic concerning the reciprocal encouragement and protection of investment (the US–Argentina BIT) (Washington, 14 November 1991; entered into force 20 October 1994), art I(1)(a); Treaty with the Czech and Slovak Federal Republic concerning the reciprocal encouragement and protection of investment (the US–Czech Republic BIT) (Washington, 22 October 1991; entered into force 19 December 1992), art I(1)(a); Treaty between the United States of America and the Republic of Ecuador concerning the reciprocal encouragement and protection of investment (the US–Ecuador BIT) (Washington, 27 August 1993; entered into force 11 May 1997), art I(1)(a); Treaty between the Government of the United States of America and the Government of Romania concerning the reciprocal encouragement and protection of investment (the US–Romania BIT) (Bucharest, 28 May 1992; entered into force 15 January 1994), art I(1)(a); Energy Charter Treaty (annex I of the Final Act of the European Energy Charter Conference) (Lisbon, 17 December 1994; 34 ILM 373), art 1(6); North American Free Trade Agreement (NAFTA) (17 December 1992; 32 ILM 296 and 605; entered into force 1 January 1994), art 1139.
[23] Or 'movable and immovable property': eg Netherlands–Venezuela BIT (n 22 above), art 1(a)(i).
[24] Significantly, some treaties—especially those concluded by the US—specifically include a 'company' or 'enterprise' as an investment. See eg United States–Czech Republic BIT (n 22 above), art I(1); Energy Charter Treaty (n 22 above), art 1(6)(b); NAFTA (n 22 above), art 1139.

(3) rights to money or any performance having economic value;[25]
(4) intellectual property rights, goodwill, and know-how;[26]
(5) rights granted in law or contract, including concessionary rights.[27]

The breadth of this illustrative class of assets is central to the wide scope of investment treaty arbitration. Unsurprisingly, it goes beyond more restrictive definitions in customary international law, which historically limited the protection of foreign-owned property to assets that are tangible[28] and directly owned.[29] More notably, investment is frequently defined to include shares in companies—or even companies or enterprises themselves—thus capturing the interests of minority shareholders.[30] In some cases, tribunals have relied on such language to allow the foreign owners of a domestic company to bring a treaty claim regarding injuries to the company itself (rather than to the shareholders directly) alongside the company's pursuit of domestic or contractual remedies.[31] This is one way in which many investment treaties open the door, quite remarkably, to parallel claims.[32]

Another element of the broad definition of investment is that it goes well beyond foreign direct investment (FDI).[33] In economic analysis, FDI is defined as cross-border investment that involves control of foreign assets.[34] This distinguishes FDI from portfolio investment, which involves the contribution of capital without foreign control or managerial influence. Statistics on investment distinguish

---

[25] This would include creditors' rights pursuant to loans, including sovereign debt.

[26] The treaties vary in the degree to which they list specific intellectual property rights as well as items such as goodwill and know how: compare Germany–Argentina BIT (n 22 above), art 1(1)(d) to United Kingdom–Egypt BIT (n 22 above), art 1(a)(iv).

[27] The treaties vary in terms of whether they refer to rights granted in 'law', 'public law', or 'contract'.

[28] eg the customary minimum standard of treatment traditionally limited the scope of protected property rights to tangible assets: AH Roth, *The Minimum Standard of International Law Applied to Aliens* (Leiden, 1949) 185–6.

[29] BA Wortley, *Expropriation in Public International Law* (Cambridge: CUP, 1959) 11; B Appleton, *Navigating NAFTA* (Scarborough: Carswell, 1994) 80–1.

[30] This effectively overrides *Barcelona Traction* to the extent that that decision bars claims of diplomatic protection on behalf of the foreign owner of a domestically incorporated enterprise: *Barcelona Traction, Light and Power Co (Belgium v Spain)*, [1970] ICJ Rep 3, 9 ILM 227, para 70 and 99–103. See *Lanco International Inc v Argentine Republic* (Jurisdiction) (8 December 1998), 40 ILM 457, para 5, 10, and 15; *GAMI Investments, Inc v Government of the United Mexican States* (Merits) (15 November 2004), 44 ILM 545, 17(2) World Trade and Arb Mat 127 [cited as *GAMI*], para 29–30 and 38; *Maffezini (Emilio Agustín) v Kingdom of Spain* (Jurisdiction) (25 January 2000), 16 ICSID Rev 212, 124 ILR 9 [cited as *Maffezini*], para 65; *Azurix Corp v Argentine Republic* (Jurisdiction) (8 December 2003), 43 ILM 262, 16(2) World Trade and Arb Mat 111 [cited as *Azurix* (Jurisdiction)], para 60; *Sempra Energy International v Argentine Republic* (Jurisdiction) (11 May 2005), ICSID Case No ARB/02/16 [cited as *Sempra*], para 92–4, online: ICSID, ITA, Investment Claims; *Continental Casualty Company v Argentine Republic* (Jurisdiction) (22 February 2006), ICSID Case No ARB/03/9, para 77–8 and 86, online: ITA.

[31] eg *CMS* (Jurisdiction) (n 5 above) para 78 and 80; *Azurix* (Jurisdiction) (n 30 above) para 99–100; *Siemens AG v Argentine Republic* (Jurisdiction) (3 August 2004), 44 ILM 138 [cited as *Siemens*], para 151 and 160; *Petrobart Ltd v Kyrgyz Republic* (Merits) (29 March 2005), SCC Rules, SCC Arbitration Institute Case No 126/2003, 65–6; *Sempra* (n 30 above) para 42 and 44.

[32] See the discussion in Ch 5 below, p 111–13.

[33] Peter (n 10 above) 17; PT Muchlinski, *Multinational Enterprises and the Law* (Oxford: Blackwell, 1999) 620.

[34] International Monetary Fund (IMF), *Foreign Direct Investment Statistics—How Countries Measure FDI* (IMF, 2001) 4 and 23.

between these two types of capital flows and the bulk of the analysis of costs and benefits of foreign investment tends to focus on FDI.[35] Yet the definition of investment in most treaties encompasses portfolio investment—such as shares or rights to money—in addition to FDI.[36] Unlike in customary international law,[37] this makes a host state's monetary policy, based on the institution of capital controls or a currency devaluation for example, reviewable by arbitrators and potentially subject to an order to compensate affected foreign capital.[38] By constraining the state's ability to regulate portfolio investment in response to a financial crisis, therefore, the treaties introduce a potentially massive and immediate risk regarding the economic stability of the state that is not present in the context of FDI.[39] In light of this, many treaties include exceptions for capital controls imposed in a balance of payments crisis.[40] Where they do not, however, the treaties offer an alternative legal avenue by which bondholders or hedge funds may pursue compensation against a state in the context of a debt renegotiation alongside IMF-sponsored refinancing or contractual remedies. In this context, the implications of investment treaty arbitration as a process of governmental decision-making may be momentous, as illustrated by the case of Argentina, discussed in Chapter 1.

Besides this expansion beyond the realm of disputes about FDI, the broad definition of investment also causes the scope of investment treaty arbitration to overlap with other areas of trade regulation, including trade in goods and trade in services.[41] A state measure that affects trade in goods will often also affect foreign investment where a multinational firm has committed capital to the production, distribution, transport, or sale of a traded product.[42] Likewise, the cross-border provision of a service always involves, at some stage, the commitment of capital.[43]

[35] eg A Mody and AP Murshid, 'Growing Up with Capital Flows' (IMF Working Paper WP/02/75, 2002) 5 and 24.
[36] *Gruslin (Philippe) v Malaysia* (Merits) (27 November 2000), 5 ICSID Rep 484.
[37] IMF (n 34 above) 7; Wortley (n 29 above) 38–9 and 46–7.
[38] As mentioned in Chapter 1, most spectacularly Argentina has faced dozens of claims arising from the devaluation of the peso in 2002, amounting to an estimated (US)$17 billion in claimed compensation.
[39] Mody and Murshid (n 35 above) 6; UNCTAD (n 13 above) 100; J Bhagwati, 'The Capital Myth: the Difference between Trade in Widgets and Dollars' (1998) 77(3) For Affairs 7, 7–8; World Bank, *World Development Report 1999/2000* (Oxford: OUP, 2000) 73–5.
[40] Dolzer and Stevens (n 5 above) 85–6.
[41] Landsmeer (n 14 above) 60–1; Afilalo (n 13 above) 5; M-F Houde and K Yannaca-Small, 'Relationships between International Investment Agreements' (OECD Working Paper on International Investment No 2004/1, May 2004) 6–7.
[42] *Pope & Talbot Inc v Government of Canada* (Jurisdiction) (26 January 2000), UNCITRAL Rules, para 26 and 33, online: DFAIT, NAFTA Claims; *Ethyl Corporation v Government of Canada* (Jurisdiction) (24 June 1998), 38 ILM 708 [cited as *Ethyl*], para 62; *ADF Group Inc v United States of America* (Merits) (9 January 2003), 18 ICSID Rev 195, 6 ICSID Rep 470, 15(3) World Trade and Arb Mat 55 [cited as *ADF*], para 155.
[43] eg *SD Myers, Inc v Government of Canada* (Merits) (13 November 2000), 40 ILM 1408, 15(1) World Trade and Arb Mat 184 [cited as *SD Myers* (Merits)], para 93 and 226; *SD Myers* (Damages) (21 October 2002), 15(1) World Trade and Arb Mat 103 [cited as *SD Myers* (Damages)], para 86 and 97–8 (characterizing, as investment, a cross-border service provider's commitment of capital to foreign sales and marketing).

This creates overlaps between investment treaties and trade agreements. In the case of a regional trade agreement that contains provisions on compulsory investment arbitration, the overlap is between different chapters of the agreement itself and between the different methods of dispute resolution used in various parts of the agreement. It is highly significant, for example, whether the North American Free Trade Agreement's investment standards (under Chapter 11 of the treaty) also apply to state measures affecting trade in goods or services (under other chapters) since only the former are subject to compulsory arbitration and the highly enforceable remedy of damages against the state.[44]

The term investment need not be defined in an all-encompassing way. It can be limited, for example, by attaching qualifiers such as a requirement that investment provide a benefit to the host economy.[45] Indeed, many ICSID tribunals have decided that, for a dispute to fall within their jurisdiction under the ICSID Convention, the relevant transaction must reflect typical features of investment, including a certain duration, a regularity of profit and return, an element of risk for both sides, a substantial commitment of capital, and a contribution to the host state's development.[46] However, the ICSID Convention itself does not prescribe a definition of investment according to these or any other factors.[47] For this reason, the issue of how to define investment is left to states to decide at the time that they

---

[44] In a number of NAFTA arbitrations, the respondent state argued that the tribunal lacked jurisdiction where the subject-matter of the dispute was covered by other NAFTA chapters; *Ethyl* (n 42 above) para 62; *Pope & Talbot* (Jurisdiction) (n 42 above) para 19; *SD Myers* (Merits) (n 43 above) para 289; *ADF* (n 42 above) para 155. Accepting this argument would have limited the overlap between investment treaty arbitration and the inter-state dispute resolution methods that apply under other chapters of the treaty. However, the argument was rejected by the tribunals on the basis that the NAFTA states' obligations under the treaty are cumulative. In reaching this conclusion, tribunals relied on the broad NAFTA definition of investment as well as WTO jurisprudence that narrows the definition of a conflict between trade obligations (*Pope & Talbot* (Jurisdiction) (n 42 above) para 25–6; *SD Myers* (Merits) (n 43 above) para 291–5 and 299; *SD Myers* (Damages) (n 43 above) para 130–8); see also *Canfor Corporation v United States of America* (Jurisdiction) (6 June 2006), UNCITRAL Rules, para 240–1, online: State Department, ITA, NAFTA Claims. Thus, investments that are incidental to trade in goods or services can also lead to claims under Chapter 11.

[45] Alternatively, an investment treaty might usefully impose an obligation on investors to reinvest the proceeds of a damages award as part of a duty to mitigate losses: DW Bowett, 'Claims Between States and Private Entities: The Twilight Zone of International Law' (1986) 35 Cath U L Rev 929, 941.

[46] *Fedax* (n 5 above) para 43; *Salini Costruttori SpA and Italstrade SpA v Kingdom of Morocco* (Jurisdiction) (23 July 2001), 42 ILM 609, 6 ICSID Rep 400, para 52; *Autopista Concesionada de Venezuela v Bolivarian Republic of Venezuela* (Jurisdiction) (27 September 2001), 16 ICSID Rev 469, para 101; *SGS Société Générale de Surveillance v Pakistan* (Jurisdiction) (6 August 2003), 18 ICSID Rev 301, 42 ILM 1290, 8 ICSID Rep 406, 16(2) World Trade and Arb Mat 167 [cited as *SGS v Pakistan*], para 133, fn 153; *SGS Société Générale de Surveillance v Philippines* (Jurisdiction) (29 January 2004), 8 ICSID Rep 518, 16(3) World Trade and Arb Mat 91 [cited as *SGS v Philippines*], para 45; *Joy Mining Machinery Ltd v Arab Republic of Egypt* (Jurisdiction) (6 August 2004), 19 ICSID Rev 486, 44 ILM 73, para 50–3; *Bayindir Insaat Turizm Ticaret Ve Sanayi Aş v Islamic Republic of Pakistan* (Jurisdiction) (14 November 2005), 18(1) World Trade and Arb Mat 163, para 130. Contrast *Saluka Investments BV v Czech Republic* (Merits) (17 March 2006), 18(3) World Trade and Arb Mat 166 [cited as *Saluka*], para 209–11.

[47] JT Schmidt, 'Arbitration Under the Auspices of the International Centre for Settlement of Investment Disputes' (1976) 17 Harv Int'l LJ 90, 99–100.

consent to arbitration, opening the door to the open-ended definitions adopted in contemporary treaties. By defining the concept to encompass 'every asset' of foreign investors—including local companies, concessionary rights, intellectual property, and short-term capital flows—investment treaties typically regulate the exercise of sovereign authority over international business in general.

Dolzer and Stevens comment that the purpose of a broad definition of investment is 'to ensure flexibility in the application of the treaty, given that the meaning of investment may change in the future'.[48] This assumes that the primary purpose of investment treaty is to evolve the review mechanism in favour of investor protection at the expense of regulatory autonomy and flexibility. The broader the definition, the more likely the treaty can credibly be applied to future forms of regulation in light of technological change or innovations in legal forms and business strategies. Put differently, a broad definition expands the discretion of arbitrators to assume jurisdiction over claims, as well as the potential liability of the state in public law. For governments, the question is what types of economic activity qualify as investments and thus engage the state's treaty obligations? Does intangible 'market share' amount to investment?[49] Does the establishment of a sales office?[50] What economic interests of multinational firms are *not* investments?[51] For public officials faced with a broad definition of investment, it becomes prudent to assume that virtually any economic loss sustained, as a result of a sovereign act or omission, by a foreign investor who owns significant assets within their jurisdiction could provoke a claim and award against the state.[52] By extension, an assessment of the likelihood of arbitrators to rule one way or another with respect to the legality of state conduct becomes an important factor in the costing and planning of much governmental activity.

The Standards of Review

An investment treaty, like any treaty, would do very little to control states and to deter abuse of governmental powers if it did not apply constraints on sovereign conduct. Typically, investment treaties apply a range of standards of review

---

[48] Dolzer and Stevens (n 5 above) 26.
[49] *Pope & Talbot Inc v Government of Canada* (Merits, Phase 1) (26 June 2000), 13(4) World Trade and Arb Mat 19 [cited as *Pope & Talbot*], para 96–8. See also *SD Myers, Inc v Government of Canada* (US Submissions) (18 September 2001), UNCITRAL Rules, para 5, online: State Department, NAFTA Claims.
[50] See n 43 above. JA Soloway, 'Environmental Regulation as Expropriation: The Case of NAFTA's Chapter 11' (2000) 33 Can Bus LJ 92, 123.
[51] eg some investment treaties expressly require that the investment be made in the territory of the host state: *SGS v Philippines* (n 46 above) para 99.
[52] P Malanczuk, 'State–State and Investor–State Dispute Settlement in the OECD Draft Multilateral Investment Agreement' (2000) 3 J Int'l Econ L 417, 437–8; P Ryan, 'David v. Goliath' (2002) 11 *National* 30, 36 (citing Peter Kirby of the law firm Fasken Martineau: it is 'practically impossible' to predict what government action will be questioned next under Chapter 11 of NAFTA).

designed to protect investors from regulation or interference by the state and it is by reference to these standards that a tribunal judges the state. The application of the standards thus determines the specific impact of the treaty: by interpreting them, arbitrators specify and elaborate the limits of sovereign power, deciding whether and how public authority may be used to restrict capital transfers, tax business, establish standards, control land use, deliver services, regulate technology, and so on.[53] Like the members of any public law body, in reviewing these sorts of measures, arbitrators rule on the legality of legislative choices, the fairness of regulation, the content of property rights, and the appropriate distribution of the costs of regulation between business and society.[54]

In this section, three core standards—national treatment, the minimum standard of treatment, and compensation for expropriation[55]—are reviewed, using various treaties as illustrations, including NAFTA, the Energy Charter Treaty, and a number of bilateral investment treaties.[56] With few exceptions

---

[53] D Schneiderman, 'Investment Rules and the New Constitutionalism' (2000) 25 Law & Social Inq 757, 771–2.

[54] eg *Olguín (Eudoro Armando) v Republic of Paraguay* (Merits) (26 July 2001), 18 ICSID Rev 143, 6 ICSID Rep 164 [cited as *Olguín*], para 65(b); *CMS Gas Transmission Company v Argentine Republic* (Merits) (12 May 2005), 44 ILM 1205, 17(5) World Trade and Arb Mat 63 [cited as *CMS* (Merits)], para 113–14, 121, and 319. FI Michelman, 'Property, Utility, and Fairness: Comments on the Ethical Foundations of "Just Compensation" Law' (1967) 80 Harv L Rev 1165, 1168–9; C Harlow and R Rawlings, *Law and Administration* (London: Butterworths, 1997) 605–6.

[55] These are the standards that are most frequently called upon in investor claims under investment treaties: in a sampling of 19 widely available damages awards to March 2006, the respondent state was sanctioned in 13 cases for a violation of the minimum standards of 'fair and inequitable' treatment or 'full protection and security'; in seven cases for an expropriation or deprivation of property without sufficient compensation; in five cases for discriminatory (or 'arbitrary') treatment of investors; and in two cases for a failure to observe contractual or other obligations (see below). Other common treaty standards oblige states to provide most favoured nation (MFN) treatment to investors; to remove restrictions on capital flows and profit repatriation; to refrain from imposing performance requirements concerning the export of goods produced, the use of local materials, and the employment of local staff; to guarantee free movement of directors and senior management; and to require states to abide by contractual and other commitments to foreign investors. These other standards, like the three core standards discussed in this chapter, regulate the exercise of public authority in relation to investors and may thus deter governmental measures. On the other hand, most are more precisely defined, making their regulatory impact less uncertain than that of the core standards. The two exceptions—both of which are open to divergent interpretations—are (1) the obligation of states to observe contractual or other obligations to investors and (2) the standard of MFN treatment, which obliges host states to treat foreign investors no less favourably than other foreign investors in like circumstances, and which may be interpreted broadly in jurisdictional terms to require a state to provide not only substantive standards included in its other investment treaties but also procedural benefits, including access to compulsory arbitration under more favourable conditions: *Maffezini* (n 30 above) para 40–2 and 64; *Siemens* (n 31 above) para 32 and 102–3. Contrast *Tecnicas Medioambientales Tecmed, SA v United Mexican States* (Merits) (29 May 2003), 19 ICSID Rev 158, 43 ILM 133 [cited as *Tecmed*], para 69; *Salini Costruttori SpA and Italstrade SpA v Hashemite Kingdom of Jordan* (Jurisdiction) (29 November 2004), 20 ICSID Rev 148, 44 ILM 573, para 115–19; *Plama Consortium Limited v Republic of Bulgaria* (Jurisdiction) (8 February 2005), 20 ICSID Rev 262, 44 ILM 721, 17(4) World Trade and Arb Mat 215 [cited as *Plama*], para 203–4 and 219–24.

[56] All the core standards examined here are contained in the selected treaties (n 22 above) although the precise language used to define them varies. Notably, unlike NAFTA and US-modelled BITs, many of the BITs do not extend to pre-establishment national treatment or apply express prohibitions on performance

and with varying legal language,[57] all of these treaties broadly require the states parties to:

(1) treat foreign investors and investments no less favourably than its own investors or investments ('national treatment');[58]

(2) treat foreign investments in accordance with international law and accord them fair and equitable treatment and full protection and security (the 'minimum standard of treatment');[59] and

(3) pay prompt, adequate and effective compensation to investors for the nationalization or expropriation or deprivation of their assets, or equivalent measures ('compensation for expropriation').[60]

These core standards were not pulled from a hat by the negotiators of the treaties. They draw on historically contested principles of public international law, although in many cases the standards' ambiguity has led tribunals to interpret them in ways that expand on the comparable standards under customary international law, as well as domestic public law.[61] Notably, the interpretative process is subject to wide discretion because the standards are defined using language that is broad enough to capture general regulatory activity that does not directly target or predominantly affect foreign investors. For this reason, it is possible to characterize a wide range

---

requirements: UNCTAD (n 4 above) 182–4 and 189–92; UNCTAD, *Bilateral Investment Treaties in the Mid-1990s* (Geneva: United Nations, 1998) 137–8; UNCTAD (n 13 above) 102 and 108.

[57] With these minor exceptions under the selected treaties (n 22 above): the Belgium–Argentina BIT does not expressly provide for treatment no less favourable than that afforded to domestic investors, although this may constitute part of the treaty's bar on discriminatory measures (art 3(2))) and guarantee of the minimum standard based on international law (art 4(1)); the Netherlands-modelled BITs limit their express mention of national treatment to 'taxes, fees, charges' and 'fiscal deductions and exemptions'; and some of the treaties (eg Peru–Paraguay BIT, art 4(1) and (2)) refer to some but not elements of the minimum standard (ie fair and equitable treatment, full protection and security, and treatment in accordance with international law).

[58] eg France–Argentina BIT (n 22 above) art 4; Germany–Argentina BIT (n 22 above) art 3(1); Mexico–Spain BIT (n 22 above) art IV(5); Netherlands–Bolivia BIT (n 22 above), art 4; Switzerland–Philippines BIT (n 22 above) art VI(2) and (3); United Kingdom–Egypt BIT (n 22 above) art 3(1); United States–Romania BIT (n 22 above) art II(1); Energy Charter Treaty (n 22 above) art 10(7); NAFTA (n 22 above) art 1102.

[59] eg France–Argentina BIT (n 22 above) art 3 and 5(1); Germany–Argentina BIT (n 22 above) art 2(3) and 4(1); Mexico–Spain BIT (n 22 above) art III(1) and IV(1); Netherlands–Bolivia BIT (n 22 above) art 3(1) and (2); Switzerland–Philippines BIT (n 22 above) art IV(1); United Kingdom–Egypt BIT (n 22 above) art 2(2); United States–Romania BIT (n 22 above) art II(2)(a); Energy Charter Treaty (n 22 above) art 10(1); NAFTA (n 22 above) art 1105.

[60] eg France–Argentina BIT (n 22 above) art 5(2); Germany–Argentina BIT (n 22 above) art 7(1); Mexico–Spain BIT (n 22 above) art V(1); Netherlands–Bolivia BIT (n 22 above), art 6; Switzerland–Philippines BIT (n 22 above) art VI(1); United Kingdom–Egypt BIT (n 22 above) art 5; United States–Romania BIT (n 22 above) art III(1); Energy Charter Treaty (n 22 above) art 13(1); NAFTA (n 22 above) art 1110.

[61] VL Been and JC Beauvais, 'The Global Fifth Amendment: NAFTA's Investment Protections and the Misguided Quest for an International 'Regulatory Takings' Doctrine' (2003) 78 NYU L Rev 30, 50–1 and 59–60. This is also because a violation of the treaty leads to a damages award rather than a more conventional public law remedy: M Lunney and K Oliphant, *Tort Law* (Oxford: OUP, 2000) 527.

of regulatory acts as unlawful on the basis that they were discriminatory, unfair, inequitable, or an indirect taking of property. This gives arbitrators the authority to sanction sovereign conduct that affects international business in numerous fields of regulation including monetary policy, taxation, regional development, land use planning, public health regulation, and environmental protection.[62]

Resolving whether the state has satisfied a treaty standard in these areas is a core element of the judicial function in public law. To illustrate, in various cases in which damages have been awarded, the impugned state measures have included: a legislative devaluation of the national currency in the face of a financial crisis,[63] a legislative ban on hazardous waste exports,[64] an administrative approval of an investment project,[65] an administrative order refusing refunds of value-added tax,[66] an administrative refusal to issue a waste disposal permit and a subsequent order establishing an ecological park,[67] an administrative denial of the authority to operate a landfill,[68] and an investigation of a firm's compliance with an export quota regime.[69] The point here is not that these measures were all sensible and pristine decisions of the state, but that they are varied in nature and, more fundamentally, that they are sovereign as opposed to commercial acts of the host state, reflecting the character of the system as a uniquely internationalized form of public law adjudication.

National treatment

Under customary international law, a state may refuse to allow foreign investors to enter its territory but must not discriminate against them once they have been allowed into the host economy.[70] Further, national treatment is a basic norm in international economic law and public law generally.[71] Thus, it is unsurprising to find the principle in all investment treaties, which typically require that states

[62] UNCTAD (n 4 above) 184–9; Schneiderman (n 53 above) 771–2; J Werksman, KA Baumert, and NK Dubash, 'Will International Investment Rules Obstruct Climate Protection Policies?' (Report for the World Resources Institute, April 2001); WW Park, 'Arbitration and the Fisc: NAFTA's "Tax Veto"' (2001) 2 Chi J Int'l L 231, 236–8; T Epps and CM Flood, 'Have We Traded Away the Opportunity for Innovative Health Care Reform? The Implications of the NAFTA for Medicare' (2002) 47 McGill LJ 747, 781–7; JR Johnson, 'How Will International Trade Agreements Affect Canadian Health Care?' (Discussion Paper No 22 for the Commission on the Future of Health Care in Canada, September 2002) 9–17 and 26–32. [63] *CMS* (Merits) (n 54 above).
[64] *SD Myers* (Damages) (n 43 above).
[65] *MTD Equity Sdn Bhd v Republic of Chile* (Merits) (25 May 2004), 44 ILM 91 [cited as *MTD*].
[66] *Occidental Exploration and Production Company v Republic of Ecuador* (Merits) (1 July 2004), 17(1) World Trade and Arb Mat 165 [cited as *Occidental*].
[67] *Metalclad Corporation v United Mexican States* (Merits) (30 August 2000) [cited as *Metalclad*], 16 ICSID Rev 168, 40 ILM 36, 5 ICSID Rep 212, 13(1) World Trade and Arb Mat 45.
[68] *Tecmed* (n 55 above).
[69] *Pope & Talbot Inc v Government of Canada* (Damages) (31 May 2002), 41 ILM 1347, 14(6) World Trade and Arb Mat 44.
[70] JB Moore, *Digest of International Law*, vol 4 (Washington: US Government Printing Office, 1906) 67; UNCTAD (n 13 above) 102.
[71] H Neufeld, *The International Protection of Private Creditors From the Treaties of Westphalia to the Congress of Vienna* (Leiden: AW Sijthoff, 1971) 96; MS McDougal, HD Lasswell, and L Chen, 'The

treat foreign investors and investments 'no less favourably' than their domestic counterparts or, put slightly differently, that investors cannot be discriminated against because they are foreign. Notably, some treaties—including NAFTA and other US-modelled BITs—go further than this by applying national treatment at the pre-establishment stage of investment. In such cases, a state must allow equal access to its economy by all investors of the other state party to the treaty, subject only to express treaty reservations that carve out particular economic sectors.[72] In US BITs, such carve outs typically apply to sectors such as air transport, banking, broadcasting, energy and power production, insurance, mining, and ocean and coastal shipping in the case of the US, although they are often less extensive for the other state party.[73]

Despite its ancient origins, application of the standard of non-discrimination in the field of investment is relatively recent.[74] Applied to investment, especially in combination with the individualization of claims, the scope of national treatment is potentially vast,[75] and this has posed interpretive challenges.[76] By definition, the standard is relative in the sense that it measures the state's treatment of foreign investors against the treatment of similarly situated domestic investors. Thus, at the heart of national treatment is the basic idea that like cases should be treated alike, as well as the dilemma of how to identify appropriate criteria for comparison.[77] Which domestic investors are in like circumstances to those of the foreign investor?[78] Does the fact that domestic investors operate in an economically depressed region distinguish them from foreign investors who operate in wealthy regions? What if the domestic investor has a better record of employing disadvantaged minorities or uses an environmentally friendly production process? Are these legitimate grounds upon which to favour domestic investors?[79] Are foreign

Protection of Aliens From Discrimination and World Public Order: Responsibility of States Conjoined with Human Rights' (1976) 70 AJIL 432, 443; JHH Weiler (n 9 above) 201.

[72] NAFTA (n 22 above) art 1102. Many BITs do not extend national treatment to the pre-establishment stage of an investment: n 55 above.

[73] US–Argentina BIT (n 22 above) s 2 and 5 (protocol); US–Czech Republic BIT (n 22 above) s 1 and 3 (annex); US–Ecuador BIT (n 22 above) s 2 and 4 (protocol); US–Romania BIT (n 22 above) s 1 and 3 (annex).

[74] Dolzer and Stevens (n 5 above) 57; UNCTAD, *National Treatment*, UNCTAD Series on Issues in International Investment Agreements (New York: United Nations, 1999) 9–13; H Mann and K von Moltke, 'NAFTA's Chapter 11 and the Environment: Addressing the Impacts of the Investor-State Process on the Environment' (Working Paper for the International Institute for Sustainable Development, 1999) 12.

[75] Dolzer and Stevens (n 5 above) 62 (noting that, for a state to violate national treatment under customary international law, the state measure had to reflect an intention to harm a foreign national); RK Paterson, 'A New Pandora's Box? Private Remedies for Foreign Investors under the North American Free Trade Agreement' (2000) 8 Willamette J Int'l L and Dispute Res 77, 95; Afilalo (n 13 above) 5.   [76] eg *Feldman* (n 5 above) para 166–7. JHH Weiler (n 9 above) 213–14.

[77] M Loughlin, *Sword and Scales* (Oxford: Hart, 2000) 20.

[78] eg *Encana Corporation v Republic of Ecuador* (Merits) (3 February 2006), London Court of International Arbitration Administered Case No UN 3481, para 40 (dissenting opinion). Dolzer and Stevens (n 5 above) 63.

[79] RD Kelemen, 'The Limits of Judicial Power—Trade-Environment Disputes in the GATT/WTO and the EU' (2001) 34 Comp Pol Studies 622, 625.

producers of canola seed pesticides that contain lindane similarly situated to domestic producers of canola seed pesticides that are lindane-free?[80] Or are they in like circumstances so long as they produce commercially substitutable products? From the outset, tribunals must distinguish between like and unlike circumstances and, the more broadly a tribunal defines likeness, the more it constrains a government's ability to differentiate between economic actors for policy reasons.

As such, the interpretation of national treatment emerges as a potentially difficult and value-laden task.[81] But this does not end the matter. Tribunals must also determine how far to cast the comparative net. Does a foreign investor have to show that any less favourable treatment of the investor reflects a pattern of conduct in the state's treatment of foreign investors *as a group*?[82] Or can a violation arise from the circumstances of a single investor?[83] On a narrow reading of the standard, a foreign investor would have to show that any less favourable treatment was not an isolated event.[84] On a broad reading, a state violates national treatment whenever it treats a foreign investor less favourably than a single domestic investor in a single instance.[85] There is a very wide gap between the consequences for governments of these two interpretations. But the issue is central because it determines the degree to which states must alter their regulatory activity in order to avoid liability.

National treatment also captures de facto as well as *de jure* discrimination.[86] Thus, a violation of the standard may occur when a state measure, though neutral on its face, has a discriminatory effect on foreign investors relative to their domestic counterparts.[87] In its original form as a standard to regulate trade in goods, the purpose of prohibiting de facto discrimination was to counter disguised protectionism against imported products.[88] Transplanted to the circumstances of a single investor (as opposed to a group of investors), de facto discrimination creates a possibility of over-inclusion by capturing regulation which only incidentally affects

---

[80] *Crompton Corp v Government of Canada* (Notice of Claim) (6 November 2001) para 28–9, online: DFAIT, NAFTA Claims.

[81] JR Johnson, 'Essential Disciplines of the National Treatment Obligation Under NAFTA Chapter Eleven' (Report on investment protection for the Ad Hoc Experts Group on Investment Rules, Department of Foreign Affairs and International Trade, 2 December 2001); JA VanDuzer, 'NAFTA Chapter 11 to Date: The Progress of a Work in Progress' in L Ritchie Dawson (ed) *Whose Rights? The NAFTA Chapter 11 Debate* (Ottawa: Centre for Trade Law and Policy, 2002) 72–3; Mann and von Moltke (n 74 above) 28–32.

[82] International Law Commission, 'Draft Articles on Responsibility of States for Internationally Wrongful Acts', *Report of the International Law Commission on the Work of Its Fifty-third Session*, UN GAOR, 56th Sess, Supp No 10, annex, UN Doc A/56/10 (2001) 43, art 15.

[83] *Feldman* (n 5 above) para 181 (award) and p 269 (dissenting opinion).

[84] Johnson (n 81 above) 8–10.

[85] *Pope & Talbot Inc v Government of Canada* (Merits, Phase 2) (10 April 2001), 13(4) World Trade and Arb Mat 61, para 70–2. PG Foy, 'Effectiveness of NAFTA's Chapter Eleven Investor-State Arbitration Procedures' (2003) 18 ICSID Rev 44, 49.

[86] eg *Feldman* (n 5 above) para 169. Contrast *In the Matter of Cross-border Trucking Services* (Merits) (6 February 2001), 13(3) World Trade and Arb Mat 121, para 291–2.

[87] UNCTAD (n 74 above) 40–1.   [88] Jackson (n 9 above) 216–18; Ehring (n 8 above) 1–2.

the foreign investor.[89] At the extreme end of the scale, de facto discrimination would bar any exercise of public authority that differentiated between investors.[90] But, of course, most governmental activity inherently involves differentiation among subjects of regulation and, if all such differentiation were prohibited, then investment treaties would scorch a wide swath of the regulatory landscape.

In this respect, it is important to highlight how the meaning of the standards of investor protection is affected by the individualization of adjudication. To date, in claims under investment treaties, investors have advocated far-reaching notions of national treatment, arguing—for instance—that the term 'like circumstances' should be read broadly and that incidental de facto discrimination violates the treaty.[91] This is not at all surprising: allowing investors to bring international claims in the context of a regulatory dispute gives a private party the discretion to make arguments in its own interest, unburdened by considerations of the home state's wider interest or by the prospect of having to defend a similar claim. Investors should be expected to argue for a broad interpretation that expands their opportunities for compensation. What is noteworthy is that by allowing investors to make these arguments, although they are often rejected by tribunals, the treaties also enable arbitrators to hear and adopt more expansive readings of the treaty, should they choose, even where this conflicts with the views of the states parties.[92]

The minimum standard of treatment

The assertion of a minimum standard of treatment for foreign nationals under customary international law has a long and contentious history.[93] Since the nineteenth century capital-exporting states traditionally asserted a minimum standard of fair treatment and protection for foreign investors, although the content of the

---

[89] *Occidental* (n 66 above) para 174–7. Paterson (n 75 above) 95 (commenting that, in the trade in goods context, discrimination is always based on nationality because imports are by definition of a different origin than the 'like' domestic product).

[90] Johnson (n 81 above) 4.

[91] *Ethyl Corporation v Government of Canada* (Investor's Submissions) (2 October 1997), UNCITRAL Rules, para 31, online: DFAIT, NAFTA Claims; *SD Myers, Inc v Government of Canada* (Investor's Submissions) (20 July 1999), UNCITRAL Rules, para 77, online: DFAIT, NAFTA Claims; *Pope & Talbot Inc v Government of Canada* (Investor's Submissions) (28 January 2000), UNCITRAL Rules, para 53–7 and 72, online: DFAIT, NAFTA Claims; *United Parcel Service of America, Inc v Government of Canada* (Investor's Submissions) (23 March 2005), UNCITRAL Rules, para 515–16, 521, 528, and 536–7, online: DFAIT, NAFTA Claims.

[92] eg *Pope & Talbot* (Merits, Phase 2) (n 85 above) para 79 (rejecting the submissions of the NAFTA Parties that Article 1102 is limited to the prohibition of discrimination *on the basis of nationality*); *GAMI* (n 30 above) para 29–30. Contrast *ADF* (n 42 above) para 177; *Noble Ventures v Romania* (Merits) (12 October 2005), ICSID Case No ARB/01/11, para 180, online: ITA, Investment Claims.

[93] MN Shaw, *International Law* (5th edn, Cambridge: CUP, 2003) 733–7; I Brownlie, *Principles of Public International Law* (6th edn, Oxford: OUP, 2003) 503–5; Center for International Environmental Law (CIEL), 'International Law on Investment: The Minimum Standard of Treatment (MST)' (Issue Brief, August 2003) 1–2.

standard was not always consistent or precise.[94] On the other hand, developing countries argued that the standard was restricted to non-discrimination based on equal access to domestic remedies once a foreign national was allowed into a state's territory.[95] Investment treaties establish a minimum standard that goes beyond simple non-discrimination, reflecting clearly the historical position of capital-exporting states.[96]

Typically, the minimum standard of treatment in investment treaties requires states to afford full protection and security, and fair and equitable treatment, according to international law. Different treaties phrase these elements of the standard in different ways, but all provide for an absolute minimum that states must provide to foreign investors. Thus, regardless of the treatment given to a state's own investors, the treatment of foreign investors must not fall below the floor set by the treaty. However, as in the case of national treatment, the minimum standard is stated in ambiguous terms:[97] the meaning of terms like 'unfair' and 'inequitable' in the acts and decisions of governments does not exactly leap from the page.[98] Perhaps for this reason, investment treaty tribunals have relied on this standard more than any other as a basis for awarding damages against a state.

Under customary international law, the minimum standard was not overly stringent out of deference to domestic courts, in particular. Ever since the decision of the US–Mexico General Claims Commission in *Neer v United Mexican States* was given in 1926 academic works on international law[99] generally refer to its description of the minimum standard, which is as follows: ' . . . the treatment of an alien, in order to constitute an international delinquency should amount to an outrage, to bad faith, to willful neglect of duty, or to an insufficiency of governmental action so far short of international standards that every reasonable and impartial man would readily recognize its insufficiency.'[100] Although this formulation may not fully reflect the evolution of international society in recent decades, and especially its greater integration of human rights standards, the continued and

---

[94] E Root, 'Elihu Root's Services to International Law' (1910) 4 Am Soc'ty Int'l L Proc 16, 21; C Eagleton, *The Responsibility of States in International Law* (New York: NYU Press, 1928) 109; McDougal, Lasswell, and Chen (n 71 above) 446–51; JC Thomas, 'Reflections on Article 1105 of NAFTA: History, State Practice and the Influence of Commentators' (2002) 17 ICSID Rev 21, 39–51.

[95] *Responsibility of States for Damage Caused in Their Territory to the Person or Property of Foreigners*, League of Nations Conference for the Codification of International Law, Bases of Discussion, vol 3, LN Doc C.75.M.69.1929.V (1929) 15. EM Borchard, 'The 'Minimum Standard' of the Treatment of Aliens' (1940) 38 Mich L Rev 445, 445–7 and 450–1; M Sornarajah, *The Pursuit of Nationalized Property* (Dordrecht: Martinus Nijhoff, 1986) 29.

[96] *Mondev International Ltd v United States of America* (Merits) (11 October 2002), 42 ILM 85, 6 ICSID Rep 192, 15(3) World Trade and Arb Mat 273 [cited as *Mondev*], para 120.

[97] Dolzer and Stevens (n 5 above) 58–9; Thomas (n 94 above) 22.

[98] UNCTAD, *Fair and Equitable Treatment*, UNCTAD Series on Issues in International Investment Agreements (New York: United Nations, 1999) 10–12.

[99] Eagleton (n 94 above) 84; G Schwarzenberger, *International Law as Applied by International Courts and Tribunals*, vol 1 (3rd edn, London: Stevens & Sons, 1957) 200; P Malanczuk, *Akehurst's Modern Introduction to International Law* (7th edn, London: Routledge, 1997) 261; Brownlie (n 93 above) 503.   [100] *Neer Claim* (*United States v Mexico*) (1926), 4 RIAA 60, 61–2.

widespread reference to the *Neer* standard by states and commentators alike indicates that a state's misconduct must be of a very serious nature before it violates the customary standard.[101]

Investors, not surprisingly, have argued for broader interpretations of the minimum standard that would import discrete standards from other treaties in order to regulate states more rigorously, while also removing established limits on the duties of a state to ensure fair treatment and full protection.[102] Much more surprising is the degree to which some tribunals have accommodated this position of claimants. To illustrate, in the early days of NAFTA arbitration, some tribunals adopted broad readings of the minimum standard that went well beyond customary international law.[103] In *Metalclad*, the tribunal read as part of the standard a general duty on the NAFTA states to ensure transparency in the regulation of foreign investment.[104] In quite sweeping language, the tribunal declared that states were obligated to ensure that 'all relevant legal requirements' are made clear to investors and to correct 'any scope for misunderstanding or confusion'.[105] Similarly, in *Pope & Talbot*, the tribunal rejected the argument that the minimum standard required evidence of state conduct that crossed a high threshold of impropriety based on the *Neer* decision,[106] and instead adopted a standard that encompassed the elements of 'fairness' under the ordinary law of the NAFTA states without any requirement that governmental conduct be egregious or otherwise extraordinary.[107] The NAFTA states objected to the *Pope & Talbot* tribunal's approach by issuing a joint interpretation of the minimum standard that bound tribunals[108] and, as a result, tribunals adopted a more restrained approach in subsequent cases.[109] Even so, the early NAFTA cases revealed that arbitrators were prepared to

[101] Schwarzenberger (n 99 above) 201; AA Fatouros, 'International Economic Development and the Illusion of Legal Certainty' (1963) 57 Am Soc'ty Int'l L Proc 117, 117–18; Thomas (n 94 above) 29–39.
[102] eg *Pope & Talbot* (Merits, Phase 2) (n 85 above) para 107; *SD Myers* (Merits) (n 43 above) para 134; *UPS* (n 3 above) para 81–2.
[103] *United Mexican States v Metalclad Corporation* (2001) 89 BCLR (3rd) 359, 38 CELR 284, 13(5) World Trade and Arb Mat 219 [cited as *United Mexican States*], para 74–6; *Pope & Talbot* (Merits, Phase 2) (n 85 above) para 110 and 115–18; *SD Myers* (Merits) (n 43 above) para 266. CIEL (n 93 above) 3–5; Thomas (n 94 above) 113–14; C Tollefson, 'Metalclad v. United Mexican States Revisited: Judicial Oversight of NAFTA's Chapter Eleven Investor–State Claim Process' (2002) 11 Minn J Global Trade 183, 207–13 and 224–5.
[104] *Metalclad* (n 67 above) para 76. See also *United Mexican* (n 103 above) para 68–73 (concluding that the *Metalclad* tribunal exceeded its jurisdiction by grounding its interpretation of Article 1105 in transparency obligations that are contained in parts of NAFTA which are not subject to compulsory investment arbitration). [105] *Metalclad* (n 67 above) para 76.
[106] *Pope & Talbot* (Merits, Phase 2) (n 85 above) para 108 and 118. See also *Pope & Talbot Inc v Government of Canada* (Canada's Submissions) (10 October 2000), UNCITRAL Rules, para 235–40, online: DFAIT, NAFTA Claims. [107] *Pope & Talbot* (Merits, Phase 2) (n 85 above) para 118.
[108] eg *Mondev* (n 96 above) para 106 and 108–10.
[109] *ADF* (n 42 above) para 179–86; *Mondev* (n 96 above) para 111; *Loewen Group, Inc and Raymond L Loewen v United States of America* (Merits) (26 June 2003), 42 ILM 811, 7 ICSID Rep 442, 15(5) World Trade and Arb Mat 97, para 131–3; *Waste Management, Inc v United Mexican States* (Jurisdiction) (26 June 2002), 41 ILM 1315, 6 ICSID Rep 549, 14(6) World Trade and Arb Mat 203 [cited as *Waste Management No 2* (Jurisdiction)], para 98; *International Thunderbird Gaming*

assume a wide-ranging authority to sanction governmental activity based on expansive readings of the minimum standard.

This is supported by the experience in BIT arbitrations, in which some tribunals have adopted a broad reading of the standard without even mentioning, let alone maintaining, the customarily deferential position in international law.[110] Frankly, some tribunals' interpretations have been nothing short of adventurous, as in *CMS*, where the tribunal concluded that the standard of 'fair and equitable treatment', although 'somewhat vague', nevertheless required Argentina to maintain a stable legal and business environment in the midst of a financial crisis, and that this was 'an objective requirement unrelated to whether [Argentina] has had any deliberate intention or bad faith . . .'.[111] Further, the tribunal—without any mention of state practice and opinio juris, or the *Neer* decision or other cases, or academic writings—incredibly concluded that its far-reaching approach to state liability was 'not different from the international law minimum standard and its evolution under customary international law'.[112] On this questionable reading of the minimum standard, the tribunal decided that Argentina's devaluation of the peso violated its BIT with the US, requiring payment of a substantial award to a US investor and heightening the prospect of further awards against that country.

The readiness of tribunals to adopt such an expansive interpretation has major implications for governments. Governments are often required to make difficult and controversial decisions when exercising public authority and their policy choices may in some cases appear to misapprehend facts, apply misguided theories, emphasize wrong-headed priorities, or create more problems than they solve. This is in many ways inherent to the dilemmas of governing. One must assume, however, that in spite of the massive growth of investment treaties, the ordinary forum to resolve disputes arising from governmental decisions remains the domestic political and legal system.[113] A broad reading of the minimum standard of treatment transforms the international law standard from a bulwark against flagrant mistreatment of foreign nationals into an all-encompassing guarantee of highly flexible notions of fairness, equity, and due process.[114] That arbitrators can

---

Corporation v United Mexican States (Merits) (26 January 2006), 18(2) World Trade and Arb Mat 59, para 192–4 and 200.

[110] eg *American Manufacturing & Trading Inc v Republic of Zaire* (Merits) (21 February 1997), 36 ILM 1534, 5 ICSID Rep 14, para 6.10–6.14; *CME Czech Republic BV v Czech Republic* (Merits) (13 September 2001), 14(3) World Trade and Arb Mat 109 [cited as *CME*], para 613–14; *Tecmed* (n 55 above) para 153–5; *MTD* (n 65 above) para 113–14; *Occidental* (n 66) para 186–92; *Eureko v Republic of Poland* (Merits) (19 August 2005), UNCITRAL Rules, para 231–5, online: ITA, Investment Claims; *Azurix Corp v Argentine Republic* (Merits) (14 July 2006), ICSID Case No ARB/01/12 [cited as *Azurix* (Merits)], para 360–1, 372, 392 and 408, online: ITA, Investment Claims.

[111] *CMS* (Merits) (n 54 above), para 274 and 280. Contrast *Olguín* (n 54 above) para 69–75.

[112] *CMS* (Merits) (n 54 above), para 284.

[113] *SD Myers* (Merits) (n 43 above) para 261. See also *Middle East Cement Shipping and Handling Co SA v Arab Republic of Egypt* (Merits) (12 April 2002), 18 ICSID Rev 602, 7 ICSID Rep 173, para 155.

[114] JC Thomas, 'The Experience of NAFTA Chapter 11 Tribunals To Date: A Practitioner's Perspective' in L Ritchie Dawson (ed) *Whose Rights? The NAFTA Chapter 11 Debate* (Ottawa: Centre for Trade Law and Policy, 2002) 113–14.

execute such a transformation of their powers of review indicates that their authority goes to the heart of public law.

Expropriation

Another deeply disputed issue in international law is whether, and the extent to which, a state is required to compensate foreign investors for an expropriation of their assets.[115] In the post-colonial era, the debate over expropriation has pitted the Western powers seeking to protect the foreign assets of their firms against newly independent states aspiring to assert more autonomy over their economy and resources.[116] Also, this debate to a degree reflects underlying social conflicts about the relationship between property, the general public, and the state.[117] In the domestic law of all countries, and under human rights treaties, this conflict has a varied legal history, especially in relation to questions of the definition of property, the recognition of a fundamental right to property, the distinction between expropriation and regulation, the existence and the extent of police powers, the incorporation of exceptions for emergency circumstances such as war or insurrection, and the extension of property protection to include compensation for non-material loss.[118] Under investment treaties, these issues are brought

---

[115] JF Williams, 'International Law and the Property of Aliens' (1928) 9 Brit Ybk Int'l L 1, 28; AP Fachiri, 'International Law and the Property of Aliens' (1929) 10 Brit Ybk Int'l L 32, 33–4 and 49–51; Wortley (n 29 above) 119–26; EF Mooney, *Foreign Seizures—Sabbatino and the Act of State Doctrine* (Lexington: University of Kentucky Press, 1967) 85; N Girvan, *Corporate Imperialism: Conflict and Expropriation* (New York: ME Sharpe, 1978) 200; R Dolzer, 'New Foundations of the Law of Expropriation of Alien Property' (1981) 75 AJIL 553, 557–72; Peter (n 10 above) 173–6; Muchlinski (n 33 above) 501–14; E Lauterpacht, 'International Law and Private Foreign Investment' (1997) 4 Indiana J Global Legal Studies 259, 263–7.

[116] FS Dunn, 'International Law and Private Property Rights' (1928) 28 Colum L Rev 166, 177–80; S Friedman, *Expropriation in International Law* (Westport, Conn: Greenwood Press, 1953) 4; SKB Asante, *Transnational Investment Law and National Development* (Lagos: University of Lagos, 1981) 31–2; C Lipson, *Standing Guard—Protecting Foreign Capital in the Nineteenth and Twentieth Centuries* (Berkeley: University of California Press, 1985) 29–30.

[117] CF Randolph, 'The Eminent Domain' (1887) 3 LQ Rev 314; Michelman (n 54 above) 1202; LS Underkuffler-Freund, 'Takings and the Nature of Property' (1996) 9 Can J Law & Jur 161.

[118] eg (United Kingdom) *Attorney General v De Keyser's Royal Hotel, Ltd* [1920] AC 508 (HL); *Gallagher v Lynn* [1937] AC 863 (HL); *France Fenwick and Co v R* [1927] 1 KB 458, 467 ('A mere negative prohibition, though it involves interference with an owner's enjoyment of property, does not . . . carry with it at Common Law any right to compensation'); H Street, *Governmental Liability* (Cambridge: CUP, 1953) 120–4. (United States) US Const amend V; *Pennsylvania Central Transportation Company v City of New York* (1978) 438 US 104; *Lucas v South Carolina Coastal Council* (1992) 505 US 1003; EV Abbot, 'The Police Power and the Right to Compensation' (1889) 3 Harv L Rev 189; RA Epstein, *Takings: Private Property and the Power of Eminent Domain* (Cambridge: Harvard University Press, 1985); WA Fischel, *Regulatory Takings: Law, Economics, and Politics* (Cambridge: Harvard University Press, 1995). (Canada) *Manitoba Fisheries Ltd v R* [1979] 1 SCR 101, 88 DLR (3rd) 462; *British Columbia v Tener* [1985] 1 SCR 533, 17 DLR (4th) 1; *A&L Investments Ltd v Ontario (Minister of Housing)* (1993) 13 OR (3rd) 799, 32 RPR (2nd) 1 (Ont CA); Ontario Law Reform Commission (OLRC), *Report on the Basis for Compensation on Expropriation* (Toronto: OLRC, 1967); ECE Todd, *The Law of Expropriation and Compensation in Canada* (2nd edn, Toronto: Carswell, 1992) 1–7. (Europe) eg *Sporrong and Lönnroth v Sweden*, Eur Ct HR Ser A,

within the discretion of arbitrators, who are often faced with the difficult task of applying the expropriation standard.

To review the historical background a bit further: in terms of the standard of actual compensation that must be paid for an expropriation under international law, capital-importing states historically asserted a right to expropriate property within their territory on payment of 'just' or 'appropriate' compensation, calculating the value of property by assessing not only its market value but also, in some cases, the host state's ability to pay and any unjust enrichment by the investor.[119] On the other hand, major capital-exporting states advanced market-based standards such as the Hull standard[120] of 'full, prompt, and adequate' compensation.[121] Virtually all investment treaties require payment of compensation for expropriation and most apply the Hull standard as a minimum.[122] Indeed, by adopting a broad definition of investment, some treaties afford protection that goes beyond the Hull standard.[123]

These treaty standards for expropriation have been widely interpreted as requiring compensation, not only for direct seizures or nationalizations of property by the state but also for indirect expropriations or 'takings' of property. Thus, the standard typically goes beyond direct seizures, although to a varying and sometimes uncertain degree.[124] In general, a broad reading of expropriation is possible under most treaties and would require compensation for any exercise of public authority that incidentally reduced the value of an investment. Anticipating this possibility, critics of investment treaty arbitration have focused on controls against expropriation as a backdoor takings doctrine that precludes proactive regulation

---

No 52, [1983] EHRR 35; *Hauer v Rheinland-Pfatz* (No 44/79), [1979] ECR 3727, (1980) 3 CML Rev 42; M Antinori, 'Does Lochner Live in Luxembourg? An Analysis of the Property Rights Jurisprudence of the European Court of Justice' (1995) 18 Fordham Int'l LJ 1778, 1803–5. (International) Friedman (n 116 above) 10; Wortley (n 29 above) 52; Muchlinski (n 33 above) 501–4.

[119] AA Fatouros, 'International Law and the Third World' (1964) 50 Virg L Rev 783, 808–9; KB Asante, 'International Law and Foreign Investment: A Reappraisal' (1988) 37 ICLQ 588, 591; GL Sandrino, 'The NAFTA Investment Chapter and Foreign Direct Investment in Mexico: A Third World Perspective' (1994) 27 Vand J Tranat'l L 259, 319.

[120] The Hull standard is named after US Secretary of State Cordell Hull, who elaborated it in correspondence with the Mexican Government responding to Mexico's nationalization of US oil companies in 1938: the correspondence is reprinted in 3 GH Hackworth, *Digest of International Law* (Washington: US Government Printing Office, 1940–4) 655–65.

[121] PM Norton, 'A Law of the Future or a Law of the Past? Modern Tribunals and the International Law of Expropriation' (1991) 85 AJIL 474, 475–9.

[122] I Delupis, *Finance and Protection of Investments in Developing Countries* (Epping: Gower Press, 1973) 39–41 (noting the absence of protection against 'creeping' expropriation in earlier BITs); Dolzer and Stevens (n 5 above) 98 (noting that many BITs provide for a more general formula than does the Hull standard, such as 'just' compensation; and that most refer to 'expropriation' or 'nationalization', although some to 'taking', 'dispossession', 'deprivation', or 'privation'); LA O'Connor, 'The International Law of Expropriation of Foreign-Owned Property: The Compensation Requirement and the Role of the Taking State' (1983) 6 Loyola LA Int'l & Comp LJ 355, 357–8 and 393.

[123] AT Guzman, 'Why LDCs Sign Treaties That Hurt Them: Explaining the Popularity of Bilateral Investment Treaties' (1998) 38 Virg J Int'l L 639, 680–1.

[124] Been and Beauvais (n 61 above) 51–9.

in public health and environmental protection.[125] Some supporters of the system have fostered a similar view by arguing that the expropriation standard requires compensation for mere prohibitions and constructive takings, including any unreasonable interference with the use, enjoyment, or disposal of the property of investors.[126] And, again, many investors have backed an expansive interpretation.[127] Thus, in *Pope & Talbot*, the claimant argued ambitiously that Article 1110 'provides the broadest protection for the investments of foreign investors who may suffer harm by being deprived of their fundamental investment rights' and that the term 'tantamount to ... expropriation' includes 'even nondiscriminatory measures of general application which have the effect of substantially interfering with the investments of investors'.[128]

A number of tribunals have favoured this expansive view.[129] An especially broad reading was adopted in the early days of NAFTA by the *Metalclad* tribunal, which concluded that expropriation included:[130]

> ... not only open, deliberate and acknowledged takings of property, such as outright seizure or formal or obligatory transfer of title in favour of the host State, but also covert or incidental interference with the use of property which has the effect of depriving the owner, in whole or in significant part, of the use or reasonably-to-be-expected economic benefit of property even if not necessarily to the obvious benefit of the host State.

Likewise, under the Spain–Mexico BIT, an expansive position was adopted in the *Tecmed* arbitration, where the tribunal declined to consider the public benefit of sovereign acts that are indirectly expropriatory as a basis for differentiating expropriation from regulation: 'we find no principle stating that regulatory administrative actions are *per se* excluded from the scope of the [BIT], even if they are beneficial to society as a whole—such as environmental protection'.[131] On the

---

[125] Been and Beauvais (n 61 above) 132–5; S Ganguly, 'The Investor–State Dispute Mechanism (ISDM) and a Sovereign's Power to Protect Public Health' (1999) 38 Colum J Transnat'l L 113, 119.

[126] eg RG Dearden, 'Arbitration of Expropriation Disputes between an Investor and the State under the North American Free Trade Agreement' (1995) 29 J World Trade 113, 117–21.

[127] eg *Waste Management Inc v United Mexican States* (Merits) (30 April 2004), 43 ILM 967, 16(4) World Trade and Arb Mat 3 [cited as *Waste Management No 2* (Merits)], para 145; *CME* (n 110 above) para 150. IA Laird, 'NAFTA Chapter 11 Meets Chicken Little' (2001) 2 Chi J Int'l L 223, 226.

[128] *Pope & Talbot* (Merits, Phase 1) (n 49 above) para 83–4.

[129] *Pope & Talbot* (Merits, Phase 1) (n 49 above) para 99; *Waste Management No 2* (Merits) (n 127 above) para 143–5; *GAMI* (n 30 above) para 131. *Compañía del Desarrollo de Santa Elena, SA v Republic of Costa Rica* (Merits) (17 February 2000), 15 ICSID Rev 169, 39 ILM 317, 5 ICSID Rep 157, 13(1) World Trade and Arb Mat 81, para 71–2 and 76 (concluding that the fact that a measure was taken for the public purpose of environmental protection made no difference as to the amount of compensation); *Tecmed* (n 55 above) para 113–15 and 121 (concluding that regulatory actions that are beneficial to society as a whole are not excluded from the duty to pay compensation); *Eureko v Republic of Poland* (Merits) (19 August 2005), UNCITRAL Rules, para 240–2, online: ITA (concluding that 'tantamount to deprivation' extends to the frustration of the benefits of an investor's contractual rights).

[130] *Metalclad* (n 67 above) para 103. See *United Mexican States* (n 103 above) para 99 (characterizing the *Metalclad* tribunal's interpretation as 'sufficiently broad to include a legitimate rezoning of property by a municipality or other zoning authority'). See also *CME* (n 110 above) para 606–9.

[131] *Tecmed* (n 55 above) para 121.

other hand, numerous tribunals—probably the majority—have sought to contain the standard by characterizing alleged expropriations as regulation or simple breach of contract, and by limiting acts that are 'tantamount' or 'equivalent' to expropriation to more familiar concepts of indirect and creeping expropriation.[132] Even so, this more restrained approach does not resolve the underlying ambiguity that infuses the standard. Perhaps inevitably, the issue tends to boomerang back to the question of how to differentiate legitimate regulation from indirect expropriation.[133] This issue has only lately fallen into the laps of investment treaty arbitrators; for a long time before, it has confounded domestic courts in cases involving constitutional and administrative law.

For governments, the priority is to be able to distinguish in advance between state measures that expropriate and those that do not, to enable reliable estimations of the cost of government measures. Left to the process of investment treaty arbitration, we shall be unlikely to reach a stable definition of expropriation for decades to come, if ever.[134] The point here is not to ask whether the security and confidence that the treaties provide to investors is desirable or to doubt the skill and dedication of arbitrators in carrying out their interpretive duties under investment treaties. It is rather that, in light of the sheer breadth of the standards of review, the state makes a major policy decision in its own right by adopting investment treaty arbitration as part of its governing apparatus.

Conclusion

Investment treaties authorize arbitrators to scrutinize virtually any sovereign act of the states that may affect the assets of a foreign investor. The ambiguity of concepts like investment, discrimination, fair treatment, and expropriation gives them a wide authority in virtually any field of public law. Moreover, because of the international principle of the unity of the state, this authority extends to legislative and judicial acts. As a result, all branches of domestic government are, in effect,

---

[132] eg *Azinian (Robert) et al v United Mexican States* (Merits) (1 November 1999), 14 ICSID Rev 538, 39 ILM 537, para 90; *Pope & Talbot* (Merits, Phase 1) (n 49 above) para 104; *SD Myers* (Merits) (n 43 above) para 281–2 and 285–6; *Feldman* (n 5 above) para 100 and 103; *Waste Management No 2* (Merits) (n 127 above) para 175; *Methanex Corporation v United States of America* (Merits) (3 August 2005), 44 ILM 1345, 17(6) World Trade and Arb Mat 61, pt IV—ch D, para 7. *Olguín* (n 54 above) para 83–4; *Generation Ukraine Inc v Ukraine* (Merits) (16 September 2003), 44 ILM 404, para 20.22 and 20.29; *Saluka* (n 46 above) para 275.

[133] eg *Saluka* (n 46 above) para 264; *Azurix* (Merits) (n 110 above) para 310. BH Weston, ' "Constructive Takings" Under International Law: A Modest Foray into the Problem of Creeping Expropriation' (1975) 16 Virg J Int'l L 103; R Dolzer, 'Indirect Expropriation of Alien Property' (1986) 1 ICSID Rev 41, 59; Soloway (n 50 above) 101–4; LY Fortier, 'Caveat Investor: The Meaning of "Expropriation" and the Protection Afforded Investors Under NAFTA' (2003) 20(1) ICSID News 1.

[134] DM Price, 'NAFTA Chapter 11—Investor–State Dispute Settlement: Frankenstein or Safety Valve?' (2001) 26 Can–US LJ 107, 111.

converted into executive entities for purposes of review and control by international tribunals, and arbitrators are empowered to overrule a country's electoral choices by declaring legislation unlawful and by awarding damages—including for purely economic loss—to investors as a remedy in public law.

Perhaps the most pressing question, therefore, is the degree to which the treaties will be read to compel states to pay compensation for general regulatory measures that do not specifically target foreign investors for abuse or discrimination. As an *ad hoc* adjudicative system, this question cannot be answered until a tribunal has ruled on a specific investor claim. Expropriation may or may not be defined broadly to include regulatory takings; the minimum standard may or may not impose a broad guarantee of regulatory fairness; national treatment may or may not oblige states to take positive steps to ensure equal treatment of individual investors. This uncertainty undermines the utility of state liability in public law as a vehicle to deter disobedience by government;[135] in a global economy, it makes a great deal of regulation inherently risky, wherever it is perceived to implicate multinational firms. Of course, a major purpose of the system is to alleviate the regulatory risks faced by foreign investors. But, in pursuit of this goal, the system makes states dependent on arbitrators to interpret the treaties in ways that are reasonably sensitive to governmental concerns. Are arbitrators capable in an institutional sense of achieving this mission?

Investment treaty arbitration is not unique in that it involves the adjudication of complex and sensitive disputes that would otherwise be resolved by legislatures or executive governments.[136] Many forms of adjudication do the same. Judges may rule on the legality of sovereign activity with major implications for the cost and viability of government, particularly when deciding whether to order payment of public compensation to an individual in matters of public law. Judges also have a say in deciding the appropriate role of the state with respect to business and, by implication, in resolving conflicts of rights and interests between investors and those who benefit from the regulation of business.[137] The question is whether the need to instill confidence in foreign investors, in the face of the regulatory risks inherent in governmental decision-making, warrants privatizing these aspects of the judicial function in public law.

---

[135] eg World Bank, *World Development Report 2005* (Washington, DC: IBRD, 2004) 179. Kennedy (n 1 above) 1692–3; C Harlow, *State Liability: Tort Law and Beyond* (Oxford: OUP, 2004) 209; Lunney and Oliphant (n 61 above) 522.

[136] LL Fuller, 'Adjudication and the Rule of Law' (1960) 54 Am Soc'ty Int'l L Proc 1, 1–5; LL Fuller, 'The Forms and Limits of Adjudication' (1978) 92 Harv L Rev 353, 354 and 363; J Goldsworthy, *The Sovereignty of Parliament* (Oxford: Clarendon, 1999) 277–8.

[137] D Cohen and JC Smith, 'Entitlement and the Body Politic: Rethinking Negligence in Public Law' (1986) 64 Can Bar Rev 1, 9–10; M Loughlin, *The Idea of Public Law* (Oxford: OUP, 2003) 148; M Koskenniemi, 'What Is International Law For?' in MD Evans (ed) *International Law* (2nd edn, Oxford: OUP, 2006) 66–7.

5
The Transformation of International Law

All treaties constrain states, one way or another, and many impose obligations that limit democratic choice at the domestic level.[1] For centuries, international courts and tribunals have scrutinized the conduct of legislatures and states in general by determining their territorial boundaries, ruling on the legality of the use of force, limiting the scope of their regulatory powers, and ordering compensation for international wrongs, including for harm done to foreign nationals. Thus, since at least the nineteenth century, international arbitrators have made decisions of great resonance for states and their people. So, one might ask, is there really anything remarkable about modern investment treaty arbitration? Are investment treaties simply a manifestation of a long and rich tradition of arbitration in international law?

The argument of this chapter is that the emergence of the system of investment treaty arbitration, when viewed against the canvass of international law, is a major (even revolutionary) transformation in international adjudication. The reason why this is so is that investment treaties uniquely combine various innovative features of international adjudication to formulate a singularly far-reaching and potent system that uses arbitration to review and control states. To be concise, the treaties draw together these features:

1. Investors can bring international claims against states in the context of regulatory disputes (unlike customary international law and most treaties).

2. The state's consent to arbitration is prospective (unlike historical claims tribunals before which foreign nationals could bring claims).

3. The main remedy is state liability in public law (unlike virtually any treaty that allows individual claims).

4. A liberal approach to forum-shopping by claimants is, in some cases, combined with the removal or limitation of the duty to exhaust local remedies (unlike virtually any treaty).

5. Awards are enforceable in domestic courts across the globe, with limited opportunity for judicial review (unlike any other adjudicative regime in public law).

---

[1] KW Abbott *et al*, 'The Concept of Legalization' in JL Goldstein *et al* (eds) *Legalization and World Politics* (Cambridge: MIT Press, 2001) 30.

Each of these elements of investment treaty arbitration, and thus of the wider adjudicative power granted to arbitrators, is examined below. Viewed as a whole, I shall argue, they establish investment treaty tribunals as the closest the world has come to an international court, albeit of judges who are themselves businessmen, that has comprehensive jurisdiction over individual claims in the regulatory sphere.

The Individualization of Claims

Customary international law presumes that the resolution of a regulatory dispute involving a foreign national is, in the first place, a matter for the domestic law of the host state.[2] States are not subject to compulsory adjudication of disputes within their territory, whether by international tribunals or foreign courts.[3] A dispute arising from one state's treatment of an investor of another state conventionally could trigger a claim of diplomatic protection by the investor's home state,[4] but the investor could not make an independent claim.[5] The international claim was that of the home state and individuals had no right to bring a claim on their own behalf.[6] Moreover, a claim of diplomatic protection by the home state could be made only after the investor had exhausted local remedies in order to give the host state the opportunity to address the investor's complaint before any resort to international law.[7] Even then, the dispute could only be referred to international adjudication with the consent of the host state.[8] With one exception, no international

---

[2] *Case Concerning the Payment of Various Serbian Loans Issued In France* (*France v Serbia*) (1921), PCIJ Ser A, No 20, para 41. I Delupis, *Finance and Protection of Investments in Developing Countries* (Epping: Gower Press, 1973) 123; W Peter, *Arbitration and Renegotiation of International Investment Agreements* (The Hague: Kluwer Law International, 1995) 167–9 (arguing that the conclusion of the ICSID Convention indicates that the dictum in *Serbian Loans* can no longer be upheld in light of the changing structure of international law).

[3] eg *Status of Eastern Carelia*, Advisory Opinion (1923), PCIJ Ser B, No 5, 27; *Ambatielos Claim* (*Greece v United Kingdom*) (1956), 12 RIAA 83 [cited as *Ambatielos*], 103.

[4] eg *Nottebohm* (*Liechtenstein v Guatemala*), [1955] ICJ Rep 4 [cited as *Nottebohm*], 23–4; *Barcelona Traction, Light and Power Co* (*Belgium v Spain*), [1970] ICJ Rep 3, 9 ILM 227 [cited as *Barcelona Traction*], para 35–6. EM Borchard, 'Basic Elements of Diplomatic Protection of Citizens Abroad' (1913) 7 AJIL 497, 576.

[5] *Mavrommattis Palestine Concessions* (*Greece v Great Britain*) (1924), PCIJ Ser A, No 2 [cited as *Mavrommattis*], 12. MO Hudson, *International Tribunals* (Washington: Carnegie Endowment for International Peace and the Brookings Institution, 1944) 67–9 and 198.

[6] *Administrative Decision No V* (1924), 7 RIAA 119, 19 AJIL 612 [cited as *Administrative Decision No V*], 626–7 (US–Germany Mixed Claims Commission); *Barcelona Traction* (n 4 above) para 79. Hudson (n 5 above) 67–9; PT Muchlinski, *Multinational Enterprises and the Law* (Oxford: Blackwell, 1999) 534–6; UNCTAD, *Bilateral Investment Treaties in the Mid-1990s* (Geneva: United Nations, 1998) 89–90.

[7] *Ambatielos* (n 3 above) 118–19; *Interhandel Case* (*Switzerland v United States*), [1959] ICJ Rep 6, 26–7. C Eagleton, *The Responsibility of States in International Law* (New York: NYU Press, 1928) 70; Hudson (n 5 above) 189–90; P Okowa, 'Admissibility and the Law on International Responsibility' in MD Evans (ed) *International Law* (2nd edn, Oxford: OUP, 2006) 498.

[8] Hudson (n 5 above) 69.

tribunal, including the International Court of Justice (ICJ), has been given comprehensive jurisdiction over disputes between states and foreign nationals.[9] The reluctance of many states to refer investment disputes to the ICJ has meant that few cases involving the regulatory relationship between states and foreign investors have come before that court.[10] Before the recent proliferation of general consents by states to investment treaty arbitration, such disputes were normally resolved by inter-state diplomacy.

This conventional method of resolving regulatory disputes in the international sphere rests on the assumption that an investor's entitlement to protection under international law in the territory of a foreign state derives from the rights of the investor's home state.[11] In seeking diplomatic protection of one of its nationals, an investor's home state was assumed to be acting on its own rights, not those of the individual.[12] Thus, a host state could moderate (or aggravate) disputes involving foreign nationals in its negotiations with the home state.[13] International claims were subject to the home state's weighing of its other interests and, in principle, to good faith considerations in international relations.[14] By authorizing investors directly to advance a claim and seek damages for an alleged violation of international law, investment treaties allow investors to decide when and how to threaten, initiate, or settle a claim; and the investor appoints counsel and approves the legal argument. Thus, the claimant is no longer a publicly representative entity but a private party with full custody of the claim, who can decide the manner and extent to which international adjudication will be used to resolve a regulatory dispute.[15]

Individualization alters the dynamic of international adjudication with various implications that may be usefully highlighted at this stage even though they are

---

[9] The exception is the Central American Court of Justice of 1907 to 1918: HM Hill, 'Central American Court of Justice' in R Dolzer et al (eds) *Encyclopedia of Public International Law*, vol 1 (Amsterdam: North-Holland Publishing, 1987) 41–2.

[10] These include: *Barcelona Traction* (n 4 above); *Elettronica Sicula SpA (United States v Italy)*, [1989] ICJ Rep 14 [cited as *ELSI*]; and *Anglo-Iranian Oil Company (United Kingdom v Iran)*, [1952] ICJ Rep 93. LB Sohn, 'The Role of Arbitration in Recent International Multilateral Treaties' in TE Carbonneau (ed) *Resolving Transnational Disputes Through International Arbitration* (Charlottesville: University of Virginia Press, 1984) 26; M Sornarajah, *The Settlement of Foreign Investment Disputes* (Boston: Kluwer, 2001) 19–20.

[11] *Barcelona Traction* (n 4 above) para 78. M Whiteman, *Damages in International Law*, vol 1 (Washington, 1937–43) 82–3.

[12] *Mavrommatis* (n 5 above) 12; *Administrative Decision No V* (n 6 above) 626–7; *Nottebohm* (n 4 above) 24; *Barcelona Traction* (n 4 above) para 78–9. But see *Iran–United States No A/18* (1984), 5 Iran–US CTR 251, 23 ILM 489, 498.

[13] Hudson (n 5 above) 191–4; JG Merrills, 'The Means of Dispute Settlement' in MD Evans (ed) *International Law* (2nd edn, Oxford: OUP, 2006) 543–4.

[14] MA Luz, 'NAFTA, Investment and the Constitution of Canada: Will the Watertight Compartments Spring a Leak' (2001) 32 Ottawa L Rev 35, 83–4.

[15] *Enron Corporation v Argentine Republic* (Jurisdiction) (2 August 2004), ICSID Case No ARB/01/3 [cited as *Enron*], para 37, online: ICSID, ITA, Investment Claims. R Baldwin and C McCrudden, *Regulation and Public Law* (London: Weidenfeld & Nicolson, 1987) 57 and 65.

not in themselves unique to investment treaty arbitration. In the first place, the protection of an investor's interests under investment treaties is no longer affected by the home state's consideration of its own interest as a representative entity.[16] Thus investors are in a position to bring claims and represent their particular interests more vigorously than the home state might because investors do not have an interest in settling or moderating a claim for reasons of the public interest.[17] The context for a private firm's decisions about a legal claim is its business strategy, not the interest of the home state, though the two may of course coincide.[18] Further, counsel to investors have a new incentive to promote treaty arbitration to generate business:[19] the market for legal services is much expanded by the individualization of claims.[20] Finally, investors, unlike states, do not face the prospect of defending a treaty claim.[21] This is particularly important because of what it reveals about the transformation of arbitration from a reciprocal method of dispute settlement into a one-way system of regulatory adjudication; one-way in that only one class of disputing party, the investor, can activate the process by bringing a claim.

A further implication of individualization is that it expands the opportunities for tribunals to adopt a broad approach to jurisdiction and to the standards of review under an investment treaty. Thus, investors have advocated a more expansive approach to state liability than that adopted by the states parties, including

---

[16] *Administrative Decision No V* (n 6 above) 626–7. Hudson (n 5 above) 191–4 and 198; DC Ohly, 'A Functional Analysis of Claimant Eligibility' in RB Lillich (ed) *International Law of State Responsibility for Injuries to Aliens* (Charlottesville: University Press of Virginia, 1983) 284.

[17] eg *Fireman's Fund Insurance Company v United Mexican States* (Jurisdiction) (17 July 2003), 15(6) World Trade and Arb Mat 3 [cited as *Fireman's Fund*], para 64 (rejecting the claimant's submission that 'as a general policy consideration, direct investor recourse to arbitration has become the rule in modern investment agreements, although there may be exceptions, and that the value of investor-state arbitral mechanism is so substantial that it should only be foreclosed when that result is unmistakably required by treaty provision'); *Siemens AG v Argentine Republic* (Jurisdiction) (3 August 2004), 44 ILM 138 [cited as *Siemens*], para 116, 120, and 135 (accepting the claimant's submission that the inclusion of a most favoured nation clause in a BIT 'implies the right [of the claimant] to select those aspects of provisions in different treaties that favor the [investor] most', thus allowing investors to pick and choose from the provisions of different treaties and to construct them into the most desirable collection of procedural and substantive rights in relation to a claim).

[18] RK Paterson, 'A New Pandora's Box? Private Remedies for Foreign Investors under the North American Free Trade Agreement' (2000) 8 Willamette J Int'l L and Dispute Res 77, 82.

[19] For an illustration of firms' promotional material: RD Bishop, SD Dimitroff, and CS Miles, 'Strategic Options Available When Catastrophe Strikes' (2001) 36 Texas Int'l LJ 635; Freshfields Bruckhaus Deringer, 'The Argentine Crisis—Foreign Investors' Rights' (Report, January 2002); Freshfields Bruckhaus Deringer, 'Dispute Resolution in the Caspian Region' (Report, June 2002).

[20] M Shapiro, 'The Globalization of Law' (1993) 1 Ind J Global Legal Studies 37, 59–60.

[21] J Paulsson, 'Arbitration without Privity' (1995) 10 ICSID Rev 232, 232; J Werner, 'The Trade Explosion and Some Likely Effects on International Arbitration' (1997) 14(2) J Int'l Arb 5, 6; JC Thomas, 'Investor–State Arbitration Under NAFTA Chapter Eleven' (Paper presented to the NAFTA Chapter 11 Investor–State Disputes: Litigating Against Sovereigns conference, Canadian Bar Association, Toronto, March 2000) 4–5; PG Foy, 'Effectiveness of NAFTA's Chapter Eleven Investor–State Arbitration Procedures' (2003) 18 ICSID Rev 44, 50.

the home state, in a number of NAFTA cases to date.[22] Of course, this is not surprising. Private claimants will naturally favour an expansive approach to investor protection and to state liability. What is noteworthy is that, by allowing investors to make the arguments, the system establishes an environment in which arbitrators are enabled to adopt a broad interpretation of the treaty even where this conflicts with the unanimous submissions of the states that negotiated and concluded it.[23] This environment does not exist in international custom and under most treaties, where access to adjudication, if permitted at all, is limited to states.

The channelling of matters once reserved for diplomacy and international relations into an individualized adjudicative process is by no means an unfortunate development. Making judicial remedies available to individuals under international law, as discussed in Chapter 1 of this book, is broadly consistent with liberal ideals of justice and fairness in a global society, and it is a major and worthwhile project of the international human rights movement, in particular. But one should not jump to the conclusion that all forms of international adjudication advance this greater cause. In consideration of this, we shall for present purposes leave aside the question of the benefits and limitations of international adjudication in order to focus on the special character of individualization under investment treaties.

The Prospective Consent

Historically, individuals were at times authorized to bring international claims against states before tribunals created in the aftermath of war or revolution.[24] Thus, states have, on occasion, allowed investor claims under international law prior to

---

[22] eg *Ethyl Corporation v Government of Canada* (Investor's Submissions) (2 October 1997), UNCITRAL Rules, para 31, online: DFAIT, NAFTA Claims; *SD Myers, Inc v Government of Canada* (Investor's Submissions) (20 July 1999), UNCITRAL Rules, para 77, online: DFAIT, NAFTA Claims; *Pope & Talbot Inc v Government of Canada* (Investor's Submissions) (28 January 2000), UNCITRAL Rules, para 53–7 and 72, online: DFAIT, NAFTA Claims; *United Parcel Service of America, Inc v Government of Canada* (Investor's Submissions) (23 March 2005), UNCITRAL Rules, para 515–16, 521, 528, and 536–7, online: DFAIT, NAFTA Claims.

[23] eg *Pope & Talbot Inc v Government of Canada* (Merits, Phase 2) (10 April 2001), 13(4) World Trade and Arb Mat 61, para 79 (rejecting the submissions of the NAFTA Parties that Article 1102 is limited to the prohibition of discrimination *on the basis of nationality*); *GAMI Investments, Inc v Government of the United Mexican States* (Merits) (15 November 2004), 44 ILM 545, 17(2) World Trade and Arb Mat 127 [cited as *GAMI*], para 29–30. Contrast *ADF Group Inc v United States of America* (Merits) (9 January 2003), 18 ICSID Rev 195, 6 ICSID Rep 470, 15(3) World Trade and Arb Mat 55, para 177.

[24] eg the Alabama Claims Arbitration established after the American Civil War, the Mixed Tribunals and Claims Commissions after the First World War, the Iran–United States Claims Commission after the Islamic revolution in Iran, and the UN Compensation Commission after the Gulf War of 1990–91. Hudson (n 5 above) 3–6 and 196–7; J Collier and V Lowe, *The Settlement of Disputes in International Law* (Oxford: OUP, 1999) c 1 and 3; A Redfern and M Hunter, *Law and Practice of International Commercial Arbitration* (4th edn, London: Sweet & Maxwell, 2004) 60–2.

the innovation of the general consent in investment treaties. Indeed, from the Jay Treaty of 1794[25] to the Iran–US Claims Tribunal,[26] states authorized international tribunals to resolve regulatory disputes arising from one state's treatment of the nationals of another and, in some cases, claims could be brought directly by investors. Nevertheless, these historical tribunals did not involve *generalized* arbitration, based on comprehensive jurisdiction, because their authority was retrospective. Adjudicative authority was given to the tribunal only after the fact, and was limited to disputes arising from a distinct period, series of events, or subject-matter.[27] Take the example of the Iran–US Claims Tribunal. In 1981, after the Islamic revolution of 1979, Iran and the United States consented to the compulsory arbitration of claims by each other's nationals arising out of 'debts, contracts ... expropriations or other measures affecting property rights'.[28] Foreign nationals could bring claims before the Tribunal if the amount in dispute was (US)$250,000 or more, and if the claim was outstanding on 19 January 1981.[29] Thus the Tribunal had compulsory jurisdiction over certain individual claims, limited to an approximately two-year period following the revolution.

This retrospective consent differs from a general consent to the arbitration of future disputes. In the case of a retrospective consent, a state is more able to anticipate the significance of its acceptance of compulsory arbitration because the consent is given after the events in question have taken place.[30] From the investor's point of view, to borrow a phrase from commercial arbitration, the general consent is like 'a blank cheque which may be cashed for an unknown amount at a future, and as yet unknown, date'.[31] By giving a prospective consent in an investment treaty, the state exposes itself in principle to claims by any multinational firm with economic interests that are subject to regulation by the state. As a result, investment treaty arbitration encompasses future disputes involving an indeterminate class of claimants in relation to a very broad range of governmental activity.

---

[25] Treaty of Amity, Commerce and Navigation between Great Britain and the United States (the Jay Treaty) (19 November 1794; 52 Cons TS 243; entered into force 28 October 1795). Hudson (n 5 above) 3–4; H Neufeld, *The International Protection of Private Creditors From the Treaties of Westphalia to the Congress of Vienna* (Leiden: AW Sijthoff, 1971) 68–77.

[26] Established by the Declaration of the Government of the Democratic and Popular Republic of Algeria concerning the Settlement of Claims by the Government of the United States of America and the Government of the Islamic Republic of Iran (the Algiers Declaration) (Algiers, 19 January 1981; 20 ILM 230 (1981)), art II(1). CD Gray, *Judicial Remedies in International Law* (Oxford: Clarendon, 1987) 181–5; M Mohebi, *The International Law Character of the Iran–United States Claims Tribunal* (The Hague: Kluwer Law International, 1991); CN Brower and D Brueschke, *The Iran–United States Claims Tribunal* (The Hague: Kluwer Law International, 1998); RB Lillich and DB Magraw, *The Iran–United States Tribunal: Its Contribution to the Law of State Responsibility* (Transnational Publishers, 1998).

[27] C Kennedy, 'Address' (1907) Am Soc'ty Int'l L Proc 100, 110–11; Hudson (n 5 above) 3–6 and 11–12.   [28] Algiers Declaration (n 26 above) art II.

[29] Algiers Declaration (n 26 above) art II.

[30] An agreement to arbitrate concluded after the dispute is typically called a *compromis*. Historically, in many states, this was the only means of consenting to arbitration even in commercial disputes: Redfern and Hunter (n 24 above) 20–1.   [31] Redfern and Hunter (n 24 above) 21.

Among others, Legum (who served as US government counsel in early arbitrations under NAFTA) has argued that the individualization of claims under contemporary investment treaties is not a major departure and that its novelty is overstated.[32] Yet all but a few of Legum's examples of other instances in which states have authorized individual claims under international law involve specific consents by states, not general consents.[33] In the case of the Jay Treaty of 1794, one of Legum's primary examples,[34] the consents to compulsory arbitration by Great Britain and the US were limited to claims by foreign creditors and ship owners that related to events within a discrete period.[35] Further, with respect to creditor claims, the Jay Treaty's process of arbitration led in the end to a lump-sum settlement without a single claim being heard, due to disagreements among the state-appointed arbitrators.[36] Legum also identifies bilateral investment treaties (BITs) as evidence that investment treaty arbitration is a common phenomenon but, as argued in Chapter 2 of this book, the rapid growth of BITs in the 1990s— and the recent explosion of investor claims—actually highlights the uniqueness of the contemporary system. Finally, Legum refers to just two historical cases in which states provided a prospective consent to international claims by foreign nationals, both dating from the early twentieth century.[37]

In fact, the state's future-oriented consent makes investment treaty arbitration a highly significant development in international law and, beyond a small number of other treaties, an innovation in international adjudication. When combined with the prospective consent, individualization has two key outcomes. First, it gives arbitrators comprehensive jurisdiction to resolve disputes concerning the legality of state conduct in the regulatory sphere. Second, it makes the analytical framework of public law more directly relevant to international adjudication, especially in matters of state liability. Both outcomes are discussed in the next section.

The Dynamic of State Liability

The expansion of international adjudication to encompass regulatory disputes between the state and private parties makes the analytical framework of public

---

[32] B Legum, 'The Innovation of Investor–State Arbitration Under NAFTA' (2002) 43 Harv Int'l LJ 531, 538; J Paulsson, *Denial of Justice in International Law* (Cambridge: CUP, 2005) 54–5 and 261; JA Rabkin, *Law Without Nations?* (Princeton: Princeton University Press, 2005) 214. See also SE Eizenstat, ' "Fast Track" needs protections for investors' *The Boston Globe* (2 May 2002).

[33] Legum (n 32 above) 535–6 (referring to individual claims under a 'significant number of treaty regimes', such as the Mixed Claims Tribunals after the First World War, the Iran–US Claims Tribunal, and regional human rights tribunals, although conceding that few of these claims were based on prospective consents by the state). [34] Legum (n 32 above) 534–5.

[35] Hudson (n 5 above) 3.

[36] H-J Schlochauer, 'Jay Treaty (1794)' in R Dolzer *et al* (eds) *Encyclopedia of Public International Law*, vol 1 (Amsterdam: North-Holland Publishing, 1987) 109–10; Neufeld (n 25 above) 70–7.

[37] Legum (n 32 above) 536 (noting states' prospective consents in the case of the Central American Court of Justice 1907 and the Upper Silesian Arbitral Tribunal of 1922).

law, as applied in domestic adjudication of regulatory disputes, more applicable than in conventional international adjudication.[38] This point was touched on in Chapter 3 of this book. It is elaborated here by a closer examination of the main remedy in investment treaty arbitration: the damages award. In making a claim under an investment treaty, an investor seeks damages for harm caused by the state's alleged breach of the treaty's standards of review.[39] Where a tribunal concludes that a state violated a standard, the tribunal may award damages to the investor.[40] Awards are compensatory and usually do not incorporate exemplary or punitive damages.[41] That said, they have a more general deterrent effect on the state because they retrospectively sanction conduct that was found unlawful by imposing a potentially crippling fiscal penalty.[42] And, while awards are always issued in response to a claim by an investor, both a finding of illegality and an award of damages may have much wider implications for the state's regulatory position because of its status as a representative entity.[43]

Individualized damages claims are exceedingly rare in international law. Outside Europe, no international regime allows individuals directly to seek damages through international adjudication in response to a state's alleged breach of international law. For example, individual claims were ruled out in the case of the World Trade Organization and non-investment chapters of regional trade agreements, which limit dispute resolution to inter-state adjudication based on non-monetary remedies such as a declaration of illegality or the suspension of concessions by

---

[38] eg *Feldman Karpa (Marvin Roy) v United Mexican States* (Jurisdiction) (6 December 2000), 18 ICSID Rev 469, 7 ICSID Rep 327, para 61–3 (referring to the domestic law of the NAFTA states on claims of estoppel to block tax enforcement); *Mondev International Ltd v United States of America* (Merits) (11 October 2002), 42 ILM 85, 6 ICSID Rep 192, 15(3) World Trade and Arb Mat 273 [cited as *Mondev*], para 149–50 (domestic law on the tortious immunity of public authorities); *SD Myers, Inc v Government of Canada* (Merits) (13 November 2000), 40 ILM 1408, 15(1) World Trade and Arb Mat 184 [cited as *SD Myers*], para 249 (domestic law on equality rights); *United Parcel Service of America, Inc v Government of Canada* (Jurisdiction) (22 November 2002), UNCITRAL Rules [cited as *UPS*], para 85 (domestic competition law), online: DFAIT, ITA, NAFTA Claims. The change here is one of degree given that international tribunals have examined or analogized issues of domestic law in the past: eg *Fabiani Case (France v Venezuela)* (1896), 10 RIAA 33 (state responsibility for the official acts of its agents).

[39] eg North American Free Trade Agreement (NAFTA) (17 December 1992; 32 ILM 296 and 605; entered into force 1 January 1994), art 1116 and 1117; Agreement between the Government of the United Kingdom of Great Britain and Northern Ireland and the Government of the Republic of India (the UK–India BIT) (London, 14 March 1994; UKTS No 27 (1995); Cmd 2797; entered into force 6 January 1995), art 9. [40] eg NAFTA (n 39 above) art 1135.

[41] eg NAFTA (n 39 above) art 1135(3).

[42] CT Oliver, 'Legal Remedies and Sanctions' in RB Lillich (ed) *International Law of State Responsibility for Injuries to Aliens* (Charlottesville: University Press of Virginia, 1983) 61–5; JHH Weiler, 'Emerging Issues on Compliance and Effectiveness of Community Law' (1997) 91 Am Soc'ty Int'l L Proc 172, 173; JA VanDuzer, 'NAFTA Chapter 11 to Date: The Progress of a Work in Progress' in L Ritchie Dawson (ed) *Whose Rights? The NAFTA Chapter 11 Debate* (Ottawa: Centre for Trade Law and Policy, 2002) 48–9.

[43] C Harlow, *State Liability: Tort Law and Beyond* (Oxford: OUP, 2004) 27, 80, and 85–6 (noting 'the possible "chilling effects"' on decision-taking' of damages awards and the risk of 'decision traps' for state).

affected states.⁴⁴ In other fields of public international law, such as humanitarian and environmental law, states have eschewed adjudication (let alone damages claims by individuals) as a means to enforce international standards or compensate those harmed by unlawful state conduct.⁴⁵ In stark contrast to the mainstream of international adjudication, therefore, investment treaties establish an individualized regime of state liability.⁴⁶

Importantly, damages claims by individuals are also the exception in international human rights law.⁴⁷ Despite the greatly expanded protection of human rights in dozens of treaties concluded since 1945, individual claims for damages are authorized only under the European Convention on Human Rights (ECHR)⁴⁸ and the American Convention on Human Rights (ACHR),⁴⁹ and in both cases the ability of individuals to claim damages is far more limited than under investment treaties. Under the ECHR, the European Court of Human Rights may afford 'just satisfaction' to an individual whose rights were violated, where considered necessary by the Court,⁵⁰ but the Court has declined to award damages for various reasons, including the adequacy of non-monetary remedies and the host state's

---

⁴⁴ Understanding on Rules and Procedures Governing the Settlement of Disputes (the WTO Dispute Settlement Understanding) (15 April 1994; 33 ILM 112), para 19 and 22; NAFTA (n 39 above) c 19 and 20. PM Nichols, 'Participation of Nongovernmental Parties in the World Trade Organization' (1996) 17 U Penn J Int'l Econ L 295, 297–8 and 302–3; BR Killmann, 'The Access of Individuals to International Trade Dispute Settlement' (1996) 13(3) J Int'l Arb 143, 164; S Dillon, *International Trade and Economic Law in the European Union* (Oxford: Hart, 2002) 372–4.

⁴⁵ EB Weiss, 'Invoking State Responsibility in the Twenty-first Century' (2002) 96 AJIL 798, 811–12; C Greenwood, 'The Law of War (International Humanitarian Law)' in MD Evans (ed) *International Law* (2nd edn, Oxford: OUP, 2006) 808–9. The United Nations Convention on the Law of the Sea [(Montego Bay, 10 December 1982; 21 ILM 1261; entered into force 16 November 1994), art 187(c) and 188(2); art 5(4) and 13(15) (annex III)] permits individuals to make claims before the International Sea-Bed Disputes Chamber, but only in contractual disputes: RR Churchill, 'Dispute Settlement in the Law of the Sea' in MD Evans, *Remedies in International Law: The Institutional Dilemma* (Oxford: Hart, 1998) 89; Sohn (n 10 above) 36–7.

⁴⁶ A Afilalo, 'Constitutionalization Through the Back Door: A European Perspective on NAFTA's Investment Chapter' (2001) 34 NYU J Int'l L & Pol 1, 6. In this book, the term 'state liability' is used rather than 'state responsibility' to highlight the distinction between a damages award in investment treaty arbitration and a damages award in conventional international adjudication. In investment treaty arbitration, damages are paid to an individual in the context of a regulatory relationship between the individual and the state. In conventional international adjudication, damages are paid to a state in the context of a reciprocal relationship between states.

⁴⁷ eg International Covenant on Civil and Political Rights (16 December 1966; 999 UNTS 171, 61 AJIL 870; entered into force 23 March 1976), art 41 (providing for an optional system of claims by states parties) and (First) Optional Protocol (1966) (providing for an optional system of individual petitions leading to the consideration of individual claims and an expression of views by an international committee, but not to compulsory arbitration or a damages award). D Shelton, *Remedies in International Human Rights Law* (Oxford: OUP, 1999) 137–8 and 142–7; Weiss (n 45 above) 809–11; R Bachand and S Rousseau, 'International Investment and Human Rights: Political and Legal Issues' (Background Paper for Rights & Democracy, 11 June 2003) 14.

⁴⁸ Convention for the Protection of Human Rights and Fundamental Freedoms (the European Convention on Human Rights [ECHR]) (4 November 1950; Eur TS 5, 213 UNTS 222; entered into force 3 September 1953), art 34.

⁴⁹ American Convention on Human Rights (ACHR) (1144 UNTS 123; entered into force 18 July 1978), art 44.   ⁵⁰ ECHR (n 48 above) art 41.

ability to pay.⁵¹ In the case of the ACHR, an individual can receive damages only if the Inter-American Commission on Human Rights decides to bring the claim before the Inter-American Court, and the Commission has refused to bring claims on behalf of corporations.⁵² Further, the Inter-American Court has adopted a cautious approach to money compensation as a remedy for human rights violations.⁵³ Importantly, both conventions (unlike investment treaties) impose a duty on individuals to exhaust local remedies before bringing a claim,⁵⁴ and, not surprisingly, neither allows individuals to choose the rules that govern the claim, to appoint members of the tribunal, or to enforce an award directly against state assets.⁵⁵

Beyond the field of human rights, the only other case in which a treaty regime guarantees the right of individuals to claim damages for violations of the treaty is under the law of the European Community. The *Francovich* doctrine⁵⁶ of the European Court of Justice, in particular, introduced the principle that individuals must be able to seek damages under domestic law for alleged violations of EC law by member states.⁵⁷ Outside investment treaty arbitration, the *Francovich* doctrine is probably the most ambitious attempt to apply treaty-based state liability in relation to international economic integration.⁵⁸ Even so, the *Francovich* doctrine is limited by various factors, including the Court's requirement that there be a 'sufficiently serious' violation of EC law for damages to be awarded.⁵⁹

Damages claims are rare in international law and viewed with caution by international courts because damages are traditionally a private law remedy not

---

⁵¹ Shelton (n 47 above) 101, 154–9, and 218–20; J-P Costa, 'The Provision of Compensation Under Article 41 of the European Convention on Human Rights' (Address to the British Institute of International and Comparative Law, 7 December 2001) 1–3 and 16–17; JA Weir, 'Human Rights and Damages' (2001) 40 Washburn LJ 412, 421–9, and 436; Harlow (n 43 above) 68 and 71.

⁵² ACHR (n 49 above) art 44. eg *Tabacalera Boquerón SA v Paraguay* (1997), Inter-Am Comm HR, Rep No 47/97, *Annual Report of the Inter-American Commission on Human Rights: 1987*, OEA/Ser.L/V/II.98/Doc.7/Rev (1998) 225, para 25 and 36. Shelton (n 47 above) 169–72.

⁵³ ACHR (n 49 above) art 63(1). Shelton (n 47 above) 221–3.

⁵⁴ ECHR (n 48 above) art 35; ACHR (n 49 above) art 46(1).

⁵⁵ Shelton (n 47 above) 90; Costa (n 51 above) 15.

⁵⁶ *Francovich and Bonifaci v Republic of Italy* (No 6 and 9/90), [1991] ECR I-5357, (1993) 2 CML Rev 66 [cited as *Francovich*].

⁵⁷ More precisely, damages must be available as a remedy before the domestic courts of the member states, subject to the overriding jurisdiction of the European Court of Justice in matters of EC law: *Francovich* (n 56 above) para 35 and 40. PP Craig and G De Búrca, *EU Law—Text, Cases, and Materials* (3rd edn, Oxford: OUP, 2003) 257–74.

⁵⁸ The *Francovich* doctrine applies to legislative acts and omissions (*Brasserie du Pêcheur SA v Germany; Secretary of State for Transport, ex parte Factortame Ltd and Others* (No 46 & 48/93), [1996] ECR I-1131, (1996) 1 CML Rev 889 [cited as *Brasserie du Pêcheur*]), administrative decisions (*R v Ministry of Agriculture and Fisheries, ex parte Hedley Lomas (Ireland) Ltd* (No 5/94), [1996] ECR I-2553), judicial decisions (*Köbler v Austria* (No C-224/01), [2003] ECR I-10239, 3 CML Rev 28), and acts of sub-national governments (*Salomone Haim v Kassenzahnärztliche Vereinigung Nordrhein* (No 424/97), [2000] ECR I-5123).

⁵⁹ *Brasserie du Pêcheur* (n 58 above) 990. See the discussion in Ch 6 below, p 147–9.

originally used to address sovereign misconduct in public law.⁶⁰ The theory of damages is based on a private law conception of the relationship between disputing parties; ie a theoretical framework based on legal relations between juridical equals. Thus, damages are classically awarded in the context of a reciprocal relationship; they are paid by one party to another for the violation of a legal duty and both the victim and the wrongdoer are protected by the law and liable to sanction.⁶¹ Either disputing party can be the claimant or the respondent in a claim.

In international law, the use of damages as a remedy does not undermine this conceptual framework because a dispute between states is more analogous to a dispute between private parties than to one between the state and an individual.⁶² (Likewise, a contractual dispute between an individual and a state is conventionally treated as private dispute, subject to the law of contract.⁶³) Thus, in inter-state adjudication, damages are awarded in the context of a dispute between juridical equals.⁶⁴ On the other hand, in investment treaty arbitration, damages are awarded as the primary remedy to a private party who is subject to the exercise of public authority.⁶⁵ The fact that state liability arises in the context of a regulatory dispute distinguishes damages awards in investment treaty arbitration from damages awards in private law and in inter-state adjudication.

⁶⁰ A Chayes, 'The Role of the Judge in Public Law Litigation' (1976) 89 Harv L Rev 1281, 1287; Gray (n 26 above) 8; Shelton (n 47 above) 38–9.

⁶¹ EJ Weinrib, *The Idea of Private Law* (Harvard: Harvard University Press, 1995) 10 and 19.

⁶² TJ Lawrence, *The Principles of International Law* (London: Macmillan & Co, 1923) 47 and 51; H Lauterpacht, *Private Sources and Analogies of International Law* (Longmans, Green & Co, 1927) 3–5; VS Mani, *International Adjudication* (The Hague: Martinus Nijhoff, 1980) 3–4.

⁶³ CN Gregory, 'Expropriation by International Arbitration' (1907) 21 Harv L Rev 23, 23; WW Willoughby, *The Fundamental Concepts of Public Law* (New York: Macmillan, 1924) 322–4; Eagleton (n 7 above) 16; Hudson (n 5 above) 188; FA Mann, 'State Contracts and State Responsibility' (1960) 54 AJIL 572, 573 and 582. See also Whiteman (n 11 above) 6–7; International Law Commission, 'Draft Articles on Responsibility of States for Internationally Wrongful Acts', *Report of the International Law Commission on the Work of Its Fifty-third Session*, UN GAOR, 56th Sess, Supp No 10, annex, UN Doc A/56/10 (2001) 43, art 42.

⁶⁴ J Dutheil de la Rochère, 'Member State Liability for Infringement of European Community Law' (1996) 11 Tul Euro Civ LF 1, 10; D Bodansky and JR Crook, 'Symposium: The ILC's State Responsibility Articles—Introduction and Overview' (2002) 96 AJIL 773, 775–6 and 785–6; Weiss (n 45 above) 798–9; C Warbrick, 'States and Recognition in International Law' in MD Evans (ed) *International Law* (2nd edn, Oxford: OUP, 2006) 222–4. But see *Legal Consequences of the Construction of a Wall in the Occupied Palestinian Territory* (Advisory Opinion) (9 July 2004), ICJ General List No 131 [cited as *Construction of a Wall*], 147 and 152 (concluding that states have an obligation, having breached a rule of customary international law that protects individuals, 'to make reparation for the damage caused to all the natural or legal persons concerned' and 'to compensate, in accordance with the applicable rules of international law, all natural or legal persons having suffered any form of material damage' as a result of the breach); *Janes Claim (United States v Mexico)* (1926), 4 RIAA 82, para 23–6 (assessing the state's liability for murder of a foreign national in terms of loss to the individuals concerned, rather than the home state, and awarding compensation to the relatives of the deceased).

⁶⁵ Eagleton (n 7 above) 3, fn 2; SJ Toope, *Mixed International Arbitration—Studies in Arbitration Between States and Private Persons* (Cambridge: Grotius Publications, 1990) 184–7.

International rules of state responsibility are in many respects more expansive than those that typically apply in the domestic public law of state liability. For example, international law adopts a flexible approach to the attribution of individual acts to the state, holding states responsible for ultra vires acts of its agents in order to encourage active supervision of public officials.[66] For similar reasons, a claimant state does not have to prove intent on the part of the respondent state in order to establish liability for acts arising from official error.[67] In general, the rules of state responsibility adopt a liberal approach to fault, relative to the domestic public law of state liability.[68] This permissive approach reflects the reciprocity of legal relations between states.[69] Every state, in principle, enjoys the protection and assumes the risk that flows from liberal rules of attribution, intent, and fault.

The reciprocity of rights and duties breaks down in the adjudication of regulatory disputes between the state and individuals.[70] In a regulatory dispute, the state wields powers and assumes responsibilities that no private person can possess.[71] Thus the protection of individuals from the exercise of public authority requires the application of norms that uniquely protect individuals from the state. In many public law systems, individuals are in some circumstances allowed to claim damages to compensate for harm they have suffered as a result of the unlawful exercise of public authority. But, in such instances, it must be understood that the individual invokes rights and entitlements that adhere to the individual against the state and not the other way round.[72] The state alone can exercise public authority over private parties, including foreign investors, within its territory. Likewise, the state has certain duties that arise only from the exercise of public authority and, as such,

---

[66] *Caire Claim (France v Mexico)* (1929), 5 RIAA 516 [cited as *Caire Claim*], 529–30. *Noble Ventures v Romania* (Merits) (12 October 2005), ICSID Case No ARB/01/11, para 81, online: ITA, Investment Claims. JA Hessbruegge, 'The Historical Development of the Doctrines of Attribution and Due Diligence in International Law' (2004) 36 NYU J Int'l L & Pol 265, 270.

[67] *Union Bridge Company Claim (United States v Great Britain)* (1924), 6 RIAA 138, 141–2. See also *Asian Agricultural Products Ltd (AAPL) v Sri Lanka* (Merits) (27 June 1990), 30 ILM 577, 4 ICSID Rep 246, para 69 and 77; *In the Matter of Cross-border Trucking Services* (Merits) (6 February 2001), 13(3) World Trade and Arb Mat 121, para 214.

[68] *Caire Claim* (n 66 above) 529–30; *Corfu Channel* (Merits) (*United Kingdom v Albania*), [1949] ICJ Rep 4, 22. See also *Tippetts v TAMS–ATTA* (1985), 6 Iran–US CTR 219, 226. Eagleton (n 7 above) 18–20; MT Ahmedouamar, 'The Liability of the Government in France as a Consequence of its Legal Activities' (1983) 11 Int'l J Legal Info 1, 6 and 10; A Nollkaemper, 'Concurrence Between Individual Responsibility and State Responsibility in International Law' (2003) 52 ICLQ 615, 633.

[69] Lauterpacht (n 62 above) 134; Eagleton (n 7 above) 5.

[70] Chayes (n 60 above) 1302; AA Fatouros, 'Transnational Enterprise in the Law of State Responsibility' in RB Lillich (ed) *International Law of State Responsibility for Injuries to Aliens* (Charlottesville: University Press of Virginia, 1983) 362–3; DW Bowett, 'Claims Between States and Private Entities: The Twilight Zone of International Law' (1986) 35 Cath U L Rev 929, 933–4; W Twining, *Globalisation and Legal Theory* (London: Butterworths, 2000) 51–3; Shelton (n 47 above) 39 and 47–50.

[71] WI Jennings, *The Law and the Constitution* (London: University of London Press, 1959) 312; D Cohen and JC Smith, 'Entitlement and the Body Politic: Rethinking Negligence in Public Law' (1986) 64 Can Bar Rev 1, 5–6; C Harlow and R Rawlings, *Law and Administration* (London: Butterworths, 1997) 5 and 41–5; Warbrick (n 64 above) 231–2.   [72] Toope (n 65 above) 388.

that cannot be compared to acts of a private party. And without the exercise of public authority the prospect of an individual claim arising out of a regulatory dispute simply does not exist.

The idea of awarding damages to individuals for sovereign wrongs raises thorny issues about the scope and purpose of state liability and the appropriate role of government.[73] Should damages be awarded to compensate individuals, or to deter inappropriate state conduct?[74] Should liability be limited by requirements of malice or fault on the part of the state,[75] or in light of the need to maintain flexibility and predictability in government?[76] Should legislative or judicial acts be exempt from liability?[77] These important questions have previously been resolved almost exclusively by domestic public law, as part of the reserved domain of domestic jurisdiction.[78] With investment treaty arbitration, they are brought within the discretion of arbitrators. In turn, approaches to state liability that evolved in domestic law become more relevant to international adjudication.[79]

During the twentieth century, in most countries, the classical doctrine of sovereign immunity from suit and from damages awards was whittled away.[80] In its place, new rules were developed to delineate the scope of state liability as a public law remedy.[81] In the common law tradition, for example, state liability was qualified by the principle of parliamentary sovereignty, which limited the legislature's liability where the passage or amendment of a law caused losses to private individuals.[82] Likewise, the liability of the courts was limited in order to promote

---

[73] C Harlow, *Compensation and Government Torts* (London: Sweet & Maxwell, 1982) 51; Ontario Law Reform Commission (OLRC), *Report on the Liability of the Crown* (Toronto: OLRC, 1989) 7; C Harlow, 'Francovich and the Problem of the Disobedient State' (1996) 2 Eur LJ 199; Dutheil de la Rochère (n 64 above); PW Hogg and PJ Monahan, *Liability of the Crown* (3rd edn, Toronto: Carswell, 2000) 151.   [74] Gray (n 26 above) 151; JHH Weiler (n 42 above) 172–3.

[75] C Morris, 'The Role of Criminal Statutes in Negligence Actions' (1949) 49 Col L Rev 21, 27–9; H Street, *Governmental Liability* (Cambridge: CUP, 1953) 66; PP Craig, 'Compensation in Public Law' (1980) 96 LQ Rev 413, 441–3; D Fairgrieve, 'The Human Rights Act 1998, Damages and Tort Law' (2001) Pub Law 695, 699–700; Harlow (n 43 above) 53–4 and 61.

[76] JM Evans et al, *Administrative Law—Cases, Text, and Materials* (4th edn, Toronto: Emond Montgomery, 1995) 1401.

[77] eg *R v Treasury, ex parte British Telecommunications* (No 392/93), [1996] ECR I-1631, 3 WLR 203, para 40 ('A restrictive approach to state liability is justified . . . in particular [because of] the concern to ensure that the exercise of legislative functions is not hindered by the prospect of actions for damages whenever the general interest requires the institutions or member states to adopt measures which may adversely affect individual interests').

[78] I Brownlie, *Principles of Public International Law* (6th edn, Oxford: OUP, 2003) 291.

[79] Harlow (1996) (n 73 above) 205–6. See the discussion in Ch 6 below, p 143–5.

[80] eg Federal Tort Claims Act 1946, 28 USC, s 1346(b), 2671–80 (USA); Crown Proceedings Act 1947 (UK). OLRC (n 73 above) 8–11; WB Lafferty, 'The Persian Gulf War Syndrome: Rethinking Government Tort Liability' (1995) 25 Stetson L Rev 137, 148–9.

[81] eg *Blanco* (8 February 1873) Rec 1er Supp 61 (recognizing the tort liability of the state in relation to its commercial activities, although noting that state liability is 'neither general, nor absolute', reflecting the need to balance the opposing and competing interests at stake). Street (n 75 above) 6–24; Ahmedouamar (n 68 above) 2–12; Weir (n 51 above) 418–20 and 428–9.

[82] Domestic courts may have the authority to award damages to individuals for legislative acts, but typically only in relation to constitutionally protected rights. Street (n 75 above) 11, 45–6, and 70–2;

impartiality and finality in judicial decision-making.[83] Administrative acts could generally lead to tort liability on the part of the state, although not where the tort flowed from a policy decision that involved the expenditure of public funds.[84] In some cases, state liability could arise from administrative acts in the context of unique public law torts but these, too, were subject to limitations on liability.[85] Thus a series of compromises was arrived at between governmental immunity and the award of damages to individuals harmed by state regulation. In every legal system, the resulting balance was specific and complex, reflecting the historical evolution of norms regarding the role of the state in society.[86]

Under an investment treaty, the award of damages to an investor can be approached simply as a form of state responsibility on the international plane. But, as noted, rules of state responsibility were developed in the context of reciprocal legal relations among states. Even in claims of diplomatic protections on behalf of a foreign national, the dispute was treated as a relationship between the host state and the home state of the foreign national.[87] The state's duty to protect a foreign national was owed to the home state and, based on Vattel's principle, a harm to the foreign national was treated as a harm to the home state.[88] In this context, international law did not confront the varied circumstances that prompted limitations on state liability in domestic public law.[89] There was less need to adapt the rules to accommodate the governmental implications of using damages as a public law remedy because no sovereign exercised public authority for the world. Only with the individualization of international claims in the regulatory sphere does the intricate dynamic of state liability fully enter the picture.

FL Morrison, 'The Liability of Governments for Legislative Acts in the United States of America' (1998) 46 Am J Comp L Supp 531, 543–6; Hogg and Monahan (n 73 above) 122 and 149–54.

[83] eg *Garnett v Ferrand* (1827) 6 B & C 611, 108 ER 576, 581 (KB); *Fray v Blackburn* (1863) 3 B & S 576, 122 ER 217, 217 (QB). Street (n 75 above) 41–5 and 69–70; Ahmedouamar (n 68 above) 6–9; OLRC (n 73 above) 18–20.

[84] The state's liability in tort for administrative acts has been limited, eg, to cases arising from 'operational' decisions by the administration, to cases in which liability is warranted for policy reasons; to cases in which non-monetary remedies are unavailable, and to cases involving more than pure economic loss. eg *Anns v Merton* (1977) [1978] AC 728, 2 All ER 492 (HL); *Nielsen v Kamloops* [1984] 2 SCR 2, 10 DLR (4th) 641; *Brown v British Columbia (Minister of Transportation and Highways* [1994] 1 SCR 420, 112 DLR (4th) 1; *Swinamer v Nova Scotia (Attorney General)* [1994] 1 SCR 445, 112 DLR (4th) 18; *Dalehite v United States* (1953) 364 US 15; *Indian Towing Co v United States* (1955) 350 US 61. Harlow (1982) (n 73 above) 53; M Lunney and K Oliphant, *Tort Law* (Oxford: OUP, 2000) 501–3.

[85] Such as the requirement that the claimant show fault or malice on the part of the public body or official in order to receive damages; or, in the case of the public law tort of breach of statutory duty, that the statutory duty be intended to benefit a particular class of the public: Lunney and Oliphant (n 84 above) 501–3 and 527; Hogg and Monahan (n 73 above) 147–8 and 151; Morrison (n 82 above) 533, 537–8, and 541; RC Evans, 'Damages for Unlawful Administrative Action: The Remedy for Misfeasance in Public Office' (1982) 31 ICLQ 640; Harlow (1996) (n 73 above) 209; Fairgrieve (n 75 above) 697–8. Note that a 'public law' tort can only arise from the exercise of public authority.

[86] Harlow and Rawlings (n 71 above) 605–6.   [87] Hudson (n 5 above) 192–3.

[88] E Vattel, *Le Droit de gens*, book II, c VI, s 74–5 and c VIII, s 108–9 (an injury to a citizen is an injury to the state).   [89] Gray (n 26 above) 8–9 and 18–19; Brownlie (n 78 above) 17.

Despite this transformation, investment treaties typically do not provide for express limits on state liability in order to temper corrective justice and thus accommodate governmental discretion.[90] As a rule, a less compromising mode of liability that originates in the reciprocity of inter-state relations is frequently applied by arbitrators in the context of the regulatory relationship, and investors are able to obtain money compensation in circumstances where they could not under domestic law.[91] For example, the treaties usually adopt open-ended language to define the standards of review without attaching an express requirement for fault on the part of the state. Also, the international principle of reparation is applied, thus boxing state liability into a private law construction of compensation.[92] Perhaps most importantly, the principle of the unity of the state is used to trump limits on state liability for legislative and judicial acts.[93] In these circumstances, combined with the far-reaching character of individual claims, the door is opened to a very expansive conception of state liability.

The Far-reaching Nature of Claims

There are various ways to extend to individuals, and to qualify, the right to bring an international claim against the state. Under investment treaties, the particular form of individualization that is adopted is far-reaching because it is prospective and because it adopts damages as a remedy. But this does not exhaust the exceptional breadth and potency of the system as an international review mechanism. In two other respects, the treaties go beyond other international arrangements that allow individual claims. First, many treaties limit or remove the duty to exhaust local remedies, allowing investors to bring a claim before the host state's courts have had the opportunity to resolve the dispute.[94] Second, many treaties

---

[90] K Roach, 'The Limits of Corrective Justice and the Potential of Equity in Constitutional Remedies' (1991) 33 Ariz L Rev 859, 864–5.

[91] VL Been and JC Beauvais, 'The Global Fifth Amendment: NAFTA's Investment Protections and the Misguided Quest for an International "Regulatory Takings" Doctrine' (2003) 78 NYU L Rev 30, 59–86.

[92] The principle was established in *The Chorzow Factory (Germany v Poland)* (1928), PCIJ Ser A, No 17, 28, based on 'the rules of international law in force between the two States concerned, and not the law governing relations between the State which has committed the wrongful act and the individual who has suffered the damage'. Regarding the application of the principle in the adjudication of an investment dispute: eg *Amoco International Finance Corp v Iran* (1987), 15 Iran–US CTR 189, para 193; *Metalclad Corporation v United Mexican States* (Merits) (30 August 2000), 16 ICSID Rev 168, 40 ILM 36, 5 ICSID Rep 212, 13(1) World Trade and Arb Mat 45, para 122; *CME Czech Republic BV v Czech Republic* (Merits) (13 September 2001), 14(3) World Trade and Arb Mat 109 [cited as *CME* (Merits)], para 616–17.

[93] Eagleton (n 7 above) 63–9; Bean and Beauvais (n 91 above) 81–2.

[94] Under some investment treaties, investors must forgo domestic remedies in order to make a claim; under others, they must first exhaust them; under others, they may pursue treaty-based and/or domestic remedies: eg *Maffezini (Emilio Agustín) v Kingdom of Spain* (Jurisdiction) (25 January 2000), 16 ICSID Rev 212, 124 ILR 9, para 19; eg *CME* (Merits) (n 92 above) para 410; *CME Czech*

encourage forum-shopping by allowing claims by foreign corporations without imposing restrictions on shareholder nationality or minimum thresholds of foreign ownership and control.[95] These two aspects are discussed below.

The removal of the duty to exhaust local remedies

First is the straightforward but essential point that many investment treaties remove the customary rule that a foreign investor must exhaust local remedies before an international claim can be brought. The duty to exhaust local remedies is well established in the international adjudication of cases involving the alleged mistreatment of foreign nationals by a state.[96] And, outside of investment treaty arbitration, no treaty that allows individual claims discards this duty. Its removal under the present system is aimed at encouraging the confidence of investors, but it also leads to other, perhaps unanticipated, implications. First, domestic courts are no longer presumed to be capable of delivering justice (even though the customary rule itself never applied where the pursuit of local remedies was obviously futile).[97] Second, investors—unlike other foreign nationals—are no longer assumed to have a duty to take into account the domestic means to redress wrongs. Third, and most importantly, the host state's legal system is often denied an opportunity itself to correct any wrongs to a foreign investor. Thus states may be found liable for acts of officials without any review by the courts or other senior decision-makers.

This makes a rich environment for creative lawyering. Above all, investors are able to bring treaty claims in the midst of domestic litigation, in effect allowing more than one bite at the adjudicative apple, even where in some cases the investor specifically agreed in an investment contract to submit to domestic remedies. This latter possibility was considered by the tribunal in *SGS v Pakistan* in the context

---

Republic BV v Czech Republic (Damages) (14 March 2003), 15(4) World Trade and Arb Mat 83 and 245 [cited as *CME* (Damages)], para 398 and 412–13; *CMS Gas Transmission Company v Argentine Republic* (Jurisdiction) (17 July 2003), 42 ILM 788, 7 ICSID Rep 492 [cited as *CMS*], para 73; *SGS Société Générale de Surveillance v Pakistan* (Jurisdiction) (6 August 2003), 18 ICSID Rev 301, 42 ILM 1290, 8 ICSID Rep 406, 16(2) World Trade and Arb Mat 167, para 151. Foy (n 21 above) 66; UNCTAD, *Dispute Settlement: Investor–State*, UNCTAD Series on Issues in International Investment Agreements (New York: United Nations, 2003) 31–7; Been and Beauvais (n 91 above) 83–6.

[95] *Tokios Tokelės v Ukraine* (Jurisdiction) (29 April 2004), 20 ICSID Rev 205, 16(4) World Trade and Arb Mat 75 [cited as *Tokios*], para 36; *CMS* (n 94 above) para 47. See also eg *Waste Management Inc v United Mexican States* (Merits) (30 April 2004), 43 ILM 967, 16(4) World Trade and Arb Mat 3 [cited as *Waste Management No 2* (Merits)], para 80; *International Thunderbird Gaming Corporation v United Mexican States* (Merits) (26 January 2006), 18(2) World Trade and Arb Mat 59, para 101–10.

[96] Eagleton (n 7 above) 79, 96, and 100; EM Borchard, 'The Access of Individuals to International Courts' (1930) 24 AJIL 359, 362–3; Okowa (n 7 above) 493–4.

[97] *Norweigen Loans (France v Norway)*, [1957] ICJ Rep 9, 39. AV Freeman, *The International Responsibility of States for Denial of Justice* (London: Longman, 1938) 74; BA Wortley, *Expropriation in Public International Law* (Cambridge: CUP, 1959) 23–4 and 140–2.

of a BIT claim based on an 'umbrella' clause in the treaty that obliged the states parties to 'constantly guarantee the observance' of their 'commitments' to investments of foreign investors. The claimant in *SGS v Pakistan* argued that the umbrella clause allowed the claimant to bring a treaty claim arising from a contract with the respondent state which provided that disputes under the contract were to be resolved by domestic arbitration. However, the tribunal rejected this reading of the umbrella clause, in part because it would establish investment treaty arbitration as a regime parallel to domestic courts in matters of both public law and contract law. According to the tribunal, the investor's approach would incorporate into the treaty 'an unlimited number of State contracts, as well as other municipal law instruments' and that by implication 'an investor may, at will, nullify any freely negotiated dispute settlement clause in a State contract' and 'the benefits of the dispute settlement provisions of a contract with a State also a party to a BIT, would flow only to the investor'.[98] To avoid this outcome, the tribunal preferred an interpretation of the treaty that would 'enhance mutuality and balance of benefits in the inter-relation of different agreements located in differing legal orders'[99] by preventing investors from being able unilaterally to override the jurisdiction of domestic courts or the agreed dispute settlement provisions of existing investment contracts. Each of these potential problems arises as a consequence, perhaps not fully anticipated when the treaties were negotiated, of the system's unprecedented removal of the duty to exhaust local remedies.

In the face of BIT claims that parallel the available domestic remedies (including those previously agreed in a contract), respondent states have argued that an investor should not be able to bring a treaty claim where local remedies have not been exhausted or where the claimant or a domestic company owned by the claimant is already pursuing such remedies. Unlike in *SGS v Pakistan*, most tribunals have rejected these arguments and read the relevant treaty to allow parallel claims.[100] They have done so in essentially two ways. First, they have distinguished the cause of action under the treaty from that of domestic law, even where

---

[98] *SGS v Pakistan* (n 94 above) para 168.   [99] *SGS v Pakistan* (n 94 above) para 168.
[100] eg *Lanco International Inc v Argentine Republic* (Jurisdiction) (8 December 1998), 40 ILM 457, para 19; *Genin (Alex) and Others v Republic of Estonia* (Merits) (25 June 2001), 17 ICSID Rev 395, 6 ICSID Rep 304, para 330–2; *Middle East Cement Shipping and Handling Co v Arab Republic of Egypt* (Merits) (12 April 2002), 18 ICSID Rev 602, 7 ICSID Rep 173, para 71; *CMS* (n 94 above) para 78 and 80; *Azurix Corp v Argentine Republic* (Jurisdiction) (8 December 2003), 43 ILM 262, 16(2) World Trade and Arb Mat 111 [cited as *Azurix*], para 99–100; *Champion Trading Company v Arab Republic of Egypt* (Jurisdiction) (21 October 2003), 19 ICSID Rev 275; *PSEG Global Inc v Republic of Turkey* (Jurisdiction) (4 June 2004), 44 ILM 465, para 158; *Occidental Exploration and Production Company v Republic of Ecuador* (Merits) (1 July 2004), 17(1) World Trade and Arb Mat 165, para 52 and 58; *Enron* (n 15 above) para 47–51; *Siemens* (n 17 above) para 151 and 160; *Petrobart Ltd v Kyrgyz Republic* (Merits) (29 March 2005), SCC Rules, SCC Arbitration Institute Case No 126/2003, 65–6; *Sempra Energy International v Argentine Republic* (Jurisdiction) (11 May 2005), ICSID Case No ARB/02/16 [cited as *Sempra*], para 42, online: ICSID, ITA, Investment Claims. C Söderlund, '*Lis Pendens, Res Judicata* and the Issue of Parallel Judicial Proceedings' (2005) 22 J Int'l Arb 301.

the claims in question arise from the same dispute and the relevant parties are the same. Second, the tribunals have differentiated treaty claims brought by the foreign owners of a domestic company from the pursuit of local or contractual remedies by the domestic company itself, thus refusing to 'pierce the corporate veil'. Such reasoning may be defensible as a form of interpretive gap-filling where the relevant treaty language is silent or ambiguous (as is usually the case) on the issue of parallel claims. But it also permits uncertain outcomes that are intolerable from a governmental perspective where it evolves treaty arbitration into a separate adjudicative system that duplicates the remedial function of domestic courts. A prudential approach, also perfectly defensible in the absence of clear treaty language to the contrary,[101] is to preclude access by investors to treaty arbitration where local remedies have not been resorted to, or not yet exhausted, by the claimant or by a domestic company that the claimant controls.[102]

Let us revisit the apprehension expressed by the International Court of Justice concerning the possible multiplication of claims in cases of diplomatic protection involving foreign investment. In *Barcelona Traction*, the ICJ declined to allow Belgium, the home state of foreign shareholders of a Canadian company, to bring a claim of diplomatic protection against Spain for the alleged expropriation of the company's assets in Spain. One of the main rationales for this ruling was the need to avoid a proliferation of international claims in light of fragmented international ownership of investments in the world economy.[103] The underlying concern was that, if parallel international claims could be brought on behalf of any foreign shareholder of an investment, then investment disputes could generate numerous claims by different states, and multinational enterprises would have an incentive to structure their investments so as to entangle as many powerful states as possible in a potential dispute.[104]

---

[101] eg *ELSI* (n 10 above) para 59, where a less strict approach to the comparison of local to treaty remedies was adopted by the ICJ in its determination of whether local remedies had been exhausted: '. . . the local remedies rule does not, indeed cannot, require that a claim be presented to the municipal courts in a form, and with arguments, suited to an international tribunal, applying different law to different parties: for an international claim to be admissible, it is sufficient if the essence of the claim has been brought before the competent tribunals and pursued as far as permitted by local law and procedures, and without success.' Based on this reasoning, the resort to remedies under an investment treaty (the text of which was ambiguous on the matter) could also be precluded—but for a denial of justice—where 'the essence of the claim' was already under consideration by a domestic court or tribunal, due to the investor's prior resort to domestic remedies.

[102] *Sedelmayer (Franz) v Russian Federation* (Merits) (7 July 1998), SCC Rules [cited as *Sedelmayer*], p 2–3 (dissenting opinion), online: ITA, Investment Claims; *Lauder (Ronald S) v Czech Republic* (Final Award) (3 September 2001), (2002) 4 World Trade and Arb Materials 35, para 287; *Joy Mining Machinery Ltd v Arab Republic of Egypt* (Jurisdiction) (6 August 2004), 19 ICSID Rev 486, 44 ILM 73, para 78–9; *Encana Corporation v Republic of Ecuador* (Merits) (3 February 2006), London Court of International Arbitration Administered Case No UN 3481 [cited as *Encana*], para 186–7 and 194; *Canfor Corporation v United States of America* (Jurisdiction) (6 June 2006), UNCITRAL Rules, para 242–3, online: State Department, ITA, NAFTA Claims.

[103] *Barcelona Traction* (n 4 above) para 96.

[104] *Administrative Decision No V* (n 6 above) 613–14. W Barnes, 'Remarks' (1907) Am Soc'ty Int'l L Proc 100, 142; Ohly (n 16 above) 283–4; Okowa (n 7 above) 484. For example, a well-known risk

Fast forward to the NAFTA arbitration in *GAMI*, involving a claim by American minority shareholders of a Mexican company that owned assets in that country's sugar industry.[105] The shareholders brought a NAFTA claim against Mexico for the alleged expropriation of their 'investment'—the Mexican company—while the Mexican company itself pursued a concurrent action for relief in Mexican courts. Both Mexico and the US submitted that, in such circumstances, the claim by the minority shareholders could be advanced under NAFTA 'only for injuries to their interests and not for injuries to the [domestic] corporation'. An understandable rationale for this, one may assume, was to avoid parallel claims arising from the same dispute as defined by the triggering act of the state. But this concern did not sway the *GAMI* tribunal, which concluded that it had jurisdiction over all of the shareholder's treaty claims, including those deriving from alleged injuries to the domestic company.[106] In adopting this approach, the tribunal opted not to temper the force of its disciplinary authority and, more broadly, it extended the reach of the system beyond what was envisaged by the governments of the affected states parties in their submissions to the tribunal, as well as beyond the prudential boundaries that were delimited by the ICJ in *Barcelona Traction*.

The facilitation of forum-shopping

A second aspect of far-reaching individualization is the way in which the system invites forum-shopping by investors.[107] To bring a claim under an investment

---

management strategy of multinational enterprises is to internationalize the economic stake in a business venture, and thus engage the nationals and governments of as many states as possible, in order to have more leverage in the event of a dispute with the host state. This can be illustrated by the case of Kennecott and the nationalization of the Chilean copper industry (Peter (n 2 above) 241–3). In the 1960s Kennecott agreed to sell 51% of its interest in the copper industry to the Chilean government and committed to the terms of a new joint venture based on a 10-year management contract. Kennecott insured, with US AID, the (US)$80 million that Kennecott had committed to the joint venture. Fresh capital was supplied by an Eximbank loan and by the Chilean Copper Corporation. Kennecott also raised funds by concluding long-term contracts for future production with European and Japanese firms, and sold the collection rights on these contracts. Peter, at 242, quotes a Kennecott executive: 'The aim of these arrangements is to ensure that nobody expropriates Kennecott without upsetting relations to customers, creditors and governments in three continents'. This strategy proved successful when, in the early 1970s, Chilean President Allende proposed to expropriate Kennecott's interest, with payment of partial compensation, due to windfall profits. In response, the assets of the Chilean national airline and Copper Corporation were seized in the US based on guarantees given by the Chilean state, and European and Asian creditors pressured the Paris Club of creditors to use the renegotiation of Chile's external debt as leverage to secure compensation for Kennecott.

[105] *GAMI* (n 23 above).
[106] *GAMI* (n 23 above) para 29 and 37–43. See also *CMS* (n 94 above) para 48; *Champion Trading Company v Arab Republic of Egypt* (Jurisdiction) (21 October 2003), 19 ICSID Rev 275, para 3.4.3; *Sempra* (n 100 above) para 77; *Bogdanov (Iurii) et al v Moldova* (Merits) (22 September 2005), SCC Rules, 18–19, online: ITA, Investment Claims. Contrast *Continental Casualty Company v Argentine Republic* (Jurisdiction) (22 February 2006), ICSID Case No ARB/03/9, para 77–9 and 86–90, online: ITA.
[107] With respect to forum-shopping, the underlying strategy of multinational firms—in adopting the nationality that is most convenient for a particular transaction, tax assessment, or legal claim—is

treaty, an investor must quality as a 'foreign' investor. In other words, the claimant must establish that it is a national of a state party to the treaty other than the host state, whether as a natural or legal person.[108] In the case of a natural person, the claimant must demonstrate that he or she is a national of another state party based on the laws of citizenship of that other state;[109] however, a legal person need satisfy only the relevant laws of incorporation or business establishment.[110] Thus the question of whether an investor is foreign is determined by the rules of nationality of the investor's home state, not those of the host state, and it is within the power of the home state to allow forum-shopping by investors by adopting liberal rules of incorporation.[111] By establishing a holding company in one state party to an investment treaty, multinational firms, though they lack a substantial business connection to that state, may acquire its nationality and obtain protection under the treaty for their assets in the other state party.

As such, investment treaties often allow claims by foreign investors regardless of whether the investor's ownership rights extend through a series of companies in

---

to exploit variations among regulatory regimes in different jurisdictions. S Timberg, 'International Combines and National Sovereigns' (1947) 95 U Penn L Rev 575, 588; S Picciotto, *International Business Taxation* (London: Weidenfeld & Nicolson, 1992) 94–6; Peter (n 2 above) 37–8; WW Bratton *et al*, 'Introduction: Regulatory Competition and Institutional Evolution' in WW Bratton *et al* (eds) *International Regulatory Competition and Coordination* (Oxford: Clarendon, 1996) 9, 21, and 40–1; R Palan, 'Trying to Have Your Cake and Eating It: How and Why the State System Has Created Offshore' (1998) 42 Int'l Studies Q 625, 630. This is the flip side of inter-state competition to attract investment: forum-shopping by international capital: UNCTAD, *Taxation*, UNCTAD Series on Issues in International Investment Agreements (New York: United Nations, 2000) 62; Fatouros (n 70 above) 362.

[108] *Nottebohm* (n 4 above) 24; *Barcelona Traction* (n 4 above) para 70. R Donner, *The Regulation of Nationality in International Law* (2nd edn, Ardsley, NY: Transnational Publishers, 1994) 19 and 34–42.

[109] eg NAFTA (n 39 above) art 1117 and 1138. *Feldman* (n 38 above) para 24–38. *Olguín (Eudoro Armando) v Republic of Paraguay* (Merits) (26 July 2001), 18 ICSID Rev 143, 6 ICSID Rep 164, para 61–2; *Soufraki (Hussein Nuaman) v United Arab Emirates* (Jurisdiction) (7 July 2004), 17(1) World Trade and Arb Mat 129 [cited as *Soufraki*], para 55. UNCTAD, *Scope and Definition*, UNCTAD Series on Issues in International Investment Agreements (New York: United Nations, 1999) 35.

[110] *Soufraki* (n 109 above) para 83. R Dolzer and M Stevens, *Bilateral Investment Treaties* (The Hague: Martinus Nijhoff, 1995) 33–6 (noting that, for companies and other legal entities, BITs rely on three basic criteria to determine nationality: the place of incorporation (eg US); the location of the seat or actual management of the company (eg Germany); and the nationality of controlling shareholders); Muchlinski (n 6 above) 622–4.

[111] *Waste Management No 2* (Merits) (n 95 above) para 80; *CME* (Merits) (n 92 above) para 419. RR Wilson, 'Postwar Commercial Treaties of the United States' (1949) 43 AJIL 262, 265–6; H Walker, 'Treaties for the Encouragement and Protection of Foreign Investment: Present United States Practice' (1956) 5 Am J Comp L 229, 233. Note that some investment treaties, including NAFTA and the Energy Charter Treaty, allow a state party—subject to prior notification and consultation—to deny the benefits of the treaty to a foreign investor of another state party, or their investments, that is a company which is owned or controlled by investors of a non-state party and which has no substantial business activities in the state in which it is established: NAFTA (n 39 above) art 1113(2); Energy Charter Treaty (annex I of the Final Act of the European Energy Charter Conference) (Lisbon, 17 December 1994; 34 ILM 373), art 17(1).

other jurisdictions.¹¹² A claim can be made at any point in the chain of international ownership, so long as the actual claimant has the nationality of another state party and, under some treaties, so long as the claimant has a minimum amount of ownership or control of the investment.¹¹³ This gives multinational firms the flexibility to choose the point in their corporate structure from which to launch a claim. Indeed, firms have an incentive to design their corporate structure in order to maximize their options to bring claims, given the degree to which different treaties open the door to parallel claims and to state liability.¹¹⁴ This does not mean that firms will necessarily adapt their corporate structures in this way. Other factors, particularly tax considerations, may take precedence over the ability to access investment treaty arbitration. Even so, variations among treaties have become a relevant factor for firms to consider and it is reasonable to anticipate that strategic forum-shopping will increasingly factor into actual claims.

By implication, it should be assumed that an investor of a state party to an investment treaty may be ultimately owned by an investor of a non-state party,¹¹⁵ or by an investor of the host state itself.¹¹⁶ In the *CME* arbitration, as discussed in Chapter 1 of this book, the US national Ralph Lauder used a Dutch holding company to launch parallel claims against the Czech Republic under two separate treaties in the same dispute, and was able to collect a substantial award, even though only one of the claims was successful.¹¹⁷ In *Tokios* a majority of the tribunal (remarkably, with the presiding arbitrator dissenting) allowed a claim against the Ukraine by a Lithuanian company that was 99 per cent owned by Ukrainians, who were thus able to leverage their ownership of a foreign firm into a claim against their own state, in effect opening the system to claims by domestic investors who shift capital to a foreign platform and then re-invest it in the home country.¹¹⁸

---

¹¹² Dolzer and Stevens (n 110 above) 35–6.
¹¹³ eg *GAMI* (n 23 above) para 29–30 and 38; *Waste Management No 2* (Merits) (n 95 above) para 85. eg *Sedelmayer* (n 102 above) para 57–9; *Compañía de Aguas del Aconquija SA & Vivendi Universal v Argentine Republic* (Annulment) (3 July 2002), 41 ILM 1135, 125 ILR, 58, 6 ICSID Rep 340 [cited as *Vivendi*], para 50; *Azurix* (n 100 above) para 21 and 42; *CMS* (n 94 above) para 47 and 55; *Siemens* (n 17 above) para 137; *Sempra* (n 100 above) para 42; *Encana* (n 102 above) para 117–18.
¹¹⁴ M-F Houde and K Yannaca-Small, 'Relationships between International Investment Agreements' (OECD Working Paper on International Investment No 2004/1, May 2004) 4; Harlow (n 43 above) 46.   ¹¹⁵ *Fireman's Fund* (n 17 above) para 5; *Mondev* (n 38 above) para 79.
¹¹⁶ *Wena Hotels Ltd v Egypt* (Jurisdiction) (25 May 1999), 41 ILM 881, 888; *Tokios* (n 95 above) para 21 and 38. But see *Vacuum Salt Products, Ltd v Republic of Ghana* (Jurisdiction) (16 February 1994), 9 ICSID Rev 72, 20 Ybk Comm'l Arb 11, para 17–20 and 29–30 (concluding in relation to an investment in Ghana that a company owned 20% by Greeks and the remainder by Ghanaians was not foreign controlled for the purposes of ICSID jurisdiction).
¹¹⁷ *CME* (Merits) (n 92 above) para 396; *CME* (Damages) (n 94 above) para 432–3 (concluding that the claimant could make claims under two investment treaties, in relation to the same underlying dispute, by channelling ownership of its investment through a holding company in the Netherlands). UNCTAD, *Most-Favoured-Nation Treatment*, UNCTAD Series on Issues in International Investment Agreements (New York: United Nations, 1999) 11.
¹¹⁸ *Tokios* (n 95 above) para 21, 38, and 80 (allowing an ICSID claim against the Ukraine by a Lithuanian company that was 99% owned by Ukrainian nationals who also comprised two-thirds of the company's management).

Most recently, in *Aguas del Tunari*, the tribunal allowed a claim by the US firm Bechtel, which, after it became apparent that there was serious public opposition to its privatized water utility in Bolivia, cleverly 'migrated' the business from the Cayman Islands to the Netherlands—again, by shifting its legal ownership to a newly created Dutch company—thus enabling it to bring a claim under the Netherlands–Bolivia BIT.[119] In each of these cases flexible rules of nationality in the treaties combined with a liberal approach by the tribunal to its jurisdiction led to a significant expansion of the system and of the supervisory remit of arbitrators.

As capital moves beyond the domestic sphere, so too does the regulatory relationship between investors and state. As foreign ownership expands and fragments, so too does the likelihood that governmental authority will trigger international claims. The ownership of assets in one country will frequently be split among investors of other countries, often leaving host states unaware of whether, and to what extent, a particular business is protected by an investment treaty.[120] Given that it is sometimes impossible for states to track foreign ownership, governments are left to assume that any economic activity in their territory involving substantial capital could lead to an international claim. The foreignness of an investor is neither identifiable nor stable where firms can legally manœuvre to alter and expand their nationalities.

In light of this, it should be emphasized that investment treaties often protect much more than *actual* flows of capital between the states parties to the treaty, since actual flows may not correspond to the legal arrangements for the ownership of assets.[121] Despite the bilateral framework of most treaties, in the stark words of the *Tokios* tribunal: 'The origin of the capital is not relevant to the existence of an investment'.[122] Investors can become foreign by a paper transfer of assets among companies without any commitment of new money to the host economy.[123] This was so in *Aguas del Tunari*, mentioned above, but also in the *Fedax* arbitration, where the tribunal allowed a Dutch company to make a BIT claim against Venezuela in a dispute concerning promissory notes issued by the Venezuelan

---

[119] *Aguas del Tunari SA v Republic of Bolivia* (Jurisdiction) (21 October 2005), 18(2) World Trade and Arb Mat 271, para 69, 73, and 237, and para 4 and 10 (dissenting opinion). See also *Vivendi* (n 113 above) para 50.
[120] *Waste Management No 2* (Merits) (n 95 above) 78–9 (dismissing Mexico's submission that local government entities in Mexico were unaware of the claimant's corporate structure, including the use of holding companies in the Cayman Islands, and that the claimant therefore failed to satisfy the NAFTA definition of 'investor'). C McLachlan, 'Commentary: The Broader Context' (2002) 18 Arb Int'l 339, 341; UNCTAD (n 109 above) 37.
[121] Peter (n 2 above) 17; UNCTAD, *World Investment Report 2004* (Geneva: United Nations, 2004) 238, fn 15; G Xiao, 'People's Republic of China's Round-Tripping FDI: Scale, Causes and Implications' (Asian Development Bank Institute Discussion Paper No 6, 2004) 2.
[122] *Tokios* (n 95 above) para 80.
[123] eg *Tradex Hellas SA v Republic of Albania* (Merits) (29 April 1999), 14 ICSID Rev 161, 5 ICSID Rep 47, para 109; *Ceskoslovenska Obchodni Banka v Slovak Republic* (Jurisdiction) (24 May 1999), 14 ICSID Rev 251, 17(3) World Trade and Arb Mat 189, para 78; *Tokios* (n 95 above) para 80–2.

government.[124] Prior to the claim the promissory notes had been transferred to the Dutch company by a Venezuelan firm; however, Venezuela's argument that the investor had not made an actual investment in the country's economy was rejected.[125] With such possibilities for forum-shopping, as well as for parallel claims, existing networks of investment treaties establish an exceptionally far-reaching mechanism of international review that engages a very broad conception of the regulatory relationship between states and international business.

International Enforceability

In an investment dispute, negotiations between a foreign investor and a state—whether before or after a claim has been filed—are informed by each party's assessment of the pressures that can be brought to bear on states to encourage compliance. As well, the force of an arbitration award ultimately rests on the prospects for its enforcement. Without a realistic hope for enforcement, claimants would rely on the goodwill of the host state to pay up, and arbitration under such conditions would have more in common with mediation or conciliation than compulsory adjudication.[126] Today, the use of force to enforce international law without authorization by the UN Security Council is legally prohibited, and in most cases practically unfeasible, thus foreclosing a significant means of enforcement in earlier eras. Nevertheless, investment treaties provide a powerful and exceptional alternative, one that taps into the collective authority of domestic courts to seize assets within the territory of their state.

Conventionally, it is very difficult for individuals to enforce public law awards and decisions in courts other than those of the state in which the dispute arose. Under international custom, courts may decline to rule on the sovereign acts of foreign states, whether for reasons of sovereign immunity, act of state, or non-justiciability.[127] The government of the investor's home might even object to its courts ruling on a foreign dispute in order to preserve its executive discretion to

---

[124] *Fedax NV v Republic of Venezuela* (Jurisdiction) (11 July 1997), 37 ILM 1378, 5 ICSID Rep 186 [cited as *Fedax*].

[125] *Fedax* (n 124 above) para 18 and 24–5. See also *Saluka Investments BV v Czech Republic* (Merits) (17 March 2006), 18(3) World Trade and Arb Mat 166, para 1, 209–11, 226, and 240–2.

[126] M Habicht, *Post-War Treaties for the Pacific Settlement of International Disputes* (Cambridge: Harvard University Press, 1931) 1035.

[127] eg *Blad v Bamfield* (1674) 3 Swan 604, 36 ER 992; *Duke of Brunswick v King of Hannover* (1844) [1848] 6 Beav 1, 2 HLC 1; *Oetjen v Central Leather Co* (1918) 246 US 297, 303–4. EF Mooney, *Foreign Seizures—Sabbatino and the Act of State Doctrine* (University of Kentucky Press, 1967) 7–9 and 22; AFM Maniruzzaman, 'Internationalization of Foreign Investment Agreements—Some Fundamental Issues of International Law' (2000) 1 J World Investment 293, 315; E Denza, 'The Relationship Between International and National Law' in MD Evans (ed) *International Law* (2nd edn, Oxford: OUP, 2006) 442–4. See generally, FA Mann, 'The International Enforcement of Public Rights' (1987) 19 NYU J Int'l L & P 603, 604.

manage foreign affairs.[128] Under investment treaties, however, the host state's general consent entails a broad waiver of its immunity from suit, not only before an international tribunal but also before a domestic court called upon to enforce an award.[129] In addition, investment treaties authorize the enforcement of awards by investors under the ICSID Convention or the New York Convention.[130] As a result, investors can seek enforcement of an award against assets of the respondent state in any state that is a party to these treaties.

Let us backtrack a little to review more closely the different ways in which awards can be enforced under investment treaties. First, if a state refuses to abide by an award, it may be subject to diplomatic and economic pressure from the home state, from other capital-exporting states, from international financial institutions, and from the international capital market. Second, investment treaties often obligate states in express terms to recognize and enforce an award issued under the treaty, which allows an investor to seek enforcement in the courts of any state party to the treaty itself.[131] Third, where an investment treaty provides for enforcement under the ICSID Convention, the Panama Convention, or the New York Convention,[132] an investor can seek enforcement in the domestic courts of any state party to these arbitration treaties. This last method of enforcement is exceptionally powerful because most states have ratified at least one of these treaties: for example, approximately 165 states are party to either the New York Convention or the ICSID Convention.

To illustrate, the investment chapter of NAFTA incorporates the enforcement structure of both the ICSID Convention and the New York Convention. The question of which treaty applies to a NAFTA award depends on the rules under which an investor files its claim. Investors may file a NAFTA claim under the

---

[128] *Banco Nacional de Cuba v Sabbatino* (1964) 376 US 398, 3 ILM 381, 398.

[129] eg under NAFTA Chapter 11, the investor's duty to exhaust local remedies is limited and arguably removed: *Waste Management, Inc v United Mexican States* (Jurisdiction) (26 June 2002), 41 ILM 1315, 6 ICSID Rep 549, 14(6) World Trade and Arb Mat 203, para 29–30; *Waste Management No 2* (Merits) (n 95 above) para 116; *Mondev* (n 38 above) para 154; *Feldman* (n 38 above) para 71–4. See also *Azinian (Robert) et al v United Mexican States* (Merits) (1 November 1999), 14 ICSID Rev 538, 39 ILM 537, para 97–9; *Loewen Group, Inc and Raymond L Loewen v United States of America* (Merits) (26 June 2003), 42 ILM 811, 7 ICSID Rep 442, 15(5) World Trade and Arb Mat 97, para 142–57; *GAMI* (n 23 above) para 29–30, 38, 101–3, and 133. GR Delaume, 'Sovereign Immunity and Transnational Arbitration' (1987) 3 Arb Int'l 28, 29–31; WS Dodge, 'National Courts and International Arbitration: Exhaustion of Remedies and Res Judicata Under Chapter Eleven of NAFTA' (2000) 23 Hast Int'l & Comp L Rev 357, 383; Foy (n 19 above) 49; PI Hansen, 'Judicialization and Globalization in the North American Free Trade Agreement' (2003) 38 Tex Int'l LJ 489, 498–9.

[130] eg NAFTA (n 39 above) art 1130 (providing that a Chapter 11 arbitration must be held in the territory of a NAFTA state that is a party to the New York Convention unless the disputing parties agree otherwise). ER Leahy, 'Enforcement of Arbitral Awards Issued by the Additional Facility of the International Centre of Settlement of Investment Disputes (ICSID)' (1985) 2(3) J Int'l Arb 15, 15–16; UNCTAD (n 94 above) 62–4.

[131] eg NAFTA (n 39 above) art 1136(2) and (4) (requiring each state party to 'abide by and comply with an award without delay' and to 'provide for the enforcement of an award in its territory').

[132] n 133 and 135 below.

ICSID Rules, the ICSID Additional Facility Rules, or the UNCITRAL Rules. If an investor selects the ICSID Rules, the arbitration proceeds under the ICSID Convention, which provides that an award has the force of a final court judgment of a state party under its domestic law and that the award cannot be reviewed by domestic courts.[133] An ICSID award is thus enforceable, independent of the New York Convention (although it is still possible that a court might decline to execute an award against state assets for reasons of sovereign immunity).[134] Alternatively, if the investor selects the ICSID Additional Facility Rules or the UNCITRAL Rules, NAFTA arbitration proceeds under the New York Convention, which provides that an award shall be recognized as binding and that domestic courts may review the award only on limited grounds.[135] Based on this structure, investment treaty awards are more widely enforceable than the rulings of any court or tribunal, international or domestic, that has the authority to resolve individual claims in regulatory disputes. For instance, the few human rights treaties that allow an international court or tribunal to hear individual claims do not authorize enforcement by domestic courts,[136] whereas judgments of the International Court of Justice are enforceable only by the UN Security Council.[137] In contrast, awards issued by investment treaty tribunals are enforceable in the courts of as many as 165 countries, which gives them a coercive force that is unrivalled in public law adjudication.

Conclusion

The customary position of individuals in international law is subordinated to decision-making by states and to inter-state dispute resolution, but this does not

---

[133] Convention on the Settlement of Investment Disputes Between States and Nationals of Other States (the ICSID Convention) (Washington, 18 March 1965; 4 ILM 524; entered into force 14 October 1966), art 54 (providing that 'Contracting States will recognise an award as if it was a final judgment of a court in that State') and 53(1) (providing that 'The award shall be binding on the parties and shall not be subject to any appeal or to any other remedy except those provided for in this Convention. Each party shall abide by and comply with the terms of the award ... '). See also *Rules Governing the Additional Facility for the Administration of Proceedings by the Secretariat of the International Centre for Settlement of Investment Disputes*, 27 September 1978, revised 1 January 2003, 1 ICSID Rep 213 [cited as ICSID Additional Facility Rules], art 53(4).

[134] Note that the enforcement of an award under the ICSID Convention is possible only where both the host state and the investor's home state are parties to that treaty. Thus, enforcement under the ICSID Convention is presently unavailable in the case of NAFTA arbitrations because neither Canada nor Mexico is party to the ICSID Convention.

[135] United Nations Convention on the Recognition and Enforcement of Foreign Arbitral Awards (the New York Convention) (New York, 10 June 1958; 330 UNTS 3; entered into force 7 June 1959), art I, III, and V. Finally, the award may also be enforced under the Inter-American Convention on International Commercial Arbitration (the Panama Convention) (Panama, 30 January 1975; 14 ILM 336), which contains provisions that are similar to those under the New York Convention: art 1, 4, and 5. [136] See n 55 above. Hudson (n 5 above) 128–9.

[137] Thus to impose enforcement of an ICJ decision, the successful state would need the support of 9 Security Council members including the 5 permanent members. Charter of the United Nations

mean that individual rights and interests do not exist on the international plane. What it means is that such rights and interests are rarely directly actionable and enforceable.[138] Based on Vattel's principle and, above all, the duty to exhaust local remedies, regulatory disputes between state and individual are filtered by the legal system of the host state so as to insulate international adjudication from many of the regulatory considerations that domestic law confronts. Where investors can bring international claims, arising from regulatory disputes, the dynamic of the adjudication changes dramatically.

This engagement with regulatory concerns is more pronounced in the case of investment treaty arbitration than in any other form of international adjudication. Virtually all investment treaties are broad in scope and apply liberal standards of review; many also invite forum-shopping while limiting the duty of investors to exhaust local remedies. As a system, the treaties greatly expand state liability in public law by extending it to legislative and judicial acts, and by allowing damages to be awarded in the absence of fault.[139] These elements take the system beyond other mechanisms of international review, with the possible exception of the European Union, that allow individual claims.

Giving investors more control over whether and how their rights and interests are protected under international law is not necessarily a bad thing. Encouraging international investment indeed justifies the removal of certain sensitive disputes from domestic legal systems as part of a wider movement towards international institutions. But the contribution of investment treaties to this movement is highly problematic. By opening the door to parallel claims and forum-shopping under so many treaties, states have moved too far and too selectively in favour of international business. It seems they have executed a transformation of international adjudication without adequate consideration of the consequences. As argued above, the transformation has been major in its scope and depth; what makes it revolutionary is that private arbitrators are given the power to resolve regulatory disputes. In the next chapter, the discussion examines the approaches thus far adopted by arbitrators in wielding this power.

(26 June 1945; UKTS No 67 (1946) (not published in the UNTS); entered into force 24 October 1945), art 94(2); DJ Harris, *Cases and Materials on International Law* (6th edn, London: Sweet & Maxwell, 2004) 1027–8; MN Shaw, *International Law* (5th edn, Cambridge: CUP, 2003) 996–7; JE Alvarez, 'The New Dispute Settlers: (Half) Truths and Consequences' (2003) 38 Texas Int'l LJ 405, 416 (remarking that ICJ cases do not always secure compliance and that the ICJ relies 'by conscious design on the most political of bodies, the Security Council, for [its] effectiveness').

[138] eg *Jurisdiction of the Courts of Danzig* (Advisory Opinion) (1928), PCIJ Ser B, No 15, 17–18; *LaGrand* (Merits) (*Germany v United States*), [2001] ICJ Rep 466, 40 ILM 1069, para 77; *Construction of a Wall* (n 64 above) para 147 and 152.

[139] Harlow (1996) (n 73 above) 205–6 and 208; Hogg and Monahan (n 73 above) 122 and 149–54.

6
Approaches and Interpretations

I have argued that the authority of arbitrators under investment treaties is wide ranging and that it goes to the heart of public law. How have arbitrators wielded this power? Four broad approaches emerge from the jurisprudence to date. Two of them emphasize a reciprocal legal framework in their conceptualization of investment treaty arbitration: the first by treating it as a form of commercial arbitration; the second as public international law. In contrast, the third and fourth approaches to the subject recognize the regulatory character of the underlying relationship between investors and state. The first does so by comparing investor protection to the protection of human rights; the second by applying a more prudential public law framework which moderates state liability in order to preserve governmental discretion. Each of these approaches is examined below, informed by the view that the appropriate approach is to accept the regulatory context for investment disputes, and thus the relevance of public law, within the boundaries set by the inter-state bargain of an investment treaty.

Any attempt to categorize adjudicative reasoning risks oversimplification. However, it is also useful to point out 'ideal type' models that inform adjudicative decisions and thus to identify the modes of execution of an adjudicative system.[1] In many cases, the choice of approaches and the analogies that an arbitrator employs will resolve questions left open by ambiguity in a treaty text, and thus affect the result in the case and the delineation of the meaning of the treaty in quite important ways. Of course, in many cases it is not possible credibly to label a set of reasons as representing one single approach; indeed, most investment treaty awards reflect more than one of the approaches I outline here. If there is a general tendency, however, it is for arbitrators either to apply the template of reciprocal adjudication, borrowed from commercial arbitration, or to read the object and purpose of investment treaties in ways that emphasize the interests of investors over competing governmental priorities. This general tendency, it is argued, is consistent with the broader critique that the system is open to a perception of bias because it deploys arbitrators to resolve regulatory disputes. That is, when arbitrators read ambiguous treaty language so as to expand their discretion and the reach of state liability, they may objectively be seen to promote treaty arbitration as an alternative to the courts and thus further the commercial aims of a private industry.

[1] M Loughlin, *Public Law and Political Theory* (Oxford: OUP, 1992) 59–61.

The Discretion of Arbitrators

Adjudication is not simply a process of rational interpretation to sensibly and consistently apply rules that govern conduct in specific cases.[2] Rather, it involves policy—and political—choices, especially in the adjudication of public law. Even so, different adjudicative processes vary in the degree to which they afford discretion to the adjudicator and delineate the subject-matter to which they apply, according to the degree of specificity of the legal language that is used to define key rules and standards.[3] Under investment treaties, it is clear that the scope and substance of the adjudicative role is expressed at a high level of generality and that this allocates considerable discretion to arbitrators.[4] As where courts interpret broadly framed public law standards that constrain government, such as in the case of human rights norms, this gives arbitrators a significant part in determining the appropriate role of government in relation to business.[5] Thus, although they are by no means alone in the world of adjudication in this regard,[6] it is none the less the case that arbitrators sometimes make choices of profound regulatory importance.

For example, what do states mean when they agree to 'encourage' and 'protect' investors or investment?[7] Did the state treat an investor 'fairly'? Was a reduction in the value of the investor's assets caused by 'legitimate' regulation? Does the investment deliver benefits to the host economy? Is the purpose of damages to deter unlawful conduct or compensate investors? What degree of fault should be attached to state liability? Is the claim a matter of business risk or governmental

---

[2] G Ganz, 'Allocation of Decision-Making Functions' (1972) Pub L 215, 215–16; LL Fuller, 'The Forms and Limits of Adjudication' (1978) 92 Harv L Rev 353, 373; JP Trachtman, 'The Domain of WTO Dispute Resolution' (1999) 40 Harv Int'l LJ 333, 336–7.

[3] D Kennedy, 'Form and Substance in Private Law Adjudication' (1976) 89 Harv L Rev 1685, 1687–9; Trachtman (n 2 above) 337–8.

[4] eg *Feldman Karpa (Marvin Roy) v United Mexican States* (Merits) (16 December 2002), 18 ICSID Rev 488, 42 ILM 625, 7 ICSID Rep 341, 15(3) World Trade and Arb Mat 157 [cited as *Feldman*], para 98. See also eg *SGS Société Générale de Surveillance v Pakistan* (Jurisdiction) (6 August 2003), 18 ICSID Rev 301, 42 ILM 1290, 8 ICSID Rep 406, 16(2) World Trade and Arb Mat 167 [cited as *SGS v Pakistan*], para 150.

[5] FI Michelman, 'Property, Utility, and Fairness: Comments on the Ethical Foundations of "Just Compensation" Law' (1967) 80 Harv L Rev 1165, 1168–71; E Schwartz and J Paulsson, 'Confronting Political and Regulatory Risks Associated with Private Investment in Infrastructure in Developing Countries' (Draft presentation to the Private Infrastructure for Development conference, Rome, 8–10 September 1999) 3; M Sornarajah, *The Settlement of Foreign Investment Disputes* (Boston: Kluwer, 2001) 16.

[6] AV Dicey, *An Introduction to the Study of the Law of the Constitution* [1885] (8th edn, London: Macmillan, 1915) 100–4; A Chayes, 'The Role of the Judge in Public Law Litigation' (1976) 89 Harv L Rev 1281, 1304; PN Bhagwati, 'Judicial Activism and Public Interest Litigation' (1985) 23 Colum J Transnat'l L 561, 562–3; JAG Griffith, 'The Brave New World of Sir John Laws' (2000) 63 Mod L Rev 159, 160 and 163; M Shapiro, 'Administrative Law Unbounded: Reflections on Government and Governance' (2001) 8 Ind J Global Leg Studies 369, 369–70.

[7] AA Fatouros, 'International Economic Development and the Illusion of Legal Certainty' (1963) 57 Am Soc'ty Int'l L Proc 117, 121.

wrong? Should the protection of investors take precedence in all cases of textual ambiguity? These questions point to the role that arbitrators play in delivering on the promise of adjudication as a purportedly neutral, rules-based system,[8] which begs the question: what are the rules and how will they be interpreted and applied?

Drafters of treaties cannot precisely anticipate all of the issues that will arise in an investment dispute. An element of discretion and policy choice is inherent in any adjudicative process and reasonable people may differ about how much discretion is appropriate.[9] Even so, the discretion that is delegated to arbitrators is quite striking in its breadth, leaving the scope and substance of investment treaty arbitration to a significant extent unclear.[10] For investors, this uncertainty is problematic because it makes it difficult to anticipate the extent to which an investor will be entitled to compensation.[11] An investor might initiate a claim that turns out to be unfounded, wasting time and money where the tribunal interprets an ambiguous provision more narrowly than anticipated. But the greater hazard is for the budgets of states.[12] States alone are ordered to pay damages for breaching the treaty and, even where the state has inadvertently violated a rule that was vague on its face or subject to inconsistent interpretations by previous tribunals, it may nevertheless be ordered to pay damages. For developing countries in particular, the potential liabilities—including the cost of defending claims[13]—can be

[8] Fatouros (n 7 above) 123; SJ Toope, *Mixed International Arbitration—Studies in Arbitration Between States and Private Persons* (Cambridge: Grotius Publications, 1990) 397–8; UNCTAD, *World Investment Report 2003* (Geneva: United Nations, 2003) 86; PT Muchlinski, *Multinational Enterprises and the Law* (Oxford: Blackwell, 1999) 11. See also eg North American Free Trade Agreement (NAFTA) (17 December 1992; 32 ILM 296 and 605; entered into force 1 January 1994), art 1115 (referring to 'due process before an impartial tribunal' as a purpose of Chapter 11 arbitration).

[9] *Mondev International Ltd v United States of America* (Merits) (11 October 2002), 42 ILM 85, 6 ICSID Rep 192, 15(3) World Trade and Arb Mat 273 [cited as *Mondev*], para 127. Fuller (n 2 above) 373; C Harlow and R Rawlings, *Law and Administration* (London: Butterworths, 1997) 100–7; Trachtman (n 2 above) 344.

[10] PG Foy, 'Effectiveness of NAFTA's Chapter Eleven Investor–State Arbitration Procedures' (2003) 18 ICSID Rev 44, 51; SD Franck, 'The Legitimacy Crisis in Investment Treaty Arbitration: Privatizing Public International Law Through Inconsistent Decisions' (2005) 73 Fordham L Rev 1521, 1523 and 1585–6.

[11] LY Fortier, 'Caveat Investor: The Meaning of "Expropriation" and the Protection Afforded Investors Under NAFTA' (2003) 20(1) ICSID News 11. Investors also face the risk of a large costs award in favour of the host state: eg *Methanex Corporation v United States of America* (Merits) (3 August 2005), 44 ILM 1345, 17(6) World Trade and Arb Mat 61 [cited as *Methanex* (Merits)], pt V, para 9–12; *International Thunderbird Gaming Corporation v United Mexican States* (Merits) (26 January 2006), 18(2) World Trade and Arb Mat 59 [cited as *International Thunderbird*], para 220–1.

[12] VL Been and JC Beauvais, 'The Global Fifth Amendment: NAFTA's Investment Protections and the Misguided Quest for an International 'Regulatory Takings' Doctrine' (2003) 78 NYU L Rev 30, 125–6.

[13] I was informed by one legal adviser to the president of a large developing country that the cost of defending a single treaty claim had consumed roughly half of the entire 2005 budget of the country's department of justice. See also UNCTAD, 'Recent developments in international investment agreements' (Research note, 30 August 2005) 15 (reporting that the Czech Republic spent $10 million on its defence in the *CME* and *Lauder* arbitrations).

crippling.¹⁴ Investors are able to weigh the costs and benefits of investment arbitration before bringing a claim; in this regard, states are at their mercy. This reflects the uniquely one-sided dynamic of state liability in public law, while highlighting again the significance of the decisions of arbitrators.

The Interpretive Approaches of Arbitrators

The analogy to commercial arbitration

It is perhaps unsurprising, given the system's reliance on a private model of adjudication, that investment treaty arbitration has been approached by many arbitrators as a modified form of commercial arbitration.¹⁵ This approach treats investor and state essentially as equal disputing parties in a reciprocally consensual adjudication. Thus: interpretation of the treaty should be based on the intent of the disputing parties, rather than the states parties.¹⁶ Or: it is appropriate for investment treaty arbitration to be kept confidential in deference to the disputing parties, rather than because the states parties so agreed in clear and express terms.¹⁷ Or: the courts should defer to the decisions of arbitration tribunals for reasons of party

---

¹⁴ To illustrate, in 19 widely available damages awards to March 2006, the average award was roughly (US)$90 million, although this figure is inflated by four catastrophic awards against Ecuador ($75 million), Argentina ($149 million), the Czech Republic ($351 million), and Slovakia ($1.05 billion). Note that in the latter award [in the *CSOB* arbitration (n 16 below)] the tribunal based its jurisdiction on the incorporation into a contract of the compulsory arbitration clause in a BIT which was not shown by the claimant to be in force—I have included the case in the data presented here because the origins of the respondent state's consent were connected to a BIT. If it is excluded, the average falls to $36 million; alternatively, if it is included but the three awards against capital-exporting states (Canada and Spain) are excluded, the average rises to $106 million. In any event, the main point is that states face the prospect of a fiscally crippling sanction because of arbitrators' power to award damages in public law.

¹⁵ W Mattli, 'Private Justice in a Global Economy: From Litigation to Arbitration' (2001) 55 Int'l Org 919, 945; DF Donovan, 'Introduction to Articles—Dallas Workshop on Arbitrating with Sovereigns' (2002) 18 Arb Int'l 229, 229; GA Alvarez and WW Park, 'The New Face of Investment Arbitration: NAFTA Chapter 11' (2003) 28 Yale J Int'l L 365, 393; CN Brower, CH Brower II, and JK Sharpe, 'The Coming Crisis in the Global Adjudicative System' (2003) 19 Arb Int'l 415, 415 and 432–5. See generally Toope (n 8 above) 389 (noting the tendency to approach investment arbitration 'purely as a subcategory of international commercial arbitration and thus infused with the values of that process').

¹⁶ *Pope & Talbot Inc v Government of Canada* (Merits, Phase 2) (10 April 2001), 13(4) World Trade and Arb Mat 61 [cited as *Pope & Talbot* (Merits, Phase 2)], para 79; *Ceskoslovenska Obchodni Banka v Slovak Republic* (Jurisdiction) (24 May 1999), 14 ICSID Rev 251, 17(3) World Trade and Arb Mat 189 [cited as *CSOB*], para 49–55. Z Douglas, 'The Hybrid Foundations of Investment Treaty Arbitration' (2003) 74 Brit Ybk Int'l L 151, 168.

¹⁷ F Orrego Vicuña, 'Arbitration in a New International Alternative Dispute Resolution' (2001) 18(2) ICSID News 1 (professor and president of the World Bank Administrative Tribunal; member of the ICSID Panels of Conciliators and Arbitrators; arguing against making investment arbitration public on the basis that it would more closely resemble ordinary court proceedings and thus cease to be an alternative).

autonomy rather than legislative intent or international comity.[18] Or: a host state's interference with an investor's business in breach of an investment treaty is akin to a private law tort.[19]

This analogy to commercial arbitration is open to the criticism that it over-emphasizes principles of private law that were developed in commercial arbitration or adjudication between states, at the expense of principles that typically apply in public law adjudication. For example, in determining the scope of the state's consent in an investment treaty arbitration, arbitrators have put the 'agreement to arbitrate' of the investor and state before the original *general* consents of the states parties in order to reject the international principle of strict interpretation (or *in dubio mitius*) in favour of the competing private law principle of party autonomy. Thus the following passage from *Amco v Indonesia*, itself a contract-based arbitration, has been widely cited in treaty awards:[20]

In the first place, like any other convention, a convention to arbitrate is not to be construed *restrictively*, nor, as a matter of fact, *broadly* or *liberally*. It is to be construed in a way which leads to find out and to respect the common will of the parties: such a method of interpretation is but the application of the fundamental principle *pacta sunt servanda*, a principle common, indeed, to all systems of internal law and to international law.

With this, the *Amco* tribunal rejected Indonesia's argument that the tribunal should adopt a restrictive interpretive approach in favour of the sovereign, applying instead the principle of *pacta sunt servanda* between investor and state (ie party autonomy). This reasoning may be appropriate in contract-based arbitration because, when interpreting an agreement to arbitrate between private parties to a contract or between states parties to a treaty, the underlying reciprocity of the private law framework is maintained. The problem arises when this analysis is transferred into the realm of treaty arbitration, as in numerous awards,[21] and more broadly when the specific consent of an investor and the general consent of the state are equated to construct artificially an agreement to arbitrate, as if in a commercial arbitration.[22]

---

[18] *United Mexican States v Feldman Karpa (Marvin Roy)* (2003), 16(2) World Trade and Arb Mat 237, para 84–5 (Ont SCJ); *United Mexican States v Marvin Roy Feldman Karpa* (2005) 193 OAC 216, 248 DLR (4th) 443, para 39 (Ont CA); WW Park, 'Duty and Discretion in International Arbitration' (1999) 93 AJIL 805, 808–10.
[19] *CME Czech Republic BV v Czech Republic* (Merits) (13 September 2001), 14(3) World Trade and Arb Mat 109, para 582. Douglas (n 16 above) 180, fn 149.
[20] *Amco Asia Corp v Indonesia* (Jurisdiction) (25 September 1983), 23 ILM 351, 89 ILR 379, 1 ICSID Rep 389, para 14.
[21] eg *AES Corporation v Argentine Republic* (Jurisdiction) (26 April 2005), ICSID Case No ARB/02/17, para 60, online: ITA, Investment Claims; *CSOB* (n 16 above) para 34; *Ethyl Corporation v Government of Canada* (Jurisdiction) (24 June 1998), 38 ILM 708, para 55; *Mondev* (n 9 above) para 43. See also C Schreuer, *The ICSID Convention: A Commentary* (Cambridge: CUP, 2001) 119–20.
[22] eg *Ethyl* (n 21 above) para 59–60; *SGS Société Générale de Surveillance v Philippines* (Jurisdiction) (29 January 2004), 8 ICSID Rep 518, 16(3) World Trade and Arb Mat 91 [cited as

By characterizing the regulatory relationship between investor and state as a reciprocal one, adjudicators also effectively eschew principles of both public law and public international law, not based on any express agreement between states directing them to do so but out of misconceived respect for party autonomy. Simply put, the principle of party autonomy, as understood in commercial arbitration, has very little place in investment treaty arbitration as a public law system. In the latter context, the investor does not agree with the host state to resolve a regulatory dispute through international arbitration. Rather, the investor acts upon the opportunity provided by an earlier inter-state bargain enabling the investor to bring a treaty claim for damages caused by a particular class of sovereign acts. As such, the investor's consent is more akin to the decision of an individual to go to court to resolve a complaint against the state under domestic administrative or constitutional law. It triggers the establishment of a tribunal and largely delineates the subject-matter of the dispute, but it is a personal consent as opposed to a sovereign authorization.

That the analogy to commercial arbitration leads to misconceptions of investment treaty arbitration is illustrated by an episode in the *Pope & Talbot* arbitration under NAFTA, in which the tribunal awarded damages to a US investor after finding that Canada's implementation of the US–Canada Softwood Lumber Agreement[23] violated NAFTA's minimum standard of treatment (Article 1105). To reach this conclusion, the tribunal adopted an expansive reading of the minimum standard, which prompted the NAFTA states to intervene by issuing a joint interpretation of the treaty.[24] In particular, the NAFTA Free Trade Commission directed that Article 1105 'prescribes the customary international law minimum standard of treatment of aliens as the minimum standard of treatment to be afforded to investments of investors of another [NAFTA] Party'.[25] This overruled the *Pope & Talbot* tribunal's interpretation, which took Article 1105 beyond the

---

SGS v Philippines], para 145 (characterizing 'as two agreements of the same character between the same parties': (1) an investment contract between host state and investor; and (2) a subsequent agreement constituted by the general consent of the host state to ICSID arbitration (in a bilateral investment treaty) 'in association with the Request for Arbitration' of the investor). Thus, investment treaty arbitration is conceptualized based on an agreement to arbitrate between investor and state, as juridical equals, to remove their dispute from the courts in favour of a forum and law of their choosing. See also eg *CSOB* (n 16 above) para 34; *Tecnicas Medioambientales Tecmed, SA v United Mexican States* (Merits) (29 May 2003), 19 ICSID Rev 158, 43 ILM 133, para 70–1 and 173 (applying the international minimum standard and good faith considerations as if the arbitration was based on an investor–state bargain). See generally Toope (n 8 above) 389.

[23] Softwood Lumber Agreement between the Government of Canada and the Government of the United States of America (Washington, 29 May 1996; CTS 1996/16, 35 ILM 1195; entered into force 29 May 1996).

[24] NAFTA (n 8 above) art 1131(2). The Free Trade Commission is made up of the US trade representative, Canada's minister of foreign trade, and Mexico's secretary of trade and industrial development.

[25] Free Trade Commission, *Notes of Interpretation of Certain Chapter 11 Provisions* (31 July 2001), 13(6) World Trade and Arb Mat 139, art B(1).

limits of customary international law, given that NAFTA provides clearly that a Free Trade Commission interpretation 'shall be binding' on NAFTA tribunals.²⁶

The *Pope & Talbot* tribunal, however, was reluctant to apply the Free Trade Commission's interpretation, evidently leading the presiding arbitrator to engage in an extended exchange of correspondence with Canada (the respondent state), and in time with the other NAFTA states, about the validity of their joint interpretation. Most importantly, the tribunal sought clarification of the circumstances in which the interpretation was issued, asking to be informed of 'what caused the Commission to take action in this manner and what the members were told about the effects of their action on this case'.²⁷ The tribunal also took the position that it was improper for Canada, as a party to the dispute, to participate in the deliberations of the Free Trade Commission.²⁸ According to the tribunal, this violated the 'rule of international law that no one shall be judge in his own case'.²⁹

The point here is that these concerns of the tribunal rest on a misconception of the character of an investment treaty dispute between an investor and a state. The concerns may have been pertinent had the tribunal been interpreting a contract in a commercial arbitration based on the intentions of the disputing parties at the time they agreed to the contract. But the authority of an investment treaty tribunal originates in an agreement between states.³⁰ NAFTA tribunals are authorized by a treaty and by the general consents of the states parties, and their authority is thus bounded by the terms of the treaty, which expressly provided in this case that the states parties, acting through the Free Trade Commission, could issue a binding interpretation of the treaty.³¹ Such a provision necessarily implies that the NAFTA states might take part in the deliberations of the Free Trade Commission while at the same time responding to Chapter 11 claims. How could they interpret the treaty other than in the context of ongoing claims? While this might appear unfair from a private law perspective, when properly viewed in terms of public law the process of the Free Trade Commission emerges as just one of the many conditions of the states parties' authorization of NAFTA arbitration, and thus as an element of the structure of the governing arrangement.³²

---

²⁶ NAFTA (n 8 above) art 1131(2).
²⁷ *Pope & Talbot Inc v Government of Canada* (Letter from Presiding Arbitrator) (17 September 2001), UNCITRAL Rules, p 2, online: DFAIT, NAFTA Claims.
²⁸ *Pope & Talbot Inc v Government of Canada* (Damages) (31 May 2002), 41 ILM 1347, 14(6) World Trade and Arb Mat 44 [cited as *Pope & Talbot* (Damages)] para 13.
²⁹ *Pope & Talbot* (Damages) (n 28 above) para 13.
³⁰ J Paulsson, 'Arbitration without Privity' (1995) 10 ICSID Rev 232, 232.
³¹ NAFTA (n 8 above) art 1131(2).
³² At the oral hearings in *Pope & Talbot*, the presiding arbitrator reportedly asked whether the NAFTA Parties 'can simply interpret [the treaty] as widely, as bizarrely ... as they like, and that must be binding on all future tribunals' (*Pope & Talbot Inc v Government of Canada* (Investor's Submissions) (14 December 2001), UNCITRAL Rules, para 29, online: DFAIT, NAFTA Claims). The answer must be 'yes' for NAFTA makes no provision for a tribunal to sit in judgment of the NAFTA Parties no matter how wrong their interpretation may appear to the tribunal.

The irony of the overlapping functions of the state manifests itself in both domestic and international law. As the repository of public authority, the state acts in a range of legal capacities based on a separation of powers.[33] In the domestic sphere, different branches of the state's governing apparatus may wield authority over each other. A decision of the administration may be overturned by the courts who are, in turn, subject to the legislature. Likewise, in the international sphere, a state may be held accountable to an international tribunal which is, in turn, subject to the authority of the states parties to a treaty. In the case of NAFTA, this irony emerges in the dual role of each NAFTA state as both potential respondent to investor claims and joint interpreter of the treaty. The *Pope & Talbot* tribunal doubted the validity of the Free Trade Commission's interpretation by restricting its view of Canada's role to that of a disputing party in a private arbitration. But Canada was taking part in an adjudicative process that Canada itself had established as part of an agreement with other states, and over which Canada exercised authority according to the terms of that agreement. From a public law perspective there was no reason for the tribunal to question the NAFTA structure by questioning the validity of the states parties' joint interpretation and, in doing so, the tribunal apparently mistook Canada's acts as a sovereign for the acts of a private party.

Let us briefly revisit the key distinction between investment treaty arbitration and commercial arbitration. The authority for commercial arbitration flows from the consents of the disputing parties to resolve their dispute through arbitration. The authority for investment arbitration, in contrast, comes from the general consents of states given as part of an international agreement. The general consent, which is both prospective and open-ended, is a sovereign act of the state as legal representative of its territory and population; it is not the act of a mere disputing party, acting in a private capacity. As such, the jurisdiction of investment treaty tribunals originates in an instrument of public international law, not private law, and the law governing the arbitration is that of the treaty rather than a contract. To turn this around by drawing analogies to commercial arbitration is to neglect the sovereign origins of the disputes that trigger investor claims, and of the regime in general.

Some investment treaties expressly provide that disputes that are subject to compulsory arbitration under the treaty are to be characterized as disputes arising from a commercial relationship for particular purposes. For example, the Mexico–Spain BIT states: 'For the purposes of Article I of the New York Convention, a claim that is submitted to arbitration in conformity with this Appendix [providing for investor claims] shall be considered to arise out of a commercial relationship or transaction'.[34] In such cases, it could be argued, the states parties have

---

[33] WW Willoughby, *The Fundamental Concepts of Public Law* (New York: Macmillan, 1924) 49–50; E Barendt, 'Separation of Powers and Constitutional Government' (1995) Pub L 599, 601.

[34] Acuerdo para la promoción y protección reciproca de inversiones entre los Estados Unidos Mexicanos y el Reino de España (the Spain–Mexico BIT) (Mexico City, 22 June 1995; entered into

agreed that investment treaty arbitration is in effect the same as commercial arbitration. But there is another, more plausible, interpretation of such clauses.

The New York Convention was originally designed to govern arbitration in the private sphere and, as such, states are allowed to limit their obligations under that treaty to arbitrations arising from commercial disputes in order to preserve domestic judicial control over the use of international arbitration in the public sphere.[35] In investment treaty arbitration, however, the requirement that an award must arise from a commercial dispute undermines the enforceability of investment treaty awards precisely because those awards arise from regulatory disputes.[36] That is, a domestic court might exercise its state's right to refuse to enforce an award under the New York Convention on the basis that the award did not arise from a commercial dispute. An express clause in an investment treaty providing that disputes under the treaty shall be considered, for purposes of the New York Convention, as arising from a commercial dispute thus facilitates the extension of the enforcement structure of commercial arbitration into the regulatory sphere. But it should not be taken further than this, so as magically to transform all regulatory disputes into commercial disputes.[37]

States have incorporated a private law model of adjudication into the architecture of investment treaties, but the rules and enforcement structure of commercial arbitration play only a subordinate and facilitative role. They were not designed to apply to the adjudication of regulatory disputes and as such they should be discarded where they conflict with the treaty or, arguably, where the treaty is silent

---

force 18 December 1996), title 8(5) (app). See also NAFTA (n 8 above) art 1136(7). The relevant 'purposes' of Article I of the New York Convention and Article I of the Panama Convention are to allow the states parties to those treaties to limit their obligations to recognize and enforce awards to the arbitration of commercial disputes. In addition, NAFTA—and many other investment treaties—expressly provide that the states parties' consents to compulsory arbitration shall also satisfy the consent requirements of other arbitration treaties, including the New York Convention, the ICSID Convention, and the Panama Convention: NAFTA, art 1122(2).

[35] United Nations Convention on the Recognition and Enforcement of Foreign Arbitral Awards (the New York Convention) (New York, 10 June 1958; 330 UNTS 3; entered into force 7 June 1959), art I. *Report of the Committee on the Enforcement of International Arbitral Awards*, UN ESC, UN Doc E/AC.42/SR.1–3, 5–6 (First Meeting, 1 March 1955) and 7–8 (Second Meeting, 23 March 1955). See the discussion in Ch 3 above, p 54–6.

[36] New York Convention (n 35 above) art I(3). eg United Nations Foreign Arbitral Awards Convention Act, RSC 1985, c 16 (Canada), s 4(1) ('The Convention applies only to difference arising out of commercial legal relationships, whether contractual or not'); Federal Arbitration Act 1925, 9 USC c 2 (USA), s 202. See also *ADF Group Inc v United States of America* (Procedural Order No 2) (11 July 2001), para 12, online: State Department, NAFTA Claims (noting the claimant's argument that US arbitration law is uncertain as to whether it calls for judicial deference to investment treaty awards, given that such awards may not be regarded as commercial arbitration awards).

[37] The narrower reading of such clauses was adopted by the NAFTA states parties, in relation to a similar provision under NAFTA, in the *ADF* arbitration, in which they took the position that NAFTA art 1136(7) deems arbitrations under NAFTA Chapter 11 to be commercial strictly for the purpose of recognition and enforcement of award, and specifically not for the purposes of court review of awards: *ADF* (Procedural Order No 2) (n 36 above) para 12.

or ambiguous and they conflict with rules of international custom.[38] The *Loewen* tribunal expressed the latter view in these terms:[39]

It is true that some aspects of the resolution of disputes arising in relation to private international commerce are imported into the NAFTA system ... and that the handling of disputes within that system by professionals experienced in the handling of major international arbitrations has tended in practice to make a NAFTA arbitration look like a more familiar kind of process. But this apparent resemblance is misleading. The two forms of process, and the rights which they enforce, have nothing in common. There is no warrant for transferring rules derived from private law into a field of international law where claimants are permitted for convenience to enforce what are in origin the rights of Party states.

Thus the tribunal considered principles of commercial arbitration to be irrelevant to NAFTA arbitration, despite the reliance on a private model of adjudication. Whatever the merits of the *Loewen* award as a whole, discussed in more detail below, in this passage the tribunal captured the key distinction between treaty arbitration and commercial arbitration. It acknowledged the use of a private law model but properly characterized this as a matter of form rather than substance.

Conceptually, the key problem with the characterization of the investor–state relationship as a reciprocal relationship is that it fundamentally alters the nature of the rights and duties of states.[40] When an adjudicator approaches the regulatory position of an investor as if it were reciprocal, this does one of two things. Either it reduces the state to the status of a private party or it elevates the investor to a quasi-sovereign status of formal equality with the state, but without any sovereign responsibilities.[41] In both cases, the concept of the state as a unique entity, endowed with authority that no private party can possess, is negated.[42] Taken to

---

[38] *Loewen Group, Inc and Raymond L Loewen v United States of America* (Merits) (26 June 2003), 42 ILM 811, 7 ICSID Rep 442, 15(5) World Trade and Arb Mat 97 [cited as *Loewen*], para 233; *United Parcel Service of America, Inc v Government of Canada* (Participation by Amicus Curiae) (1 August 2003), UNCITRAL Rules, para 70, online: DFAIT, NAFTA Claims. See also *Banro American Resources, Inc and Société Aurifère du Kivu et du Maniema SARL v Democratic Republic of the Congo* (Jurisdiction) (1 September 2000), 17 ICSID Rev 382, para 24; *CME Czech Republic BV v Czech Republic* (Damages) (14 March 2003), 15(4) World Trade and Arb Mat 83 and 245, para 74 (separate opinion); *SGS v Philippines* (n 22 above) para 142; *Tokios Tokelés v Ukraine* (Jurisdiction) (29 April 2004), 20 ICSID Rev 205, 16(4) World Trade and Arb Mat 75, para 24 and 28 (dissenting opinion).

[39] *Loewen* (n 38 above) para 233.

[40] W Friedmann, *Law in a Changing Society* (2nd edn, London: Stevens & Sons, 1964) 276–7; Harlow and Rawlings (n 9 above) 41–5.

[41] AA Fatouros, 'Transnational Enterprise in the Law of State Responsibility' in RB Lillich (ed) *International Law of State Responsibility for Injuries to Aliens* (Charlottesville: University Press of Virginia, 1983) 385.

[42] This is reminiscent of the debate about whether contracts between foreign investors and host states could be 'internationalized', thus elevating contractual obligations between private parties (one of which was the state) to the status of international obligations falling within the pubic sphere. See *Texaco Overseas Petroleum Co and California Asiatic Oil Co v Libya* (Merits) (1977), 53 ILR 389, 17 ILM 1, para 40–7. DW Bowett, 'Claims Between States and Private Entities: The Twilight Zone

its logical outcome, this approach ignores the regulatory relationship and destroys the notion of public law. That private arbitrators are able to execute this conceptual transformation of juridical sovereignty and redraw the boundaries of the regulatory sphere, without effective judicial supervision, is one of the more perilous aspects of the present system.

The analogy to public international law

An antidote to the misconception of investment treaty arbitration as private law is to reinvigorate the actual reciprocal relationship that underlies investment treaties: the inter-state bargain.[43] Put differently, the promise of international arbitration as an institution lies in the ideal of neutrality between states, not between investors and states. By understanding investment treaty arbitration as a bargain between states, subject to international law, one advances its neutrality as an international institution. By analogizing investment treaty arbitration to commercial arbitration, one promotes it as a private ordering of relations between state and investors.[44] The former is a founding principle of the system; the latter an ill-advised policy choice. In investment treaty arbitration, the principle of neutrality demands equal treatment of foreign investors relative to each other and regardless of each investor's home state. Likewise, neutrality requires equal treatment of governments relative to each other, regardless of the relative importance of the host state. What neutrality specifically does not require is equal treatment between investors and governments. Investment treaty arbitration is a matter of *pacta sunt servanda* between states parties, not between disputing parties. Ultimately, the obligations of one state under the treaty correspond to the rights of another.[45]

Thus to implement the inter-state bargain, adjudicators need look to the intentions of the parties to the treaty. And where the states parties make unanimous submissions about how the treaty should be interpreted, tribunals should adopt

---

of International Law' (1986) 35 Cath U L Rev 929, 931; M Sornarajah, 'The UNCITRAL Model Law: A Third World Viewpoint' (1989) 6(4) J Int'l Arb 7, 18; Toope (n 8 above) 387; R Lillich, 'The Law Governing Disputes Under Economic Development Agreements: Re-examining the Concept of "Internationalization"' in R Lillich and CN Brower (eds), *International Arbitration in the 21st Century: Towards Judicialization and Uniformity?* (Ardsley, NY: Transnational Publishers, 1994) 64; Muchlinski (n 8 above) 494–6.

[43] eg NAFTA (n 8 above) art 1115 (describing the purpose of Chapter 11 arbitration as being 'to assure equal treatment *among investors* of the Parties in accordance with the principle of international reciprocity and due process before an impartial procedure' [emphasis added]). The reference is to equal treatment among investors, not between investors and states; and to international reciprocity and due process, not reciprocity between private parties and respect for party autonomy.

[44] eg CH Brower II, 'Investor–State Disputes Under NAFTA: The Empire Strikes Back' (2001) 40 Colum J Transnat'l L 43, 72–3; CN Brower and LA Steven, 'Who Then Should Judge? Developing the International Rule of Law under NAFTA Chapter 11' (2001) 2 Chi J Int'l L 193, 196.

[45] Toope (n 8 above) 388–9; JC Thomas, 'A Reply to Professor Brower' (2002) 40 Col J Transnat'l L 433, 460.

their view as a matter of course.[46] In particular, a tribunal should be cautious about adopting interpretations in favour of investor protection that go beyond the submissions of the investor's home state.[47] Investors are simply not parties to investment treaty arbitration as an inter-state bargain. It is true that most of the treaties favour the historical position of capital-exporting states and, as such, investor protection, but there remains much room for discretion.

The public international law framework, which emphasizes the legal relationship between the states parties to the treaty, has been resolutely applied by tribunals in a number of cases. For example, in *Tokios*, the presiding arbitrator offered these reasons for his dissenting opinion that Ukrainian investors should not be able to bring a treaty claim before ICSID, against their own government, by channelling ownership of their assets in the Ukraine through a Lithuanian holding company:[48]

Since the object and purpose of this provision—and, for that matter, the whole ICSID Convention and mechanism—is to protect *foreign* investment, it should not be interpreted so as to allow domestic, national corporations to evade the application of their domestic, national law and the jurisdiction of their domestic, national tribunals ...

When it comes to mechanisms and procedures involving States and implying, therefore, issues of public international law, economic and political reality is to prevail over legal structure, so much so that the application of the basic principles and rules of public international law should not be frustrated by legal concepts and rules prevailing in the relations between private economic and juridical players.

According to this reasoning, then, a gap in the language of the treaty—namely, its omission of express language prohibiting claims by foreign companies owned by nationals of the respondent state—should not be filled in a way that contradicts the purpose of ICSID.

Alternatively, tribunals favouring this approach have filled gaps in the treaty language by defaulting to rules of customary international law. In *SGS v Pakistan*,

---

[46] *ADF Group Inc v United States of America* (Merits) (9 January 2003), 18 ICSID Rev 195, 6 ICSID Rep 470, 15(3) World Trade and Arb Mat 55, para 177 (concluding in relation to the unanimous submissions of the NAFTA states parties: '... we have the Parties themselves—all the Parties—speaking to the Tribunal. No more authentic and authoritative source of instruction on what the Parties intended to convey in a particular provision of NAFTA, is possible.'). *Methanex Corporation v United States of America* (Jurisdiction) (7 August 2002), 14(6) World Trade and Arb Mat 109, para 130–4 and 147; *United Parcel Service of America, Inc v Government of Canada* (Jurisdiction) (22 November 2002), UNCITRAL Rules [cited as *UPS*], para 59, 79, and 96, online: DFAIT, ITA, NAFTA Claims.

[47] eg *Pope & Talbot* (Merits, Phase 2) (n 16 above) para 114; *GAMI Investments, Inc v Government of the United Mexican States* (Merits) (15 November 2004), 44 ILM 545, 17(2) World Trade and Arb Mat 127 [cited as *GAMI*], para 29–30 (both tribunals rejecting the submissions of the investor's home state (the US) in favour of the more ambitious interpretation of NAFTA advanced by the investor). See also *Enron Corporation v Argentine Republic* (Jurisdiction) (2 August 2004), ICSID Case No ARB/01/3, para 39, online: ICSID, ITA, Investment Claims; *Sempra Energy International v Argentine Republic* (Jurisdiction) (11 May 2005), ICSID Case No ARB/02/16 [cited as *Sempra*], para 142–3, online: ICSID, ITA, Investment Claims.

[48] *Tokios* (n 38 above) para 23–4 (dissenting opinion) [emphasis in original].

an award that has been openly criticized by some arbitrators, the tribunal read down an umbrella clause in the Swiss–Pakistan BIT and limited the tribunal's own jurisdiction by concluding that it could not hear a treaty claim arising from an alleged breach of contract.[49] The tribunal supported this decision in part by referring to the international principle of *in dubio mitius*, which, the tribunal noted, has been adopted by the ICJ and the WTO Appellate Body.[50] For example, the principle is evident in the *ELSI* case, in which a chamber of the ICJ rejected the argument that a US–Italy commercial treaty implicitly removed the duty to exhaust local remedies, ruling that it was 'unable to accept that an important principle of customary international law should be held to have been tacitly dispensed with, in the absence of any words making clear an intention to do so.'[51] Similarly, in the *Hormones* case, the WTO Appellate Body—in the course of interpreting the degree to which the Agreement on the Application of Sanitary and Phytosanitary Measures required domestic sanitary and phytosanitary measures to be 'based on' international standards—said this:[52]

We cannot lightly assume that sovereign states intended to impose upon themselves the more onerous, rather than the less burdensome, obligation by mandating conformity or compliance with such standards ... To sustain such an assumption and to warrant such a far-reaching interpretation, treaty language far more specific and compelling than that found in Article 3 of the SPS Agreement would be necessary.

This interpretive stance assumes that the jurisdiction of international tribunals is bounded by the framework of international custom unless a tribunal is authorized to go further than custom by express language in a treaty.[53] In other words, a state's right to withhold consent should be carefully guarded.[54] Customary international law does not allow individuals to make claims against states; thus, clear language is needed before a state can be found to have exposed itself to such claims.[55]

---

[49] *SGS v Pakistan* (n 4 above) para 167–73.

[50] *SGS v Pakistan* (n 4 above) para 171. See also *Noble Ventures v Romania* (Merits) (12 October 2005), ICSID Case No ARB/01/11 [cited as *Noble Ventures*], para 55, online: ITA, Investment Claims. [51] *Elettronica Sicula SpA (United States v Italy)*, [1989] ICJ Rep 14, para 50.

[52] WTO, *EC Measures Concerning Meat and Meat Products (Hormones)* (16 January 1998), WTO Docs WT/DS26/AB/R and WT/DS48/AB/R (Appellate Body report) para 165.

[53] *Methanex* (Jurisdiction) (n 46 above) para 106; *ADF* (n 46 above) para 147; *Loewen* (n 38 above) para 234; *Waste Management, Inc v United Mexican States* (Jurisdiction) (2 June 2000), 15 ICSID Rev 214, 40 ILM 56, 121 ILR 30 [cited as *Waste Management No 1*], para 27–8 and 31; *UPS* (n 46 above) para 68; *Plama Consortium Limited v Republic of Bulgaria* (Jurisdiction) (8 February 2005), 20 ICSID Rev 262, 44 ILM 721, 17(4) World Trade and Arb Mat 215, para 203–4 and 227.

[54] *Loewen* (n 38 above) para 230, 233–4, and 238. *Tokios* (n 38 above) para 16 (dissenting opinion). JC Thomas, 'Investor–State Arbitration Under NAFTA Chapter Eleven' (Paper presented to the NAFTA Chapter 11 Investor–State Disputes: Litigating Against Sovereigns conference, Canadian Bar Association, Toronto, March 2000) 16–19 and 29–30; Schwartz and Paulsson (n 5 above) 13–14.

[55] *Azinian (Robert) et al v United Mexican States* (Merits) (1 November 1999), 14 ICSID Rev 538, 39 ILM 537 [cited as *Azinian*], para 82–4; *UPS* (n 46 above) para 60–9; *Loewen* (n 38 above) para 226; *Fireman's Fund Insurance Company v United Mexican States* (Jurisdiction) (17 July 2003), 15(6)

This deferential approach was also relied on by the *Loewen* tribunal, acting under NAFTA, which effectively adopted in its reasons a presumption that ambiguity or silence in the treaty should be resolved by default to international custom. The dispute in *Loewen* arose after a massive Mississippi jury award of (US)$500 million was delivered against a Canadian funeral homes company.[56] The Canadian investor argued that the US court process that led to the jury award violated the NAFTA minimum standard of treatment, and the tribunal agreed, finding that '[b]y any standard of measurement' the trial was 'a disgrace' and that the trial judge's failure to ensure due process constituted a denial of justice under international law.[57] Even so, the *Loewen* tribunal dismissed the investor's claim on the ground that the investor did not exhaust local remedies.[58] Although the text of NAFTA can be read as providing that investors need not exhaust local remedies before bringing a NAFTA claim,[59] the tribunal concluded that the duty remained applicable as a substantive element of the NAFTA minimum standard, given the definition of denial of justice under customary international law.[60] The tribunal also stressed the ICJ's statement in *ELSI* that clear language is required to override customary rules.[61]

In addition, the *Loewen* tribunal expressly rejected the comparison between NAFTA arbitration and private law in order to position investment treaty arbitration as a matter of public international law:[62]

Rights of action under private law arise from personal obligations (albeit they may be owed by or to a State) brought into existence by domestic law and enforceable through domestic tribunals and courts. NAFTA claims have a quite different character, stemming from a corner of public international law in which, by treaty, the power of States under that law to take international measures for the correction of wrongs done to its nationals has been replaced by an ad hoc definition of certain kinds of wrong, coupled with specialist means of compensation. These means are both distinct from and exclusive of the remedies for wrongful acts under private law ...

World Trade and Arb Mat 3, para 64. *SGS v Pakistan* (n 4 above) para 161, 167, and 171; *Tokios* (n 38 above) para 8 (dissenting opinion).

[56] *Loewen* (n 38 above) para 39.

[57] *Loewen* (n 38 above) para 119, 139 and 141 (dismissing independent claims of violations of NAFTA Articles 1102 and 1110, respectively).   [58] *Loewen* (n 38 above) para 217.

[59] NAFTA (n 8 above) art 1121.

[60] *Loewen* (n 38 above) para 153–6. See also *Waste Management Inc v United Mexican States* (Merits) (30 April 2004), 43 ILM 967, 16(4) World Trade and Arb Mat 3 [cited as *Waste Management No 2* (Merits)], para 116 and 174; *GAMI* (n 47 above) para 133. *Generation Ukraine Inc v Ukraine* (Merits) (16 September 2003), 44 ILM 404, para 20.30 and 20.33; *Encana Corporation v Republic of Ecuador* (Merits) (3 February 2006), London Court of International Arbitration Administered Case No UN 3481 [cited as *Encana*], para 186–7 and 194. Contrast *CME* (Damages) (n 38 above) para 398 and 412–13.

[61] *Loewen* (n 38 above) para 160 and 162. See also *SGS v Pakistan* (n 4 above) para 169. Contrast *SGS v Philippines* (n 22 above) para 122; *Tokios* (n 38 above) para 52; *Saluka Investments BV v Czech Republic* (Merits) (17 March 2006), 18(3) World Trade and Arb Mat 166, para 229.

[62] *Loewen* (n 38 above) para 233.

This passage reveals both the utility and the weakness of the analogy to public international law. The *Loewen* tribunal used the analogy appropriately to distinguish treaty arbitration from commercial adjudication by differentiating treaty claims from 'rights of action under private law'. But the tribunal also characterized the distinction as a contrast between 'a corner of public international law' and 'personal obligations brought into existence by domestic law'. This latter distinction is less than compelling because domestic law is not limited to actions under private law. Rather, domestic law extends to encompass individual rights to seek judicial review or bring constitutional claims in disputes arising from sovereign acts of the state. These individual rights of action in domestic law are akin to treaty rights of action 'for the correction of . . . certain kinds of wrongs, coupled with specialist means of compensation'. In either case, the right is exercised directly by the individual, not by the state (or states) that delegate or enforce the authority of the adjudicator who rules on the claim. The more apt distinction, therefore, is between regulatory and private, not between international and domestic .

Put differently, the *Loewen* tribunal's reasoning denies the transformative impact of individualization. It struggles to reincarnate Vattel's principle of formalized state representation in a habitat where it simply cannot survive. The individualization of claims, especially in as far-reaching a form as under investment treaties, transforms international adjudication by expanding the degree to which it engages the regulatory sphere, thus superimposing the analytical framework of public law. This means that international principles which originate in the adjudication of disputes between states must be modified or jettisoned. In particular, as discussed in Chapter 5 of this book, one must distinguish state liability under investment treaties from state responsibility in public international law. The latter is defined broadly in part because damages are awarded in disputes between juridical equals.[63] Investment treaties, on the other hand, lead to damages awards to investors and against the state but not the other way around, calling for special consideration of the governmental implications of liability. It is the altered dynamic of international adjudication, as opposed to the fall-back position of inter-state relations, that most clearly warrants a deferential approach to the sovereign interests at stake. This does not mean that the prudentialist steps taken in *SGS v Pakistan* and *Loewen*—to invigorate the principle of *in dubio mitius*, for instance—are misguided. On the contrary, they become all the more important when one considers the profound transformation that is wrought by far-reaching individualization, in relation to issues like parallel claims and state liability in public law. In light of this transformation, it is consistent with a public international law approach to characterize

---

[63] VS Mani, *International Adjudication* (The Hague: Martinus Nijhoff, 1980) 3–4.

investment treaty arbitration as an exceptional remedy and to reserve its use for flagrant treaty violations.⁶⁴

The investor rights approach

In Chapter 5 of this book, investment treaty arbitration was compared to individualized adjudication under human rights treaties, although stressing the relatively limited scope and ambition of the latter in terms of both the duty of victims of human rights violations to exhaust local remedies and the conditional availability of damages as a remedy. The analogy to human rights treaties has been taken much further, however, by commentators and some arbitrators who regard investment treaties as creating fundamental rights for investors; thus, in the *Mondev* arbitration under NAFTA, the tribunal saw fit to refer to court decisions under Article 6(1) of the European Convention on Human Rights—which (somewhat ironically) affirms the right of individuals to a fair and public hearing by an independent and impartial tribunal—as providing 'guidance by analogy as to the possible scope of NAFTA's guarantee' of fair and equitable treatment for investors.⁶⁵ This likening of investment treaty standards to human rights is consistent with the wider proposition in relation to the European Union and the WTO that the destiny of international economic law is to establish the economic interests of individuals as fundamental rights in support of international business freedom and a liberal economy and society,⁶⁶ a view

---

⁶⁴ *Azinian* (n 55 above) para 90; *ADF* (n 46 above) para 157, 184, and 191; *Loewen* (n 38 above) para 242; *Waste Management No 2* (Merits) (n 60 above) para 115, 130, and 139; *GAMI* (n 47 above) para 83–4, 104, 108, and 114. Fatouros (n 7 above) 124; Thomas (n 54 above) 42; PT Muchlinski, 'The Rise and Fall of the Multilateral Agreement on Investment: Where Now?' (2000) 34 Int'l Lawyer 1033, 1051–2.

⁶⁵ eg *Mondev* (n 9 above) para 143–4. See also *SD Myers, Inc v Government of Canada* (Merits) (13 November 2000), 40 ILM 1408, 15(1) World Trade and Arb Mat 184 [cited as *SD Myers* (Merits)], para 229 (separate opinion); *Tecmed* (n 22 above) para 122; *Azurix Corp v Argentine Republic* (Jurisdiction) (8 December 2003), 43 ILM 262, 16(2) World Trade and Arb Mat 111 [cited as *Azurix*], para 72; *CMS Gas Transmission Company v Argentine Republic* (Jurisdiction) (17 July 2003), 42 ILM 788, 7 ICSID Rep 492 [cited as *CMS* (Jurisdiction)], para 45; *Siemens AG v Argentine Republic* (Jurisdiction) (3 August 2004), 44 ILM 138 [cited as *Siemens*], para 141. Lillich (n 42 above) 67–8; TW Wälde, 'Investment Arbitration Under the Energy Charter Treaty—From Dispute Settlement to Treaty Implementation' (1996) 12 Arb Int'l 429, 434–6 and 444; Brower II (n 44 above) 87–8; CH Brower II, 'NAFTA's Investment Chapter: Initial Thoughts About Second-Generation Rights' (2003) 36 Vanderbilt J Transnat'l L 1533, 1546–8; Alvarez and Park (n 15 above) 394; JP Trachtman and PM Moreman, 'Costs and Benefits of Private Participation in WTO Dispute Settlement: Whose Right Is It Anyway?' (2003) 44 Harv Int'l LJ 221, 225; O Spiermann, 'Individual Rights, State Interests and the Power to Waive ICSID Jurisdiction under Bilateral Investment Treaties' (2004) 20 Arb Int'l 179, 187; Z Douglas, 'Nothing if Not Critical for Investment Treaty Arbitration: *Occidental, Eureko* and *Methanex*' (2006) 22 Arb Int'l 27, 37.

⁶⁶ E Sik, 'Concept of Acquired Rights in International Law' (1977) 44 Neth Int'l L Rev 120, 127–9; Lillich (n 42 above) 112–13; T Cottier, 'Trade and Human Rights: A Relationship to Discover' (2002) 5 J Int'l Econ L 111, 114–15 and 129–31; EU Petersmann, 'Taking Human Dignity, Poverty and Empowerment of Individuals More Seriously: Rejoinder to Alston' (2002) 13 Eur J Int'l L 845, 850.

that is contested in these other contexts as well as that of investment treaty arbitration.⁶⁷

The investor rights approach is demonstrated at times by explicit statements of tribunals emphasizing the independent status of private investors, while rejecting the framework of state-based representation. Thus, according to the *Azurix* tribunal, acting pursuant to the US–Argentina BIT: 'The issues before this Tribunal concern not diplomatic protection under customary international law but the rights of investors, including shareholders, as determined by treaty...'.⁶⁸ Likewise, it is often argued that the predominant aim of the system is to protect investors from arbitrary, discriminatory, and other inappropriate treatment by the state.⁶⁹ Allowing investors to bring treaty claims gives effect to investor rights, therefore, by enabling a neutral tribunal ('neutral' meaning beyond the domestic arena) to scrutinize the state and decide whether an investor is entitled to compensation. Encouraging business confidence takes precedence over other concerns, such as the possible disruption of government or the legitimacy of economic integration.⁷⁰ As such, other purposes of investment treaties are subordinated to norms rooted in concepts of private adjudication and individualized corrective justice, leading to a very liberal stance in relation to both investor protection and state liability in public law.⁷¹

---

⁶⁷ Fatouros (n 41 above) 372–3; M Sornarajah, 'Power and Justice in Foreign Investment Arbitration' (1997) 14(3) J Int'l Arb 103, 133; P Alston, 'Resisting the Merger and Acquisition of Human Rights by Trade Law: A Reply to Petersmann' (2002) 13 Eur J Int'l L 815; A Afilalo, 'Constitutionalization Through the Back Door: A European Perspective on NAFTA's Investment Chapter' (2001) 34 NYU J Int'l L & Pol 1, 31–43; P Juillard, 'Freedom of Establishment, Freedom of Capital Movements, and Freedom of Investment' (2000) 15 ICSID Rev 322, 326–9; DZ Cass, *The Constitutionalization of the World Trade Organization* (Oxford: OUP, 2005) c 5.

⁶⁸ *Azurix* (n 65 above) para 72. See also *CMS* (Jurisdiction) (n 65 above) para 28 and 45; *Occidental Exploration and Production Company v Republic of Ecuador* (Merits) (1 July 2004), 17(1) World Trade and Arb Mat 165, para 49; *Siemens* (n 65 above) para 102 and 141. R Bruno and JHH Weiler, 'Access of Private Parties to International Dispute Settlement: A Comparative Analysis' (Harvard Jean Monnet Working Paper 13/97, New York University School of Law, 1997).

⁶⁹ J Byrne, 'NAFTA Dispute Resolution: Implementing True Rule-Based Diplomacy Through Direct Access' (2000) 35 Texas Int'l LJ 415, 416–20; MM Hart and WA Dymond, 'NAFTA Chapter 11: Precedents, Principles, and Prospects' in LR Dawson (ed) *Whose Rights? The NAFTA Chapter 11 Debate* (Ottawa: Centre for Trade Law and Policy, 2002) 149–51; T Weiler, 'NAFTA Investment Arbitration and the Growth of International Economic Law' (2002) 3 Bus Law Int'l 158, 189; RG Dearden, 'Arbitration of Expropriation Disputes between an Investor and the State under the North American Free Trade Agreement' (1995) 29 J World Trade 113, 113; Brower II (n 44 above) 77–80 and 88; IA Laird, 'NAFTA Chapter 11 Meets Chicken Little' (2001) 2 Chi J Int'l L 223, 229.

⁷⁰ *Metalclad Corporation v United Mexican States* (Merits) (30 August 2000), 16 ICSID Rev 168, 40 ILM 36, 5 ICSID Rep 212, 13(1) World Trade and Arb Mat 45 [cited as *Metalclad*], para 76; *Waste Management No 2* (Merits) (n 60 above) para 78–85; *GAMI* (n 47 above) para 94. *Compañía del Desarrollo de Santa Elena, SA v Republic of Costa Rica* (Merits) (17 February 2000), 15 ICSID Rev 169, 39 ILM 317, 5 ICSID Rep 157, 13(1) World Trade and Arb Mat 81, para 71–2; *CME* (Merits) (n 19 above) para 419, 602, and 613; *Siemens* (n 65 above) para 120. T Weiler (n 69 above) 173; RK Paterson, 'A New Pandora's Box? Private Remedies for Foreign Investors under the North American Free Trade Agreement' (2000) 8 Willamette J Int'l L and Dispute Res 77, 120; Brower *et al* (n 15 above) 428–35.

⁷¹ *Asian Agricultural Products Ltd (AAPL) v Sri Lanka* (Merits) (27 June 1990), 30 ILM 577, 4 ICSID Rep 246, para 69 and 77; *Tecmed* (n 22 above) para 70–1; *Metalclad* (n 70 above) para 76; *Waste*

138   *Approaches and Interpretations*

That said, even where tribunals do not boldly declare their colours for the investor rights position, they advance it none the less by the common practice of resolving doubts arising from ambiguity in the treaty in favour of investor protection. A clear statement of this presumption was enunciated by the tribunal in *SGS v Philippines*:[72]

> The object and purpose of the BIT supports an effective interpretation of Article X(2). The BIT is a treaty for the promotion and reciprocal protection of investments. According to the preamble it is intended 'to create and maintain favourable conditions for investments by investors of one Contracting Party in the territory of the other'. It is legitimate to resolve uncertainties in its interpretation so as to favour the protection of covered investments.

The same presumption has been adopted by other tribunals, usually to support a finding in favour of jurisdiction,[73] but also to require the respondent state to answer for official conduct where there is prima facie evidence of harm to an investor[74] or to found a substantive violation of the treaty.[75] In this vein, tribunals have relied on the object and purpose of investor protection to override the principle of *in dubio mitius* and to dismiss decisions of other tribunals applying that principle in support of a more prudential approach.[76] Adoption of these interpretive presumptions in favour of investor protection evokes the rights-based school of interpretation that deems it appropriate to resolve legal uncertainty in favour of the protection of individuals from the state.[77]

Management No 2 (Merits) (n 60 above) para 79; *GAMI* (n 47 above) para 94; *CMS Gas Transmission Company v Argentine Republic* (Merits) (12 May 2005), 44 ILM 1205, 17(5) World Trade and Arb Mat 63 [cited as *CMS* (Merits)], para 186; *Azurix Corp v Argentine Republic* (Merits) (14 July 2006), ICSID Case No ARB/01/12 [cited as *Azurix* (Merits)], para 374–7, 393, and 408, online: ITA, Investment Claims. Vicuña (n 17 above); Laird (n 69 above) 229; Brower and Steven (n 44 above) 195–7.

[72] *SGS v Philippines* (n 22 above) para 116.

[73] eg *Sedelmayer (Franz) v Russian Federation* (Merits) (7 July 1998), SCC Rules, para 58–9, online: ITA, Investment Claims; *Maffezini (Emilio Agustín) v Kingdom of Spain* (Jurisdiction) (25 January 2000), 16 ICSID Rev 212, 124 ILR 9, para 54–6 and 64; *CSOB* (n 16 above) para 57 and 64; *Tokios* (n 38 above) para 31–2 and 52 (majority opinion); *Siemens* (n 65 above) para 85 and 120; *Noble Ventures* (n 50 above) para 52; *Continental Casualty Company v Argentine Republic* (Jurisdiction) (22 February 2006), ICSID Case No ARB/03/9, para 80, online: ITA; *Waste Management No 1* (n 53 above) para 33–4 (dissenting opinion); *Petrobart Ltd v Kyrgyz Republic* (Merits) (29 March 2005), SCC Rules, SCC Arbitration Institute Case No 126/2003, 62–3; *Sempra* (n 47 above), para 94; *Aguas del Tunari SA v Republic of Bolivia* (Jurisdiction) (21 October 2005), 18(2) World Trade and Arb Mat 271, para 244–7 [cited as *Aguas del Tunari*]. R Dolzer and M Stevens, *Bilateral Investment Treaties* (The Hague: Martinus Nijhoff, 1995) 17; WS Dodge 'National Courts and International Arbitration: Exhaustion of Remedies and Res Judicata Under Chapter Eleven of NAFTA' (2000) 23 Hast Int'l & Comp L Rev 357, 383.

[74] *Feldman* (n 4 above) para 173 and 176–8. Dearden (n 69 above) 119–20.

[75] *MTD Equity Sdn Bhd v Republic of Chile* (Merits) (25 May 2004), 44 ILM 91, para 104 and 113; *CMS* (Merits) (n 73 above) para 274; *Eureko v Republic of Poland* (Merits) (19 August 2005), UNCITRAL Rules [cited as *Eureko*], para 248, online: ITA, Investment Claims.

[76] eg *SGS v Philippines* (n 22 above) para 122; *Tokios* (n 38 above) para 52 (majority opinion); *Eureko* (n 75 above) para 258; *Aguas del Tunari* (n 73 above) para 91 and 153.

[77] An obvious parallel is to the liberal interpretation of human rights in favour of the protection of individuals: Human Rights Committee, *General Comment 24 on Reservations to the International*

The investor rights approach is defensible above all because it accepts the regulatory character of the disputes that are subject to investment treaty arbitration. Its emergence is also an unsurprising outcome of individualization, combined with the proclivity of many lawyers to focus on the threats to individuals that come from the state, rather than the privileges and benefits.[78] But the approach overreaches by treating investor protection as a rights-based trump card. Obviously, if one defines a 'right' as merely a legally enforceable claim,[79] then treaty standards that are enforced through compulsory arbitration clearly pass muster (indeed, few if any international standards which protect individuals are as enforceable, and thus as obviously a right, as those adopted in investment treaties). But behind the investor rights approach is a normative construction of investor protection as something so vital, so dominant, as to be treated an end in itself,[80] or at least as something that benefits states and their people more or less as a rule without the need for any detailed inquiry into the implications of particular interpretations for governments.[81] Because investment treaties use such broad language to define core concepts, the presumption in favour of investor protection systematically favours an expansive approach to jurisdiction or, in the case of the standards of review, to state liability.[82] This elevates the norm of investor protection in the same way that doctrines of human rights prioritize certain individual rights over those of the state, and the result is to exaggerate the importance of investor protection in relation to the other values and concerns that are at stake in governmental decision-making.[83]

Covenant on Civil and Political Rights (1994), (1995) 15 HRLJ 464, 2 IHRR 10, para 10–11 and 17. G Huscroft, 'Rights, Bills of Rights, and the Role of Courts and Legislatures' in G Huscroft and P Rishworth (eds) *Litigating Rights* (Oxford: Hart, 2002) 3–4; A Nollkaemper, 'Concurrence Between Individual Responsibility and State Responsibility in International Law' (2003) 52 ICLQ 615, 630–1.

[78] eg MS McDougal, HD Lasswell, and L Chen, 'The Protection of Aliens From Discrimination and World Public Order: Responsibility of States Conjoined with Human Rights' (1976) 70 AJIL 432, 435–6; P Allott, 'State Responsibility and the Unmaking of International Law' (1988) 29 Harv Int'l LJ 1, 14–16. See generally MM Carrow, *The Background of Administrative Law* (Newark: Associated Lawyers, 1948) 20–1; P McAuslan, 'Administrative Law, Collective Consumption, and Judicial Policy' (1983) 46 Mod L Rev 1, 11–12; D Bodansky and JR Crook, 'Symposium: The ILC's State Responsibility Articles—Introduction and Overview' (2002) 96 AJIL 773, 775.

[79] eg World Bank, *Report of the Executive Directors on the Convention on the Settlement of Investment Disputes Between States and Nationals of Other States* (18 March 1965), reprinted in *Convention, Regulations and Rules* (Washington: ICSID, 2003) para 26 (commenting that a 'legal dispute', for the purposes of the ICSID Convention, concerns 'the existence or scope of a legal right or obligation, or the nature or extent of the reparation to be made for breach of a legal obligation').

[80] *Metalclad* (n 70 above) para 75–6, 89, and 99; *Pope & Talbot* (Merits, Phase 2) (n 16 above) para 42, 72, and 116. Brower II (n 44 above) 87–8; Lillich (n 42 above) 67–8; Brower II (n 65 above) 1546–8.

[81] eg *Siemens* (n 65 above) para 81; *Bogdanov (Iurii) et al v Moldova* (Merits) (22 September 2005), SCC Rules, 16, online: ITA, Investment Claims. Donovan (n 15 above) 229; T Weiler (n 69 above) 181.

[82] See n 73–5 above. See also *Wena Hotels Ltd v Egypt* (Jurisdiction) (25 May 1999), 41 ILM 881, 888; *Waste Management No 2* (Merits) (n 60 above) para 85.

[83] eg Brower *et al* (n 15 above) 430–5. See JE Alvarez, 'Critical Theory and the North American Free Trade Agreement's Chapter Eleven' (1997) 28 U Miami Inter-Am L Rev 303, 307–8.

This does not in any way deny that states have concluded investment treaties so as to protect more effectively foreign investors under international law, in support of business confidence and security in the international economy. As much is clearly stated in the preambles of treaties calling for 'a treaty aiming to promote and protect investment ... to stimulate the initiative of investors' (Belgium–Luxembourg BIT), for 'the encouragement and reciprocal protection of investment' in order to 'stimulate the flow of private capital and the economic development of the Parties' (US-modelled BITs), or for 'the stimulation of business initiative' by creating 'favourable conditions for greater economic co-peration ... in particular for investments' (UK-modelled BITs; Germany-modelled BITs). But the preambles of investment treaties also connect the economic justifications for investor protection to wider public interest objectives; such as, to 'stimulate the transfer of capital and technology between the two countries in the interest of their economic development' (France-modelled BITs; Netherlands-modelled BITs); to 'promote the economic prosperity' of the states parties (Swiss-modelled BITs; Peru–Paraguay BIT); or to maintain 'maximum effective utilization of economic resources' and 'contribute to the well-being of workers' (US-modelled BITs). These treaties do not affirm the rights and interests of international business as an inherent good; they utilize investor protection as a means to an end.[84]

Read with care, and in light of the representative role of the state as juridical sovereign, the preambular language of investment treaties does not provide a basis for adopting a presumption in favour of safeguarding the claimant against the state. It is also noteworthy that investment treaties in the great majority of cases do not use bold rights-affirming language to describe the standards that constrain states in order to protect foreign investors.[85] Human rights treaties usually declare in unambiguous terms the rights and freedoms of individuals.[86] Compare investment treaties to, for instance, the language of the Declaration on the Human Rights of Individuals Who are not Nationals of the Country in which They Live, the preamble of which recognizes that 'all human beings are born free and equal in dignity and rights' and refers to the need to protect the human rights and fundamental freedoms of all consistent with the Charter of the United Nations and the

---

[84] eg NAFTA (n 8 above) preamble (describing the purpose of the treaty as being to encourage economic opportunities, growth, competition, and employment in the NAFTA states). *Loewen* (n 38 above) para 222; *Salini Costruttori SpA and Italstrade SpA v Kingdom of Morocco* (Jurisdiction) (23 July 2001), 42 ILM 609, 6 ICSID Rep 400 [cited as *Salini v Morocco*], para 52. Fatouros (n 41 above) 364; PI Hansen, 'Judicialization and Globalization in the North American Free Trade Agreement' (2003) 38 Texas Int'l LJ 489, 502–3.

[85] *Jurisdiction of the Courts of Danzig* (Advisory Opinion) (1928), PCIJ Ser B, No 15 [cited as *Courts of Danzig*], 17–19; *LaGrand* (Merits) (*Germany v United States*), [2001] ICJ Rep 466, 40 ILM 1069, para 77–8; *Legal Consequences of the Construction of a Wall in the Occupied Palestinian Territory* (Advisory Opinion) (9 July 2004), ICJ General List No 131 [cited as *Construction of a Wall*], para 126–31, 134, and 137. McDougal, Lasswell, and Chen (n 78 above) 460–4; M Koskenniemi, 'What Is International Law For?' in MD Evans (ed) *International Law* (2nd edn, Oxford: OUP, 2006) 73.

[86] eg *Construction of a Wall* (n 85 above) para 126–31.

Universal Declaration of Human Rights. In this instrument, the interests of foreign nationals that are affirmed and protected—including the right to life and security of the person, the right to equality before the courts, and the right to own property—are given the indisputable status of 'rights' in the tradition of human rights.[87] The omission of similar language from investment treaties, although not determinative in itself, is an additional factor that indicates that investor protection was not meant to have the same level of governmental priority as do fundamental rights.[88]

More importantly, there is a difference between a legally enforceable right and a fundamental or human right.[89] Human rights are universal in that they protect all by the nature of the human condition and by the common entitlement of everyone to dignity and protection, and, for this reason, they are given a higher recognition by the community. Because they are universal, human rights treaties normally protect all persons from those sovereign acts that are prohibited[90] and, on this basis, rights-based systems of state liability should in principle be open to any individual.[91] However, if investment treaties are taken to bestow rights, then those rights are strongly restricted to individuals who have enough foreign wealth to contemplate bringing claims. For one, most humans and many companies do not own foreign assets and therefore do not qualify as investors under the treaties;[92] further, among those that do, few own enough ever to credibly threaten a claim given that a claimant must front half the cost of an arbitration.[93] In NAFTA awards thus far, where arbitration costs were reported by the tribunal, they averaged about

---

[87] Declaration on the Human Rights of Individuals Who are not Nationals of the Country in which They Live, GA Res 40/144, UN GAOR, 40th Sess, Supp No 53, UN Doc A/40/53 (1985) 252, art 5.

[88] M Sornarajah, *The Pursuit of Nationalized Property* (Dordrecht: Martinus Nijhoff, 1986) 31–2; Juillard (n 67 above) 338 and 329.

[89] PP Craig, 'Once Upon a Time in the West: Direct Effect and the Federalization of EEC Law' (1992) 12 Ox J Legal Studies 453, 453–8; JA Weir, 'Human Rights and Damages' (2001) 40 Washburn LJ 412, 419–20 and 445–6; J Allan, 'Rights, Paternalism, Constitutions and Judges' in G Huscroft and P Rishworth (eds) *Litigating Rights* (Oxford: Hart, 2002) 34–5.

[90] D Shelton, *Remedies in International Human Rights Law* (Oxford: OUP, 1999) 39–40.

[91] C Eagleton, *The Responsibility of States in International Law* (New York: NYU Press, 1928) 139–41; C Harlow, 'Francovich and the Problem of the Disobedient State' (1996) 2 Eur LJ 199, 204–15.

[92] Investment treaties adopt different definitions of 'investor' but virtually all make access to arbitration available to both natural and legal persons who qualify as investors. Typically, the claimant is a foreign corporation, established in one state party to the treaty, that owns assets in another state party to the treaty. The claimant could also be a natural person, public entity, or other business vehicle such as a trust or partnership: eg NAFTA (n 8 above) art 201 and 1139 (definitions of 'enterprise' and 'investor of a Party'). *Azinian* (n 55 above) para 77; *SD Myers* (Merits) (n 65 above) para 222–31 (majority opinion); *UPS* (n 46 above) para 6 and 18–21; *Mondev* (n 9 above) para 49–50 and 80; *Waste Management No 2* (Merits) (n 60 above) para 77.

[93] The cost of an investor claim typically includes not only legal fees but also 50% of the fees of the arbitrators as well as administrative fees charged by the arbitration institution (eg ICSID charges (US)$25,000 to file a claim): LE Peterson, 'Bilateral Investment Treaties and Development Policy-Making' (Report for the International Institute for Sustainable Development, November 2004) 24–6.

(US)$1.5 million a claim, which one assumes is beyond the means of many who do business abroad. In the *CME* case, under the Netherlands–Czech Republic BIT, the arbitrator fees alone were (US)$1.35 million, divided equally between the investor and the host state.[94] Thus, access to the system is limited in practical terms to foreign investors that have a significant economic interest in the outcome of a regulatory dispute. In most cases, these are multinational firms.[95]

All legalized systems of rights can be criticized on the grounds that 'the rich and powerful not only have more rights but also have the means to enforce them' and the same goes for investment treaty arbitration.[96] But under investment treaties, unlike other public law systems, wealth is a legal as well as practical precondition of access to justice. The jurisdiction of tribunals to review state conduct is limited to foreign nationals *who own investment*.[97] Thus, a foreign-owned business could bring a claim against a repressive government, while a foreign national who was arbitrarily imprisoned and tortured, but who did not own local assets, could not. If an investment treaty establishes rights, therefore, it is a bill of rights that only property owners may enforce in the courts. Finally, and rather absurdly, the main class of claimants under investment treaties are firms that can vary the nature and content of the rights they enjoy by using holding companies to forum-shop among treaty regimes.

More than anything, it is this selectivity of the legal entitlement to protection that undermines the investor rights view. As a human rights system, investment treaty arbitration would establish the right to property and freedom of contract as the only actionable rights[98] and prioritize the implementation of investor rights (ie property and economic rights) over all other rights in circumstances where the former directly conflict with human rights that depend on state action and the regulation of business for their realization.[99] In this respect, investor protection can be as much an obstacle to human rights as a strand in the wider rights movement.

As alluded to above, another way to understand the role of individual investors in the present system that is also consistent with the regulatory nature of investment treaty disputes is to conclude that investment treaties give exceptional powers to certain individuals, but for a public purpose.[100] From this point of

---

[94] *CME* (Damages) (n 38 above) para 650 (summary of decision).
[95] Sornarajah (n 5 above) 8; Douglas (n 16 above) 152.   [96] Griffith (n 6 above) 172–3.
[97] Alvarez (n 83 above) 304–5 and 307–8.
[98] Sornarajah (n 88 above) 31; JE Stiglitz, 'The Broken Promise of NAFTA' *The New York Times* (6 January 2004).
[99] D Cohen and JC Smith, 'Entitlement and the Body Politic: Rethinking Negligence in Public Law' (1986) 64 Can Bar Rev 1, 12; E Drake *et al*, 'The Multilateral Agreement on Investment: A Step Backward in International Human Rights' (Report for the Human Rights Clinical Project Program, Harvard Law School, undated); R Bachand and S Rousseau, 'International Investment and Human Rights: Political and Legal Issues' (Background Paper for Rights and Democracy, 11 June 2003) 18–19; Koskenniemi (n 85 above) 109–10.
[100] *UPS* (n 46 above) para 80; *SGS v Philippines* (n 22 above) para 154. See also *LaGrand* (n 85 above) para 77–8 ('Although under modern international law, treaties may confer rights, substantive and procedural, on individuals, they will normally do so in order to achieve some public interest').

view, investment treaty arbitration is a legal mechanism to enforce international standards as part of an inter-state bargain, and the role of the claimant is more like that of a private attorney-general than the victim of a rights violation.[101] This approach lends itself to a more cautious approach to the individualization of international claims and to state liability in light of the governmental implications of a damages award, in part because it rejects investor protection as a fundamental norm.[102] I expand on this public law perspective in the next section.

The public law framework

Each of the approaches discussed above faces conceptual difficulties arising from the expansion of international adjudication into the regulatory sphere and, for different reasons, each tends to undermine the system's viability as a governing arrangement based on the promise of neutral, rules-based decision-making. The commercial arbitration analogy treats the respondent state as a private party, although the conduct of states that is subject to review is clearly sovereign in nature, and thus disregards the very notion of public law. The public international law approach underestimates the manner in which far-reaching individualization injects public law considerations directly and fully into the forum of international adjudication. The investor rights position recognizes that investor–state disputes adjudicated pursuant to a treaty are regulatory disputes, but treats investor protection as the dominant aim of the system and, in doing so, discards the ongoing need to accommodate democratic choice and governmental discretion.

Adjudicators should, therefore, not give pride of place to any of these approaches. Rather, the appropriate way to implement the adjudicative function under an investment treaty is to adapt a public law framework to the novel context of regulatory adjudication under international law.[103] This approach follows from the recognition that a claim brought by an individual against the state in a dispute arising from a sovereign act falls within a unique realm of governmental adjudication that is distinct from private law as well as classical public international law. It analogizes the international adjudication of regulatory disputes to the adjudication of individual claims in public law generally, and calls for the application of principles developed domestically and, to a lesser extent, in the international sphere in cases where courts and tribunals directly resolve regulatory disputes between

---

[101] C Tollefson, 'Metalclad v United Mexican States Revisited: Judicial Oversight of NAFTA's Chapter Eleven Investor–State Claim Process' (2002) 11 Minn J Global Trade 183, 203–5; Wälde (n 65 above) 435–6 and 444; JHH Weiler, 'Emerging Issues on Compliance and Effectiveness of Community Law' (1997) 91 Am Soc'ty Int'l L Proc 172, 172.

[102] eg *CME* (Damages) (n 38 above) para 74–8 (separate opinion); *SGS v Pakistan* (n 4 above) para 171; *Saluka Investments v Czech Republic* (Merits) (17 March 2006), 18(3) World Trade and Arb Mat 166 [cited as *Saluka*], para 300; *Azinian* (n 55 above) para 99; *Loewen* (n 38 above) para 242.

[103] Chayes (n 6 above) 1284; K Roach, 'The Limits of Corrective Justice and the Potential of Equity in Constitutional Remedies' (1991) 33 Ariz L Rev 859, 860; R Jackson, 'Sovereignty in World Politics' (1999) 47 Pol Studies 431, 454; B Legum, 'Trends and Challenges in Investor–State Arbitration' (2003) 19 Arb Int'l 143, 147.

individuals and the state. Thus, it is only to the extent that they directly engage relevant matters of public law that domestic and international law offer proper comparators for resolving ambiguity in the scope and content of the standards of review or the appropriateness of an award of damages as a remedy against the state. The primary reference point in this regard must be domestic law, both as a source of analogous rules and principles and as evidence of the practice of the states parties to the treaty, given that in the case international law it is often not possible to disentangle distinctively 'public law' principles from awards and decisions that have been made in the context of reciprocally consensual adjudication between states.

The public law framework calls for detailed review of how rules and principles of the administrative and constitutional law of business regulation in different countries, and especially in the dominant capital-exporting states, govern the myriad issues that arise in the adjudication of regulatory disputes. Such a detailed review is beyond the scope of the present work, although it is possible to signal some general directions as to how this might be pursued by adjudicators. First, as a general principle, and given that the system is designed to regulate states, it is necessary for the treaties to be interpreted in ways that promote predictability not only for investors but also for government.[104] Thus, tribunals should be cognizant of wider regulatory concerns, including the countervailing interests that are represented by public opposition to particular business activity; the implications of a particular investment for the host economy; the impact on the host state's ability to prioritize social stability, public health and morals, and environmental concerns over the objectives of economic efficiency and investor confidence; and the overall coherence and legitimacy of the integration project.[105] It is not an excess of jurisdiction to take these concerns into account; on the contrary, is it an integral part of any official decision-making process, including public law adjudication. Further, where a dispute tests the limits of the adjudicative process in general, because of its complexity or the treaty's ambiguity, adjudicators should afford a margin of appreciation to the discretionary policy choices of domestic

---

[104] *Methanex* (Jurisdiction) (n 46 above) para 130 and 137–8. *SGS v Pakistan* (n 4 above) para 167. JC Thomas, 'Reflections on Article 1105 of NAFTA: History, State Practice and the Influence of Commentators' (2002) 17 ICSID Rev 21, 29; Center for International Environmental Law (CIEL), 'International Law on Investment: The Minimum Standard of Treatment (MST)' (CIEL Issue Brief, August 2003) 6–7.

[105] eg *Genin (Alex) and Others v Republic of Estonia* (Merits) (25 June 2001), 17 ICSID Rev 395, 6 ICSID Rep 304 [cited as *Genin*], para 370; *Salini v Morocco* (n 84 above) para 52; *SGS v Pakistan* (n 4 above) para 167–8; *Tecmed* (n 22 above) para 133 and 146–8; *Waste Management No 2* (Merits) (n 60 above) para 101 and 111–12; *Loewen* (n 38 above) para 242; see also *Noble Ventures* (n 50 above) para 182; *International Thunderbird* (n 11 above) para 127. AA Fatouros, 'International Law and the Third World' (1964) 50 Virg L Rev 783, 813–14; JA McKinney, *Created from NAFTA—The Structure, Function, and Significance of the Treaty's Related Institutions* (Armonk, NY: ME Sharpe, 2000) 231; C Tollefson, 'Games without Frontiers: Claims and Citizen Submissions Under the NAFTA Regime' (2002) 27 Yale J Int'l L 141, 153; UNCTAD (n 8 above) 117.

institutions,[106] and defer to governmental decisions that are not specifically abusive or discriminatory.[107] The aim should be to preserve a reasonably predictable space, consistent with the public law of most, if not all, legal systems, for the state to exercise public authority undeterred by the prospect of a retrospective damages award. In particular, in delineating the scope of state liability, it is appropriate to consider the relevant public law of the host state but also, and more significantly, the investor's home state.[108] Affording a multinational firm greater access to state compensation for regulatory acts in the host state than that available in the firm's own state is a one-sided approach that undermines the ideal of neutrality in international adjudication.

The use of damages as a public law remedy, including for unlawful legislative and judicial acts, makes it especially appropriate to use treaty arbitration to deter state conduct that flaunts international standards, but not to sanction general regulation.[109] This rejects the agenda of investor rights on the assumption that the treaties aim to encourage foreign investment for an overarching wider public purpose and that the adjudicator's task when faced with ambiguity in the treaty is to define more specific elements of that purpose. Presuming that ambiguity should be interpreted in favour of investor protection is a governmental decision that defines investor protection as the singular purpose of the state in the context of business regulation. Instead, arbitrators should recognize that investor protection is a means to a public end and that it should not be championed at the expense of other governmental priorities or the viability of the state itself.[110] As signatories to treaties, states retain ultimate responsibility for public welfare.[111]

This more cautious approach is not wholly absent from the reasoning of investment treaty tribunals, although it does usually take a back seat to the other approaches identified above. The clearest example of a tendency towards prudence is the trend in the NAFTA jurisprudence towards a more cautious interpretation of the NAFTA minimum standard of treatment[112] and expropriation standard,[113]

---

[106] eg *Saluka* (n 102 above) para 305; *Encana* (n 60 above) para 194. Fuller (n 2 above); RSJ Macdonald, 'The Margin of Appreciation' in RSJ Macdonald, F Matscher, and H Petzold (eds) *The European System for the Protection of Human Rights* (Dordrecht: Martinus Nijhoff, 1993) 122–4; JHH Weiler, 'Epilogue: Towards a Common Law of International Trade' in JHH Weiler (ed) *The EU, the WTO, and the NAFTA* (Oxford: OUP, 2000) 202–3; Weir (n 89 above) 433–4.

[107] eg *SD Myers* (Merits) (n 65 above) para 261–3 (majority opinion). Harlow and Rawlings (n 9 above) 96–7; JHH Weiler (2000) (n 106 above) 207–10.

[108] CD Gray, *Judicial Remedies in International Law* (Oxford: Clarendon, 1987) 9.

[109] McKinney (n 105 above) 230–1; JHH Weiler (n 101 above) 173–4.

[110] *CME* (Damages) (n 38 above) para 75 and 78 (separate opinion). D Rodrik, *The Global Governance of Trade As If Development Really Mattered* (Report for the UN Development Programme, October 2001) 22.

[111] *Azinian* (n 55 above) para 87; *ADF* (n 46 above) para 170 and 173; *Loewen* (n 38 above) para 242; *Waste Management No 2* (Merits) (n 60 above) para 161; *GAMI* (n 47 above) para 114.

[112] *ADF* (n 46 above) para 179–86; *Mondev* (n 9 above) para 111; *Loewen* (n 38 above) para 131–3; *Waste Management No 2* (Merits) (n 60 above) para 98.

[113] eg by distinguishing expropriation from regulation or from breach of contract, and by limiting the concept of 'tantamount to' expropriation to indirect or creeping expropriation: *Azinian* (n 55 above)

following the states parties' objections[114] to the expansive readings adopted by early tribunals.[115] A few NAFTA tribunals have even assumed as a starting-point that the exercise of public authority is not objectionable in the absence of clear evidence of an abuse of authority that specifically targets foreign investors.[116] On the other hand, evidence of a similar tendency in BIT arbitration is scarce; only a small handful of awards has clearly favoured it, led by *SGS v Pakistan* (in which the tribunal read down an umbrella clause out of respect for the autonomy of the domestic legal order).[117] One explanation for this is that only under NAFTA has a dominant capital-exporting state, the US, had to respond to a wave of investor claims. This generated a significant political backlash to the system and prompted the NAFTA states to temper the interpretations that were urged on tribunals by investors. But there is no principled reason for tribunals that are constituted under BITs to wait for joint submissions by the states parties or a political storm in Western Europe before also acting to contain the impact of state liability.

On this note, it must be acknowledged that the adoption of a prudential position that insulates states from retroactive liability under NAFTA and other investment treaties appears, at times, to be motivated by concerns that themselves undermine the inter-state bargain upon which the system is founded. In particular, an apparent motivation has been the desire to accommodate states in order to guard the system against political threats to its existence.[118] The *Loewen* tribunal, in particular, anticipated the likely criticism that its award left a Canadian investor who suffered injustice in US courts without a remedy, and responded with this pre-emptive statement:[119]

As we have sought to make clear, we find nothing in NAFTA to justify the exercise by this Tribunal of an appellate function parallel to that which belongs to the courts of the host nation. In the last resort, a failure by that nation to provide adequate means of remedy may amount to an international wrong but only in the last resort. . . . Too great a readiness to step from outside into the domestic arena, attributing the shape of an international wrong

---

para 90; *Pope & Talbot Inc v Government of Canada* (Merits, Phase 1) (26 June 2000), 13(4) World Trade and Arb Mat 19, para 104; *SD Myers* (Merits) (n 65 above) para 281–2 and 285–6 (majority opinion); *Feldman* (n 4 above) para 100 and 103; *Waste Management No 2* (Merits) (n 60 above) para 175.

[114] eg *Mondev* (n 9 above) para 106 and 108–10.

[115] *Metalclad* (n 70 above) para 74–6; *Pope & Talbot* (Merits, Phase 2) (n 16 above) para 110 and 115–18; *SD Myers* (Merits) (n 65 above) para 266 (majority opinion). CIEL (n 104 above) 3–5; Thomas (n 104 above) 113–14; Tollefson (n 101 above) 207–13 and 224–5.

[116] *ADF* (n 46 above) para 156–7; *Loewen* (n 38 above) para 135; *Waste Management No 2* (Merits) (n 60 above) para 115 and 130–2; *Methanex* (Merits) (n 11 above) pt IV—ch E, para 22.

[117] *SGS v Pakistan* (n 4 above) para 168. See also *Genin* (n 105 above) para 367; *Joy Mining Machinery Ltd v Arab Republic of Egypt* (Jurisdiction) (6 August 2004), 19 ICSID Rev 486, 44 ILM 73, para 58 and 81; *Encana* (n 60 above) para 184–98.

[118] *Azinian* (n 55 above) para 87 and 99; *Loewen* (n 38 above) para 242. Paulsson (n 30 above) 257; Alvarez and Park (n 15 above) 399; J Werner, 'Some Comments on the NAFTA Chapter 11 Case—*ADF Group Inc and United States of America*' (2003) 4 J World Investment 113, 123–4.

[119] *Loewen* (n 38 above) para 242. See also *Empresas Lucchetti, SA v Lucchetti Peru, SA* (Merits) (7 February 2005), 19 ICSID Rev 359, 17(3) World Trade and Arb Mat 161, para 61.

to what is really a local error (however serious), will damage both the integrity of the domestic judicial system and the viability of NAFTA itself. The natural instinct, when someone observes a miscarriage of justice, is to step in and try to put it right, but the interests of the international investing community demand that we must observe the principles which we have been appointed to apply, and stay our hands.

The reference here to the 'viability of NAFTA' and to 'the interests of the international investing community' as justification for prudence suggests that arbitrators may choose to limit state liability only where a damages award could provoke controversy among decision-makers and the public in the major states. If so, this would be the right result for the wrong reason. By encouraging adjudicators to tread softly on powerful governments while maintaining strict disciplinary standards for those less powerful, such reasoning jeopardizes the neutrality of treaty arbitration. The inter-state bargain gives way to an accommodation of states based on the degree to which their support is believed critical to maintain the system.[120] If this were to become commonplace, then investment treaty arbitration would be associated with a bias in favour of international business and capital-exporting states, and investment treaties would emerge as simply the new capitulation treaties.[121] Thus, out of respect for international reciprocity, it is necessary to extend the consideration of sovereign priorities to all respondent states.

A compelling example of the prudential position that follows from the application of a public law framework in international adjudication is offered by the only other international regime that relies, like investment treaties, on individualized claims and state liability to enforce rules of economic integration. This example is the *Francovich* doctrine of the European Court of Justice, which, as noted in Chapter 5 of this book, requires that an EC member state's law allow for damages awards to individuals who have suffered harm from the member state's violation of EC law. The *Francovich* doctrine is a judge-made doctrine—'an assertion of power or even act of defiance by the ECJ', in Harlow's words—and it reflects the tendency of that court to interpret EC law expansively so as to support European integration.[122] It is all the more telling, therefore, that the ECJ found it necessary to restrict state liability under *Francovich* to 'sufficiently serious' violations of EC law by member states. In particular, in its decision in *Brasserie de Pêcheur*, the Court ruled that various factors may be taken into account to preclude a damages award, including the level of clarity of the rule breached, the measure of discretion left by that rule to public authorities, whether the infringement and the damage caused was intentional or involuntary of the state, whether any error of law was

---

[120] Paulsson (n 30 above) 246 and 257.
[121] M Sornarajah, 'The Clash of Globalisations and the International Law on Foreign Investment' (Presentation to the Centre for Trade Policy and Law, Ottawa, 12 September 2002) 18, online: Centre for Trade Law and Policy (Carleton University) http://www.carleton.ca/ctpl/pdf/papers/sornarajah.pdf; B Kingsbury, N Krisch, and RB Stewart, 'The Emergence of Global Administrative Law' (2005) 68 Law & Contemporary Problems 15, 52.
[122] C Harlow, *State Liability: Tort Law and Beyond* (Oxford: OUP, 2004) 57–8.

excusable or inexcusable, the fact that the position taken by a Community institution may have contributed towards the omission, and the adoption or retention of state measures contrary to EC law.[123] Subsequently, in *Bergaderm*, the Court clarified further that 'the decisive test' for the imposition of state liability was whether the state 'manifestly and gravely disregarded the limits of its discretion' under EC law.[124]

These essentially fault-based limitations are very much an outgrowth of the checks on state liability that have evolved in the domestic law of EC member states (most of which adopt a civil law approach to state liability, which is typically more generous to individuals than is the common law tradition).[125] In the proceedings in *Brasserie de Pêcheur*, in which the ECJ spelled out the limits on the *Francovich* doctrine, the ECJ received submissions by eight of the EC member states, all informed by each state's own law of state liability. Moreover, all of these submissions favoured limiting the doctrine to cases of manifest breach of the law, with frequent mention of the difficulties that arise from retroactive damages awards against the state. The Danish and UK governments, along with the EC Commission, expressed the following concern:[126]

If questions of interpretation are shrouded in uncertainty and a Member State exercises its discretion in a reasonable way, it would seem unreasonable for it to incur liability if it is later held that Community law precludes the national law or administrative practice in question. Unblameworthy legal mistakes should not lead to liability to make reparation.

In receiving such elaborate submissions from states, the ECJ obtained a detailed outline of how different legal systems manage the thorny issues that arise in relation to state liability in public law. Under investment treaties, as argued here, the states parties to the treaty should likewise be encouraged to make submissions on matters of treaty interpretation, even where the treaty and the arbitration rules do not expressly provide a mechanism for doing so.[127] Also, tribunals should take notice of relevant rules and principles of state liability that are common to the public law of the states parties. Doing so, it is suggested, will support a more cautious

---

[123] *Brasserie du Pêcheur SA v Germany; Secretary of State for Transport, ex parte Factortame Ltd and Others* (No 46 & 48/93), [1996] ECR I-1131, (1996) 1 CML Rev 889, para 56.

[124] *Laboratoires Pharmaceutiques Bergaderm and Goupil v Commission* (No 352/98), [2000] ECR I-5291.

[125] D Fairgrieve, 'The Human Rights Act 1998, Damages and Tort Law' [2001] Pub Law 695, 698–9; Harlow (n 122 above) 59–61. Note that 'fault' has a broader meaning than the concept of 'intent to harm', which is much-maligned in investment treaty arbitration [eg Douglas (n 65 above) 49].

[126] *Brasserie du Pêcheur SA v Germany; Secretary of State for Transport, ex parte Factortame Ltd and Others* (No 46 & 48/93), Report for the Hearing, [1996] ECR I-1034, (1996) 1 CML Rev 889, para 57.

[127] The approach adopted by the *Aguas del Tunari* tribunal—which solicited the views of the government of the home state (the Netherlands) about an official answer it had given to a parliamentary question about the BIT—was constructive but unduly narrow, informed as it was by the tribunal's predominantly private law view of investment treaty arbitration: *Aguas del Tunari* (n 73 above) para 47 and 258.

reading than that which emerges from the binary dynamic of investor versus respondent state. This is particularly so for the interpretation of the standards of review where they constrain acts of the host state's legislature or courts, although it applies to all cases that affect the general viability of government in matters of broad public concern.[128]

Notably, in contrast to the *Francovich* doctrine of the ECJ, other limiting factors beyond the requirement for a sufficiently serious breach are also absent from investment treaties. In particular, the availability of damages under EC law is based on domestic rules of liability in the member state responsible for the breach, subject to minimum requirements of effectiveness and non-discrimination,[129] and domestic courts play a key role in determining whether liability should be imposed in specific cases.[130] This has allowed the courts in the United Kingdom, for instance, to decline to award compensation out of a fear that claimants 'might thereby side-step limitations on liability in domestic tort law'.[131] I do not suggest that the domestic courts of host states should play a direct role in interpreting investment treaties, at least in the first instance. The point here is simply that the residual role of domestic courts in the implementation of EC law cushions the impact of treaty-based state liability.[132] The absence of this cushion in investment treaty arbitration is yet another reason for prudence, particularly where a tribunal is urged by a claimant to interpret ambiguous treaty language so as to remove the duty to exhaust local remedies.

Conclusion

The ratification of so many investment treaties in recent years attests to a wide convergence of views among states as to the desirability of protecting investment in support of a liberalized global economy. But states should not be assumed by the conclusion of these treaties to have mandated a transformation of the juridical

---

[128] *Azinian* (n 55 above) para 87; *SD Myers* (Merits) (n 65 above) para 261–3 and 282 (majority opinion); *ADF* (n 46 above) para 170 and 173; *Loewen* (n 38 above) para 242; *Waste Management No 2* (Merits) (n 60 above) para 161. J Kurtz, 'A General Investment Agreement in the WTO? Lessons from Chapter 11 of NAFTA and the OECD Multilateral Agreement on Investment' (Jean Monnet Working Paper, New York University School of Law, 2002) 69; D Brown, 'Commentary' in L Ritchie Dawson (ed) *Whose Rights? The NAFTA Chapter 11 Debate* (Ottawa: Centre for Trade Policy and Law, 2002) 40–1; JA VanDuzer, 'NAFTA Chapter 11 to Date: The Progress of a Work in Progress' in L Ritchie Dawson (ed) *Whose Rights? The NAFTA Chapter 11 Debate* (Ottawa: Centre for Trade Law and Policy, 2002) 95.

[129] *Francovich and Bonifaci v Republic of Italy* (No 6 and 9/90), [1991] ECR I-5357, (1993) 2 CML Rev 66 [cited as *Francovich*], para 43.

[130] *Rewe-Zentral Finanz eG v Lanschwirtschaftskammer für das Saarland* (No 33/76), [1976] ECR 1989. Harlow and Rawlings (n 9 above) 632–3; T Tridimas, 'Liability for Breach of Community Law: Growing Up and Mellowing Down?' (2001) 38 CML Rev 301, 317–21 and 331–2.

[131] M Lunney and K Oliphant, *Tort Law* (Oxford: OUP, 2000) 524–5.

[132] Lunney and Oliphant (n 131 above) 524–5. See also Tridimas (n 130 above) 317–21 and 331–2.

nature of the state or the sacrifice of all other governmental priorities for the benefit of more efficient capital flows. Ironically, an affirmation of the ongoing role of government is inherent in any state's decision to use adjudication to resolve regulatory disputes. Part of the public law character of investment treaty arbitration is the recognition that the aims of investment treaties also depend on how values other than property rights and the sanctity of contract are advanced within the adjudicative process.

This does not mean that the host state should always win. But in all domestic legal systems there is a regulatory space in which individuals cannot receive damages for unlawful state conduct, and it would be very surprising if this space did not exist at the international level.[133] When sovereign acts of the state are equated to acts of a private party, investment treaty arbitration by definition infringes on this fiscally risk-free domain of government. In determining the extent to which such a domain exists in the international sphere, it is suggested that arbitrators bear in mind the well-established limits in domestic law on the adjudication of regulatory disputes and on damages as a public law remedy.[134] Investment treaties constrain the policy options of domestic governments without establishing international institutions to regulate multinational firms,[135] meaning that the state remains the primary repository of regulatory authority in a world that calls for proactive government for reasons beyond the encouragement of international investment, however important the latter objective may be.[136]

Unfortunately, some arbitrators and many commentators seem to act aggressively when protecting investors while downplaying the implications for the respondent state. This converts investment treaty arbitration into a regime that governs the public sphere by private law rules or rights-based norms and, as such, it skews the system in favour of business and against other individuals and the

---

[133] Even if one accepts the human rights analogy, then it should be considered that, in human rights instruments, rights to property and contract are subject to exceptions relating to the public welfare and thus balanced against other public interests and individual rights. eg Universal Declaration of Human Rights, GA Res 217A, UN GAOR, 3rd Sess, Part I, UN Doc A/810 (1948) 71, art 17 and 29.

[134] Cohen and Smith (n 99 above) 8 and 11–12; R Baldwin and C McCrudden, *Regulation and Public Law* (London: Weidenfeld & Nicolson, 1987) 60–1; Harlow (n 91 above) 220; JHH Weiler (n 101 above) 173–4; Loughlin (n 1 above) 48–52; JHH Weiler (n 106 above) 230; JG Merrills, 'The Means of Dispute Settlement' in MD Evans (ed) *International Law* (2nd edn, Oxford: OUP, 2006) 547–8.

[135] AC Aman, 'Globalization, Democracy, and the Need for a New Administrative Law' (2003) 10 Ind J Global Legal Studies 125, 139–40.

[136] Fatouros (n 41 above) 364–5; R Kozul-Wright and R Rowthorn, 'Spoilt for Choice? Multinational Corporations and the Geography of International Production' (1998) 14 Ox Rev Econ Pol 74, 84–5; S Picciotto, 'Introduction: What Rules for the World Economy?' in S Picciotto and R Mayne (eds) *Regulating International Business* (Houndmills: Macmillan, 1999) 4–5 and 19–20; Rodrik (n 110 above) 15–16 and 27; UNCTAD, *World Investment Report 2004* (New York: United Nations, 2004) 233 and 236.

community as a whole.[137] What might explain this tendency? As is argued in the next chapter of this book, the most important reason not to allocate to arbitrators the ultimate authority to resolve core matters of public law is that the financial incentives of private lawyers and academics, as distinct from judges, may be seen to encourage them whilst sitting as arbitrators to eschew a prudential approach to state liability.

[137] W Twining, *Globalisation and Legal Theory* (London: Butterworths, 2000) 51; WW Bratton *et al*, 'Introduction: Regulatory Competition and Institutional Evolution' in WW Bratton *et al* (eds) *International Regulatory Competition and Coordination* (Oxford: Clarendon, 1996) 3; A Claire Cutler, 'Critical Reflections on the Westphalian Assumptions of International Law and Organization: A Crisis of Legitimacy' (2001) 27 Rev Int'l Studies 133, 143–50; F Snyder, 'The Gatekeeper: The European Courts and WTO Law' (2003) 40 CML Rev 313, 365.

7
The Businessman's Court

The predominant theme of this book is that investment treaty arbitration must be distinguished from both commercial arbitration and inter-state adjudication on the basis that it is more akin to a public law system of adjudication, albeit constituted in a unique way at the international level. Drawing this distinction does not require one to deny that private law may raise issues of broad public concern or that public international law may affect matters in the regulatory sphere. Neither claim has been made nor would it be sustainable. However, the distinction does explain why certain disputes involving claims by individuals against the state are not suited to arbitration in the manner of a commercial or a conventional international dispute because they concern the legality of sovereign acts and the right of private business to receive state compensation for losses that are caused by governmental activity.

In this chapter, I elaborate on this public law approach by examining what it contributes to the ongoing and often fractious debate about investment treaty arbitration. In particular, four criteria of public law adjudication—accountability, openness, coherence, and independence—are reviewed in order to identify flaws with the present system.[1] First, in terms of accountability, it is argued that the key problem is that arbitrators can interpret public law without the possibility of a judge reviewing their decisions for errors of law. Second, as is widely acknowledged, the system does not satisfy the standard of openness because it requires that essential information about the process be withheld as a matter of course from the public. Third, in terms of coherence, the lack of an appellate body to review awards makes it difficult, if not impossible, to unify the jurisprudence into a stable system of state liability. Fourth, and most critically, it is argued that arbitrators are financially dependent on executive governments and on prospective claimants—and thus not independent in the manner of a judge—because they do not have security of tenure and because investment treaty arbitration is one-sided in that only investors bring claims and only states are ordered to pay damages for breach of treaty. That is, as merchants of adjudicative services, arbitrators have a financial stake in furthering the system's appeal to claimants and, as a result, the system is

---

[1] M Taggart, 'The Province of Administrative Law Determined' in M Taggart (ed) *The Province of Administrative Law* (Oxford: Hart, 1997) 4; M Aronson, B Dyer, and M Groves, *Judicial Review of Administrative Action* (3rd edn, North Ryde: LBC Information Services, 2004) 1.

tainted by an apprehension of bias in favour of allowing claims and awarding damages against governments.

Each of these flaws in the system is a consequence of the unhappy marriage of international arbitration and public law. The purpose of elaborating them is not categorically to reject the use of international adjudication to resolve regulatory disputes or to suggest that all of the criticisms of investment treaties hold water. It is rather to focus on precise and unique failings of the system in order to develop a clear and viable framework for reform. At root, the critique is not an attack on arbitration but a defence of accountable and independent courts, in accordance with the straightforward proposition that public law adjudication must satisfy basic standards of judicial decision-making in a democratic society. Otherwise, the global economy becomes but a convenient excuse for a method of adjudication that is tainted, in an objective sense, and that consequently fails to deliver on the promise of the rule of law.

Four Criteria of Public Law Adjudication

Accountability

Accountability is a broad concept that can incorporate many different checks and restraints on judicial power, from the general approbation of the legislature or the general public, to specific legal controls such as the duty to give reasons or disciplinary processes for serious misconduct by individual judges. Not surprisingly, then, a variety of complaints about investment treaty arbitration can be collected under the accountability umbrella, including the rather unpersuasive argument that arbitrators should not have the authority to resolve the important policy issues that arise in investment disputes because their background is often in commercial law or because their decisions are taken very distantly from those affected.[2]

This criticism has a degree of resonance, especially when combined with recognition of the exceptional aspects of investment treaty arbitration—compared to other international regimes—as well as the underlying selectivity of the system's protection of investors. But it is diluted by the fact it could apply to virtually any form of adjudication including the courts. For instance, the WTO Appellate Body is condemned for being unresponsive to local and national priorities, just as it is said that unelected judges should not have the power to overturn legislatures in order to protect individual rights.[3] And while it is true that nearly all

---

[2] B Stern, 'Comments—International Economic Relations and the MAI Dispute Settlement System' (1999) 16(2) J Int'l Arb 118, 128; M Sornarajah, 'The Clash of Globalisations and the International Law on Foreign Investment' (Presentation to the Centre for Trade Policy and Law, Ottawa, 12 September 2002) 17.

[3] RI Martin, *The Most Dangerous Branch* (Montreal: McGill-Queen's University Press, 2003).

arbitrators are white males from a relatively narrow professional and class background, the same goes for most judges.[4] Simply, these are much broader issues than those raised uniquely by the advent of investment treaty arbitration as a system of public law, and they merge into a wider debate about the role that adjudication should play in the control of government. At times, they even blend into an anti-internationalist position that is incongruous to the expansion of the international economy and to the ensuing social integration. In the case of investment treaties, this last version of the accountability critique is effectively answered by the argument that, while investment treaty arbitration is far from ideal, it is nevertheless an essential instrument to resolve investor–state disputes in a way that is detached from the legal systems of individual states.[5]

Recognizing these vulnerabilities of the broader critique, I shall limit the notion of accountability to the narrower point that an adjudicator can be made accountable to the public for the interpretation of public law, as in domestic legal systems, simply by allowing for the appeal of awards to the courts in matters of legal interpretation. It is this more specific accountability that is absent from investment treaty arbitration because of the system's incorporation of the enforcement structure of international commercial arbitration. Transferred into the regulatory sphere under investment treaties, this enforcement structure allows arbitrators to rule on critical issues of public law without the possibility of judicial review to correct errors of law. Moreover, where arbitrators are authorized to select the jurisdictional seat of an arbitration,[6] this structure allows them to choose the general standard of review to which they will themselves be subject. In this respect, the system enables arbitrators to decide to what degree their formulations of public law should occur beyond the supervision of state-appointed and publicly accountable courts. Again, this is an anomalous situation that arises in the present system because of its unique reliance on a private model of international adjudication in the regulatory sphere.

It is, of course, true that investment treaties subject tribunals to review by domestic courts or, in ICSID arbitrations, by an annulment committee whose members are appointed by ICSID.[7] But in both cases the grounds for judicial

---

[4] JAG Griffith, *The Politics of the Judiciary* (5th edn, London: Fontana Press, 1997) 18–22 and 338.
[5] J Paulsson, *Denial of Justice in International Law* (Cambridge: CUP, 2005) 228 and 233.
[6] Tribunals are frequently required to select the seat of the arbitration in accordance with the arbitration rules under which the investor claim is filed. The UNCITRAL Rules [(n 33 below) art 16(1)] and the ICSID Additional Facility Rules [(n 33 below) art 21 of sch C] grant tribunals the authority to choose the seat of the arbitration unless the parties agree otherwise. Arbitrations under the ICSID Rules are held at the seat of the ICSID, in Washington DC, unless the parties agree to hold the arbitration at an institution with which ICSID has made arrangements [ICSID Convention (n 8 below) art 62–3] or at another institution with the approval of the tribunal [ICSID Rules (n 33 below) r 13(3)]. Some investment treaties [eg NAFTA (n 15 below) art 1130] specifically designate the jurisdictions that are eligible to be chosen as the seat of the arbitration.
[7] SD Franck, 'The Legitimacy Crisis in Investment Treaty Arbitration: Privatizing Public International Law Through Inconsistent Decisions' (2005) 73 Fordham L Rev 1521, 1547–57.

review, as laid out in the ICSID Convention, the New York Convention, and other instruments, are very limited.[8] Further, most states have enacted legislation since the 1980s (for the distinct purpose of encouraging agreements to arbitrate in order to stimulate international commerce) that directs their courts to defer to foreign arbitration awards,[9] and since then the trend in the jurisprudence in North America and Western Europe, at least, is to show a high level of deference to international arbitrators.[10] In general, domestic courts will overturn an award only where they find a jurisdictional error, procedural impropriety, or serious violation of public policy, and, crucially, the courts are typically not authorized to correct errors of law by tribunals in their interpretation of broadly framed

---

[8] Convention on the Settlement of Investment Disputes Between States and Nationals of Other States (the ICSID Convention) (Washington, 18 March 1965; 4 ILM 524; entered into force 14 October 1966), art 53–5; United Nations Convention on the Recognition and Enforcement of Foreign Arbitral Awards (the New York Convention) (New York, 10 June 1958; 330 UNTS 3; entered into force 7 June 1959), art V; Inter-American Convention on International Commercial Arbitration (the Panama Convention) (Panama, 30 January 1975; 14 ILM 336), art 4–5. See also *Model Law on International Commercial Arbitration*, 21 June 1985, UNCITRAL, UN Doc A/40/17, annex I, 24 ILM 1302, art 34–5; *Report of the Secretary-General: Analytical Commentary on Draft Text of a Model Law on International Commercial Arbitration*, UN, UN Doc A/CN.9/264 (25 March 1985), 16 Ybk UNCITRAL 104, para 44.

[9] eg Federal Arbitration Act 1925, 9 USC c 2 (USA) (governing actions in a US federal court to vacate awards (c 1, s 10) and to recognize and enforce awards under the New York Convention (c 2, s 207) and the Panama Convention (c 3, s 304)); Arbitration Act 1996 (UK) s 67–9; Commercial Arbitration Act, RSC 1985, c 17 (2nd Supp) (Canada), art 34–6 of sch (Commercial Arbitration Code); Código de Comercio, Title IV, c 1–9 (Commercial Arbitration), as amended 1989 and 1993 (Mexico), art 1415–63. Many US states have adopted arbitration laws based on the Uniform Arbitration Act, itself modelled on the Federal Arbitration Act, and some have adopted arbitration statutes based on the UNCITRAL Model Law. Canadian federal and provincial legislation (with the exception of Québec) and the relevant provisions of Mexico's arbitration legislation are also based on the UNCITRAL Model Law. MJ Mustill, 'Arbitration: History and Background' (1989) 6(2) J Int'l Arb 43, 51–3; S Kierstead, 'Referral to Arbitration Under Article 8 of the UNCITRAL Model Law: The Canadian Approach' (1998) 31 Can Bus LJ 98, 100–2; WM Reisman, *Systems of Control in International Adjudication and Arbitration* (Durham: Duke University Press, 1992) 125–6; D Enix-Ross and DW Rivkin for the NAFTA Advisory Committee on Private Commercial Disputes, *Summary of US Arbitration Law* (June 1995) 1; M Tenenbaum, 'International Arbitration of Trade Disputes in Mexico—The Arrival of the NAFTA and New Reforms to the Commercial Code' (1995) 12 J Int'l Arb 53, 59–60 and 73–4; K-H Böckstiegel, 'An Introduction to the New German Arbitration Act Based on the UNCITRAL Model Law' (1998) 14 Arb Int'l 19, 28–31; R Nishikawa, 'Arbitration Law Reform in Japan' (2004) 21 J Int'l Arb 303, 305–6.

[10] eg *Bremen v Zapata Offshore Co* (1972) 407 US 1, 92 S Ct 1907; *Scherk v Alberto-Culver Co* (1907) 417 US 506; *Mitsubishi Motors Corp v Soler Chrysler Plymouth Inc* (1985) 473 US 614, 627–37; *Shearson/American Express, Inc v McMahon* (1987) 482 US 220; *Quintette Coal Ltd v Nippon Steel Corp* (1990) 50 BCLR (2nd) 207 (BC CA); *Gulf Canada Resources Ltd v Arochem International Inc* (1992) 11 BCAC 145, 43 CPR (3rd) 390 (BC CA); *Corporacion Transnacional de Inversiones v STET International* (1999) 45 OR (3rd) 183 (Ont SCJ), aff'd 49 OR (3rd) 414 (Ont CA). MA Scodro, 'Arbitrating Novel Legal Questions: A Recommendation for Reform' (1996) 105 Yale LJ 1927, 1929–37; C Reymond, 'The Channel Tunnel Case and the Law of International Arbitration' (1993) 109 LQ Rev 337, 341; A Redfern and M Hunter, *Law and Practice of International Commercial Arbitration* (4th edn, London: Sweet & Maxwell, 2004) 329.

standards of investor protection.[11] As one judge in British Columbia found in deciding whether to set aside the *Metalclad* award under NAFTA:[12]

The Tribunal gave an extremely broad definition of expropriation for the purposes of Article 1110. In addition to the more conventional notion of expropriation involving a taking of property, the Tribunal held that expropriation under the NAFTA includes covert or incidental interference with the use of property which has the effect of depriving the owner, in whole or in significant part, of the use or reasonably-to-be-expected economic benefit of property. This definition is sufficiently broad to include a legitimate rezoning of property by a municipality or other zoning authority. However, the definition of expropriation is a question of law with which this Court is not entitled to interfere under the *International Commercial Arbitration Act* [of British Columbia].

Thus, arbitrators autonomously resolve core questions of public law: whether legislation is discriminatory, whether regulation is expropriation, whether a court decision is unfair or inequitable. The difficulty here is not that these issues are resolved by international adjudication but that they are resolved by a private adjudicator without adequate supervision by public judges.[13] This lack of judicial supervision renders the arbitrator's interpretation of public law—itself a fundamentally sovereign act—unaccountable in the conventional sense.

A review of how arbitration awards are enforced by domestic courts pursuant to the New York Convention sheds further light on this point. First, it is necessary to distinguish between the jurisdictional seat of arbitration and the place of enforcement, given that arbitration awards can be reviewed by courts in either location. The seat of an arbitration is the place in which the arbitration is located by the arbitration tribunal for purposes of domestic jurisdiction. Under the New York Convention, an arbitration is subject to supervision by domestic courts in the seat of the arbitration, and a respondent state may apply to set aside an award only in the courts of that seat based on its domestic law. Importantly, it is this domestic law that dictates the level of supervision that a court may exercise over an arbitration tribunal. Thus where a tribunal selects the respondent state as the seat of the arbitration, the tribunal is subject to supervision by the courts of that state and its relevant laws. Where a foreign state is chosen as the seat of the arbitration, the arbitration is subject to supervision by foreign courts, subject to a foreign domestic

---

[11] *United Mexican States v Metalclad Corporation* (2001) 89 BCLR (3rd) 359, 38 CELR 284, 13(5) World Trade and Arb Mat 219, para 50–6; *United Mexican States v Marvin Roy Feldman Karpa* (2003) 16(2) World Trade and Arb Mat 237, para 77–86 (Ont SCJ); *United Mexican States v Marvin Roy Feldman Karpa* (2005) 193 OAC 216, 248 DLR (4th) 443, para 34–43 (Ont CA); *Attorney General of Canada v SD Myers, Inc* [2004] 3 FCR 368, 5 CELR (3rd) 166 (Fed Ct TD), para 42–4; *Ecuador v Occidental Exploration and Production Co* [2006] 1 Lloyd's Rep 773 (QB), para 124–5. See also Franck (n 7 above) 1546.

[12] *United Mexican States v Metalclad Corporation* (n 11 above) para 99. International Commercial Arbitration Act, RSBC 1996, c 233 (British Columbia).

[13] Some arbitrators argue that investment treaty tribunals are accountable via domestic court supervision while in the same breath advocating judicial deference to the system as a whole. They cannot have it both ways. To be accountable, tribunals must at least be subject to judicial review for errors of legal interpretation, as well as errors of jurisdiction and procedural impropriety.

law.[14] By selecting the seat of the arbitration, therefore, arbitrators indirectly determine whether investment treaty arbitration constitutes an extra-territorial arrangement by which the sovereign conduct of one state is subject to review by a tribunal established in the jurisdiction of a foreign state, which may or may not be the home state of the investor. Such was the case in the *UPS* arbitration under NAFTA, for example, in which the tribunal was constituted to review acts of the Canadian government, subject to the supervisory jurisdiction of US courts in that the seat of arbitration chosen by the tribunal was Washington, DC.[15]

The place of enforcement, on the other hand, is the jurisdiction in which an investor seeks enforcement of an award against assets of the respondent state. For an award to be executed under the New York Convention, it must be recognized and enforced by the courts in the place where enforcement is sought.[16] A court in the place of enforcement has the discretion to refuse to enforce an award based on the limited grounds laid out in the New York Convention.[17] It appears that this includes the discretion to enforce an award even where the award was already set aside in the seat of the arbitration.[18] Thus, an investor can seek enforcement of an award against assets of the respondent state before the domestic courts of any state party to the New York Convention, regardless of whether the courts of either the respondent state itself or the seat of the arbitration have upheld the award.[19] Considering that there are hundreds of states parties to the New York Convention, an investor has myriad opportunities to chase the assets of the respondent state against which it has won an award.[20]

The key significance of this enforcement structure for the principle of accountability in public law is that it fragments and restricts judicial supervision of arbitrators. Judicial supervision is fragmented because investors can pursue the

---

[14] Where the foreign state in question is the home state of the investor, then the tribunal is supervised by the courts of the investor's state. In such instances, investment treaty arbitration is more reminiscent of the capitulation treaties of the nineteenth and early twentieth centuries; see the discussion in Ch 2 above, p 15.

[15] Under NAFTA, a tribunal must locate the seat of a Chapter 11 arbitration in a NAFTA state that is a party to the New York Convention: North American Free Trade Agreement (NAFTA) (17 December 1992; 32 ILM 296 and 605; entered into force 1 January 1994), art 1130. To June 2005, 8 NAFTA arbitrations had been located in Canada, 7 in the US (including all of the claims against the US), and 0 in Mexico. Under many BITs, typically the seat of the arbitration, barring an agreement to the contrary by the disputing parties, is Washington, DC, which is the default location for ICSID arbitrations: ICSID Convention (n 8 above) art 62. This removes the discretion of arbitrators to select the seat of the arbitration, while also reflecting US dominance of ICSID.

[16] New York Convention (n 8 above) art V.

[17] New York Convention (n 8 above) art V. See also UNCITRAL Model Law (n 8 above) art 34 and 35.   [18] New York Convention (n 8 above) art V(1)(e).

[19] eg *Sonatrach v Ford Bacon & Davis Inc* (1990) 11 Ybk Comm'l Arb 370; *Hilmarton I* (1995) 20 Ybk Comm'l Arb 663; *Chromalloy Aeroservices v Arab Republic of Egypt* (1996) 939 F Supp 907, 12(4) Int'l Arb R B-1 (DDC). Reisman (n 9 above) 113–16; CN Brower, CH Brower II, and JK Sharpe, 'The Coming Crisis in the Global Adjudicative System' (2003) 19 Arb Int'l 415, 428.

[20] On the other hand, many courts would presumably be reluctant to enforce awards that were previously set aside by a court in the seat of the arbitration. Redfern and Hunter (n 10 above) 404 and 468–70.

enforcement of awards in any state party to the New York Convention, thus dividing supervisory responsibility among the courts of many different countries.[21] More importantly, judicial supervision is restricted because the enforcement structure limits the setting aside or non-recognition of awards to the narrow grounds enumerated in the New York Convention and relevant domestic legislation. In international commercial arbitration, this restriction on judicial supervision is justifiable on the basis that the courts should not interfere with the choices of private parties to resolve commercial disputes in a forum of their choosing. Under investment treaties, though, the structure operates to insulate the authority of arbitrators to interpret public law.

Perversely, the use of this enforcement structure also gives arbitrators and investors a substantial measure of control over the degree of accountability of tribunals to courts. Tribunals in many cases choose the seat of the arbitration, thus determining the domestic law that will apply to an application by the respondent state to pre-empt the arbitration or set aside an award.[22] Also, investors decide where to seek enforcement, thus determining the domestic law that will apply to the enforcement of the award.[23] In both cases, arbitrators and investors have a smorgasbord of jurisdictions from which to choose a legal system that is likely to defer to, and enforce, an award. In this regard, many states have, in recent decades, adopted liberal rules of enforcement for foreign arbitration awards in an effort to make themselves more attractive as centres for international arbitration, typically at the urging of their own arbitration industry.[24] This presents an additional challenge to accountability. The practice has been condemned by commercial arbitrators, such as Reisman, on grounds of unfair competition:[25]

> The 'Belgians,' as it were, will take advantage of the more stringent jurisdictional practices of other jurisdictions to attract a quantity of arbitral business that would otherwise not have selected their venue. They are free riders, in the economic sense, benefiting from a general regime but refusing to pay their dues. They are ... engaging in an unfair trade practice by exploiting a noneconomic variable in order to make themselves more attractive to a class of potential customers of services.

Here, Reisman's criticism speaks of the tendency of competition among states to undermine court supervision of international commercial arbitration. But the dynamic of regulatory competition poses a far greater threat to accountability where the contest becomes a race to limit judicial oversight of public law.

---

[21] *Ecuador v Occidental Exploration and Production Co* [2005] 2 Lloyd's Rep 240 (QB), para 76 and 84. Brower *et al* (n 19 above) 419.

[22] W Peter, *Arbitration and Renegotiation of International Investment Agreements* (2nd edn, The Hague: Kluwer Law International, 1995) 284–5; Reisman (n 9 above) 127.

[23] Presumably, the investor's decision would be driven first by the location of assets of the state and, second, by the enforceability of awards in that jurisdiction.

[24] Y Dezaley, 'Between the State, Law, and the Market: The Social and Professional Stakes in the Construction and Definition of a Regulatory Arena' in WW Bratton *et al* (eds) *International Regulatory Competition and Coordination* (Oxford: Clarendon, 1996) 84–6; Peter (n 22 above) 284–5.   [25] Reisman (n 9 above) 131.

Openness

There has been widespread criticism of investment treaty arbitration for its lack of openness, and rightly so, for this issue goes to the heart of the problem of using arbitration to resolve regulatory disputes.[26] Here, I refer to openness both as the principle that the public should have access to information about adjudicative decision-making and the notion that, in some cases, the legitimacy of adjudicative decisions which affect regulatory concerns may require views other than those of the claimant and respondent to be represented in the process.

Public *access* to information is widely recognized as a fundamental principle of judicial decision-making in domestic and international courts.[27] It requires that adjudication take place in the public eye, subject to specifically enumerated exceptions, and that judicial decisions and relevant documents filed in a litigation be placed on the public record. If adjudication—above all in public law—were not fully open and transparent, it would be immune from public scrutiny and matters affecting the community at large could routinely be decided in secret. For this reason, openness is a precondition of both accountability and independence in adjudication.[28] In contrast, *participation* by non-parties in adjudication is not as fundamental a principle, and it is approached differently in different legal systems.[29] For example, the practice of courts to appoint amicus curiae to assist in the consideration of outside interests that are affected by a dispute, and that would not otherwise be represented by the disputing parties, is largely an innovation of US law that has spread to other jurisdictions, including, as we shall see, investment treaty arbitration.[30]

---

[26] PI Hansen, 'Judicialization and Globalization in the North American Free Trade Agreement' (2003) 38 Texas Int'l LJ 489, 500–1; CG Garcia, 'All the Other Dirty Little Secrets: Investment Treaties, Latin America, and the Necessary Evil of Investor–State Arbitration' (2004) 16 Florida J Int'l L 301, 354–5; A Cosbey et al, *Investment and Sustainable Development* (Report by the International Institute for Sustainable Development, 2004) 4–5; J Atik, 'Legitimacy, Transparency and NGO Participation in the NAFTA Chapter 11 Process' in T Weiler (ed) *NAFTA, Investment Law and Arbitration* (Ardsley, NY: Transnational Publishers, 2004) 149–50.

[27] eg Convention for the Protection of Human Rights and Fundamental Freedoms (the European Convention on Human Rights [ECHR]) (4 November 1950; Eur TS 5, 213 UNTS 222; entered into force 3 September 1953), art 40 (providing that hearings of the court shall take place in public and that documents deposited with the Registry shall be made accessible to the public). S Shetreet, 'Judicial Independence: New Conceptual Dimensions and Contemporary Challenges' in S Shetreet and J Deschênes (eds) *Judicial Independence: The Contemporary Debate* (Dordrecht: Martinus Nijhoff, 1985) 656–7.

[28] T Meron, 'Judicial Independence and Impartiality in International Criminal Tribunals' (2005) 99 AJIL 359, 360.

[29] C Harlow, 'Global Administrative Values: The Quest for Principles and Values' (2006) 17 EJIL 187, 202–4. Thus, while the International Institute for Sustainable Development in its critique of investment treaties [Cosbey et al (n 26 above) 4] is right to describe openness as one of the 'essential safeguards used by most democratic societies to ensure the legitimacy and accountability of judicial proceedings', it is an exaggeration to extend this proposition to participation by third parties and, in particular, to amicus curiae representation.

[30] M Shapiro, 'The Globalization of Law' (1993) 1 Ind J Global Legal Studies 37, 57–60.

In terms of public access, the system falls well short of openness, although notable improvements have been made, mainly at the instance of the US and Canada. The nub of the problem is that openness conflicts with party autonomy, reflected in the right of a disputing party to keep the arbitration of a dispute confidential.[31] In commercial arbitration, it is usually assumed that the existence of the dispute, its subject-matter, the identity of the arbitrators, the materials submitted, and the award itself must all be kept confidential unless both disputing parties agree otherwise; indeed, confidentiality is one of the selling points of commercial arbitration as an alternative to the courts.[32] This element of the principle of party autonomy is reflected in the provisions on confidentiality that are contained in the different sets of arbitration rules that are incorporated into investment treaties, including the ICSID Rules, the ICSID Additional Facility Rules, the UNCITRAL Rules, the ICC Rules, and the Stockholm Rules.[33] But while this closed approach may be tolerable in the resolution of commercial disputes that relate exclusively or overwhelmingly to the disputing parties alone, and that do not raise issues of broad public concern, its transplantation into investment treaty arbitration allows the meaning of public law to be determined finally in secret. Thus, the *New York Times* reported with respect to NAFTA arbitration:[34]

Their meetings are secret. Their members are generally unknown. The decisions they reach need not be fully disclosed. Yet the way a small group of international tribunals handles disputes between investors and foreign governments has led to national laws being revoked, justice systems questioned and environmental regulations challenged. And it is all in the name of protecting the rights of foreign investors....

One should not overstate the level of secrecy that exists in the system at present. A large proportion of awards, perhaps the majority, is issued under the auspices of

---

[31] Respect for party autonomy is the primary rationale for confidentiality in international commercial arbitration: *Report of the Secretary-General: Revised Draft Set of Arbitration Rules for Optional Use in Ad Hoc Arbitration Relating to International Trade (UNCITRAL Arbitration Rules)*, UN, UN Doc A/CN.9/112/Add.1 (12 December 1975), 7 Ybk UNCITRAL 166, 175 (art 22(4), commentary); *Report of the Secretary-General: Analytical Commentary on Draft Text of a Model Law on International Commercial Arbitration*, UN, UN Doc A/CN.9/264 (25 March 1985), 16 Ybk UNCITRAL 104 [cited as *Model Law Report*] 124 (art 19, commentary).

[32] L Mistelis, 'Confidentiality and Third Party Participation in Investment Arbitration' (2005) 21 Arb Int'l 205, 213; A Redfern, 'Investor–State Arbitrations—A Bridge Too Far?' in G Aksen *et al* (eds) *Global Reflections on International Law, Commerce and Dispute Resolution* (International Chamber of Commerce, 2005) 671–2.

[33] eg ICSID Convention (n 8 above) art 48(5); ICSID *Administrative and Financial Regulations*, reprinted in *Convention, Regulations and Rules* (Washington: ICSID, 2003) 51, reg 22(2); ICSID, *Rules of Procedure for Arbitration Proceedings*, revised 26 September 1984 and 1 January 2003 (original rules 1968), reprinted in *Convention, Regulations and Rules* (Washington: ICSID, 2003) [cited as ICSID Rules] r 48(4) and 6(2); *Rules Governing the Additional Facility for the Administration of Proceedings by the Secretariat of the International Centre for Settlement of Investment Disputes*, revised 1 January 2003 (original rules 1978), 1 ICSID Rep 213 [cited as ICSID Additional Facility Rules] art 4(5) and art 13(2) and 53(3) (sch C); *Arbitration Rules of the United Nations Commission on International Trade Law*, UN GA Res 31/98, UN GAOR, 31st Sess, Supp No 17, UN Doc A/31/17, c V, s C (1976) [cited as UNCITRAL Rules] art 25(4) and 32(5).

[34] A DePalma, 'NAFTA's Powerful Little Secret' *The New York Times* (11 March 2001).

ICSID, which routinely publishes the existence of an arbitration; the identity of the parties, their legal agents, and the arbitrators; and the general nature of the dispute.³⁵ Also, the internet has made investment treaty awards at ICSID and elsewhere far more available to the public than the most widely disseminated court decisions in days of old.³⁶ But public access is about more than how many people can get their hands on a decision. It is about the parties and the adjudicator knowing that their views and arguments can be read and picked apart by anyone, so that they will more assuredly consider the implications of what they do or decide for their reputation and for that of the system.³⁷ This knowledge is integral to the accountability and independence of judges, especially where they are deciding questions of sovereign authority and the allocation of taxpayer funds. So, it is most unfortunate that in many cases, including at ICSID, the content of submissions and awards is kept secret where either of the disputing parties does not consent to publication. Worse, outside of ICSID the mere existence of a claim and identity of the arbitrators may also be withheld. The norm of public access is thus subordinated to rules of confidentiality that are alien to public law.

The fact that investment treaties do not provide for the compulsory publication of all relevant information in investment treaty arbitration indicates that state officials did not fully appreciate the implications of using international arbitration in the regulatory sphere when they concluded the treaties.³⁸ How else does one explain their failure to adjust the rules to preserve this basic premiss of public law? This conclusion is supported by the early debate that occurred over openness in NAFTA arbitration, in which the issue of confidentiality arose in a number of cases, leading to divergent approaches by different tribunals.³⁹ The NAFTA text, as in most investment treaties, does not resolve the issue of public access one way or the other.⁴⁰ However, the applicable arbitration rules appeared to support a

---

³⁵ Mistelis (n 32 above) 212.   ³⁶ Redfern (n 32 above) 671–2.
³⁷ *Scott v Scott* [1913] AC 417, 477 (HL) (Lord Shaw citing Jeremy Bentham): 'Publicity is the very soul of justice. It is the keenest spur to exertion and the surest of all guards against improbity. It keeps the judge himself while trying under trial.'). See also *Home Office v Harman* [1983] 1 AC 280, 303 (HL) (Lord Diplock) and 316 (Lord Scarman); *Attorney-General v Leveller Magazine Limited* [1979] AC 440, 450 (Lord Diplock).
³⁸ H Mann and K von Moltke, 'Protecting Investor Rights and the Public Good: Assessing NAFTA's Chapter 11' (Report for the International Institute for Sustainable Development, 2002) 21.
³⁹ *SD Myers, Inc v Government of Canada* (Procedural Order No 3 and 11) (10 June 1999 and 11 November 1999), UNCITRAL Rules [cited as *SD Myers*], online: DFAIT, NAFTA Claims; *Pope & Talbot Inc v Government of Canada* (Merits, Phase 2) (10 April 2001), 13(4) World Trade and Arb Mat 61 [cited as *Pope & Talbot*], para 17. Compare *Loewen Group, Inc and Raymond L Loewen v United States of America* (Jurisdiction) (5 January 2001), 7 ICSID Rep 421, para 25–6; *Feldman Karpa (Marvin Roy) v United Mexican States* (Procedural Order No 5) (6 December 2000), ICSID Case No ARB(AF)/99/1, para 10–11, online: NAFTA Claims. B Legum, 'Trends and Challenges in Investor–State Arbitration' (2003) 19 Arb Int'l 143, 144–5.
⁴⁰ In particular, annex 1137:4 of NAFTA provides that, in a NAFTA Chapter 11 claim against Canada or the United States, either the host state or the investor can make an award public. Because this applies only to the publication of awards, it leaves open the possibility that other materials relating to a Chapter 11 claim may not be released without the consent of both the respondent state and the investor. This state of affairs was addressed by the Free Trade Commission's interpretation of 31 July 2001 (n 43 below).

presumption in favour of confidentiality.[41] Applying these rules, some tribunals declined to publish materials or allow public access to the proceedings without the consent of the disputing parties.[42] In 2002 the NAFTA states intervened by announcing that they would publish all documents submitted to, or issued by, NAFTA tribunals, and that they interpreted the treaty such that it did not prevent the states parties from releasing materials relating to NAFTA claims against them.[43] In this respect, the rules of arbitration were subordinated to the states parties' reading of the treaty, putting openness before party autonomy.

Moreover, the release of documents filed in NAFTA arbitrations enabled NAFTA tribunals and the states parties to take the additional step of allowing participation by non-parties in the process. In a seminal decision in 2001 the *Methanex* tribunal found that it had the power under the UNCITRAL Rules to allow non-governmental organizations to make submissions based on documents that were already in the public domain.[44] In this respect, the tribunal also noted the importance of bearing in mind the burden that this could impose by increasing the number of participants in an arbitration.[45] This is a unique concern in private arbitration because the cost of the process is borne by the disputing parties and, as a result, participation by non-parties raises access concerns that do not exist in the courts. On the other hand, the *Methanex* tribunal decided that, without the consent of the parties, it did not have the authority to add third parties to the proceedings or hold public hearings.[46] Subsequently, in October 2003, the NAFTA states issued a joint statement that supported public participation by recommending procedures for how tribunals should respond to submissions by non-participating parties, but which also signalled that NAFTA hearings would remain closed to the public in the absence of party consent.[47] However, in June 2004, the *Methanex* tribunal opened its hearings in Washington, DC to the public for the first time in an investment treaty arbitration.

---

[41] UNCITRAL Rules (n 33 above) art 32(5) ('The award may be made public only with the consent of both parties'); ICSID Additional Facility Rules, art 44(2).

[42] *Ethyl Corporation v Government of Canada* (Procedural Orders) (13 October 1997 and undated), UNCITRAL Rules, para 9 and para 2 and 3, respectively, online: DFAIT, NAFTA Claims; *SD Myers* (n 39 above); *Pope & Talbot* (n 39 above).

[43] Free Trade Commission, *Notes of Interpretation of Certain Chapter 11 Provisions* (31 July 2001), 13(6) World Trade and Arb Mat 139, art A, online: DFAIT www.dfait-maeci.gc.ca/tna-nac/NAFTA-Interpr-en.asp.

[44] *Methanex Corporation v United States of America* (Participation by Amicus Curiae) (15 January 2001), UNCITRAL Rules [cited as *Methanex*], para 30–1 and 46–7, online: State Department, ITA, NAFTA Claims. See also *United Parcel Service of America, Inc v Government of Canada* (Participation by Amicus Curiae) (1 August 2003), UNCITRAL Rules, online: DFAIT, NAFTA Claims; *Glamis Gold, Ltd v United States of America* (Participation by Amicus Curiae) (16 September 2005), UNCITRAL Rules, online: State Department, NAFTA Claims.

[45] *Methanex* (n 44 above) para 35–7 and 50.   [46] *Methanex* (n 44 above) para 29 and 42.

[47] Free Trade Commission, *Statement of the Free Trade Commission on non-disputing party participation* (17 October 2003), online: DFAIT http://www.dfait-maeci.gc.ca/nafta-alena/Nondisputing-en.pdf.

These reforms of the NAFTA regime to ensure greater openness were a very important improvement. Even if they fall short of the openness of court proceedings and of the power of judges to appoint amicus curaie,[48] they have assured the possibility of public scrutiny and allowed arbitrators an additional means to inform themselves about what are often complex regulatory disputes.[49] Recently two tribunals established under other treaties (but presided over by the same arbitrator) followed the lead by allowing written submissions by non-parties, while keeping the hearings closed to the public.[50] However, it is important to emphasize that the inclusion in the process of NGOs claiming to represent aspects of the public interest more effectively than government does nothing to address more fundamental failings of system. All investment treaties, including NAFTA, are still beset by deeper problems of accountability and independence. Moreover, at least one BIT tribunal—in *Aguas del Tunari*—has remained faithful to the misplaced ideal of party autonomy and preserved confidentiality in the process, in the context of a dispute that garnered major public attention and opposition.[51] In particular, the tribunal decided that the interplay of the Netherlands–Bolivia BIT and the ICSID Convention, along with the consensual nature of arbitration, made it 'manifestly clear to the Tribunal that it does not, absent the agreement of the Parties, have the power to join a non-party to the proceedings; to provide access to hearings to non parties and, *a fortiori*, to the public generally; or to make the documents of the proceedings public.'[52] This decision catalogues the reasons why the system as a whole still fails to meet the criterion of openness in public law. Moreover, without intervention by the states parties to BITs to require the release of documents, more diverse representation of the public is a non-starter. Genuine public participation, after all, can only follow public access.

To summarize, it appears that investment treaties were negotiated without adequate consideration of the need to ensure openness in the process. Second, this can be resolved by state intervention (as in the case of NAFTA) and by the inclusion of provisions in new investment treaties (as in recent treaties concluded by the US with Singapore, Morocco, Peru, and Central American countries, for example) that mandate the disclosure of documents, open the hearings to the

---

[48] VL Been and JC Beauvais, 'The Global Fifth Amendment: NAFTA's Investment Protections and the Misguided Quest for an International "Regulatory Takings" Doctrine' (2003) 78 NYU L Rev 30, 46–7; CH Brower II, 'Structure, Legitimacy, and NAFTA's Investment Chapter' (2003) 36 Vand J Transnat'l L 37, 72–3.

[49] DM Gruner, 'Accounting for the Public Interest in International Arbitration: The Need for Procedural and Structural Reform' (2003) 41 Colum J Transnat'l L 923, 955–6.

[50] *Aguas Argentinas, SA v Argentine Republic* (Participation by Amicus Curiae) (19 May 2005), ICSID Case No ARB/03/19, online: ICSID, ITA, Investment Claims; *Aguas Provinciales de Santa Fe SA v Argentine Republic* (Participation by Amicus Curiae) (17 March 2006), ICSID Case No ARB/03/17, online: ICSID, ITA, Investment Claims.

[51] *Aguas del Tunari SA v Republic of Bolivia* (Jurisdiction) (21 October 2005), 18(2) World Trade and Arb Mat 271 [cited as *Aguas del Tunari*].

[52] *Aguas del Tunari* (n 51 above) para 17 and app III.

public, and affirm the power of tribunals to allow non-party submissions.⁵³ Third, the positive steps of a few states on this issue do not resolve the system's ongoing failings with respect to openness. Confidentiality is still the dominant principle in the treaties of most countries. The Europeans, in particular, have failed to follow the North American lead by adjusting their model BITs and using their bargaining power to press for the reinterpretation or amendment of existing treaties. And while it is true that some other international courts and tribunals, such as WTO panels, maintain elements of confidentiality, it should be remembered that these are inter-state forms of arbitration which take place in the classical context of reciprocal relationships between states. Also, other bodies, including the WTO, regularly publish the existence of claims by states and the content of decisions. In short, investment treaty arbitration is alone among all international bodies that adjudicate regulatory disputes in its blanket suppression of essential information about the process.

Coherence

Another concern with the present system, expressed among others by many arbitrators, is that it lacks coherence.⁵⁴ I shall deal with this concern only briefly, given that it is less specifically a public law concern than the other issues discussed in this chapter.

Coherence may be defined as the capability of an adjudicative system to resolve inconsistencies that arise from different decisions, and to ensure that the law is interpreted in a uniform and relatively predictable manner to allow those affected by the rules to plan their conduct.⁵⁵ The difficulty in investment treaty arbitration arises from the system's fragmented and individualized structure (as discussed above) and, specifically, from the absence of an appellate institution with jurisdiction to review awards issued by the disparate tribunals under the many different treaties and to correct errors of law made in the first instance. And, with so many treaties in place, it is inevitable that tribunals will interpret core standards and

---

⁵³ eg Singapore–United States Free Trade Agreement (Washington, 6 May 2003), art 15.19(3) and 15.20; Chile–United States Free Trade Agreement (6 June 2003), art 10.19(3) and 10.20; Morocco–United States Free Trade Agreement (Washington, 15 June 2004), art 10.19(3) and 10.20; The Dominican Republic–Central America–United States Free Trade Agreement (CAFTA) (Washington, 5 August 2004; entered into force 1 March 2006 [US, El Salvador], 1 April [Honduras, Nicaragua], and 1 July 2006 [Guatemala]; 16(6) World Trade and Arb Mat 87), art 10.20(3) and 10.21; Peru–United States Trade Promotion Agreement (Washington, 12 April 2006), art 10.20(3) and 10.21.

⁵⁴ J Werner, 'Making Investment Arbitration More Certain—A Modest Proposal' (2003) 4 J World Investment 767; Brower *et al* (n 19 above) 429–30; G Kaufmann–Kohler, 'Annulment of ICSID Awards in Contract and Treaty Arbitrations: Are There Differences?' in E Gaillard and Y Banifatemi (eds) *Annulment of ICSID Awards* (Huntington, NY: Juris Publishing, 2004) 219; Garcia (n 26 above) 340 and 348–51; Redfern (n 32 above) 672–4; Paulsson (n 4 above) 241.

⁵⁵ TM Franck, *Fairness in International Law and Institutions* (New York: Clarendon Press, 1995) 38; Meron (n 28 above) 361.

concepts in different ways.⁵⁶ To be sure, the system provides for the supervision of tribunals by domestic courts (ie in arbitrations pursuant to the New York Convention and related instruments) or by the ICSID annulment process.⁵⁷ These avenues provide an important means to promote greater coherence in the law, although certainly not as much as a hierarchical system that gives a single judicial body the power to correct legal errors by lower courts.⁵⁸ Further, because the system is internationalized, the supervisory role of domestic courts is divided among many jurisdictions that exercise varying degrees of review, but that typically defer to arbitrators.⁵⁹ This is hardly a recipe for a coherent jurisprudence, compared to domestic public law regimes. Werner's quip, comparing investment treaty arbitration to a casino in which investors and states roll the dice on whether a tribunal will award damages, thus has a small grain of truth to it.⁶⁰

Even so, coherence is a live issue in all forms of adjudication, including international commercial arbitration, which is subject to the very same regime of internationalized enforcement and review. Interpreting the law in ways that are predictable but still flexible is one of the great challenges of any court. As Price argues, one cannot expect arbitrators to outperform the US Supreme Court, which has worked for over 150 years to distinguish unlawful expropriation from legitimate regulation without producing a clear takings doctrine.⁶¹ Several NAFTA tribunals have, in fact, done a commendable job in their efforts to unify the jurisprudence under Chapter 11,⁶² whereas tribunals established under other treaties typically defer to earlier decisions, if sometimes rather selectively. At the international level, the challenge of coherence confronts all treaty-based adjudication, given that there is no way to appeal decisions to a single body, such as the International Court of Justice, for a final decision.⁶³ Decisions of the WTO Appellate Body may conflict with decisions of the UN Tribunal on the Law of the

---

⁵⁶ eg *SGS Société Générale de Surveillance v Pakistan* (Jurisdiction) (6 August 2003), 18 ICSID Rev 301, 42 ILM 1290, 8 ICSID Rep 406, 16(2) World Trade and Arb Mat 167 [cited as *SGS v Pakistan*], para 168 and 171 (treating a dispute resolution clause in an investment contract as a jurisdictional limit on BIT arbitration) versus *SGS Société Générale de Surveillance v Philippines* (Jurisdiction) (29 January 2004), 16(3) World Trade and Arb Mat 91 [cited as *SGS v Philippines*], para 97 (treating such a clause as an issue of admissibility and distinguishing *SGS v Pakistan* 'on issues of the interpretation of arguably similar language': 'In the Tribunal's view, although different tribunals constituted under the ICSID system should in general seek to act consistently with each other, in the end it must be for each tribunal to exercise its competence in accordance with the applicable law, which will by definition be different for each BIT and each Respondent State'). See also *BP America Production Co v Argentine Republic* (Jurisdiction) (27 July 2006), ICSID Case No ARB/04/8, para 104–5, online: ITA; Franck (n 7 above) 1558. ⁵⁷ See n 7–8 above.
⁵⁸ PS Atiyah, *Law & Modern Society* (2nd edn, Oxford: OUP, 1995) 19–20.
⁵⁹ Garcia (n 26 above) 341–5.   ⁶⁰ Werner (n 54 above) 782.
⁶¹ DM Price, 'NAFTA Chapter 11—Investor–State Dispute Settlement: Frankenstein or Safety Valve?' (2001) 26 Can–US LJ 107, 111. See also Paulsson (n 4 above) 243–4.
⁶² eg *Feldman Karpa (Marvin Roy) v United Mexican States* (Merits) (16 December 2002), 18 ICSID Rev 488, 42 ILM 625, 7 ICSID Rep 341, 15(3) World Trade and Arb Mat 157, para 143–52; *GAMI Investments, Inc v Government of the United Mexican States* (Merits) (15 November 2004), 44 ILM 545, 17(2) World Trade and Arb Mat 127, para 124–31. Brower II (n 48 above) 63.
⁶³ Y Shany, *The Competing Jurisdictions of International Courts and Tribunals* (Oxford: OUP, 2003).

Sea, which may conflict with decisions of the ECJ. Incoherence in international law, as such, is a product of the growth of international courts and tribunals in general, not just under investment treaties. The grand question in this context, not tackled here, is whether the value of international adjudication in resolving disputes and promoting respect for legal rules justifies whatever heightened prospects exist for inconsistent decisions.

Thus, investment treaty arbitration may generate incoherence but it generally does not raise unique problems in this respect. The one significant exception arises from the system's use of arbitration to resolve individual damages claims in public law. In particular, because only states are ordered to pay compensation for violating investment treaties, the system puts a special burden on those states (presently the vast majority) that host substantial assets of multinational firms. These states cannot look to the decisions of a single adjudicative body with a stable membership to draw together diverse readings of the treaties, many of which will establish varying bases for investor entitlements to compensation, into a firm jurisprudence. Incoherence poses a particular problem for states in this context because of the system's unique combination of state liability and international arbitration. Thus, Blackaby's condemnation of the conflicting awards against the Czech Republic in *CME* and *Lauder* applies most acutely to the position of the state: 'Any system where diametrically opposed decisions can legally coexist cannot last long. It shocks the sense of rule of law or fairness.'[64]

This impact on state decision-making is accentuated in the context of regulation of international business. All governmental decision-making depends to a degree on the ability of legislatures and administrations to know the boundaries of sovereign power and the consequences of the unlawful use of that power. Introducing damages as a remedy in public law heightens the fiscal uncertainty that accompanies regulation. Where the subjects of regulation are multinational firms with substantial legal resources, however, there is much greater likelihood that litigation will be used as a defence against regulatory initiatives that impose costs on business. In the words of one US lawyer, the ability to sue under an investment treaty is 'an open invitation to unhappy investors, tempted to complain that a financial or business failure was due to improper regulation, misguided macroeconomic policy, or discriminatory treatment by the host government and delighted by the opportunity to threaten the national government with a tedious expensive arbitration'.[65] Thus the incoherence that arises from the mixture of international arbitration and state liability in public law benefits large firms in their political bargaining with government, by exacerbating the regulatory chill that is otherwise generated by the threat of a damages award against

---

[64] N Blackaby, of Freshfields Bruckhaus Deringer, quoted in MD Goldhaber, 'Wanted: A World Investment Court' (Summer 2004) *The American Lawyer*.

[65] W Rogers, 'Emergence of the International Centre for Settlement of Investment Disputes (ICSID) as the Most Significant Forum for Submission of Bilateral Investment Treaty Disputes' (Presentation to the Inter-American Development Bank Conference, 26–7 October 2000).

the state.66 In some cases, depending on the degree of foreign ownership in the affected sector of a host economy, regulation carries the risk of fiscal ruin. For this reason, the burden of incoherence is borne most by those countries that lack the legal and administrative capacity effectively to fight off, or deter, investor claims (just as the risk of a costs award—although not of a damages award—falls most heavily on small and mid-sized firms contemplating a claim against a large state that can extensively litigate every stage of the dispute).67

Despite these important practical implications of incoherence, the alarm bell does not ring as loudly on this point as for the other principles of public law that are jeopardized by the system. States could address incoherence, as proposed by ICSID in 2004, merely by establishing an appellate body while leaving intact the private character of the system as a whole.68 For reasons of accountability, openness, and above all independence this would be a mistake.

Independence

I turn now to the most troubling issue that arises from the use of private arbitration to resolve regulatory disputes: the threat to judicial independence. Despite its importance, this issue has largely escaped the attention of states, arbitrators, and critics of the system. However, because it is unique in its character to investment treaty arbitration, the threat to judicial independence is all the more pressing. In the first place, this threat cannot be separated from the issues of accountability, openness, and coherence discussed above, each of which poses its own challenges to judicial independence.69 Even so, a more fundamental challenge arises for the interrelated reasons that arbitrators lack security of tenure and that the system is one-sided in that it allows only investors to bring claims and requires only states to pay damages for treaty violations. As I shall discuss, these aspects of the system make arbitrators dependent on both executive governments and prospective claimants in ways that tenured judges are not.

In democratic societies, public courts are respected as institutions of government in large part because they are perceived to be independent from other branches of the state and from powerful non-state interests.70 This is reinforced in most cases by the fact that judges are chosen by officials who are responsible to the electorate or by the electorate directly, and that their decisions are open to public comment and subject to appeal. Above all, however, the perception of independence rests on the perceived freedom of judges from inappropriate influences[71]

---

[66] Been and Beauvais (n 48 above) 132–5; C Harlow, *State Liability: Tort Law and Beyond* (Oxford: OUP, 2004) 27–8 and 56.   [67] Legum (n 39 above) 146–7.
[68] ICSID, 'Possible Improvements of the Framework for ICSID Arbitration' (Discussion Paper, 22 October 2004).   [69] Meron (n 28 above) 360–1.
[70] Shetreet (n 27 above) 656–7.
[71] UN Basic Principles on the Independence of the Judiciary (adopted by the Seventh United Nations Congress on the Prevention of Crime and the Treatment of Offenders, Milan,

and, as is long and widely recognized, on judicial security of tenure.[72] To make them independent from financial or business entanglements, judges are appointed for a set term of office and assured a secure income regardless of how they perform in individual cases. In disputes involving business or the state, in particular, security of tenure isolates the judge from the temptation to further his or her career by interpreting the law in ways that will appease powerful forces in government and industry.[73] The longer a judge's term of tenure, the less concern he or she will be seen to have about future employment.

No court is perfectly independent, of course: judges are subject to outside influence in various ways from other judges, from their family, or from the media, for example, and the courts may be subject to administrative and funding pressure from other branches of government.[74] Notably, where they are expected to seek work as arbitrators after retiring from the courts, judges may be seen to have a degree of bias in favour of arbitration while on the bench. Judges are human after all. But the judiciary remains the closest that modern constitutional democracy has come to an institution that is free from the economic levers that are controlled by senior decision-makers in government and business.[75] This in part explains why it is acceptable in democratic societies for the courts to check the power of elected legislatures.[76] No public decision-makers are more shielded from pressures to modify their conduct at work in order to improve their prospects for future enrichment.

Do arbitrators satisfy this standard of independence where, like judges, they are given comprehensive jurisdiction to exercise vital functions in public law? Unfortunately, they do not. Arbitrators are appointed under investment treaties on a case-by-case basis, either by one of the disputing parties or by an external

---

26 August–6 September 1985; endorsed by GA Res 40/32 and 40/146, UN GAOR, 40th Sess, UN Doc A/RES/40/32 and A/RES/40/146 (1985) [cited as UN Basic Principles], art 2 ('The judiciary shall decide matters before them impartially... without any restrictions, improper influences, inducements, pressures, threats or interferences, direct or indirect, from any quarter or for any reason'), endorsed by UN GA Res 40/32 and 40/146, UN GAOR, 40th Sess, UN Doc A/RES/40/32 and A/RES/40/146 (1985).

[72] UN Basic Principles (n 71 above) art 11–15 ('The term of office of judges, their independence, security, adequate remuneration, conditions of service, pensions and the age of retirement shall be adequately secured by law .... Judges, whether appointed or elected, shall have guaranteed tenure until a mandatory retirement age or the expiry of their term of office, where such exists.'). Judicial tenure dates from the Act of Settlement of 1701 in the UK and, in the US, from the first constitutions of the 13 states: Shetreet (n 27 above) 600–3; WS Carpenter, *Judicial Tenure in the United States* (New Haven: Yale University Press, 1918) 4 and 155–6. See also the compilation of country studies and pronouncements on judicial independence in S Shetreet and J Deschênes (eds) *Judicial Independence: The Contemporary Debate* (Dordrecht: Martinus Nijhoff, 1985).

[73] G Borrie, 'Judicial Conflicts of Interest in Britain' (1970) 18 Am J Comp L 697, 698.

[74] K Malleson, *The New Judiciary* (Aldershot: Dartmouth, 1999) 47–56; Atiyah (n 58 above) 14–16; Griffith (n 4 above) 292–3; B Friedman, 'The Politics of Judicial Review' (2005) 84 Texas L Rev 257, 270–4, 308–11, and 320–5.

[75] J Hampden Dougherty, *Power of Federal Judiciary Over Legislation* (New York: GP Putnam's Sons, 1912) 106–10 ('Human invention never devised a better method than the appointive system with tenure during good behavior'). [76] Carpenter (n 72 above) 1–2.

authority. This method of appointment was designed for the consensual arbitration of disputes arising from a reciprocal legal relationship between juridical equals, in which either of the disputing parties is capable of bringing a claim.[77] This method is acceptable in this context where the parties have freely decided to resolve disputes between them in a way that is not genuinely independent, in the judicial sense, agreeing instead that each will have a say in appointing the arbitrator(s) and that any disagreements between them will be resolved by a designated authority. In public law adjudication, on the other hand, where only investors bring the claims that trigger the appointments, this method of appointment seriously undermines judicial independence by foreclosing security of tenure. As a result, arbitrators are made dependent on two powerful actors in the system: executive officials and prospective claimants. I shall discuss each in turn.

First is the dependence of arbitrators on senior officials at the organizations that are designated as appointing authorities under investment treaties.[78] The key role of these officials is to appoint presiding arbitrators of tribunals in cases where the parties or the party-appointed arbitrators do not themselves agree. The importance of this power should not be underestimated. In tripartite arbitration the decision-making process generally turns on the presiding arbitrator given that the party-appointed arbitrators are more likely to take opposing views and that the president usually drafts the award.[79] In addition, negotiations between the disputing parties about who they should agree to appoint as president will be influenced by their estimation of how the designated authority will exercise its power to appoint, if called upon to do so.

Lacking tenure, arbitrators who wish to win future appointments to tribunals have an interest in safeguarding their reputation among those who select arbitrators at the designated organizations.[80] Neglect of their reputation in such quarters will naturally dim their prospects for more business. The most important of the organizations designated as an appointing authority is the International Centre for Settlement of Investment Disputes (ICSID), which has made more publicly reported appointments than any other external authority, and which is probably designated under more investment treaties than any other organization.[81] At ICSID, appointments are made either by the Chairman of the ICSID Administrative Council or by the ICSID Secretary-General.[82] In both cases, the

---

[77] AS Rau, 'Integrity in Private Judging' (1997) 38 South Texas L Rev 455, 523–4.

[78] These include the International Centre for Settlement of Investment Disputes, the International Court of Justice, the International Court of Arbitration of the International Chamber of Commerce, and the Arbitration Institute of the Stockholm Chamber of Commerce.

[79] Friedman (n 74 above) 291–2.

[80] Rau (n 77 above) 488 and 521; AF Lowenfeld, 'The Party-Appointed Arbitrator in International Controversies: Some Reflections' (1995) 30 Tex Int'l LJ 59, 65.

[81] ICSID has appointed at least 18 presiding arbitrators to date in publicly reported investment treaty arbitrations.

[82] eg treaties designating the Secretary-General of ICSID as appointing authority: NAFTA (n 15 above) art 1124(1); Treaty with the Czech and Slovak Federal Republic concerning the reciprocal

authority is exercised by a World Bank officer who ultimately owes his or her position to the major capital-exporting states, which effectively control decision-making at the World Bank based on the Bank's system of weighted voting.[83]

Specifically, the ICSID Administrative Council is chaired *ex officio* by the President of the World Bank, who is nominated by the US government and confirmed by the Bank's Board of Directors, and who is by convention a US national.[84] At the moment, this appointing authority is exercised by former US Deputy Secretary of Defense Paul Wolfowitz. Similarly, the Secretary-General of ICSID (usually also the Bank's Legal Vice President and General Counsel) is nominated by the Chairman of the Administrative Council and approved by a two-thirds vote of the Administrative Council.[85] In both cases, appointing authority is vested in an official who is customarily chosen by the US Administration with the

encouragement and protection of investment (the US–Czech Republic BIT) (Washington, 22 October 1991; entered into force 19 December 1992), art VI(3)(b)(ii); Acuerdo para la promoción y protección recíproca de inversiones entre los Estados Unidos Mexicanos y el Reino de España (the Spain–Mexico BIT) (Mexico City, 22 June 1995; entered into force 18 December 1996), title 4(3) (app). See also eg treaties authorizing investor claims pursuant to the ICSID Rules and thus designating the Chairman of the ICSID Administrative Council as appointing authority (ICSID Convention (n 8 above) art 38): Treaty between the United States of America and the Argentine Republic concerning the reciprocal encouragement and protection of investment (the US–Argentina BIT) (Washington, 14 November 1991; entered into force 20 October 1994), art VII(3)(a)(i); Agreement between the Government of the United Kingdom of Great Britain and Northern Ireland and the Government of the Democratic Socialist Republic of Sri Lanka for the promotion and protection of investments (the UK–Sri Lanka BIT) (Colombo, 13 February 1980; UKTS No 14 (1981); Cmd 8186; entered into force 18 December 1980), art 8(1); Accord entre le Gouvernement de la République Française et le Gouvernement de la République Argentine sur l'encouragement et la protection réciproques des investissements (the France–Argentina BIT) (Paris, 3 July 1991; entered into force 3 March 1993), art 8(3); Tratado entre la República Federal de Alemania y la República Argentina sobre promoción y protección recíproca de inversiones (the Germany–Argentina BIT) (Bonn, 9 April 1991; entered into force 8 November 1993), art 10(4); and Agreement on encouragement and reciprocal protection of investments between the Kingdom of the Netherlands and the Republic of Venezuela (the Netherlands–Venezuela BIT) (22 October 1991; entered into force 1 November 1993), art 9(2).

[83] Voting at the World Bank is weighted according to each member state's approved shareholding in the Bank. At present, the Bank has 24 Executive Directors—who select the Bank's President—11 of whom are nationals of significant capital-exporting countries (US, Japan, Germany, France, UK, Belgium, Spain, Netherlands, Canada, Italy, and Switzerland), who together cast 61.5% of the votes.

[84] IBRD Articles of Agreement, art V, 5(a).

[85] ICSID Convention (n 8 above) art 10(1). See also AR Parra, 'New Amendments of the Regulations and Rules of the International Centre for Settlement of Investment Disputes' (2002) 19 ICSID News 1, 9.

The serving and most recent Secretaries-General are: Secretary-General Ana Palacio, who was formerly Foreign Minister of Spain under Prime Minister Jose Maria Aznar; Scott B White (2006), an American national who was previously Deputy General Counsel of the World Bank before being appointed as General Counsel; Roberto Dañino (2005–6), who previously served as prime minister of Peru and its ambassador to the United States, after a career as a corporate lawyer in the US and Peru, and who resigned in January 2006; and Ko-Yung Tung (2000–5), who was born in China, raised in Japan, and educated at Harvard Law School, who was previously a senior partner at the international law firm O'Melveny & Myers, where his practice concentrated on cross-border corporate transactions, and who formerly served as a member of the US Presidential Commission on International Trade and Investment.

concurrence of other major states. Arbitrators who aspire to an appointment as president of an ICSID tribunal are thus objectively dependent on a small group of senior officials who are themselves selected by capital-exporting countries, led by the US. It would not be surprising, as suggested to me by one arbitrator, if most arbitrators studiously avoided criticizing ICSID;[86] arbitrators are more likely to publicly defend ICSID and identify themselves as part of its constituency.[87] One must keep in mind, however, that in doing so arbitrators open themselves to the perception that they are making a pitch for governments to continue to contract out fundamental functions of the courts in a way that profits arbitrators.

Other institutions designated under investment treaties as appointing authorities have different arrangements for exercising the power to appoint, and the ICSID process is neither best nor worst at insulating itself from outside political pressure. Some treaties designate the International Court of Justice as appointing authority, thus ensuring that arbitrators are at least appointed by an international judge rather than an executive official.[88] On the other hand, other treaties give the power to appoint arbitrators to the International Chamber of Commerce (ICC) and the Stockholm Chamber of Commerce (SCC), which are not public authorities at all.[89] In doing so, they empower a group of business representatives to choose directly those who will decide the legality of sovereign acts and order states to compensate private investors.[90] Frankly, this is an affront to judicial independence.

---

[86] This arbitrator expressed to me his view, for instance, that ICSID exceeds its authority by appointing to tribunals individuals who have not been nominated to the ICSID roster of arbitrators: ICSID Convention (n 8 above) art 13 and 40(1).

[87] In June 2006 prominent arbitrator VV Veeder reportedly gave a passionate defence of ICSID at an arbitration conference in Dallas, calling for the World Bank to fund the institution adequately so as not to jeopardize its continued existence and high quality: R Alford, 'The Looming Crisis at ICSID', online: www.opiniojuris.org.

[88] eg Agreement among the Government of Brunei Darussalam, the Republic of Indonesia, Malaysia, the Republic of the Philippines, the Republic of Singapore and the Kingdom of Thailand for the Promotion and Protection of Investments (ASEAN Agreement for the Promotion and Protection of Investments) (Manila, 15 December 1987; 27 ILM 612), art X(4); Agreement between the Government of the United Kingdom of Great Britain and Northern Ireland and the Government of the Republic of India (the UK–India BIT) (London, 14 March 1994; UKTS No 27 (1995); Cmd 2797; entered into force 6 January 1995), art 9(3)(c)(ii).

[89] eg Agreement on encouragement and reciprocal protection of investments between the Kingdom of the Netherlands and the Republic of Bolivia (the Netherlands–Bolivia BIT) (10 March 1992; entered into force 1 November 1994), art 9(4) (designating the President of the Court of Arbitration of the Paris International Chamber of Commerce as appointing authority); Agreement on encouragement and reciprocal protection of investments between the Kingdom of the Netherlands and the Czech and Slovak Republic (the Netherlands–Czech Republic BIT) (22 October 1991; entered into force 19 December 1992), art 8(4) (designating the President of the Arbitration Institute of the Stockholm Chamber of Commerce).

[90] Under the ICC Rules, arbitrators are appointed by the ICC International Court of Arbitration, the members of which are nominated by the ICC world council of business representatives on the recommendation of the ICC Executive Board (*Rules of Arbitration of the International Chamber of Commerce*, revised 1 January 1998, art 1 and 9(3); and app I (Statute of the International Court of Arbitration of the ICC), art 3). Individual candidates are put forward by a national committee of the

This brings us to the dependency of arbitrators on prospective claimants. Again, because of specific design flaws in investment treaty arbitration, arbitrators are dependent on those investors that have enough foreign wealth and access to legal resources to contemplate claims, because it is they who decide whether and when to activate the system. Unlike in commercial arbitration, this dependence is not cured by allowing two of three arbitrators on a tribunal to be appointed by the claimant and respondent, respectively, since the size of the pool of opportunities that is open to *all* arbitrators—regardless of who appoints them—will always reflect the system's attractiveness to international business. The more investors see the system delivering benefits for them, the more claims will be brought, and the more contracts will be available for arbitrators.[91] Here, it seems, is an instance where the independence of the judiciary is endangered, as Shetreet warned decades ago, not by 'parliaments and monarchs' but by 'the steady growth of corporate giants'.[92] At least, the need to insulate investment treaty arbitration from a perception of dependence on corporate interests was not properly accounted for when the system was designed, seeing as arbitrators do business only if the system provides satisfaction to its main customers: multinational firms.[93]

Because they interpret public law in response to claims by private investors, arbitrators are perceptibly beholden to international business in ways that tenured judges are not. However, arbitrators are also subject to influence by business in other ways as a result of their lack of tenure. Not surprisingly, as practising lawyers or consultants, many arbitrators provide a range of other services to firms, and it is not uncommon for prominent arbitrators to adjudicate one case, while representing a claimant in another, while generally advising private clients on matters of investment law.[94] Arbitrators are members of an industry the purpose of which is

---

ICC that the Court considers appropriate. The Court was founded in 1922 'by businessmen who wrestled with the practical difficulties of designing a dispute resolution process acceptable to merchants of different national backgrounds': WL Craig, WW Park, and J Paulsson, *International Chamber of Commerce Arbitration* (New York: Oceana Publications, 1990) xxi (statement does not appear in most recent edition). See also MS Rosenthal, 'Arbitration in the Settlement of International Trade Disputes' (1946) 11 Law & Contemporary Problems 808, 817.

Under the SCC Rules, arbitrators are chosen by the Arbitration Institute of the SCC, the members of which are appointed by the business representatives on the SCC Board of Directors (*Rules of the Arbitration Institute of the Stockholm Chamber of Commerce*, revised 1 April 1999, art 16). See also E Müller, 'How Do International Institutions Select Arbitrators?' (2000) 17 J Int'l Arb 157.

[91] M Sornarajah, 'Power and Justice in Foreign Investment Arbitration' (1997) 14(3) J Int'l Arb 103, 117.

[92] S Shetreet, *Judges on Trial* (Amsterdam: North Holland Publishing Co, 1976) 17–18.

[93] W Mattli, 'Private Justice in a Global Economy: From Litigation to Arbitration' (2001) 55 Int'l Org 919, 921–2.

[94] *Republic of Ghana v Telekom Malaysia Berhad* (18 October 2004 and 5 November 2004, No HA/RK 2004.667 and HA/RK 2004.788) (DC The Hague) (concluding that a party-nominated arbitrator in an investment arbitration under the UNCITRAL Rules could not concurrently act as counsel to an unrelated party in an ICSID annulment proceeding that raised similar legal issues). *Compañía de Aguas del Aconquija SA & Vivendi Universal v Argentine Republic* (Decision on Challenge to the President) (3 October 2001), 17 ICSID Rev 168, 125 ILR 46, 6 ICSID Rep 330, para 21, citing *Amco Asia Corp v Republic of Indonesia* (Decision) (24 June 1982), ICSID Case No

to supply adjudicative services in exchange for (lucrative) remuneration.[95] Franck argues that this makes arbitrators accountable through 'the impact of the "arbitrator marketplace" where professional credibility and word-of-mouth recommendations play a role in both the appointment and re-appointment of arbitrators'.[96] But such market-based accountability is rather weak if those who direct arbitration business down the industry ladder are themselves dependent on prospective claimants and corporate patrons. The club of arbitrators is very different from a bench of judges whose perception of themselves as independent officers of the state adapts the newcomer to 'a whole new universe of judicial thinking and action', in the words of one international jurist.[97]

Some arbitrators have been repeatedly appointed to tribunals by investors and host states alike. This is no doubt because they have an impeccable reputation for fairness and balance. But the problem here is one of perceived bias, not actual impartiality.[98] Even the most reputable arbitrator is open to the reproach that he will favour claimants, one way or another, so as to encourage claims. However well a tribunal does its job, its interpretations of the law will carry an inherent perception of bias against the interests of host states because of the objective link between interpreting the treaty and furthering the industry.[99] Regardless of whether they are 'distinguished former judges', 'respected scholars and practitioners', or 'former government officials',[100] all arbitrators lack the independence of the most junior tenured judge. This is an outcome of combining a public law system of state liability with private arbitration.

The dependence of arbitrators on government and business belies the claim that investment treaty arbitration removes sensitive disputes from the political realm and subjects them to the rule of law.[101] The argument that it does so attempts to exploit the credibility of the courts and, in particular, the widely held belief that judges are better able to make certain governmental decisions because they are removed from electoral and other pressures that confront legislators and ministers.[102] Thus, Brower and Steven advocate NAFTA arbitration in these terms: 'What the NAFTA Parties set out to accomplish—the protection and

---

ARB/81/1 [unpublished]. Y Dezaley and BG Garth, *Dealing in Virtue: International Commercial Arbitration and the Construction of a Transnational Legal Order* (Chicago: University of Chicago Press, 1996) 49–50; Garcia (n 26 above) 353–4; O Guglielmino, 'Analista señala arbitrariedad del sistema judicial; Demandas inverosímiles' *La Nación* [Argentina] (17 January 2005).

[95] Dezaley and Garth (n 94 above) 33; Dezaley (n 24 above) 84–6; J Werner, 'The Trade Explosion and Some Likely Effects on International Arbitration' (1997) 14(2) J Int'l Arb 5, 10; Rau (n 77 above) 488, 496–7 and 521.

[96] Franck (n 7 above) 1596–7.   [97] Meron (n 28 above) 360.

[98] *R v Valente (No 2)* [1985] 2 SCR 673, 23 CCC (3rd) 193, 24 DLR (4th) 161, para 15 (concluding that judicial independence 'connotes not merely a state of mind or attitude in the actual exercise of judicial functions, but a status or relationships to others, particularly to the executive branch of government, that rests on objective conditions or guarantees').   [99] Sornarajah (n 2 above) 18.

[100] Franck (n 7 above) 1597–8.   [101] Paulsson (n 5 above) 233 and 265.

[102] CL Eisgruber, *Constitutional Self-Government* (Cambridge: Harvard University Press, 2001) 58.

promotion of investment through the uniform application of rules and guarantees in all three NAFTA countries—can best be sustained through the enforcement of Chapter 11 *by independent and impartial international tribunals.*'[103] The problem with this claim is that adjudication is neither independent nor impartial where the adjudicator is appointed by a political or corporate entity on a case-by-case basis. Can it really be said that appointments by ICSID or by the International Chamber of Commerce are not 'political'? They most certainly are, just as the appointment of judges is political; in both cases, the decision whom to appoint calls for an evaluation of how different candidates are likely to rule on important issues and how this will reflect on whoever made the original appointment. What ICSID and the ICC are not is free from unwarranted influences and control by executive officials in government or in business, as the case may be. It is precisely because they are not appointed and assured tenure by the state that arbitrators are exposed to undue political pressures. There can be no rule of law without an independent judiciary.[104]

As indicated above, I have not elaborated these criticisms in order to impugn the integrity of individual arbitrators, many of whom have an outstanding reputation. Indeed, it is a testament to the sense of fairness of arbitrators that the reasoning in most awards is not strongly skewed in favour of claimants and that it often reflects an appreciation of the complex policy issues that arise in regulatory adjudication. Awards that defer to host governments, such as *Loewen* and *SGS v Pakistan*, demonstrate clearly that many arbitrators will put their integrity and that of the system ahead of the interests of their industry.[105] On the other hand, the fact that many awards narrow the object and purpose of investment treaty arbitration to that of investor protection[106] lends support to the perception of bias that I have elaborated. Arbitrator bias offers a credible explanation for the tendency of tribunals to adopt a broad reading of their jurisdiction and of the standards of review,[107] thus expanding the system's compensatory promise for

---

[103] CN Brower and LA Steven, 'Who Then Should Judge? Developing the International Rule of Law under NAFTA Chapter 11' (2001) 2 Chi J Int'l L 193, 200 [emphasis added]. See also *Aguas del Tunari* (n 51 above) para 153 (concluding that 'a primary objective of the BIT... is agreement upon ICSID as an independent and neutral forum for the resolution of investment disputes'); J Byrne, 'NAFTA Dispute Resolution: Implementing True Rule-Based Diplomacy Through Direct Access' (2000) 35 Texas Int'l LJ 415, 415–16 and 428–9.

[104] International Commission of Jurists (Summary of discussions, Conference on the Independence of Judges and Lawyers, Caracas, 16–18 January 1989); Meron (n 28 above) 359.

[105] Notably, tribunals that tend towards a more cautious approach to investment treaty arbitration are often presided over by former judges. eg *Loewen Group, Inc and Raymond L Loewen v United States of America* (Merits) (26 June 2003), 42 ILM 811, 7 ICSID Rep 442, 15(5) World Trade and Arb Mat 97 [cited as *Loewen*], para 222–3 and 233 (presided over by Sir Anthony Mason); *ADF Group Inc v United States of America* (Merits) (9 January 2003), 18 ICSID Rev 195, 6 ICSID Rep 470, 15(3) World Trade and Arb Mat 55 (Judge FP Feliciano); *SGS Société Générale de Surveillance v Pakistan* (Jurisdiction) (6 August 2003), 18 ICSID Rev 307, 16(2) World Trade and Arb Mat 167 (Judge FP Feliciano). [106] See the discussion in Ch 6 above, p 136–8.

[107] AFM Maniruzzaman, 'Internationalization of Foreign Investment Agreements—Some Fundamental Issues of International Law' (2000) 1 J World Investment 293, 311; E Gaillard,

investors. And the simple fact that this explanation has currency is enough to conclude that the system does not satisfy the requirement of judicial independence in public law.

The Options for Reform

The aim of this book has been to explain why investment treaty arbitration is a form of public law adjudication and, in the present chapter, to identify problems that arise from the use of arbitration to resolve regulatory disputes. The purpose has not been to elaborate a comprehensive proposal for reform of the system. That said, any review of systemic flaws begs the question of alternatives. In this last section, therefore, a framework is outlined for reform of the system, as informed by the discussion above. Also, where they appear relevant to this proposal for reform, some explanations are offered for why states have not yet established a system that satisfies basic criteria of public law.

To begin, the problems with the present system are structural and they cannot be solved by appointing different people, thought by ICSID or some other organization to have more integrity, as arbitrators. The failings go beyond that of the rogue tribunal or the cowboy arbitrator, in spite of the murmuring of some to this effect. Regardless of how prudently a tribunal acts in an individual case, the system as a whole lacks accountability and openness in fundamental ways, and above all it is open to a perception of bias so long as arbitrators earn appointments by the claim. This can only be remedied be moving away from private arbitration and back to the model of public courts.

The limits of domestic responses

There are two broad options in this regard: the first domestic and the second international. I shall discuss each in turn, although they are not mutually exclusive. The first is for domestic courts to assert greater control over investment treaty arbitration in a co-ordinated way and, notably, to establish that courts may overrule errors of law by tribunals, in addition to errors of jurisdiction or procedural improprieties. This would not address all of the system's flaws;[108] it is rather a minimum that is required to ensure independence and accountability in the interpretation of public law and in the award of public funds to private business.

The difficulty with this option is that the assertion of sufficient control by domestic courts will not be consistent, in key enforcing countries, with legislative

---

'Commentary' (2002) 18 Arb Int'l 247, 249; C McLachlan, 'Commentary: The Broader Context' (2002) 18 Arb Int'l 339, 340; T-H Cheng, 'Power, Authority and International Investment Law' (2005) 20 Am U Int'l L Rev 465, 474.

[108] Ideally, this step would be accompanied by action by states to mandate openness under all investment treaties in the manner of NAFTA.

directions for the courts to defer to foreign arbitration awards. To date, where investment treaty awards have been reviewed by domestic courts, no court has found that it had the authority to carry out the required intensity of review, and the courts have generally not been swayed by the argument that the relevant laws were enacted by legislatures in order to facilitate international commercial arbitration, well before the prospect of investment treaty arbitration came to light.[109] This does not bode well for the emergence of a co-ordinated response by the courts across the major jurisdictions.[110] It also indicates that if legislatures do not amend domestic statutes implementing the New York Convention and ICSID Convention to stipulate specific exceptions to deference for investment treaty awards, then the courts would either have to widen existing grounds for review or act autonomously under their constitutional law. While neither is beyond the realm of the possible, especially where the courts are authorized to set aside awards for reasons of public policy (or non-arbitrability),[111] it is more likely to be the exception than the rule. This suggests that, although domestic courts may play an important role in identifying problems with the system, they are not in a strong position to address its structural flaws.[112]

Beyond the courts, one may look to domestic legislatures or executive governments to implement reform. Here it is the major capital exporters, the US and the Western Europeans in particular, which occupy the commanding position to instigate reform of the system, just as they drove its creation and expansion. As discussed, significant steps were taken by the NAFTA states to open Chapter 11 arbitration to the public, but other problematic aspects were left untouched. Moreover, the UK, Germany, France, and other key players in Western Europe have done little, if anything, to adjust their investment treaty programmes even after many of the problems with the system were revealed in the negotiations towards the proposed Multilateral Agreement on Investment.[113] To explain this lack of response, it is necessary to revisit the motivations of the major states in pushing for the system in the first place.

It is by now trite to say that an overarching purpose of investment treaty arbitration is to encourage cross-border investment by protecting multinational firms from various forms of regulatory treatment by host states, and that the vehicle for doing so has been to establish international adjudication as a method of control alongside domestic courts, by allowing investors to bring treaty claims against sovereigns in ways that go well beyond customary international law. So goes the

---

[109] See cases at n 11 above.   [110] Franck (n 7 above) 1601.
[111] HR Evans, 'The Nonarbitrability of Subject Matter Defense to Enforcement of Foreign Arbitral Awards in United States Federal Courts' (1989) 21 NYU J Int'l L & Pol 329; Gruner (n 49 above) 932–6.
[112] eg *Council of Canadians v Canada* (8 July 2005, Pepall J, Docket No 01-CV-208141), para 31 (Ont SCJ).
[113] eg C Lalumière and J-P Landau, 'Report on the Multilateral Agreement on Investment (MAI)' (Interim report to the Government of France, September 1998).

mantra. Reciting it, however, does not bring us much closer to an explanation for why the major states chose arbitration to resolve investor claims instead of an international court. Past proposals in the field, which emanated from the capital-exporting countries, often called for the creation of an international judicial body.[114] Why then did the major states opt instead to support the privatization of the judicial function in public law?

One explanation, alluded to in Chapter 2 of this book, assesses the present system against the backdrop of Western imperialism, which relied on international arbitration as an element of an extra-territorial legal system designed to control the governments of newly independent countries. To illustrate, in 1926 Dunn collected concessionary contracts between US businesses and Central American or Caribbean governments which provided in a number of cases for disputes to be resolved by an arbitration tribunal, the president of which was to be appointed by the US Secretary of State.[115] Such a one-sided set-up is similar to current arrangements that designate ICSID or the ICC as the appointing authority in investment treaty arbitration. Moreover, it shows that there has been a degree of continuity in the efforts of the capital-exporting states to establish a system of international adjudication that is slanted against host governments, perhaps primarily on the assessment that capital-exporting states are unlikely to face claims. That the US has been forced to respond to claims by Canadian investors under NAFTA is something of an anomaly in this respect, and it offers a rationale for why the US Congress saw fit to revise that country's treaty programme.[116]

If this assessment of the motivations of major states holds any water, then it need be said that the selective abandonment of judicial independence in the adjudication of claims for compensation by Western firms against developing countries is cynical and short-sighted. It stands in stark contrast to the professed commitments of the same countries to encourage the rule of law and democratic development in their relations with the developing world. Further, it is doubtful that the interests of investors, as much as anyone, are served by a system that lacks legitimacy, when put under scrutiny, for its secrecy and bias. Pitted against this rationale for the present system, based on the self-interest of the capital-exporters, the case for reform is powerful indeed.

This leads to the peripheral question of whether the implications of investment treaties in public law were widely appreciated by legislatures and governments in the major states, let alone the general public, when the treaties were ratified. For example, there was little, if any, public debate of the ramifications of the US having to respond to claims under investment treaties until 15 years after the US

---

[114] eg AS Miller, 'Protection of Private Foreign Investment by Multilateral Convention' (1959) 53 AJIL 371, 374.

[115] RW Dunn, *American Foreign Investments* (New York: BW Huebsch and Viking Press, 1926) 357–8, 368.

[116] GA Alvarez and WW Park, 'The New Face of Investment Arbitration: NAFTA Chapter 11' (2003) 28 Yale J Int'l L 365, 383–8.

Administration adopted its BIT programme.[117] Likewise, in Western Europe, a public debate on investment treaties took place only after a draft of the OECD's Multilateral Agreement on Investment was leaked to and distributed by non-governmental organizations, and this was 25 years after the region's early BITs were concluded. In such circumstances, until the mid-1990s at least, it is reasonable to assume that major gaps of discussion and analysis lay behind the decisions of the major states to delegate core sovereign power to arbitrators, and that the constituencies most likely to object, including elected officials, were largely unaware of what was taking place.

That said, obviously someone negotiated the treaties with a degree of appreciation of their consequences and recommended their approval by ministers or by the governing party in the legislature. An important part was played in this respect by the specialized staff of the particular government departments—ministries of trade, commerce, and foreign affairs, for the most part—that worked to establish and expand the system over decades, sometimes at the urging of the local arbitration industry or national business lobbies or the International Chamber of Commerce. Notably, some individuals who were involved as treaty negotiators or advisers to government in the 1990s now serve as counsel or arbitrators within the system.[118] On the other hand, the role played by individual officals in the negotiating process does not make for a conspiracy: in capital-exporting states, the mandate of the relevant government departments has long included the aim to protect foreign assets of their nationals from expropriation and other regulatory threats, and investment treaties are very much consistent with this objective. It is also hardly surprising that lawyers and other professionals would support legal reforms that create business opportunities for their professions and themselves. The question here is the degree to which states as representative entities made a deliberated choice to create a system of investor protection that reforms judicial decision-making in fundamental respects. It may have been convenient, in the negotiation of investment treaties, to rely on the existing structure of international commercial arbitration to provide a framework for investor–state arbitration rather than to confront the sensitivities that surround the creation of new international courts.[119] But an implication of doing so is that the profound consequences of a few lines in a treaty are obscured from wider scrutiny.

---

[117] eg comment of Abner Mikva, former Congressman and Chief Justice of the US Court of Appeals for the District of Columbia Circuit, and member of the *Loewen* tribunal: 'If Congress had known that there was anything like this [Chapter 11 arbitration] in NAFTA, they would never have voted for it' (A Liptak, 'Review of US Rulings by NAFTA Tribunals Stirs Worries' *New York Times* (18 April 2004) 20); D Brown, 'Commentary' in L Ritchie Dawson (ed) *Whose Rights? The NAFTA Chapter 11 Debate* (Ottawa: Centre for Trade Policy and Law, 2002) 40–1; Been and Beauvais (n 48 above) 137–9; P Sands, *Lawless World* (London: Penguin, 2005) 121–2 and 140; A Capling and K Richard Nossal, 'Blowback: Investor–State Dispute Mechanisms in International Trade Agreements' (2006) 19 *Governance* 151, 165.

[118] N Majeed, 'Investor–State Disputes and International Law: From the Far Side' (2004) 98 Am Soc'ty Int'l L Proceedings 30, 31.

[119] HT King *et al*, 'Dispute Settlement Under the North American Free Trade Agreement' (1992) 26 Int'l Lawyer 855, 861; A Porges, 'Step by Step to an International Trade Court' in DLM

The lack of public debate about the system prior to its establishment at least gives some reason for optimism that major states may come to support reform if a wider debate on the system takes place. That said, both the US and Canadian governments have extensively debated investment treaty arbitration and, for the most part, they continue to back the same horse by favouring arbitrators over judges in the resolution of investment disputes. A number of further explanations for this preference are suggested in the literature. One is that states wish to avoid the expense of new institutions and that they welcome the system's high cost to investors as a means to deter claims.[120] Another is that states are convinced by the argument that arbitrators are more capable than judges in matters of international investment.[121] None of these explanations does much to justify the privatization of the judiciary, however. Efficient public spending is important, but it is not a reason to contract out the adjudication of public law claims and, in doing so, to forgo judicial accountability and independence. Further, an international court could just as easily apply deterrents to claims by investors if states wished to impose them. Finally, the argument that arbitrators are more skilled than judges in the resolution of investment disputes seems misplaced given that the same experts who serve as arbitrators could just as well be appointed to an international court.

A more likely explanation for the continued support of major states for investment treaty arbitration stems from the competitive pressure they face to protect their own investors relative to those of other capital-exporting states. In Chapter 2 of this book, it was argued that inter-state competition to attract foreign investment provides a rationale for why capital-importing countries have submitted to such rigorous regulation of their governments under investment treaties. The competition among capital-exporting states to protect investors operates in much the same way: they, like their counterparts in the southern hemisphere and Eastern Europe, are induced to appease international capital in response to its mobility in a global economy. Thus, the expansion of the system since the 1970s has largely tracked the efforts of US and European negotiators to keep up with one another by securing more intensive controls on host governments.[122] Over time, this competition has produced a system that ensures a high level of investor protection, with the unfortunate by-product that it favours investors so heavily as to undermine core principles of public law. The same dynamic also deters

Kennedy and JD Southwick (eds) *The Political Economy of International Trade Law* (Cambridge: CUP, 2002) 535–6.

[120] Brower and Steven (n 103 above) 196, n 7.
[121] Redfern (n 32 above) 671; Franck (n 7 above) 1598.
[122] UNCTAD, *Bilateral Investment Treaties in the Mid-1990s* (Geneva: United Nations, 1998) 139–40. See eg D Vis-Dunbar, 'Germany seeks revisions and addition of investor-state arbitration to Pakistan BIT' *Investment Treaty News* (31 May 2006); D Vis-Dunbar and LE Peterson, 'European Commission makes another play for power to negotiate investment pacts' *Investment Treaty News* (19 July 2006) (reporting that the European Commission has referred to the need to compete with NAFTA countries as reason for it to assume greater responsibility over the negotiation of investment treaties by EC member states).

capital-exporting states from acting unilaterally to reform their investment treaties where doing so may expose their internationally oriented firms to regulatory risks against which the competition is protected.[123]

An international investment court

The response should therefore be one that precludes such rivalry but that is flexible enough to allow states to opt in to reform when the time is right for each. Also, given the long history of failed proposals for a multilateral treaty on investment, and the large number of bilateral treaties that are now in force, an ambitious, wholesale reform of the system is unlikely to succeed. For this reason, the proposal for reform that is outlined here is aimed at issues of institutional design rather than the system's scope and substance or the conditions for investor claims. These other matters are left for existing treaties in order to focus on reforms that will ensure that investment treaties, regardless of their terms, are interpreted and applied in a way that is consistent with basic judicial standards.

The strategy is to encourage states—especially the major capital-exporting states—to support a multilateral code that would establish an international court with comprehensive jurisdiction over the adjudication of investor claims.[124] The court would have jurisdiction in the first instance over all claims filed by investors (or, as a less attractive alternative, it could have appellate jurisdiction over the awards and decisions of tribunals[125]) pursuant to any investment treaty between states that were also party to the multilateral code. To ensure its independence, the court would be staffed by judges appointed by states for a set term based on the model of other international courts.[126] Given the rapid proliferation of investor claims in recent years, now at roughly 25 to 30 per year at ICSID, perhaps 12 or 15 judges would be required to allow several three-judge tribunals to sit simultaneously. The judges would be selected for tribunals on a rotating basis either by the president of the court or by random assignment, and challenges to a judge's impartiality would be decided by other members of the court.[127] The judges

---

[123] Complementing this is the competition among states to attract arbitration business (n 24–5 above). Arbitrators sometimes signal in relation to the decision where to locate an arbitration that they will boycott jurisdictions that do not defer to awards. In this context, some states may be prepared to put the integrity of the judicial system ahead of the interests of their own arbitration industry and foreign investors, but one should not expect all to do so.

[124] S Timberg, 'An International Trade Tribunal—A Step Forward Short of Surrender of Sovereignty' (1945) 33 Georgetown LJ 373, 386–9.

[125] This latter option is less attractive because it does not ensure accountability, openness, and independence in the first instance of the adjudication of claims.

[126] eg ECHR (n 27 above) art 23.1 and 24. See also JH Ralston, 'Some Suggestions as to the Permanent Court of Arbitration' (1907) 1 AJIL 321, 322–4 and 328–9; R Mackenzie and P Sands, 'International Courts and Tribunals and the Independence of the International Judge' (2003) 44 Harv Int'l LJ 271.   [127] UN Basic Principles (n 71 as above) art 14.

would also be expressly barred from taking part in activities that are incompatible with their independence.[128] Finally, the judges would adopt rules of the court to replace the various sets of rules that now govern claims, so that the court itself—guided by overarching principles laid out by the states parties to the multilateral code—can address anomalies in the present system, such as the presumption of confidentiality and the ability of claimants to pick the procedural rules that apply to their claim.

The court's decisions in the first instance on matters of jurisdiction, procedure, and legal interpretation could be appealed to a special assembly of the court, representing a majority of its members. To protect against baseless appeals and delay, the right of appeal might exist only with leave by the court. With this arrangement for appeal, the annulment process of the ICSID Convention is made redundant in relation to investment treaty claims, although ICSID would retain its role in other forms of investment arbitration. Removing ICSID from investment treaty arbitration is desirable on the basis that an international court is best segregated from current appointing authorities under investment treaties, given that they are heavily dominated by capital-exporting states and, in some cases, by international business. On the other hand, the court's awards should remain enforceable under both the ICSID Convention and the New York Convention so as to maintain their coercive authority, and thus awards would continue to be subject to review by domestic courts in the place of enforcement based on the existing grounds for review. There would be no need to designate a specific jurisdictional seat for each claim brought before the court or to allow applications to set aside awards in that seat, since the court would be an international court rather than an ad hoc tribunal. Even so, it would not be unduly burdensome to instruct the court to designate a seat for each investor claim, considering that domestic courts have thus far deferred to investment treaty tribunals and that the courts in the place of enforcement could enforce an award even if it was set aside in the seat of the arbitration. Above all, the decision where to locate claims for purposes of domestic court review would be made by an independent judicial body.

Perhaps the most difficult question is how to appoint members of the court in a manner that balances representation of the different interests at stake in regulatory disputes between international business and states. Let us begin with the method of appointment. In international courts, judges are typically nominated and elected by states, acting through an international organization.[129] In the case of the International Court of Justice, judges are elected by a majority vote of

---

[128] eg ECHR (n 27 above) art 21.1 (providing that judges 'shall be of high moral character and must either possess the qualifications required for appointment to high judicial office or be jurisconsults of recognised competence') and art 21.3 (providing that judges, during their term of office, 'shall not engage in any activity which is incompatible with their independence, impartiality or with the demands of a full-time office'). JG Wetter, *The International Arbitral Process—Public and Private*, vol 3 (Dobbs Ferry, NY: Oceana Publications, 1979) 355; Rau (n 77 above) 493–4.

[129] Meron (n 28 above) 361.

the UN General Assembly and Security Council from lists of candidates submitted by national groups of states.[130] At the European Court of Human Rights, they are elected by the Parliamentary Assembly of the Council of Europe from a list of three candidates put forward by the state party whose judge is to be elected.[131] At the International Criminal Court, judges are elected by an assembly of the states parties;[132] whereas at the International Criminal Tribunal for the Former Yugoslavia, they are nominated by UN member states, short-listed by the Security Council, and elected by the General Assembly.[133] In other words, there are various methods to appoint judges to international courts, but in all cases the authority rests with states or organizations of states. Notably, unlike in domestic law, international judges do not hold tenure for life (as in US federal courts) or until a mandatory retirement age (as in the UK). Instead, they are appointed for a specified term—nine years at the ICJ and the International Criminal Court, six years at the ECJ, and four years at the ICTY—sometimes with the possibility of re-election.[134] Each of these arrangements is far superior to the present system of case-by-case appointment in investment treaty arbitration. However, it is preferable for reasons of independence that the judges' term of office be as long as possible and that it preclude reappointment.[135]

Appointment for a set term is essential to make judges independent; appointment by states is essential to make them accountable. This is not because states are flawlessly representative of the interests of their people, but because they are the entities deemed in law to possess the formal authority to act for their populations on the international plane. Just as states, by concluding a treaty, can effectively privatize aspects of the judicial function, so too can they re-establish the pre-eminence of the courts in international law. Some commentators have argued against state-based appointments to an appellate body in investment law on the basis that states will not appoint expert and unbiased personnel.[136] In light of the experience of many other courts—which are staffed by talented and responsible jurists—we shall have to trust that states will not appoint nincompoops to an international investment court. For some, state-appointed judges can be reduced to mere ' "faceless bureaucrats" *imposed* upon parties' as opposed to 'arbitrators *selected* by the disputants in international arbitrations involving states'.[137] But at least states have a defensible claim to represent the interests of their people, unlike

---

[130] Statute of the International Court of Justice (Statute of the ICJ) 59 Stat 1055, art 4–10.
[131] ECHR (n 27 above) art 22.
[132] Rome Statute of the International Criminal Court (Statute of the ICC) (Rome, 17 July 1998; 2187 UNTS 3), art 36.
[133] Statute of the International Criminal Tribunal for the Former Yugoslavia (Statute of the ICTY) (annex to UN Security Council Res No 827) (25 May 1993, 32 ILM 1203 (1993)), art 13 *bis*.
[134] Statute of the ICJ (n 130 above) art 13(1); Statute of the ICC (n 132 above) art 36(9)(a) and (b); ECHR (n 27 above) art 23.1; Statute of the ICTY (n 133 above) art 13 *bis* (3).
[135] Meron (n 28 above) 362.   [136] eg Paulsson (n 5 above) 245.
[137] Paulsson (n 5 above) 242 [emphasis in original].

the agents of international business who currently make appointments under many treaties. In short, a system of tenured appointment by states is the best means to assure judicial accountability in a democratic society.

More difficult is the question of how this authority should be allocated among different groups of states. To encourage ratification of the proposed code, as a guiding principle the system of appointment should not unduly favour capital-exporting or (above all) capital-importing states.[138] Just as it is wrong to require developing countries to accept that appointments to an international body of such importance be made by a bloc of capital-exporting countries or by a business lobby, the major states should not be expected to accept a system of judicial election based on country or population-based votes. The simple fact remains that the great majority of companies that own substantial assets outside their home jurisdiction are based in a small number of countries which hold a minority of the world's people. To bridge the political gap on this issue will require the willingness of developing countries pragmatically to set aside many objections that they have raised in past negotiations on investment law in exchange for the commitment of the major states to accept judicial independence as a condition for investor claims in international law. Both outcomes are more likely if the proposed code provides for its entry into force only after a modest quorum[139] of states have consented to it, and then for it to be open to ratification by others at a time of their choosing. To be clear, once it entered into force the code would apply to claims initiated by investors under any investment treaty between states that were also party to the code.

Is such a proposal likely to succeed? For capital-importing countries, an international court in which they have some say in the appointment process is much preferable to a system of private arbitration, biased against host governments, in which they have little say at all. For the major capital-exporting states and their firms, the proposal asks them to sacrifice little in exchange for an international judicial body that is more likely to have political staying power than the current system. Thus, the proposal does not ask that investors be barred from bringing claims, that damages be foreclosed as a public law remedy, or that the standards of investor protection be rewritten. All it requires is that investors be subject to the rule of law as applied by an independent judiciary. And for those who are opposed

---

[138] For this reason, appointments should not be made by institutions, such as the World Bank, that clearly favour capital-exporting states. To illustrate, one alternative would be a combined procedure whereby candidates were nominated by groups of capital-exporting and capital-importing states representing different regions of the world, for approval by a majority vote of both the UN Security Council and the UN General Assembly.

[139] For example, the code might take effect following ratification by at least 20 states whose nationals collectively own at least 20% of the world's total foreign direct investment (FDI) outward stock. This would allow the code to enter into force with the agreement of either the US (20.7% of world FDI outward stock in 2004) or a collection of the other top capital-exporters including: the UK (14.2%), Germany (8.6%), France (7.9%), and the Netherlands (5.6%). UNCTAD, *World Investment Report 2005* (Geneva: United Nations, 2003), annex, table B.2.

in principle to the multiplication of international courts, it should be kept in mind that the proposal would consolidate hundreds of (inadequate) tribunals into a proper judicial body. For these reasons, all states have good reason to support an international investment court that is open and accountable, capable of delivering coherence, and genuinely independent. Ultimately, however, the prospects for the present proposal depend on whether key constituencies in the major states make it a priority to reform the system not so much because it fits their particular interests (although in most cases it will) but because they wish to defend long-cherished principles of judging in public law.

Bibliography

DOCUMENTS OF INTERNATIONAL ORGANIZATIONS

Economic Commission for Latin America and the Caribbean (ECLAC), *Foreign Investment in Latin America and the Caribbean, 2003*, UN Doc E/04/II/G.54 (2004).

Free Trade Commission (NAFTA), *Notes of Interpretation of Certain Chapter 11 Provisions* (31 July 2001), 13(6) World Trade and Arb Mat 139, online: DFAIT www.dfait-maeci.gc.ca/tna-nac/NAFTA-Interpr-en.asp.

Free Trade Commission (NAFTA), *Statement of the Free Trade Commission on non-disputing party participation* (17 October 2003), online: DFAIT http://www.dfait-maeci.gc.ca/nafta-alena/Nondisputing-en.pdf.

Human Rights Committee, *General Comment 24 on Reservations to the International Covenant on Civil and Political Rights* (1994), (1995) 15 Human Rights LJ 464, 2 IHRR 10.

International Centre for Settlement of Investment Disputes (ICSID), *Rules of Procedure for Arbitration Proceedings*, revised 26 September 1984 and 1 January 2003 (original rules 1968), reprinted in *Convention, Regulations and Rules* (Washington: ICSID, 2003) [ICSID Rules], online: ICSID www.worldbank.org/icsid/basicdoc/basicDoc.htm.

ICSID, *Model Clauses Relating to the Convention on the Settlement of Investment Disputes Designed for Use in Bilateral Investment Agreements* (1969), 8 ILM 1341.

ICSID, *Rules Governing the Additional Facility for the Administration of Proceedings by the Secretariat of the International Centre for Settlement of Investment Disputes*, revised 1 January 2003 (original rules 1978), 1 ICSID Rep 213 [ICSID Additional Facility Rules], online: ICSID www.worldbank.org/icsid/facility-archive/1.htm.

ICSID, *Administrative and Financial Regulations*, reprinted in *Convention, Regulations and Rules* (Washington: ICSID, 2003).

International Commission of Jurists (Summary of discussions, Conference on the Independence of Judges and Lawyers, Caracas, 16–18 January 1989).

International Joint Commission, *Protection of the Waters of the Great Lakes—Final Report to the Governments of Canada and the United States* (IJC, February 2002).

International Law Commission, *Summary Records of the 9th Session*, 1957, UN Doc A/CN.4/106, [1957] 1 Ybk Int'l Law Comm 155.

International Law Commission, *Commentary to its Final Draft Articles* [1966] 2 Ybk Int'l L Comm.

International Law Commission, 'Draft Articles on Responsibility of States for Internationally Wrongful Acts', *Report of the International Law Commission on the Work of Its Fifty-third Session*, UN GAOR, 56th Sess, Supp No 10, annex, UN Doc A/56/10 (2001).

International Monetary Fund, *Foreign Direct Investment Statistics—How Countries Measure FDI* (IMF, 2001).

League of Nations, *Responsibility of States for Damage Caused in Their Territory to the Person or Property of Foreigners*, Conference for the Codification of International Law, Bases of Discussion, vol 3, LN Doc C.75.M.69.1929.V (1929).

NAFTA Advisory Committee on Private Commercial Disputes, *Summary of US Arbitration Law* by D Enix-Ross and DW Rivkin (June 1995).

Organization for Economic Cooperation and Development (OECD), *The MAI Negotiating Text*, Paris (1998).

OECD, *OECD Guidelines for Multinational Enterprises*, Revision 2000 (Paris: OECD, 2000).

United Nations, *Report of the Committee on the Enforcement of International Arbitral Awards*, UN ESC, UN Doc E/AC.42/SR.1 (First Meeting, 1 March 1955).

UN, *Report of the Committee on the Enforcement of International Arbitral Awards*, UN ESC, UN Doc E/AC.42/SR.2 (Second Meeting, 23 March 1955).

UN, *Report of the Committee on the Enforcement of International Arbitral Awards*, UN ESC, UN Doc E/AC.42/SR.3 (Third Meeting, 23 March 1955).

UN, *Report of the Committee on the Enforcement of International Arbitral Awards*, UN ESC, UN Doc E/AC.42/4/Rev.1 (28 March 1955).

UN, *Report by the Secretary-General on the Recognition and Enforcement of Foreign Arbitral Awards*, annex I and II, UN ESC, UN Doc E/2822 (31 January 1956).

UN, *Comments by Governments on the draft Convention on the Recognition and Enforcement of Foreign Arbitral Awards*, UN ESC, UN Doc E/2822/Add.4 (3 April 1956).

UN, *Report of the Secretary-General: Preliminary Draft Set of Arbitration Rules for Optional Use in Ad Hoc Arbitration Relating to International Trade (UNCITRAL Arbitration Rules)*, UN, UN Doc A/CN.9/97 (4 November 1974), 6 Ybk UNCITRAL 163.

UN, *Report of the Secretary-General: Revised Draft Set of Arbitration Rules for Optional Use in Ad Hoc Arbitration Relating to International Trade (UNCITRAL Arbitration Rules)*, UN, UN Doc A/CN.9/112/Add.1 (12 December 1975), 7 Ybk UNCITRAL 166.

UN, *Arbitration Rules of the United Nations Commission on International Trade Law*, UN GA Res 31/98, UN GAOR, 31st Session, Supp No 17, UN Doc A/31/17, c V, s C (1976) [UNCITRAL Rules].

UN, *Note by the Secretariat: Further Work in respect of International Commercial Arbitration*, UN, UN Doc A/CN.9/169 (11 May 1979).

UN, *Report of the Secretary-General: Possible Features of a Model Law on International Commercial Arbitration*, UN, UN Doc A/CN.9/207 (14 May 1981), (1981) 12 Ybk UNCITRAL 77.

UN, *Note by the Secretariat: Model Law on International Commercial Arbitration: Draft Articles 1 to 24 on Scope of Application, Arbitration Agreement, Arbitrators, and Arbitral Procedure*, UN, UN Doc A/CN.9/WG.II/WP.37 (1982).

UN, *Report of the Secretary-General: Analytical Compilation of Comments by Governments and International Organizations on the Draft Text of a Model Law on International Commercial Arbitration*, UN, UN Doc A/CN.9/263 and Add 1–3 (1985).

UN, *Report of the Secretary-General: Analytical Commentary on Draft Text of a Model Law on International Commercial Arbitration*, UN, UN Doc A/CN.9/264 (25 March 1985), 16 Ybk UNCITRAL 104.

UNCITRAL, *Model Law on International Commercial Arbitration*, 21 June 1985, UN Doc A/40/17, annex I, 24 ILM 1302.

United Nations Conference on Trade and Development (UNCTAD), *International Investment Instruments: A Compendium*, vol 3 (New York: United Nations, 1996).
UNCTAD, *World Investment Report 1996* (Geneva: United Nations, 1997).
UNCTAD, *Bilateral Investment Treaties in the Mid-1990s* (Geneva: United Nations, 1998).
UNCTAD, *Fair and Equitable Treatment*, UNCTAD Series on Issues in International Investment Agreements (New York: United Nations, 1999).
UNCTAD, *Most-Favoured-Nation Treatment*, UNCTAD Series on Issues in International Investment Agreements (New York: United Nations, 1999).
UNCTAD, *National Treatment*, UNCTAD Series on Issues in International Investment Agreements (New York: United Nations, 1999).
UNCTAD, *Scope and Definition*, UNCTAD Series on Issues in International Investment Agreements (New York: United Nations, 1999).
UNCTAD, *Trends in International Investment Agreements: An Overview*, UNCTAD Series on Issues in International Investment Agreements (New York: United Nations, 1999).
UNCTAD, *Bilateral Investment Treaties—1959–1999* (New York: United Nations, 2000).
UNCTAD, *Taxation*, UNCTAD Series on Issues in International Investment Agreements (New York: United Nations, 2000).
UNCTAD, *Dispute Settlement: Investor-State*, UNCTAD Series on Issues in International Investment Agreements (New York: United Nations, 2003).
UNCTAD, *World Investment Report 2003* (New York: United Nations, 2003).
UNCTAD, *World Investment Report 2004* (New York: United Nations, 2004).
UNCTAD, 'Occasional Note: Many BITs Have Yet to Enter Into Force' (New York, United Nations, 2005).
UNCTAD, 'Recent Developments in International Investment Agreements' (Research note, 30 August 2005).
UNCTAD, *World Investment Report 2005* (New York: United Nations, 2005).
United Nations Development Programme (UNDP), *Human Development Report 2005* (New York: UNDP, 2005).
United States Department of Commerce, Office of the Chief Counsel for International Commerce, *International Arbitration* (1998).
World Bank, *Memorandum of the meeting of the Committee of the Whole, December 27, 1962*, World Bank, UN Doc SID/62-2 (7 January 1963), reprinted in ICSID, *Convention on the Settlement of Investment Disputes between States and Nationals of Other States—Documents Concerning the Origins and the Formulation of the Convention*, vol 2 (World Bank, 1968).
World Bank, *First Preliminary Draft of a Convention on the Settlement of Investment Disputes, Annotated Text*, World Bank, UN Doc SID/63-15 (9 August 1963), reprinted in ICSID, *Convention on the Settlement of Investment Disputes between States and Nationals of Other States—Documents Concerning the Origins and the Formulation of the Convention*, vol 2 (World Bank, 1968).
World Bank, *Report of the Executive Directors on the Convention on the Settlement of Investment Disputes Between States and Nationals of Other States* (18 March 1965), reprinted in *Convention, Regulations and Rules* (Washington: ICSID, 2003).
World Bank, *World Development Report 1999/2000* (Oxford: OUP, 2000).
World Bank, *World Development Report 2005* (Washington, DC: IBRD, 2004).

SECONDARY SOURCES

EV Abbot, 'The Police Power and the Right to Compensation' (1889) 3 Harv L Rev 189.

AF Abbott, 'Latin America and International Arbitration Conventions: The Quandary of Non-Ratification' (1976) 17 Harv Int'l LJ 131.

KW Abbott *et al*, 'The Concept of Legalization' in JL Goldstein *et al* (eds) *Legalization and World Politics* (Cambridge: MIT Press, 2001).

H Abs and H Shawcross, 'The Proposed Convention to Protect Private Foreign Investment' (1960) 9 J Public L 115.

A Afilalo, 'Constitutionalization Through the Back Door: A European Perspective on NAFTA's Investment Chapter' (2001) 34 NYU J Int'l L & Pol 1.

MT Ahmedouamar, 'The Liability of the Government in France as a Consequence of its Legal Activities' (1983) 11 Int'l J Legal Info 1.

R Alford, 'The Looming Crisis at ICSID', online: www.opiniojuris.org.

J Allan, 'Rights, Paternalism, Constitutions and Judges' in G Huscroft and P Rishworth (eds) *Litigating Rights* (Oxford: Hart, 2002).

P Allott, 'State Responsibility and the Unmaking of International Law' (1988) 29 Harv Int'l LJ 1.

P Alston, 'Resisting the Merger and Acquisition of Human Rights by Trade Law: A Reply to Petersmann' (2002) 13 Eur J Int'l L 815.

A Alvarez, 'Latin America and International Law' (1909) 3 AJIL 269.

JE Alvarez, 'Critical Theory and the North American Free Trade Agreement's Chapter Eleven' (1997) 28 Inter-Am L Rev 303.

JE Alvarez, 'The New Dispute Settlers: (Half) Truths and Consequences' (2003) 38 Texas Int'l LJ 405.

GA Alvarez and WW Park, 'The New Face of Investment Arbitration: NAFTA Chapter 11' (2003) 28 Yale J Int'l L 365.

AC Aman, 'The Limits of Globalization and the Future of Administrative Law: From Government to Governance' (2001) 8 Ind J Global Legal Studies 379.

AC Aman, 'Globalization, Democracy, and the Need for a New Administrative Law' (2003) 10 Ind J Global Legal Studies 125.

R Anderson, 'Tribunal to rule on Czech bank failure' *Financial Times* (8 April 2005) 27.

A Anghie, 'Finding the Peripheries: Sovereignty and Colonialism in Nineteenth-Century International Law' (1999) 40 Harv Int'l LJ 1.

M Antinori, 'Does Lochner Live in Luxembourg? An Analysis of the Property Rights Jurisprudence of the European Court of Justice' (1995) 18 Fordham Int'l LJ 1778.

B Appleton, *Navigating NAFTA* (Scarborough: Carswell, 1994).

M Aronson, B Dyer, and M Groves, *Judicial Review of Administrative Action* (3rd edn, North Ryde: LBC Information Services, 2004).

SKB Asante, *Transnational Investment Law and National Development* (Lagos: University of Lagos, 1981).

SKB Asante, 'International Law and Foreign Investment: A Reappraisal' (1988) 37 ICLQ 588, 591–5.

SKB Asante, 'International Law and Investments' in M Bedjaouni (ed) *International Law: Achievements and Prospects* (Paris and Dordrecht: UNESCO and Martinus Nijhoff, 1991).

J Atik, 'Legitimacy, Transparency and NGO Participation in the NAFTA Chapter 11 Process' in T Weiler (ed) *NAFTA, Investment Law and Arbitration* (Ardsley, NY: Transnational Publishers, 2004).

PS Atiyah, *Law & Modern Society* (2nd edn, Oxford: OUP, 1995) 14–16.

RS Avi-Yonah, 'Globalization, Tax Competition, and the Fiscal Crisis of the Welfare State' (2000) 113 Harv L Rev 1573.

R Bachand and S Rousseau, 'International Investment and Human Rights: Political and Legal Issues' (Background paper for Rights & Democracy, 11 June 2003).

A Baines, 'Capital Mobility and European Financial and Monetary Integration: A Structural Analysis' (2002) 28 Rev Int'l Studies 337.

R Baldwin and C McCrudden, *Regulation and Public Law* (London: Weidenfeld & Nicolson, 1987).

E Barendt, 'Separation of Powers and Constitutional Government' (1995) Pub L 599.

M Barlow and T Clark, *MAI: The Multilateral Agreement on Investment and the Threat to Canadian Sovereignty* (Toronto: Stoddart: 1997).

W Barnes, 'Remarks' (1907) Am Soc'ty Int'l L Proc 100.

M Barrow, 'Argentina puts bankers to the test' *The Times* (7 August 2001) 21.

VL Been and JC Beauvais, 'The Global Fifth Amendment: NAFTA's Investment Protections and the Misguided Quest for an International "Regulatory Takings" Doctrine' (2003) 78 NYU L Rev 30.

MS Bergman, 'Bilateral Investment Protection Treaties: An Examination of the Evolution and Significance of the US Prototype Treaty' (1983) 16 NYU J Int'l L & Pol 1.

J Bhagwati, 'The Capital Myth: the Difference between Trade in Widgets and Dollars' (1998) 77(3) For Affairs 7.

PN Bhagwati, 'Judicial Activism and Public Interest Litigation' (1985) 23 Colum J Transnat'l L 561.

RD Bishop, SD Dimitroff, and CS Miles, 'Strategic Options Available When Catastrophe Strikes' (2001) 36 Texas Int'l LJ 635.

L Biucovic, 'Impact of the Adoption of the Model Law in Canada: Creating a New Environment for International Arbitration' (1998) 30 Can Bus LJ 376.

AK Bjorklund, 'Contract Without Privity: Sovereign Offer and Investor Acceptance' (2001) 2 Chi J Int'l L 183.

K-H Böckstiegel, 'An Introduction to the New German Arbitration Act Based on the UNCITRAL Model Law' (1998) 14 Arb Int'l 19.

D Bodansky and JR Crook, 'Symposium: The ILC's State Responsibility Articles—Introduction and Overview' (2002) 96 AJIL 773.

EM Borchard, 'Basic Elements of Diplomatic Protection of Citizens Abroad' (1913) 7 AJIL 497.

EM Borchard, 'Governmental Responsibility in Tort, V' (1927) 36 Yale LJ 757.

EM Borchard, 'Governmental Responsibility in Tort: VII' (1928) 28 Colum L Rev 577.

EM Borchard, 'The Access of Individuals to International Courts' (1930) 24 AJIL 359, 362–3.

EM Borchard, ' "Responsibility of States," At the Hague Codification Conference' (1930) 24 AJIL 517.

EM Borchard, 'The "Minimum Standard" of the Treatment of Aliens' (1940) 38 Mich L Rev 445.

G Borrie, 'Judicial Conflicts of Interest in Britain' (1970) 18 Am J Comp L 697.
JW Boscariol, 'Canada and the New International Investment Regime—Canada's Foreign Investment Protection Agreements' (Presentation to the Canadian Bar Association—Ontario International Law Section, March 1999).
EH Bouzari, 'The Public Policy Exception to Enforcement of International Arbitral Awards: Implications for Post-NAFTA Jurisprudence' (1995) 30 Texas Int'l LJ 205.
DW Bowett, 'Claims Between States and Private Entities: The Twilight Zone of International Law' (1986) 35 Cath U L Rev 929.
J Braithwaite and P Drahos, *Global Business Regulation* (Cambridge: CUP, 2000).
WW Bratton *et al*, 'Introduction: Regulatory Competition and Institutional Evolution' in WW Bratton *et al* (eds) *International Regulatory Competition and Coordination* (Oxford: Clarendon, 1996).
JL Brierly, *The Law of Nations* (6th edn, Oxford: Clarendon Press, 1963).
A Broches, 'An Analysis of the Bank's Tentative Proposals and of the Principal Issues Raised Thereby', World Bank, UN Doc SID/63-2 (18 February 1963), reprinted in ICSID, *Convention on the Settlement of Investment Disputes between States and Nationals of Other States—Documents Concerning the Origins and the Formulation of the Convention*, vol 2 (World Bank, 1968).
A Broches, 'Development of International Law by the International Bank for Reconstruction and Development' (1965) 59 Am Soc'ty Int'l L Proc 33.
CH Brower II, 'Investor–State Disputes Under NAFTA: The Empire Strikes Back' (2001) 40 Colum J Transnat'l L 43.
CH Brower II, 'NAFTA's Investment Chapter: Initial Thoughts About Second-Generation Rights' (2003) 36 Vanderbilt J Transnat'l L 1533.
CN Brower, CH Brower II, and JK Sharpe, 'The Coming Crisis in the Global Adjudicative System' (2003) 19 Arb Int'l 415.
CN Brower and D Brueschke, *The Iran–United States Claims Tribunal* (The Hague: Kluwer Law International, 1998).
CN Brower and LA Steven, 'Who Then Should Judge? Developing the International Rule of Law under NAFTA Chapter 11' (2001) 2 Chi J Int'l L 193.
D Brown, 'Commentary' in LR Dawson (ed) *Whose Rights? The NAFTA Chapter 11 Debate* (Ottawa: Centre for Trade Law and Policy, 2002).
I Brownlie, *Principles of Public International Law* (6th edn, Oxford: OUP, 2003).
R Bruno and JHH Weiler, 'Access of Private Parties to International Dispute Settlement: A Comparative Analysis' (Harvard Jean Monnet Working Paper No 13/97, New York University School of Law, 1997).
A Bucher, 'Court Intervention in Arbitration' in R Lillich and CN Brower (eds) *International Arbitration in the 21st Century: Towards Judicialization and Uniformity?* (Ardsley, NY: Transnational Publishers, 1994).
J Byrne, 'NAFTA Dispute Resolution: Implementing True Rule-Based Diplomacy Through Direct Access' (2000) 35 Texas Int'l LJ 415.
S Calloni, 'Frágil, el equilibrio politico, económico y social en Argentina' *La Jornada* [Mexico] (21 January 2002).
C Calvo, *Le Droit international* (5th edn, Paris: A Rousseau, 1896).
A Capling and K Richard Nossal, 'Blowback: Investor–State Dispute Mechanisms in International Trade Agreements' (2006) 19 *Governance* 151.
WS Carpenter, *Judicial Tenure in the United States* (New Haven: Yale University Press, 1918).

MM Carrow, *The Background of Administrative Law* (Newark: Associated Lawyers, 1948).
JP Carver, 'The Strengths and Weaknesses of International Arbitration Involving a State as a Party: Practical Implications' (1985) 1 Arb Int'l 179.
DZ Cass, *The Constitutionalization of the World Trade Organization* (Oxford: OUP, 2005).
J Castaneda, 'The Underdeveloped Nations and the Development of International Law' (1961) 15 Int'l Org 38.
Center for International Environmental Law (CIEL), 'International Law on Investment: The Minimum Standard of Treatment (MST)' (Issue Brief, August 2003).
PG Cerny, 'Paradox of the Competition State: the Dynamics of Political Globalization' (1997) 32 Gov't and Opposition 251.
A Chayes, 'The Role of the Judge in Public Law Litigation' (1976) 89 Harv L Rev 1281.
T-H Cheng, 'Power, Authority and International Investment Law' (2005) 20 Am U Int'l L Rev 465.
RR Churchill, 'Dispute Settlement in the Law of the Sea' in MD Evans, *Remedies in International Law: The Institutional Dilemma* (Oxford: Hart, 1998).
P Civello, 'The TRIMs Agreement: A Failed Attempt at Investment Liberalization' (1999) 8 Minn J Global Trade 97.
A Claire Cutler, 'Critical Reflections on the Westphalian Assumptions of International Law and Organization: A Crisis of Legitimacy' (2001) 27 Rev of Int'l Studies 133.
S Clarkson, 'Systemic or Surgical? Possible Cures for NAFTA's Investor–State Dispute Process' (2002) 36 Can Bus LJ 368.
D Cohen and JC Smith, 'Entitlement and the Body Politic: Rethinking Negligence in Public Law' (1986) 64 Can Bar Rev 1.
J Collier and V Lowe, *The Settlement of Disputes in International Law* (Cambridge: CUP, 1999).
CM Correa, 'Bilateral Investment Agreements: Agents of New Global Standards for the Protection of Intellectual Property Rights?' (Report for GRAIN, August 2004).
A Cosbey *et al*, 'Investment and Sustainable Development' (Report by the International Institute for Sustainable Development, 2004).
J-P Costa, 'The Provision of Compensation Under Article 41 of the European Convention on Human Rights' (Address to the British Institute of International and Comparative Law, 7 December 2001).
T Cottier, 'Trade and Human Rights: A Relationship to Discover' (2002) 5 J Int'l Econ L 111.
PP Craig, 'Compensation in Public Law' (1980) 96 LQ Rev 413.
PP Craig, 'Once Upon a Time in the West: Direct Effect and the Federalization of EEC Law' (1992) 12 Ox J Legal Studies 453.
PP Craig and G De Búrca, *EU Law—Text, Cases, and Materials* (3rd edn, Oxford: OUP, 2003).
WL Craig, WW Park, and J Paulsson, *International Chamber of Commerce Arbitration* (New York: Oceana Publications, 1990).
BM Cremades and DJA Cairns, 'The Brave New World of Global Arbitration' (2002) 3 J World Investment 173.
JH Dalhuisen, *Dalhuisen on International Commercial, Financial and Trade Law* (Oxford: Hart, 2000).
CK Dalrymple, 'Politics and Foreign Direct Investment: The Multilateral Investment Guarantee Agency and the Calvo Clause' (1996) 29 Cornell Int'l LJ 161.

M Daly, 'Some Taxing Questions for the Multilateral Agreement on Investment (MAI)' (1997) 20 World Economy 787.

M Damaška, 'Activism in Perspective' (1983) 92 Yale LJ 1189.

RG Dearden, 'Arbitration of Expropriation Disputes between an Investor and the State under the North American Free Trade Agreement' (1995) 29 J World Trade 113.

C Deblock and D Brunelle, 'Globalization and New Normative Frameworks—The Multilateral Agreement on Investment', Cahier de recherche 98–2 (Groupe de recherche sur l'intégration continentale, Université de Québec à Montréal, 1998).

GR Delaume, 'ICSID Arbitration and the Courts' (1983) 77 AJIL 784.

GR Delaume, 'Sovereign Immunity and Transnational Arbitration' (1987) 3 Arb Int'l 28.

I Delupis, *Finance and Protection of Investments in Developing Countries* (Epping: Gower Press, 1973).

E Denza, 'The Relationship Between International and National Law' in MD Evans (ed) *International Law* (2nd edn, Oxford: OUP, 2006).

A DePalma, 'NAFTA's Powerful Little Secret' *The New York Times* (11 March 2001).

Y Dezaley, 'Between the State, Law, and the Market: The Social and Professional Stakes in the Construction and Definition of a Regulatory Arena' in WW Bratton *et al* (eds) *International Regulatory Competition and Coordination* (Oxford: Clarendon, 1996).

Y Dezaley and B Garth, *Dealing in Virtue: International Commercial Arbitration and the Construction of a Transnational Legal Order* (Chicago: University of Chicago Press, 1996).

AV Dicey, *An Introduction to the Study of the Law of the Constitution* [1885] (8th edn, London: Macmillan, 1915).

W Diebold, 'The End of the ITO' in *Essays in International Finance*, no 16 (Princeton: Princeton University Press, 1952).

S Dillon, *International Trade and Economic Law in the European Union* (Oxford: Hart, 2002).

WS Dodge, 'National Courts and International Arbitration: Exhaustion of Remedies and Res Judicata Under Chapter Eleven of NAFTA' (2000) 23 Hast Int'l & Comp L Rev 357.

R Dolzer, 'New Foundations of the Law of Expropriation of Alien Property' (1981) 75 AJIL 553.

R Dolzer, 'Indirect Expropriation of Alien Property' (1986) 1 ICSID Rev 41.

R Dolzer and M Stevens, *Bilateral Investment Treaties* (The Hague: Kluwer Law International, 1995).

R Donner, *The Regulation of Nationality in International Law* (2nd edn, Ardsley, NY: Transnational Publishers, 1994).

DF Donovan, 'Introduction to Articles—Dallas Workshop on Arbitrating with Sovereigns' (2002) 18 Arb Int'l 229.

Z Douglas, 'The Hybrid Foundations of Investment Treaty Arbitration' (2003) 74 Brit Ybk Int'l L 151.

Z Douglas, 'Nothing if Not Critical for Investment Treaty Arbitration: *Occidental, Eureko* and *Methanex*' (2006) 22 Arb Int'l 27.

L Drago, 'State Loans in Their Relations to International Policy' (1907) 1 AJIL 692.

E Drake *et al*, 'The Multilateral Agreement on Investment: A Step Backward in International Human Rights' (Report for the Human Rights Clinical Project Program, Harvard Law School, undated).

FS Dunn, 'International Law and Private Property Rights' (1928) 28 Colum L Rev 166.
RW Dunn, *American Foreign Investments* (New York: BW Huebsch and Viking Press, 1926).
J Dunning, *International Production and the Multinational Enterprise* (London: Allen & Unwin, 1981).
R Dussault and L Bourgeat, *Administrative Law—A Treatise* (Toronto: Carswell, 1985).
J Dutheil de la Rochère, 'Member State Liability for Infringement of European Community Law' (1996) 11 Tul Euro Civ LF 1.
C Eagleton, *The Responsibility of States in International Law* (New York: NYU Press, 1928).
P Egger and M Pfaffermayr, 'The Impact of Bilateral Investment Treaties on Foreign Direct Investment' (2004) 32 J Comp Economics 788.
L Ehring, 'De Facto Discrimination in WTO Law: National and Most-Favored-Nation Treatment—or Equal Treatment?' (Jean Monnet Working Paper No 12/01, New York University School of Law, 2001).
B Eichengreen *et al*, 'Liberalizing Capital Movements: Some Analytical Issues', Economic Issues No 17 (IMF, 1999).
CL Eisgruber, *Constitutional Self-Government* (Cambridge: Harvard University Press, 2001).
SE Eizenstat, '"Fast Track" needs protections for investors' *The Boston Globe* (2 May 2002).
T Epps and CM Flood, 'Have We Traded Away the Opportunity for Innovative Health Care Reform? The Implications of the NAFTA for Medicare' (2002) 47 McGill LJ 747.
RA Epstein, *Takings: Private Property and the Power of Eminent Domain* (Cambridge, Mass: Harvard University Press, 1985).
JM Evans *et al*, *Administrative Law—Cases, Text, and Materials* (4th edn, Toronto: Emond Montgomery, 1995).
HR Evans, 'The Nonarbitrability of Subject Matter Defense to Enforcement of Foreign Arbitral Awards in United States Federal Courts' (1989) 21 NYU J Int'l L & Pol 329.
RC Evans, 'Damages for Unlawful Administrative Action: The Remedy for Misfeasance in Public Office' (1982) 31 ICLQ 640.
AP Fachiri, 'International Law and the Property of Aliens' (1929) 10 Brit Ybk Int'l L 32.
JK Fairbank, *The United States and China* (Cambridge, Mass: Harvard University Press, 1959).
D Fairgrieve, 'The Human Rights Act 1998, Damages and Tort Law' (2001) Pub Law 695.
TJ Farer, 'Economic Development Agreements: A Functional Analysis' (1971) 10 Colum J Transnat'l L 200.
MJ Farrelly, 'Recent Questions of International Law' (1894) 10 LQ Rev 254.
AA Fatouros, 'An International Code to Protect Private Investment—Proposals and Perspectives' (1961) 14 U Toronto LJ 77.
AA Fatouros, *Government Guarantees to Foreign Investors* (New York: Columbia University Press, 1962).
AA Fatouros, 'International Economic Development and the Illusion of Legal Certainty' (1963) 57 Am Soc'ty Int'l L Proc 117.
AA Fatouros, 'International Law and the Third World' (1964) 50 Virg L Rev 783.
AA Fatouros, 'On Domesticating Giants: Further Reflections on the Legal Approach to Transnational Enterprise' (1976) 15 U Western Ontario L Rev 151.

AA Fatouros, 'Transnational Enterprise in the Law of State Responsibility' in RB Lillich (ed) *International Law of State Responsibility for Injuries to Aliens* (Charlottesville: University Press of Virginia, 1983).

WA Fischel, *Regulatory Takings: Law, Economics, and Politics* (Cambridge, Mass: Harvard University Press, 1995).

OM Fiss, 'Against Settlement' (1984) 93 Yale LJ 1073.

JP Fitzpatrick, 'The Future of the North American Free Trade Agreement: A Comparative Analysis of the Role of Regional Economic Institutions and the Harmonization of Law in North America and Western Europe' (1996) 19 Houston J Int'l L 1.

LY Fortier, 'Delimiting the Spheres of Judicial and Arbitral Power' (2000) 80 Can Bar Rev 143.

LY Fortier, 'Caveat Investor: The Meaning of "Expropriation" and the Protection Afforded Investors Under NAFTA' (2003) 20(1) ICSID News 1.

PG Foy, 'Effectiveness of NAFTA's Chapter Eleven Investor–State Arbitration Procedures' (2003) 18 ICSID Rev 44.

SD Franck, 'The Legitimacy Crisis in Investment Treaty Arbitration: Privatizing Public International Law Through Inconsistent Decisions' (2005) 73 Fordham L Rev 1521.

TM Franck, *Fairness in International Law and Institutions* (New York: Clarendon Press, 1995).

S François-Poncet and C Mouawad, 'Final Arbitral Award Rendered in 2003 in SCC Case 49/2002' (2004) 2004:1 Stockholm Arbitration Report 141.

J Freeman, 'The Private Role in Public Governance' (2000) 75 NYU L Rev 543.

Freshfields Bruckhaus Deringer, 'The Argentine Crisis—Foreign Investors' Rights' (Report, January 2002).

Freshfields Bruckhaus Deringer, 'Dispute Resolution in the Caspian Region' (Report, June 2002).

B Friedman, 'The Politics of Judicial Review' (2005) 84 Texas L Rev 257.

S Friedman, *Expropriation in International Law* (Westport, Conn: Greenwood Press, 1953).

W Friedmann, *Law in a Changing Society* (London: Stevens & Sons, 1959).

LL Fuller, 'Consideration and Form' (1941) 41 Colum L Rev 799.

LL Fuller, 'Adjudication and the Rule of Law' (1960) 54 Am Soc'ty Int'l L Proc 1.

LL Fuller, 'The Forms and Limits of Adjudication' (1978) 92 Harv L Rev 353.

E Gaillard, 'Commentary' (2002) 18 Arb Int'l 247.

N Gal-Or, 'Private Party Direct Access: A Comparison of the NAFTA and EU Disciplines' (1998) 21 BC Int'l & Comp L Rev 1.

G Gamini, 'Argentina faces debt default as IMF stops loan' *The Times* (7 December 2001) 21.

G Gamini, 'Rioters killed as Argentina slides into chaos' *The Times* (20 December 2001) 17.

G Gamini, 'Argentina slides deeper into mire of debt' *The Times* (15 November 2002) 22.

S Ganguly, 'The Investor–State Dispute Mechanism (ISDM) and a Sovereign's Power to Protect Public Health' (1999) 38 Colum J Transnat'l L 113.

G Ganz, 'Allocation of Decision-Making Functions' (1972) Pub L 215.

CG Garcia, 'All the Other Dirty Little Secrets: Investment Treaties, Latin America, and the Necessary Evil of Investor–State Arbitration' (2004) 16 Florida J Int'l L 301.

Y Ghai, R Luckham, and F Snyder, 'Introduction' in Y Ghai, R Luckham, and F Snyder (eds) *The Political Economy of Law* (Oxford: OUP, 1987).
PS Gibbs, 'Prospects for Sustainable Liberalization of Foreign Investment Laws as a Concomitant of Hemispheric Integration in the Americas' (1996) 28 Inter-Am L Rev 95.
N Girvan, *Corporate Imperialism: Conflict and Expropriation* (New York: ME Sharpe, 1978).
PH Gleick et al, 'The New Economy of Water' (Report for the Pacific Institute for Studies in Development, Environment, and Security, 2002).
MD Goldhaber, 'Wanted: A World Investment Court' (Summer 2004) *The American Lawyer*.
J Goldsworthy, *The Sovereignty of Parliament* (Oxford: Clarendon, 1999).
U Goni, 'Debt-ridden middle classes ready to desert Argentina' *The Sunday Times* (6 January 2002) 24.
CD Gray, *Judicial Remedies in International Law* (Oxford: Clarendon, 1987).
CN Gregory, 'Expropriation by International Arbitration' (1907) 21 Harv L Rev 23.
C Greenwood, 'The Law of War (International Humanitarian Law)' in MD Evans (ed) *International Law* (2nd edn, Oxford: OUP, 2006).
JAG Griffith, *The Politics of the Judiciary* (5th edn, London: Fontana Press, 1997).
JAG Griffith, 'The Brave New World of Sir John Laws' (2000) 63 Mod L Rev 159.
WE Grigsby, 'The Mixed Court of Egypt' (1896) 12 LQ Rev 252.
DM Gruner, 'Accounting for the Public Interest in International Arbitration: The Need for Procedural and Structural Reform' (2003) 41 Colum J Transnat'l L 923.
O Guglielmino, 'Analista señala arbitrariedad del sistema judicial; Demandas inverosímiles' *La Nación* [Argentina] (17 January 2005).
AT Guzman, 'Why LDCs Sign Treaties That Hurt Them: Explaining the Popularity of Bilateral Investment Treaties' (1998) 38 Virg J Int'l L 639.
M Habicht, *Post-War Treaties for the Pacific Settlement of International Disputes* (Cambridge: Harvard University Press, 1931).
S Haggard, *Developing Nations and the Politics of Global Integration* (Washington, DC: Brookings Institution, 1995).
M Hallward-Driemeier, 'Do Bilateral Investment Treaties Attract Foreign Direct Investment? Only a Bit . . . and They Could Bite' (World Bank Policy Research Working Paper No 3121, Washington, June 2003).
J Hampden Dougherty, *Power of Federal Judiciary Over Legislation* (New York: GP Putnam's Sons, 1912).
PI Hansen, 'Judicialization and Globalization in the North American Free Trade Agreement' (2003) 38 Tex Int'l LJ 489.
C Harlow, '"Public" and "Private" Law: Definition Without Distinction' (1980) 43 Mod L Rev 241.
C Harlow, *Compensation and Government Torts* (London: Sweet & Maxwell, 1982).
C Harlow, 'Francovich and the Problem of the Disobedient State' (1996) 2 Eur LJ 199.
C Harlow, *State Liability: Tort Law and Beyond* (Oxford: OUP, 2004).
C Harlow, 'Global Administrative Values: The Quest for Principles and Values' (2006) 17 EJIL 187.
C Harlow and R Rawlings, *Law and Administration* (London: Butterworths, 1997).

DJ Harris, *Cases and Materials on International Law* (6th edn, London: Sweet & Maxwell, 2004).

M Hart, 'A Multilateral Agreement on Foreign Direct Investment—Why Now?' in P Sauvé and D Schwanen (eds) *Investment Rules for the Global Economy* (Toronto: CD Howe Institute, 1996).

MM Hart and WA Dymond, 'NAFTA Chapter 11: Precedents, Principles, and Prospects' in LR Dawson (ed) *Whose Rights? The NAFTA Chapter 11 Debate* (Ottawa: Centre for Trade Law and Policy, 2002).

D Held and A McGrew, 'Globalization' (1999) 5 Glob Governance 483.

T Hennigan, 'Argentina defaults on $2.9 billion debt' *The Times* (10 September 2003) 13.

AS Hershey, 'The Calvo and Drago Doctrines' (1907) 1 AJIL 26.

JA Hessbruegge, 'The Historical Development of the Doctrines of Attribution and Due Diligence in International Law' (2004) 36 NYU J Int'l L & Pol 265.

J Hewko, 'Foreign Direct Investment—Does the Rule of Law Matter?' (Report to the Carnegie Endowment for International Peace, Rule of Law Series, Report No 26, April 2002).

R Higgins, 'Conceptual Thinking about the Individual in International Law' (1978) 4 Brit J Int'l Studies 1.

HM Hill, 'Central American Court of Justice' in R Dolzer *et al* (eds) *Encyclopedia of Public International Law*, vol 1 (Amsterdam: North-Holland Publishing, 1987).

SM Hill, 'Growth of International Law in Africa' (1900) 16 LQ Rev 249.

J Hillary, 'Divide and Rule: The EU and US Response to Developing Country Alliances at the WTO' (Report for Action Aid International, 2004).

M Hirsh, *The Arbitration Mechanism of the International Centre for Settlement of Investment Disputes* (Dordrecht: Martinus Nijhoff, 1993).

E Hobsbawm, *Industry and Empire* (London: Penguin, 1968).

PW Hogg and PJ Monahan, *Liability of the Crown* (3rd edn, Toronto: Carswell, 2000).

M Hood, *Gunboat Diplomacy 1895–1905* (London: George Allen & Unwin, 1975).

GN Horlick and AL Marti, 'NAFTA Chapter 11B: A Private Right of Action to Enforce Market Access through Investments' (1997) 14 J Int'l Arb 43.

JF Hornbeck, 'The Argentine Financial Crisis: A Chronology of Events' (US Congressional Research Service Report No RS21130, 31 January 2002).

K Hossain, 'Introduction' in K Hossain and SR Chowdhury (eds) *Permanent Sovereignty over Natural Resources in International Law* (London: Pinter, 1984).

M-F Houde and K Yannaca-Small, *Relationships between International Investment Agreements* (OECD Working Paper on International Investment No 2004/1, May 2004).

MO Hudson, 'The Rendition of the International Mixed Court at Shanghai' (1927) 21 AJIL 451.

MO Hudson, *International Tribunals* (Washington: Carnegie Endowment for International Peace and the Brookings Institution, 1944).

G Huscroft, 'Rights, Bills of Rights, and the Role of Courts and Legislatures' in G Huscroft and P Rishworth (eds) *Litigating Rights* (Oxford: Hart, 2002).

International Chamber of Commerce (ICC), *Rules of Arbitration of the International Chamber of Commerce*, revised 1 January 1998 (original rules 1922) [ICC Rules], online: ICC www.iccwbo.org/court/english/arbitration/rules.asp.

ICC, 'Fair Treatment for Foreign Investments: International Code' (ICC Brochure No 129, 1949).

ICC, 'Multilateral rules for investment' (Doc No 103/179, Rev, 30 April 1996).
ICC, 'ICC's expectation regarding a WTO investment agreement' (Policy statement of the ICC Commission on Trade and Investment Policy, 7 March 2003).
C Issawi, *The Economic History of Turkey 1800–1914* (Chicago: University of Chicago Press, 1980).
JH Jackson, *The World Trading System* (2nd edn, Cambridge, Mass: MIT Press, 1997).
JH Jackson, WJ Davey, and AO Sykes, Jr, *Legal Problems of International Economic Relations* (4th edn, St Paul, Minn: West Group, 2002).
R Jackson, 'Sovereignty in World Politics: A Glance at the Conceptual and Historical Landscape' (1999) 47 Pol Studies 431.
G Jaenicke, 'The Prospects for International Arbitration: Disputes Between States and Private Enterprises' in AHA Soons, *International Arbitration: Past and Prospects* (Dordrecht, Martinus Nijhoff, 1990).
A James, *Sovereign Statehood: The Basis of International Society* (London: Allen & Unwin, 1986).
WI Jennings, *The Law and the Constitution* (London: University of London Press, 1959).
JR Johnson, 'Essential Disciplines of the National Treatment Obligation Under NAFTA Chapter Eleven' (Report on investment protection for the Ad Hoc Experts Group on Investment Rules, Department of Foreign Affairs and International Trade, 2 December 2001), online: DFAIT http://www.dfait-maeci.gc.ca/tna-nac/treatment-en.asp.
JR Johnson, 'How Will International Trade Agreements Affect Canadian Health Care?' (Discussion Paper No 22 for the Commission on the Future of Health Care in Canada, September 2002).
WR Johnston, *Sovereignty and Protection: A Study of British Jurisdictional Imperialism in the Late Nineteenth Century* (Durham, NC: Duke University Press, 1973).
GS Jones, 'The History of US Imperialism' in R Blackburn (ed) *Ideology in Social Science* (Glasgow: Fontana/Collins, 1972).
P Juillard, 'MAI: A European View' (1998) 31 Cornell Int'l LJ 477.
P Juillard, 'Freedom of Establishment, Freedom of Capital Movements, and Freedom of Investment' (2000) 15 ICSID Rev 322.
D Kalderimis, 'IMF Conditionality as Investment Regulation: A Theoretical Analysis' (2004) 13 Social & Leg Studies 103.
M Kantor, 'The New Draft Model US BIT: Noteworthy Developments' (2004) 21 J Int'l Arb 383.
G Kaufmann-Kohler, 'Annulment of ICSID Awards in Contract and Treaty Arbitrations: Are There Differences?' in E Gaillard and Y Banifatemi (eds) *Annulment of ICSID Awards* (Huntington, NY: Juris Publishing, 2004).
Z Kawaciukova, 'State ordered to pay 10 billion Kc' *The Prague Post* (19 March 2003).
RD Kelemen, 'The Limits of Judicial Power—Trade-Environment Disputes in the GATT/WTO and the EU' (2001) 34 Comp Pol Studies 622.
T Kellner, 'The Informer: Call It the Ronald *Lauder* Tax', 171(9) *Forbes Magazine* (28 April 2003).
J Kelsey, 'The Denationalization of Money: Embedded Neoliberalism and the Risks of Implosion' (2003) 12 Social & Leg Studies 155.
C Kennedy, 'Address' (1907) Am Soc'ty Int'l L Proc 100.
D Kennedy, 'Form and Substance in Private Law Adjudication' (1976) 89 Harv L Rev 1685.

E Kentin, 'Prospects for Rules on Investment in the New WTO Round' (2002) 29 Leg Issues Econ Integration 61.

S Kierstead, 'Referral to Arbitration Under Article 8 of the UNCITRAL Model Law: The Canadian Approach' (1998) 31 Can Bus LJ 98.

BR Killman, 'The Access of Individuals to International Trade Dispute Settlement' (1996) 13 J Int'l Arb 143.

HT King et al, 'Dispute Settlement Under the North American Free Trade Agreement' (1992) 26 Int'l Lawyer 855.

B Kingsbury, 'Sovereignty and Inequality' (1998) 9 EJIL 599.

B Kingsbury, N Krisch, and RB Stewart, 'The Emergence of Global Administrative Law' (2005) 68 Law & Contemporary Problems 15.

N Komesar, *Imperfect Alternatives—Choosing Institutions in Law, Economics and Public Policy* (Chicago: University of Chicago Press, 1994).

M Koskenniemi, 'The Future of Statehood' (1991) 32 Harv Int'l LJ 397.

M Koskenniemi, 'What Is International Law For?' in MD Evans (ed) *International Law* (2nd edn, Oxford: OUP, 2006).

R Kozul-Wright and R Rowthorn, 'Spoilt for Choice? Multinational Corporations and the Geography of International Production' (1998) 14 Ox Rev Econ Policy 74.

N Krisch, 'International Law in Times of Hegemony' (2005) 16 EJIL 369.

AK Kuhn, 'The International Conference on the Treatment of Foreigners' (1930) 24 AJIL 570.

J Kurtz, 'A General Investment Agreement in the WTO? Lessons from Chapter 11 of NAFTA and the OECD Multilateral Agreement on Investment' (Jean Monnet Working Paper, New York University School of Law, 2002).

WB Lafferty, 'The Persian Gulf War Syndrome: Rethinking Government Tort Liability' (1995) 25 Stetson L Rev 137.

IA Laird, 'NAFTA Chapter 11 Meets Chicken Little' (2001) 2 Chi J Int'l L 223.

C Lalumière and J-P Landau, 'Report on the Multilateral Agreement on Investment (MAI)' (Interim report to the Government of France, September 1998).

A Landsmeer, 'Movement of Capital and Other Freedoms' (2001) 28 Legal Issues of Economic Integration 57.

C Larsen, 'International Commercial Arbitration' *ASIL Insights* (April 1997).

JH Latané, 'Address' (1907) Am Soc'ty Int'l L Proc 100.

AM Latter, 'The Government of Foreigners in China' (1903) 19 LQ Rev 316.

E Lauterpacht, 'International Law and Private Foreign Investment' (1997) 4 Indiana J Global Legal Studies 259.

H Lauterpacht, *Private Sources and Analogies of International Law* (Longmans, Green & Co, 1927).

TJ Lawrence, *The Principles of International Law* (London: Macmillan & Co, 1923).

ER Leahy, 'Enforcement of Arbitral Awards Issued by the Additional Facility of the International Centre of Settlement of Investment Disputes (ICSID)' (1985) 2 J Int'l Arb 15.

B Legum, 'The Innovation of Investor–State Arbitration Under NAFTA' (2002) 43 Harv Int'l LJ 531.

B Legum, 'Trends and Challenges in Investor–State Arbitration' (2003) 19 Arb Int'l 143.

D Lemieux and A Stuhec, *Review of Administrative Action Under NAFTA* (Scarborough: Carswell, 1999).
T Levi, 'NAFTA's Provision for Compensation in the Event of Expropriation: A Reassessment of the "Prompt, Adequate and Effective" Standard' (1995) 31 Stanf J Int'l L 423.
R Lillich, 'The Law Governing Disputes Under Economic Development Agreements: Re-examining the Concept of "Internationalization"' in R Lillich and CN Brower (eds) *International Arbitration in the 21st Century: Towards Judicialization and Uniformity?* (Ardsley, NY: Transnational Publishers, 1994).
RB Lillich and DB Magraw, *The Iran–United States Tribunal: Its Contribution to the Law of State Responsibility* (Transnational Publishers, 1998).
C Lipson, *Standing Guard—Protecting Foreign Capital in the Nineteenth and Twentieth Centuries* (Berkeley: University of California Press, 1985).
A Liptak, 'Review of US Rulings by NAFTA Tribunals Stirs Worries' *New York Times* (18 April 2004) 20.
V Lowe, 'Some Comments on Procedural Weaknesses in International Law' (2004) 98 Am Soc'ty Int'l L Proc 37.
AF Lowenfeld, 'The Party-Appointed Arbitrator in International Controversies: Some Reflections' (1995) 30 Tex Int'l LJ 59.
M Loughlin, *Public Law and Political Theory* (Oxford: Clarendon, 1992).
M Loughlin, *Sword and Scales* (Oxford: Hart, 2000).
M Loughlin, *The Idea of Public Law* (Oxford: OUP, 2003).
M Lunney and K Oliphant, *Tort Law* (Oxford: OUP, 2000).
MA Luz, 'NAFTA, Investment and the Constitution of Canada: Will the Watertight Compartments Spring a Leak' (2001) 32 Ottawa L Rev 35.
RSJ Macdonald, 'The Margin of Appreciation' in RSJ Macdonald, F Matscher, and H Petzold (eds) *The European System for the Protection of Human Rights* (Dordrecht: Martinus Nijhoff, 1993).
N Majeed, 'Investor–State Disputes and International Law: From the Far Side' (2004) 98 Am Soc'ty Int'l L Proceedings 30.
FW Maitland, 'The Crown as Corporation' (1901) 17 LQ Rev 131.
P Malanczuk, *Akehurst's Modern Introduction to International Law* (7th edn, London: Routledge, 1997).
P Malanczuk, 'State–State and Investor–State Dispute Settlement in the OECD Draft Multilateral Investment Agreement' (2000) 3 J Int'l Econ L 417.
K Malleson, *The New Judiciary* (Aldershot: Dartmouth, 1999).
VS Mani, *International Adjudication* (The Hague: Martinus Nijhoff, 1980).
AFM Maniruzzaman, 'Internationalization of Foreign Investment Agreements—Some Fundamental Issues of International Law' (2000) 1 J World Investment 293.
FA Mann, 'State Contracts and State Responsibility' (1960) 54 AJIL 572.
FA Mann, 'The International Enforcement of Public Rights' (1987) 19 NYU J Int'l L & P 603.
H Mann and K von Moltke, 'NAFTA's Chapter 11 and the Environment: Addressing the Impacts of the Investor-State Process on the Environment' (Working Paper for the International Institute for Sustainable Development, 1999).
H Mann and K von Moltke, 'Protecting Investor Rights and the Public Good: Assessing NAFTA's Chapter 11' (Report for the International Institute for Sustainable Development, 2002).

G Marceau and JP Trachtman, 'The Technical Barriers to Trade Agreement, the Sanitary and Phytosanitary Measures Agreement, and the General Agreement On Tariffs and Trade' (2002) 36 J World Trade 811.

RI Martin, *The Most Dangerous Branch* (Montreal: McGill-Queen's University Press, 2003).

RJ Mataloni, Jr, 'A Guide to BEA Statistics on US Multinational Companies' (March 1995) Survey Current Bus 38.

W Mattli, 'Private Justice in a Global Economy: From Litigation to Arbitration' (2001) 55 Int'l Org 919.

P McAuslan, 'Administrative Law, Collective Consumption, and Judicial Policy' (1983) 46 Mod L Rev 1.

MS McDougal, HD Lasswell, and L Chen, 'Nationality and Human Rights: The Protection of the Individual in External Arenas' (1973) 83 Yale LJ 900.

R Mackenzie and P Sands, 'International Courts and Tribunals and the Independence of the International Judge' (2003) 44 Harv Int'l LJ 271.

JA McKinney, *Created from NAFTA—The Structure, Function, and Significance of the Treaty's Related Institutions* (Armonk, NY: ME Sharpe, 2000).

C McLachlan, 'Commentary: The Broader Context' (2002) 18 Arb Int'l 339.

T Meron, 'Judicial Independence and Impartiality in International Criminal Tribunals' (2005) 99 AJIL 359.

JG Merrills, *International Dispute Settlement* (3rd edn, Cambridge: CUP, 1998).

JG Merrills, 'The Means of Dispute Settlement' in MD Evans (ed) *International Law* (2nd edn, Oxford: OUP, 2006).

FI Michelman, 'Property, Utility, and Fairness: Comments on the Ethical Foundations of "Just Compensation" Law' (1967) 80 Harv L Rev 1165.

AS Miller, 'Protection of Private Foreign Investment by Multilateral Convention' (1959) 53 AJIL 371.

L Mistelis, 'Confidentiality and Third Party Participation in Investment Arbitration' (2005) 21 Arb Int'l 205.

A Mody and AP Murshid, 'Growing Up with Capital Flows' (IMF Working Paper, Doc No WP/02/75, 2002).

M Mohebi, *The International Law Character of the Iran–United States Claims Tribunal* (The Hague: Kluwer Law International, 1991).

EF Mooney, *Foreign Seizures—Sabbatino and the Act of State Doctrine* (University of Kentucky Press, 1967).

JB Moore, *Digest of International Law*, vol 4 (Washington: US Government Printing Office, 1906).

G Morón, *A History of Venezuela* (London: George Allen & Unwin, 1964).

C Morris, 'The Role of Criminal Statutes in Negligence Actions' (1949) 49 Col L Rev 21.

O Morrissey, 'Investment and Competition Policy in the WTO: Issues for Developing Countries' (2001) 20 Development Policy Rev 63.

FL Morrison, 'The Liability of Governments for Legislative Acts in the United States of America' (1998) 46 Am J Comp L Supp 531.

PT Muchlinski, *Multinational Enterprises and the Law* (Oxford: Blackwell, 1999).

PT Muchlinski, 'The Rise and Fall of the Multilateral Agreement on Investment: Where Now?' (2000) 34 Int'l Lawyer 1033.

PT Muchlinski, 'Globalisation and Legal Research' (2003) 37 Int'l Lawyer 221.

D Mullan, 'Damages for Violation of Constitutional Rights—A False Spring?' (1995) 6 Nat'l J Constitutional Law 105.

D Mullan and A Ceddia, 'The Impact on Public Law of Privatization, Deregulation, Outsourcing, and Downsizing: A Canadian Perspective' (2003) 10 Ind J Global Legal Studies 199.

E Müller, 'How Do International Institutions Select Arbitrators?' (2000) 17 J Int'l Arb 157.

MJ Mustill, 'Arbitration: History and Background' (1989) 6 J Int'l Arb 43.

National Association of Manufacturers, 'The Havana Charter for an International Trade Organization' (1949).

National Foreign Trade Council, 'Position of the NTC with Respect to the Havana Charter for an ITO' (1950).

H Neufeld, *The International Protection of Private Creditors From the Treaties of Westphalia to the Congress of Vienna* (Leiden: AW Sijthoff, 1971).

PM Nichols, 'Participation of Nongovernmental Parties in the World Trade Organization' (1996) 17 U Penn J Int'l Econ L 295.

R Nishikawa, 'Arbitration Law Reform in Japan' (2004) 21 J Int'l Arb 303.

A Nollkaemper, 'Concurrence Between Individual Responsibility and State Responsibility in International Law' (2003) 52 ICLQ 615.

PM Norton, 'A Law of the Future or a Law of the Past? Modern Tribunals and the International Law of Expropriation' (1991) 85 AJIL 474.

A Nussbaum, 'Treaties on Commercial Arbitration' (1942) 56 Harv L Rev 219.

E Obadia, 'ICSID, Investment Treaties and Arbitration: Current and Emerging Issues' (2001) 18(2) ICSID News 4.

LA O'Connor, 'The International Law of Expropriation of Foreign-Owned Property: The Compensation Requirement and the Role of the Taking State' (1983) 6 Loyola LA Int'l & Comp LJ 355.

DC Ohly, 'A Functional Analysis of Claimant Eligibility' in RB Lillich (ed) *International Law of State Responsibility for Injuries to Aliens* (Charlottesville: University Press of Virginia, 1983).

P Okowa, 'Admissibility and the Law on International Responsibility' in MD Evans (ed) *International Law* (2nd edn, Oxford: OUP, 2006).

CT Oliver, 'Legal Remedies and Sanctions' in RB Lillich (ed) *International Law of State Responsibility for Injuries to Aliens* (Charlottesville: University Press of Virginia, 1983).

Ontario Law Reform Commission (OLRC), *Report on the Basis for Compensation on Expropriation* (Toronto: OLRC, 1967).

OLRC, *Report on the Liability of the Crown* (Toronto: OLRC, 1989).

C Osakwe, 'The Soviet Position on International Arbitration as a Method of Resolving Transnational Disputes' in TE Carbonneau (ed) *Resolving Transnational Disputes Through International Arbitration* (Charlottesville: University of Virginia Press, 1984).

A Ostrovsky, R Speed, and E Tuerk, 'GATS, Water and the Environment' (Report for the Center for International Environmental Law and the World Wide Fund for Nature, 2003).

R Palan, 'Trying to Have Your Cake and Eating It: How and Why the State System Has Created Offshore' (1998) 42 Int'l Studies Q 625.

WW Park, 'Duty and Discretion in International Arbitration' (1999) 93 AJIL 805.

WW Park, 'Arbitration and the Fisc: NAFTA's "Tax Veto"' (2001) 2 Chi J Int'l L 231.

AR Parra, 'The Role of ICSID in the Settlement of Investment Disputes' (1999) 16(1) ICSID News 5.
AR Parra, 'ICSID and Bilateral Investment' (2000) 17(1) ICSID News 7.
AR Parra, 'New Amendments of the Regulations and Rules of the International Centre for Settlement of Investment Disputes' (2002) 19 ICSID News 1.
L Paterson, 'Argentina holds make-or-break talks with IMF' *The Times* (8 December 2001) 56.
RK Paterson, 'A New Pandora's Box? Private Remedies for Foreign Investors under the North American Free Trade Agreement' (2000) 8 Willamette J Int'l L and Dispute Res 77.
JE Pattison 'The United States–Egypt Bilateral Investment Treaty: A Prototype for Future Negotiations' (1983) 16 Cornell Int'l LJ 305.
J Paulsson, 'Arbitration without Privity' (1995) 10 ICSID Rev 232.
J Paulsson, *Denial of Justice in International Law* (Cambridge: CUP, 2005).
WL Penfield, 'Address: Is the Forcible Collection of Contract Debts in the Interest of International Justice and Peace?' (1907) 1 Am Soc'ty Int'l L Proc 129.
W Peter, *Arbitration and Renegotiation of International Investment Agreements* (The Hague: Kluwer Law International, 1995).
EU Petersmann, 'Taking Human Dignity, Poverty and Empowerment of Individuals More Seriously: Rejoinder to Alston' (2002) 13 Eur J Int'l L 845.
LE Peterson, 'Investors emboldened by arbitral verdict against Czech Republic' *Investment Law and Policy Weekly News Bulletin* (11 April 2003).
LE Peterson, 'Swedish court affirms award against Czech Republic; damages could be taxable' *Investment Law and Policy Weekly News Bulletin* (16 May 2003).
LE Peterson, 'Bilateral Investment Treaties and Development Policy-Making' (Report for the International Institute for Sustainable Development, November 2004).
LE Peterson, 'Argentine bondholders girding for multi-billion dollar investment treaty claim' *Investment Law and Policy News Bulletin* (10 June 2005).
S Picciotto, *International Business Taxation* (London: Weidenfeld & Nicolson, 1992).
S Picciotto, 'A Critical Assessment of the MAI' in S Picciotto and R Mayne (eds) *Regulating International Business* (Houndmills: Macmillan, 1999).
S Picciotto, 'Introduction: What Rules for the World Economy?' in S Picciotto and R Mayne (eds) *Regulating International Business* (Houndmills: Macmillan, 1999).
F Pollock, 'Sovereignty in English Law' (1894) 8 Harv L Rev 243.
A Porges, 'Step by Step to an International Trade Court' in DLM Kennedy and JD Southwick (eds) *The Political Economy of International Trade Law* (Cambridge: CUP, 2002).
ME Porter, *The Competitive Advantage of Nations* (New York: The Free Press, 1990).
A Prakash, 'Beyond Seattle: Globalization, the Nonmarket Environment and Corporate Strategy' (2002) 9 Rev Int'l Pol Econ 513.
DM Price, 'NAFTA Chapter 11—Investor–State Dispute Settlement: Frankenstein or Safety Valve?' (2001) 26 Can–US LJ 1.
DM Price, Testimony Before the Subcommittee on Trade of the House Committee on Ways and Means, Hearing on the Summit of the Americas and Prospects for Free Trade in the Hemisphere (Statement on behalf of the US Council for International Business, 8 May 2001).
JA Rabkin, *Law Without Nations?* (Princeton: Princeton University Press, 2005).

JH Ralston, 'Some Suggestions as to the Permanent Court of Arbitration' (1907) 1 AJIL 321.
BB Ramaiah, 'Towards a Multilateral Framework on Investment' (1997) 6 Transnat'l Corp 117.
CF Randolph, 'The Eminent Domain' (1887) 3 LQ Rev 314.
S Rao and A Ahmad, 'Formal and Informal Investment Barriers in the G-7 Countries' in P Sauvé and D Schwanen (eds) *Investment Rules for the Global Economy* (Toronto: CD Howe Institute, 1996).
AS Rau, 'Integrity in Private Judging' (1997) 38 South Texas L Rev 455.
A Redfern, 'Investor–State Arbitrations—A Bridge Too Far?' in G Aksen *et al* (eds) *Global Reflections on International Law, Commerce and Dispute Resolution* (International Chamber of Commerce, 2005).
A Redfern and M Hunter, *Law and Practice of International Commercial Arbitration* (3rd edn, London: Sweet & Maxwell, 1999).
A Redfern and M Hunter, *Law and Practice of International Commercial Arbitration* (4th edn, London: Sweet & Maxwell, 2004).
WM Reisman, *Systems of Control in International Adjudication and Arbitration* (Durham, NC: Duke University Press, 1992).
C Reymond, 'The Channel Tunnel Case and the Law of International Arbitration' (1993) 109 LQ Rev 337.
K Roach, 'The Limits of Corrective Justice and the Potential of Equity in Constitutional Remedies' (1991) 33 Ariz L Rev 859.
JAG Roberts, *A History of China* (London: Macmillan, 1999).
NS Rodley, 'Corporate Nationality and the Diplomatic Protection of Multinational Enterprises: The *Barcelona Traction* Case' (1971) 47 Indiana LJ 70.
D Rodrik, *The Global Governance of Trade as if Development Really Mattered* (Report for the UN Development Programme, October 2001).
W Rogers, 'Emergence of the International Center for Settlement of Investment Disputes (ICSID) as the Most Significant Forum for Submission of Bilateral Investment Treaty Disputes' (Presentation to the Inter-American Development Bank Conference, 26–7 October 2000).
E Root, 'Elihu Root's Services to International Law' (1910) 4 Am Soc'ty Int'l L Proc 16.
MS Rosenthal, 'Arbitration in the Settlement of International Trade Disputes' (1946) 11 Law & Contemporary Problems 808.
AH Roth, *The Minimum Standard of International Law Applied to Aliens* (Leiden, 1949).
AM Rugman and M Gestrin, 'A Conceptual Framework for a Multilateral Agreement on Investment: Learning from the NAFTA' in P Sauvé and D Schwanen (eds) *Investment Rules for the Global Economy* (Toronto: CD Howe Institute, 1996).
P Ryan, 'David v. Goliath' (2002) 11 *National* 30.
JW Salacuse, 'BIT by BIT: The Growth of Bilateral Investment Treaties and Their Impact on Foreign Investment in Developing Countries' (1990) 14 Int'l Lawyer 655.
JW Salacuse, 'Toward a Global Treaty on Foreign Investment: The Search for a Grand Bargain' in N Horn (ed) *Arbitrating Foreign Investment Disputes* (The Hague: Kluwer Law International, 2004).
GL Sandrino, 'The NAFTA Investment Chapter and Foreign Direct Investment in Mexico: A Third World Perspective' (1994) 27 Vand J Tranat'l L 259.

P Sands, *Lawless World* (London: Penguin, 2005).

S Sassen, 'Losing Control? The State and the New Geography of Power?' (1999) 1 Global Dialogue 78.

S Sassen, 'Globalization or Denationalization?' (2003) 10 Rev Int'l Pol Econ 1.

Lord Saville, 'Denning Lecture 1995: Arbitration and the Courts' (1995) 61 Arbitration: J Institute of Chartered Arbitrators 157.

H-J Schlochauer, 'Jay Treaty (1794)' in R Dolzer *et al* (eds) *Encyclopedia of Public International Law*, vol 1 (Amsterdam: North-Holland Publishing, 1987).

JT Schmidt, 'Arbitration Under the Auspices of the International Centre for the Settlement of Investment Disputes' (1976) 17 Harv Int'l LJ 90.

D Schneiderman, 'Investment Rules and the New Constitutionalism' (2000) 25 Law & Social Inq 757.

C Schreuer, *The ICSID Convention: A Commentary* (Cambridge: CUP, 2001).

E Schwartz and J Paulsson, 'Confronting Political and Regulatory Risks Associated with Private Investment in Infrastructure in Developing Countries' (Draft presentation to the Private Infrastructure for Development conference, Rome, 8–10 September 1999).

G Schwarzenberger, *International Law as Applied by International Courts and Tribunals*, vol 1 (3rd edn, London: Stevens & Sons, 1957).

G Schwarzenberger, 'The Abs-Shawcross Draft Convention on Investments Abroad: A Critical Commentary' (1960) 9 J Public L 147.

MA Scodro, 'Arbitrating Novel Legal Questions: A Recommendation for Reform' (1996) 105 Yale LJ 1927.

H Scoffield, 'France pulls out of MAI talks' *The Globe and Mail* [Toronto] (15 October 1998) B1.

L Sek, 'Fast-Track Authority for Trade Agreements (Trade Promotion Authority): Background and Developments in the 107th Congress' (US Congressional Research Service Report No IB10084, 17 January 2002).

Y Shany, *The Competing Jurisdictions of International Courts and Tribunals* (Oxford: OUP, 2003).

M Shapiro, 'The Globalization of Law' (1993) 1 Ind J Global Legal Studies 37.

M Shapiro, 'Administrative Law Unbounded: Reflections on Government and Governance' (2001) 8 Ind J Global Leg Studies 369.

MN Shaw, *International Law* (5th edn, Cambridge: CUP, 2003).

DR Shea, *The Calvo Clause* (Minneapolis: University of Minnesota Press, 1955).

D Shelton, *Remedies in International Human Rights Law* (Oxford: OUP, 1999).

S Shetreet, *Judges on Trial* (Amsterdam: North Holland Publishing Co, 1976).

S Shetreet, 'Judicial Independence: New Conceptual Dimensions and Contemporary Challenges' in S Shetreet and J Deschênes (eds) *Judicial Independence: The Contemporary Debate* (Dordrecht: Martinus Nijhoff, 1985).

S Shetreet and J Deschênes (eds) *Judicial Independence: The Contemporary Debate* (Dordrecht: Martinus Nijhoff, 1985).

E Sik, 'Concept of Acquired Rights in International Law' (1977) 44 Neth Int'l L Rev 120.

AC Sinclair, 'The Origins of the Umbrella Clause in the International Law of Investment Protection' (2004) 20 Arb Int'l 411.

I Sinclair, *The Vienna Convention and the Law of Treaties* (Manchester: Manchester University Press, 1984).

R Singh, 'The Impact of the Central American Free Trade Agreement on Investment Treaty Arbitrations: A Mouse that Roars?' (2004) 21 J Int'l Arb 329.

LC Situmbeko and J Jones Zulu, 'Zambia: Condemned to Debt' (Report by the World Development Movement, April 2004).

Q Skinner, 'Hobbes and the Purely Artificial Person of the State' (1999) 7 J Pol Phil 1.

H Smit and V Pechota, *World Arbitration Reporter*, vol 2 (Huntington, NY: Juris, 2002).

S de Smith and R Brazier, *Constitutional and Administrative Law* (8th edn, London: Penguin, 1998).

E Smythe, 'Domestic and International Sources of Regime Change: Canada and the Negotiation of the OECD Multilateral Agreement on Investment' (Paper presented to the Annual Meeting of the Canadian Political Science Association, St John's, Nfld, 8 June 1997).

F Snyder, 'Governing Economic Globalisation: Global Legal Pluralism and European Law' (1999) 5 Eur LJ 334.

F Snyder, 'The Gatekeeper: The European Courts and WTO Law' (2003) 40 CML Rev 313.

C Söderlund, '*Lis Pendens*, *Res Judicata* and the Issue of Parallel Judicial Proceedings' (2005) 22 J Int'l Arb 301.

LB Sohn, 'The Role of Arbitration in Recent International Multilateral Treaties' in TE Carbonneau (ed) *Resolving Transnational Disputes Through International Arbitration* (Charlottesville: University of Virginia Press, 1984).

JA Soloway, 'Environmental Regulation as Expropriation: The Case of NAFTA's Chapter 11' (2000) 33 Can Bus LJ 92.

M Sornarajah, *The Pursuit of Nationalized Property* (Dordrecht: Martinus Nijhoff, 1986).

M Sornarajah, 'The UNCITRAL Model Law: A Third World Viewpoint' (1989) 6 J Int'l Arb 7.

M Sornarajah, 'The Climate of International Arbitration' (1991) 8 J Int'l Arb 47.

M Sornarajah, *The International Law on Foreign Investment* (Cambridge: CUP, 1994).

M Sornarajah, 'Power and Justice in Foreign Investment Arbitration' (1997) 14 J Int'l Arb 103.

M Sornarajah, *The Settlement of Foreign Investment Disputes* (Boston: Kluwer, 2001).

M Sornarajah, 'The Clash of Globalisations and the International Law on Foreign Investment' (Presentation to the Centre for Trade Policy and Law, Ottawa, 12 September 2002), online: Centre for Trade Law and Policy (Carleton University) http://www.carleton.ca/ctpl/pdf/papers/sornarajah.pdf

O Spiermann, 'Individual Rights, State Interests and the Power to Waive ICSID Jurisdiction under Bilateral Investment Treaties' (2004) 20 Arb Int'l 179.

MJ Staff and CW Lewis, 'Arbitration Under NAFTA Chapter 11: Past, Present, and Future' (2003) 25 Houston J Int'l L 301.

B Stern, 'Comments—International Economic Relations and the MAI Dispute Settlement System' (1999) 16 J Int'l Arb 118.

JE Stiglitz, 'The Broken Promise of NAFTA' *The New York Times* (6 January 2004).

Stockholm Chamber of Commerce (SCC), *Rules of the Arbitration Institute of the Stockholm Chamber of Commerce*, revised 1 April 1999 [Stockholm Rules], online: SCC www.sccinstitute.com/uk/Rules.

H Street, *Governmental Liability* (Cambridge: CUP, 1953).

A Sweet Stone, 'Islands of Transnational Governance' in M Shapiro and A Sweet Stone (eds) *Law, Politics, and Judicialization* (Oxford: OUP, 2002).

M Taggart, 'The Province of Administrative Law Determined' in M Taggart (ed) *The Province of Administrative Law* (Oxford: Hart, 1997).

M Tenenbaum, 'International Arbitration of Trade Disputes in Mexico—The Arrival of the NAFTA and New Reforms to the Commercial Code' (1995) 12 J Int'l Arb 53.

C Thomas, 'Balance-of-Payments Crises in the Developing World: Balanced Trade, Finance and Development in the New Economic Order' (2000) 15 Am U Int'l L Rev 1249.

JC Thomas, 'Investor–State Arbitration Under NAFTA Chapter Eleven' (Paper presented to the NAFTA Chapter 11 Investor–State Disputes: Litigating Against Sovereigns conference, Canadian Bar Association, Toronto, March 2000).

JC Thomas, 'The Experience of NAFTA Chapter 11 Tribunals To Date: A Practitioner's Perspective' in L Ritchie Dawson (ed) *Whose Rights? The NAFTA Chapter 11 Debate* (Ottawa: Centre for Trade Law and Policy, 2002).

JC Thomas, 'Reflections on Article 1105 of NAFTA: History, State Practice and the Influence of Commentators' (2002) 17 ICSID Rev 21.

JC Thomas, 'A Reply to Professor Brower' (2002) 40 Col J Transnat'l L 433.

JC Thomas, 'Notes on Investor–State Arbitration in the North American Context' (Address to the International Bar Association conference, San Francisco, 9–14 September 2003).

A Thomson, 'Argentine creditors toughen stance' *The Financial Times* (17 February 2005) 39.

A Thomson, 'Argentina revels in power of peso' *The Financial Times* (30 June 2005) 43.

J Thornton, 'Environmental Liability—A Shrinking Mirage or the Most Realistic Attempt So Far' (2003) J Planning & Enviro L 272.

S Timberg, 'An International Trade Tribunal—A Step Forward Short of Surrender of Sovereignty' (1945) 33 Georgetown LJ 373.

S Timberg, 'International Combines and National Sovereigns' (1947) 95 U Penn L Rev 575.

J Tobin and S Rose-Ackerman, 'Foreign Direct Investment and the Business Environment in Developing Countries: the Impact of Bilateral Investment Treaties' (Working paper, Yale University, 3 January 2005).

MP Todaro and SC Smith, *Economic Development* (8th edn, Harlow: Pearson, 2003).

ECE Todd, *The Law of Expropriation and Compensation in Canada* (2nd edn, Toronto: Carswell, 1992).

C Tollefson, 'Games without Frontiers: Claims and Citizen Submissions Under the NAFTA Regime' (2002) 27 Yale J Int'l L 141.

C Tollefson, 'Metalclad v. United Mexican States Revisited: Judicial Oversight of NAFTA's Chapter Eleven Investor–State Claim Process' (2002) 11 Minn J Global Trade 183.

SJ Toope, *Mixed International Arbitration—Studies in Arbitration Between States and Private Persons* (Cambridge: Grotius Publications, 1990).

JP Trachtman, 'The Domain of WTO Dispute Resolution' (1999) 40 Harv Int'l LJ 333.

JP Trachtman and PM Moreman, 'Costs and Benefits of Private Participation in WTO Dispute Settlement: Whose Right Is It Anyway?' (2003) 44 Harv Int'l LJ 221.

M Trebilcock and R Howse, *The Regulation of International Trade* (London: Routledge, 1995).

T Tridimas, 'Liability for Breach of Community Law: Growing Up and Mellowing Down?' (2001) 38 CML Rev 301.

W Twining, *Globalisation and Legal Theory* (London: Butterworths, 2000).

LS Underkuffler-Freund, 'Takings and the Nature of Property' (1996) 9 Can J Law & Jur 161.

AJ Van den Berg, *The New York Convention of 1958* (Antwerp: Kluwer, 1981).

KJ Vandevelde, 'The Bilateral Treaty Program of the United States' (1988) 21 Cornell Int'l LJ 201.

KJ Vandevelde, 'The Political Economy of a Bilateral Investment Treaty' (1998) 92 AJIL 621.

KJ Vandevelde, 'Sustainable Liberalism and the International Investment Regime' (1998) 19 Mich J Int'l L 373.

JA VanDuzer, 'NAFTA Chapter 11 to Date: The Progress of a Work in Progress' in L Ritchie Dawson (ed) *Whose Rights? The NAFTA Chapter 11 Debate* (Ottawa: Centre for Trade Law and Policy, 2002).

E Vattel, *Le Droit de gens*, book II.

F Orrego Vicuña, 'Arbitration in a New International Alternative Dispute Resolution' (2001) 18(2) ICSID News 1.

F Orrego Vicuña, 'Of Contracts and Treaties in the Global Market' (2004) 8 Max Planck Ybk UN Law 341

D Vis-Dunbar, 'Germany seeks revisions and addition of investor–state arbitration to Pakistan BIT' *Investment Treaty News* (31 May 2006).

D Vis-Dunbar and LE Peterson, 'European Commission makes another play for power to negotiate investment pacts' *Investment Treaty News* (19 July 2006).

C Vogel, 'Lauder Pays $135 Million, a Record, for a Klimt Portrait' *The New York Times* (19 June 2006).

B Von Hase, 'Do the Right Thing' *The Times Magazine* [London] (13 September 2003) 50.

R Von Hennigs, 'European Convention on State Immunity and Other International Aspects of Sovereignty Immunity' (2001) 9 Willamette J Int'l L & Disp Resol 185.

R Wai, 'Transnational Liftoff and Juridical Touchdown: The Regulatory Function of Private International Law in an Era of Globalization' (2002) 40 Colum J Transnat'l L 209.

TW Wälde, 'Investment Arbitration Under the Energy Charter Treaty—From Dispute Settlement to Treaty Implementation' (1996) 12 Arb Int'l 429.

H Walker, 'Treaties for the Encouragement and Protection of Foreign Investment: Present United States Practice' (1956) 5 Am J Comp L 229.

T Walker, 'Argentina panics as banks close' *The Sunday Times* (21 April 2002) 25.

A Walter, 'Globalisation and Policy Convergence: The Case of Direct Investment Rules' in RA Higgott *et al* (eds) *Non-State Actors and Authority in the Global System* (London: Routledge, 2000).

A Walter, 'NGOs, Business, and International Investment: The Multilateral Agreement on Investment, Seattle, and Beyond' (2001) 7 Glob Governance 51.

C Warbrick, 'States and Recognition in International Law' in MD Evans (ed) *International Law* (2nd edn, Oxford: OUP, 2006).

JHH Weiler, 'Emerging Issues on Compliance and Effectiveness of Community Law' (1997) 91 Am Soc'ty Int'l L Proc 172.
JHH Weiler, 'Epilogue: Towards a Common Law of International Trade' in JHH Weiler (ed) *The EU, the WTO, and the NAFTA* (Oxford: OUP, 2000).
T Weiler, 'NAFTA Investment Arbitration and the Growth of International Economic Law' (2002) 3 Bus Law Int'l 158.
EJ Weinrib, *The Idea of Private Law* (Harvard: Harvard University Press, 1995).
JA Weir, 'Human Rights and Damages' (2001) 40 Washburn LJ 412.
EB Weiss, 'Invoking State Responsibility in the Twenty-first Century' (2002) 96 AJIL 798.
J Werksman, KA Baumert, and NK Dubash, 'Will International Investment Rules Obstruct Climate Protection Policies?' (Report for the World Resources Institute, April 2001).
J Werner, 'The Trade Explosion and Some Likely Effects on International Arbitration' (1997) 14 J Int'l Arb 5.
J Werner, 'Making Investment Arbitration More Certain—A Modest Proposal' (2003) 4 J World Investment 767.
J Werner, 'Some Comments on the NAFTA Chapter 11 Case—*ADF Group Inc and United States of America*' (2003) 4 J World Investment 113.
BH Weston, ' "Constructive Takings" Under International Law: A Modest Foray into the Problem of Creeping Expropriation' (1975) 16 Virg J Int'l L 103.
G Wetter, 'The Present Status of the International Court of Arbitration of the ICC: An Appraisal' (1990) 1 Am Rev Int'l Arb 91.
JG Wetter, *The International Arbitral Process—Public and Private*, vol 3 (Dobbs Ferry, NY: Oceana Publications, 1979).
P Wheatcroft, 'Argentina loan' *The Times* (23 August 2001) 23.
M Whiteman, *Damages in International Law*, vol 1 (Washington, 1937–43).
C Wilcox, *A Charter for World Trade* (New York: Macmillan, 1949).
M Wilkins, 'Defining a Firm: History and Theory' in P Hertner and G Jones (eds) *Multinationals: Theory and History* (Aldershot: Gower, 1986).
JF Williams, 'International Law and the Property of Aliens' (1928) 9 Brit Ybk Int'l L 1.
K Williams, 'British Re-Nationalization and Regulation: The Government's Liability to Shareholders' (1993) 14 U Penn J Int'l Bus L 243.
WW Willoughby, *The Fundamental Concepts of Public Law* (New York: Macmillan, 1924).
GM Wilner, 'Acceptance of Arbitration by Developing Countries' in TE Carbonneau (ed) *Resolving Transnational Disputes Through International Arbitration* (Charlottesville: University of Virginia Press, 1984).
RR Wilson, 'Postwar Commercial Treaties of the United States' (1949) 43 AJIL 262.
LH Woolsey, 'The Problem of Foreign Investment' (1948) 42 AJIL 121.
BA Wortley, *Expropriation in Public International Law* (Cambridge: CUP, 1959).
G Xiao, 'People's Republic of China's Round-Tripping FDI: Scale, Causes and Implications' (Asian Development Bank Institute Discussion Paper No 6, 2004).
DR Young, 'Governmental Regulation of Foreign Investment' (1969) 47 Texas L Rev 421.
H-L Yu and L Shore, 'Independence, Impartiality, and Immunity of Arbitrators—US and English Perspectives' (2003) 52 ICLQ 935.
'A decline without parallel—Argentina's collapse' *The Economist* (2 March 2002).
'Liberty's great advance' *The Economist* (28 June 2003).
'The Secret Trade Courts', Editorial *New York Times* (27 September 2004) 26.

Index

Abs-Shawcross Draft Convention on
 Investments Abroad 1959 20–1, 43
accountability 4–6
 public law adjudication 152–9
Agreement on the Application of Sanitary and
 Phytosanitary Measures (SPS
 Agreement) 133
Agreement on Trade-Related Investment
 Measures (TRIMs Agreement) 21, 75
Aguas del Tunari v Bolivia 163
Alabama Claims Arbitration 99n
Algiers Declaration 100n
Amco v Indonesia 125
American Convention on Human Rights
 103–4
amicus curiae *see* participation by non parties
Anglo-Turkish Convention 1838 15
arbitration
 awards
  enforcement 117–19
  judicial review 95
  treaty structure 35–6, 38
 contract-based 25, 111
 legislation-based 25
 as reciprocally consensual adjudication 169
 seat of arbitration 154, 156–8, 181
 treaty-based 25
arbitration treaties *see* investment arbitration
 treaties
arbitrators
 accountability 152–9
 appointment 169–170
 authority 61n
 bias 153, 168, 171, 173–5
 delegation of authority by legislation 25
 discretion 122–3, 132
  supervisory discretion 73
 financial dependence 152
 interpretative approaches
  as commercial arbitration 124–31
  as public law adjudication 131–6
 judicial independence 167–75
 jurisdiction 72
  comprehensive jurisdiction 5
Argentina
 claims against 2–3, 33
 financial crisis and peso devaluation 1–3
 invitation to foreign investors 41
Asia 32
Azurix v Argentine Republic 137

Barcelona Traction Light and Power Co v Spain
 77n, 112
Bechtel 116
Belgium 158
Belt, Guillermo 12
Bergaderm v Commission 148
bilateral investment treaties 25–7, 29, 140,
 163–4
 economic liberalization 41
 history 25–26
 international system of investment treaty
  arbitration 6
 sample studied 29–30
 standards of review 89, 92–3
 umbrella clauses 111, 133
 variations among 27–8
Bipartisan Trade Promotion Authority Act
 2002 40n
BITs *see* bilateral investment treaties
Bolivia 116
Brasserie du Pecheur SA v Germany 147–8
Brazil 23
British Columbia 156
British Virgin Islands 39
business regulation 1, 18, 43, 122, 125, 144–5

Calvo doctrine 17
Canada 26, 32–3, 177
 openness 160
canola 85
capital exporting states, 177–80, 183
 a category, as 14n
 assertion of minimum standard of treatment
  145–6
 claims against 27
 conclusion of investment treaties 6, 27–8
 control of World Bank decision making 170
 economic strategies 40
 proposals for a multilateral investment code
  16–17, 18–20, 23
 reform of the system 179–80
 role in expansion of system 43
capital flows
 deregulation 38–9, 42
capital importing states 183
 a category, as 13n
 claims against 32
 conclusion of investment treaties 27
 economic strategies 39
 opposition to MAI

capital importing states (*cont.*)
  proposals for a multilateral investment code 17, 19, 23
  reform of the system 179–80
capitulation treaties 15, 157n
Caribbean 177
Castro, Cipriano 16
Cavallo, Domingo 2
Cayman Islands 116
Central America 163, 177
Central American Court of Justice (1907–1918) 97n
Chile 112–13n
China 15, 32
CME v Czech Republic 7–8, 115, 142
CMS v Argentine Republic 89
coherence 164–7
colonial companies 69n
colonialism *see* empires
commercial arbitration
  coherence 164–7
  conceptual framework 59–62
  confidentiality 160–4
  international commercial arbitration 5, 50
  interpretative approach to investment treaty arbitration, as 124–31
  investment arbitration as sub-category 25
  openness 159–64
  private dispute resolution 48
commercial presence 21n, 75
common law 148
compensation 123, 134–7, 145, 149, 166, 177
competition among states 158, 179–80
concessionary contracts 177
confidentiality 160–4, 181
consent
  general consent by state 24–6, 28, 30, 40, 62–5, 100, 118, 125, 128
  private parties, by 62, 68–70, 125–6
  prospective consent 95, 99–101
  retrospective consent 99–100
Convention on the Execution of Foreign Arbitral Awards 1927 (Geneva Convention) 51
Convention on the Settlement of Investment Disputes Between States and Nationals of Other States 1965 (ICSID Convention) 27, 34–6, 55–6
  annulment process 34
  appointment of arbitrators 34, 169–71
    perception of bias 171, 174
  claims
    analysis of claims 30–3
    spike in number of claims 4n
  coherence 167
  definition of investment 79
  enforcement of awards 118, 181

ICSID Additional Facility 35
ICSID Additional Facility Rules 37
ICSID Arbitration Rules 37
ratification by major capital-importers 27n
removal from international investment arbitration 181
role in the system 34–8
corporations *see* investors
corrective justice 137
Council of Europe 182
Court of Arbitration of the International Chamber of Commerce 30, 171n
courts
  deference to international arbitrators 155, 176
  public law competence 5, 111
Cuaderno, Miguel 12
Cuba 12
customary international law 96
  diplomatic protection 9
  exhaustion of local remedies 110
  individual damages claims 102–3
  individual rights 119–20
  intention to harm 84n
Czech Republic 7–8, 115, 166

damages 102–9
  as public law remedy 145
  awards to March 2006 124n
  mitigation of loss 79n
debt (sovereign)
  Argentina 1–3
Declaration on the Human Rights of Individuals Who are not Nationals of the Country in which They Live 1985 140
Developing countries 177, 183
  conclusion of investment treaties 39–40
  exclusion from MAI negotiations 21–2
  hostility to arbitration 16
  strategy on foreign investment 39
diplomatic protection 112, 137, 166
Draft Convention on the Protection of Foreign Property 1967 21
Draft Convention on the Treatment of Foreigners 1929 19–20
Drago doctrine 17
due process 134
  see also standards of review
duty to exhaust local remedies 110–13
  differences among treaties 28

Egypt 23
ELSI Case 133–4
empires 14–15, 177
  Ottoman empire 15
Energy Charter Treaty 26, 29–30, 40
  standards of review 81

Index

enforcement of arbitration awards *see* arbitration
environmental protection 40
errors of jurisdiction 175
errors of law 152, 154–6, 164–5, 175
European Convention on Human Rights 1950 103, 136
European Court of Human Rights
  judicial election 182
European Court of Justice 147
European Union 10
expropriation 81, 90–4, 145, 156, 165, 178
  see also standards of review
extraterritorial law 15–17

fair and equitable treatment 81n, 136
  see also minimum standard of treatment
fault 122, 148–9
Fedax v Venezuela 116
foreign direct investment 77–8
fork in the road clauses 28
former communist countries 27, 29, 32, 40
forum shopping 8, 40–1, 109, 113–17
France 22, 29, 176
Francovich doctrine 104, 147–9
Free Trade Commission (NAFTA) 126–7
full protection and security 81n
  see also minimum standard of treatment

GATS *see* General Agreement on Trade in Services
GATT
  Uruguay Round 21
General Agreement on Trade in Services 1994 21, 75
Geneva Convention *see* Convention on the Execution of Foreign Arbitral Awards 1927
Geneva Protocol *see* Protocol on Arbitration Clauses in Commercial Matters 1923
Germany 16, 20, 29, 33
Great Britain 16

Havana Charter 1948 19n, 20, 23
  Article 12 20
Herbert Smith 32
Hong Kong 39
Hormones Case 133
Hull standard 91
human rights 121–2, 140–1
  individualization 10n
  investor rights approach 136–42

ICC *see* International Chamber of Commerce
ICSID Convention *see* Convention on the Settlement of Investment Disputes Between States and Nationals of Other States 1965

impartiality
  arbitrators' impartiality 173
  judicial impartiality 180
imperial law *see* empires
independence (judicial) 165–75
India 23, 32
in dubio mitius 125, 133, 135, 138
individualization
  of adjudication 86
  of claims 84, 96–9, 101, 108–9, 135, 139, 143
  exceptionality in international law 9–10, 96–7
  facilitation of forum shopping 113
Indonesia 125
international arbitration 16
  resolution of regulatory disputes 47
international business
  proposals for a multilateral investment code 18–23
International Chamber of Commerce (ICC) 19, 21, 37, 51–2, 178
  appointment of arbitrators 171, 174
  ICC Rules 37
  investor lobby, as 19, 56
  see also commercial arbitration
international comity 125
international commercial arbitration *see* commercial arbitration
International Convention for the Mutual Protection of Private Property Rights in Foreign Countries 12
International Court of Justice 165
  Abs-Shawcross Draft Convention on Investments Abroad 1959 43
  appointment of arbitrators 20, 37, 171
  judicial election 181
international courts
  judicial appointment 181–3
  see also specific courts
International Criminal Court
  judicial election 182
  jurisdiction 69n
International Criminal Tribunal for the Former Yugoslavia
  judicial nomination 182
international financial markets
  liberalization of markets 38–9
international investment court 180–3
international investment disputes
  history 8–9, 14, 16–17
international law *see* customary international law
International Monetary Fund 41–2
International Trade Organization 19
inter-state adjudication 152
investment
  definition 73–8
  foreign investment 20, 40, 77
  benefits 39, 41, 79

investment treaties
  alternatives to 180–4
  definition of investment 75–80
  exhaustion of local remedies 28, 109–13
  fork in the road clauses 69
  forum shopping 109
  interpretation 124–51
  object and purpose 121, 132, 138
  standards of review 72, 80–3
investment treaty arbitration 17
  access to the system 69–70, 142
  accountability 153–8
  appointing authorities 36
  claims
    cost of claims 141n, 162, 179
    parallel claims 111–12
    rate of claims 4, 27, 180
  coherence 152, 164–7
  commercial arbitration, as 124–31
  compulsory character 45n, 96–7, 100–1, 117
  definition 3n
  expansion 43
  general consent by state 24–6, 28, 30, 40, 63–5, 100, 118
  history 13–23
  international system 6
  investor rights adjudication, as 137–43
  multinational firms 18, 38
  openness of the system 152, 159–64
  private law model of adjudication 58, 129–30, 134, 150
  process 37–8
  prospective consent by state 95, 99–101
  public law model of adjudication 4, 28, 43, 47–50, 131–6, 143–9
    accountability 152–9
  reform
    domestic reform 175–80
    international reform 180–4
  retrospective consent by state 99–100
  scope 73–80
  subject matter of claims 4
  a system, as 8
    explanations for emergence 38
investors
  authority to bring claims 3–4, 10n
    exhaustion of local remedies 28, 109–13
    individualization of claims 98–9, 135
    minority shareholders 77
  foreign investors 114
  investor protection 42, 136–43, 145, 179–80
  investor rights 3, 137
  multinational firms 38
Iran 100
Iran–US Claims Tribunal 70n, 100–1

Japan 13, 16
Jay Treaty 1794 100
judicial independence 167–75

Kennecott 112–13n

labour rights 40
Latin America 16, 32, 40
Lauder, Ralph 7–8
Lauder v Czech Republic 166
League of Nations 19
Lithuania 115
Loewen v United States 130, 134–5, 174

MAI *see* Multilateral Agreement on Investment
Malaysia 23, 33
Menem, Carlos 2
Metalclad v United Mexican States 156
Methanex v United States 162
Mexico 26, 64–5, 68, 113
Middle East 32
minimum standard of treatment 81–2, 86–9
mitigation of loss 79n
mixed tribunals 99n
Mondev v United States 136
Morocco 163
most favoured nation treatment 43n, 81n
Multilateral Agreement on Investment (MAI) 22–3, 176, 178
multilateral investment treaties, 13
  definition 12
  historical failure to conclude 18, 22–3, 180–1
multinational firms 142, 145, 150, 166
  definition 4–5n
  emergence of investment arbitration treaty system 38–9
  global investors 38
  nationality 115
  risk management strategy 113

NAFTA *see* North American Free Trade Agreement
National Association of Manufacturers 19n
National Foreign Trade Council 19n
national treatment *see* standards of review
nationality 110, 114–16
Neer v United Mexican States 87–9
Netherlands 7–8, 115–16, 140, 142
neutrality 131, 145
New International Economic Order 17
New York Convention *see* United Nations Convention on the Recognition and Enforcement of Foreign Arbitral Awards 1958
non-governmental organizations 162
North Africa 32

North American Free Trade Agreement
   (NAFTA) 26–7, 29, 64–5, 126–7
   claims 26n, 31–3
      minority shareholder claims 113
   coherence 165
   enforcement of awards 118–19
   expropriation 156
   openness 161–3
   public law adjudication 134
   standards of review 81, 88–9, 92, 145–6
   waiver of legal remedies 69–70

OECD *see* Organization for Economic
   Co-operation and Development
openness 159–64
operational decisions 108n
Organization for Economic Co-operation and
   Development 21–2
Ottoman empire *see* empires

pacta sunt servanda (principle of) 125, 131
Pakistan 133
Panama Convention 1975
   enforcement of awards 118
parallel claims 111–12,115, 117, 120
participation by non parties 159, 162–3
party autonomy (principle of) 125–6, 160, 162–3
performance requirements 21n, 28
Persia 15
Philippines 12, 29, 33
place of enforcement 156–7, 181
Pope & Talbot v Canada 126–8
Porter Convention 1907 16
private law 127
   tortious liability of the state 108n, 125
   see also investment treaty arbitration
property
   protection of foreign owners 19, 21
Protocol on Arbitration Clauses in Commercial
   Matters 1923 (Geneva Protocol) 50–1
public access to information 159–62
public health 40, 144
public law 45, 152–3, 157–75
   interpretation 154–6, 181
public policy 155, 176

regional trade agreements 28, 79
regulatory relationship 32
reparation (principle of) 109
rule of law 153, 166, 173–4, 177, 184
Russia 32
   see also Soviet Union

seat of arbitration *see* arbitration
secrecy *see* confidentiality
SGS v Pakistan 132, 135, 146, 174
SGS v Philippines 138

Singapore 163
Softwood Lumber Agreement 126
sovereign immunity 46–7, 49, 107, 118
sovereignty
   conceptual framework 48
   public disputes 48
   regulatory disputes 48–50
   sovereign acts
      application of investment treaty
         arbitration 72, 83
Soviet Union 8, 32, 42
Spain 32
standards of review 72, 80–3
   compensation for expropriation 12, 19–20,
      81, 90–4, 145
   minimum standard of treatment 81, 86,
      126, 145
   national treatment 19, 22, 28, 81, 83–6
SPS Agreement *see* Agreement on the
   Application of Sanitary and
   Phytosanitary Measures
state liability 106–8, 121–4, 135, 137, 139,
   141, 145–9
   limitations 5, 109
state measures 65n
Stockholm Chamber of Commerce 37
   appointment of arbitrators 58n, 171
Sub-Saharan Africa 32

takings doctrine *see* expropriation
tax havens 39
Tecmed v United Mexican States 92
Tokios v Ukraine 132
TRIMs Agreement *see* Agreement on
   Trade-Related Investment Measures

Uganda 23
Ukraine 115, 132
ultra vires 106
UN Commission on International Trade Law
   (UNCITRAL)
   UNCITRAL Model Law 53–4
      definition of commercial 56n
   UNCITRAL Rules 30, 37, 54
      comparison with other rules 54n
      openness 160, 162
UN Tribunal on the Law of the Sea 165
UNCITRAL *see* UN Commission on
   International Trade Law
United Nations
   General Assembly 182
   Secretary General 20, 34
   Security Council 117, 182
United Nations Convention on the Recognition
   and Enforcement of Foreign Arbitral
   Awards 1958 (New York Convention)
   34, 51–2, 54–6

United Nations Convention (*cont.*)
  enforcement of awards 118, 156–7, 181
  incorporation into investment treaties 128–9
  judicial review 155
United States 26, 32, 116, 177
  Bipartisan Trade Promotion Authority Act 2002 40n
  BIT programme 27n, 41
  claims 32–3, 40
  CME Czech Republic Case 7–8
  Congress 20, 40
  Havana Charter
    rejection of 20, 23
  NAFTA 40
  openness 160
unity of the state (principle of) 93
Universal Declaration of Human Rights 1948 141
UPS v Canada 157
US–Canada Softwood Lumber Agreement 1996 126

US Council for International Business 21
US–Mexico General Claims Commission 87
US Supreme Court 165
use of force 16–18

Vattel's principle 108, 120, 135
Venezuela 16, 116

Washington DC 157, 162
water 74–5
Western Europe 20, 32, 41
Wolfowitz, Paul 170
World Bank 34, 41–2
  appointment of arbitrators 170–1
  voting 170n
World Trade Organization (WTO) 21, 164
  Cancun ministerial conference 2003 22–3
  WTO Appellate Body 43, 53, 153
World War Two 19
WTO *see* World Trade Organization

Index

North American Free Trade Agreement (NAFTA) 26–7, 29, 64–5, 126–7
  claims 26n, 31–3
    minority shareholder claims 113
  coherence 165
  enforcement of awards 118–19
  expropriation 156
  openness 161–3
  public law adjudication 134
  standards of review 81, 88–9, 92, 145–6
  waiver of legal remedies 69–70

OECD *see* Organization for Economic Co-operation and Development
openness 159–64
operational decisions 108n
Organization for Economic Co-operation and Development 21–2
Ottoman empire *see* empires

pacta sunt servanda (principle of) 125, 131
Pakistan 133
Panama Convention 1975
  enforcement of awards 118
parallel claims 111–12, 115, 117, 120
participation by non parties 159, 162–3
party autonomy (principle of) 125–6, 160, 162–3
performance requirements 21n, 28
Persia 15
Philippines 12, 29, 33
place of enforcement 156–7, 181
Pope & Talbot v Canada 126–8
Porter Convention 1907 16
private law 127
  tortious liability of the state 108n, 125
  see also investment treaty arbitration
property
  protection of foreign owners 19, 21
Protocol on Arbitration Clauses in Commercial Matters 1923 (Geneva Protocol) 50–1
public access to information 159–62
public health 40, 144
public law 45, 152–3, 157–75
  interpretation 154–6, 181
public policy 155, 176

regional trade agreements 28, 79
regulatory relationship 32
reparation (principle of) 109
rule of law 153, 166, 173–4, 177, 184
Russia 32
  see also Soviet Union

seat of arbitration *see* arbitration
secrecy *see* confidentiality
SGS v Pakistan 132, 135, 146, 174
SGS v Philippines 138

Singapore 163
Softwood Lumber Agreement 126
sovereign immunity 46–7, 49, 107, 118
sovereignty
  conceptual framework 48
  public disputes 48
  regulatory disputes 48–50
  sovereign acts
    application of investment treaty arbitration 72, 83
Soviet Union 8, 32, 42
Spain 32
standards of review 72, 80–3
  compensation for expropriation 12, 19–20, 81, 90–4, 145
  minimum standard of treatment 81, 86, 126, 145
  national treatment 19, 22, 28, 81, 83–6
SPS Agreement *see* Agreement on the Application of Sanitary and Phytosanitary Measures
state liability 106–8, 121–4, 135, 137, 139, 141, 145–9
  limitations 5, 109
state measures 65n
Stockholm Chamber of Commerce 37
  appointment of arbitrators 58n, 171
Sub-Saharan Africa 32

takings doctrine *see* expropriation
tax havens 39
Tecmed v United Mexican States 92
Tokios v Ukraine 132
TRIMs Agreement *see* Agreement on Trade-Related Investment Measures

Uganda 23
Ukraine 115, 132
ultra vires 106
UN Commission on International Trade Law (UNCITRAL)
  UNCITRAL Model Law 53–4
    definition of commercial 56n
  UNCITRAL Rules 30, 37, 54
    comparison with other rules 54n
    openness 160, 162
UN Tribunal on the Law of the Sea 165
UNCITRAL *see* UN Commission on International Trade Law
United Nations
  General Assembly 182
  Secretary General 20, 34
  Security Council 117, 182
United Nations Convention on the Recognition and Enforcement of Foreign Arbitral Awards 1958 (New York Convention) 34, 51–2, 54–6

United Nations Convention (*cont.*)
  enforcement of awards 118, 156–7, 181
  incorporation into investment treaties 128–9
  judicial review 155
United States 26, 32, 116, 177
  Bipartisan Trade Promotion Authority Act 2002 40n
  BIT programme 27n, 41
  claims 32–3, 40
  CME Czech Republic Case 7–8
  Congress 20, 40
  Havana Charter
    rejection of 20, 23
  NAFTA 40
  openness 160
unity of the state (principle of) 93
Universal Declaration of Human Rights 1948 141
UPS v Canada 157
US–Canada Softwood Lumber Agreement 1996 126

US Council for International Business 21
US–Mexico General Claims Commission 87
US Supreme Court 165
use of force 16–18

Vattel's principle 108, 120, 135
Venezuela 16, 116

Washington DC 157, 162
water 74–5
Western Europe 20, 32, 41
Wolfowitz, Paul 170
World Bank 34, 41–2
  appointment of arbitrators 170–1
  voting 170n
World Trade Organization (WTO) 21, 164
  Cancun ministerial conference 2003 22–3
  WTO Appellate Body 43, 53, 153
World War Two 19
WTO *see* World Trade Organization

Printed in France by Amazon
Brétigny-sur-Orge, FR